THE FEAR OF INVASION

-

The Fear of Invasion

Strategy, Politics, and British War Planning, 1880–1914

DAVID G. MORGAN-OWEN

OXFORD
UNIVERSITY PRESS

OXFORD
UNIVERSITY PRESS

Great Clarendon Street, Oxford, OX2 6DP,
United Kingdom

Oxford University Press is a department of the University of Oxford.
It furthers the University's objective of excellence in research, scholarship,
and education by publishing worldwide. Oxford is a registered trade mark of
Oxford University Press in the UK and in certain other countries

© David G. Morgan-Owen 2017

The moral rights of the author have been asserted

First Edition published in 2017

Impression: 2

Published in the United States of America by Oxford University Press
198 Madison Avenue, New York, NY 10016, United States of America

British Library Cataloguing in Publication Data
Data available

Library of Congress Control Number: 2017932097

ISBN 978–0–19–880519–9

Printed and bound by
CPI Group (UK) Ltd, Croydon, CR0 4YY

Acknowledgements

This book has benefited from the insight and support of a great many people, all of whom it would be impossible to list. To any I omit, your help has not gone unappreciated.

I would like to thank the staff at the numerous archives and institutions I visited during the course of researching this work. For access and permission to quote from materials held in their care, I extend my kindest appreciation to the British Library, The National Archives, the National Maritime Museum, the National Army Museum, the Cadbury Research Library Special Collections, the Trustees of the Liddell Hart Centre for Military Archives, the Master and Fellows of Churchill College, Cambridge, the Chatsworth House Trust, the National Library of Scotland, the University of Southampton, the National Museum of the Royal Navy and Royal Marines Museums, the University of Buckingham, the National Records of Scotland, the Bodleian Libraries, and the Trustees of the Imperial War Museum. Heather Johnson at the National Museum of the Royal Navy, Ben Fellows at the National Army Museum, and Anthony Richards at the Imperial War Museum deserve special mention for their kindness and help during my research at their respective institutions. I would also like to thank the Robertson family, the current Lord Selborne, Richard W. Haldane, Roderick Balfour, Michael Brander, and Tony Maxse for allowing me to quote from material for which they hold the copyright. Every effort has been made to secure the necessary permissions for copyrighted material. My sincerest apologies for any lapses, which are entirely inadvertent.

I am grateful to the staff at the History Department at the University of Exeter who provided a wonderful environment in which to explore my interest in the past and who set me on the path on which I now find myself. Maria Fusaro and Jeremy Black were a regular source of encouragement and advice during my studies and Henry French kindly granted me a university fellowship following the completion of my Ph.D. which provided ongoing access to vital materials. Mike Duffy was a wonderful, patient, and insightful supervisor to a diffuse and often recalcitrant student, and sharpened many of the ideas which underpin this work. Richard Toye and Matthew Seligmann provided a wealth of useful suggestions when they examined my doctoral thesis and their encouragement to explore the broader implications of that project was crucial in my decision to write this book.

Duncan Redford gave invaluable support after I completed my doctoral studies and I would like to thank him, Dominic Tweddle, and the National Museum of the Royal Navy for their award of a Visiting Research Fellowship in 2014. This post provided crucial additional research and writing time and a very convivial atmosphere in which to work.

My colleagues and students at the Joint Services Command and Staff College have been a constant source of ideas, advice, and support, and have posed many thought-provoking questions which have caused me to re-examine aspects of this project and sharpened parts of the argument. The department funded a research trip to Edinburgh in 2015 which gleaned much useful information from the Ewart and Haldane Papers and supported additional research elsewhere. I would particularly like to thank Ellen Hallams for making sure I finished, and Rachael Kelly for making me realize that I had finally done so.

This work has benefited from conversations with Richard Dunley, Jonathan Fennell, Anna Brinkman, Aimée Fox-Godden, Helen McCartney, and Bob Foley. Chris Tripodi, Greg Kennedy, Nick Lloyd, and James Goldrick all read the manuscript, made helpful suggestions, and saved me from numerous errors.

This book is dedicated to my parents, for whom education was always the best investment and without whom none of this would have been possible. Thank you.

David G. Morgan-Owen

Contents

List of Abbreviations   ix

Introduction   1

1. The Command of the Sea   11

2. The Military Resources of the Empire   43

3. 'Practical Politics'   71

4. Preparing for War   99

5. The German Threat   131

6. The North Sea Guard   155

7. A Growing Burden   179

8. Surrendering the Initiative   203

Conclusion   227

Bibliography   235
Index   247

Contents

List of Abbreviations

AG	Adjutant General
AoP	Admiral of Patrols
BEF	British Expeditionary Force
CGS	Chief of the General Staff
CID	Committee of Imperial Defence
CIGS	Chief of the Imperial General Staff
C-in-C	Commander-in-Chief
CoS	Chief of Staff
DGMI	Director General of Mobilization and Intelligence
DMI	Director of Military Intelligence
DMO	Director of Military Operations
DNI	Director of Naval Intelligence
HPDC	Home Ports Defence Sub-Committee
NID	Naval Intelligence Department
RUSI	Royal United Services Institute
TF	Territorial Force
WF	War Office 'With France' scheme

BRITISH & GERMAN NORTH
SEA BASES — 1914

Taken from Arthur J. Marder, *From the Dreadnought to Scapa Flow, The Royal Navy in the Fisher Era 1904–1919 – Volume I: The Road to War, 1904–1914*, London: OUP, 1961, pp. 422–32. By permission of Oxford University Press.

Introduction

The image of a hostile army disgorging onto British shores, violating the peace and prosperity of the English countryside, and subjugating her people to foreign rule was a familiar spectre of late Victorian and Edwardian society. The periodic 'invasion scares' which swept the country were a reflection of how Britain and her inhabitants perceived their relationship with the outside world. Unlike the other Great Powers, Britain could boast of having suffered no foreign intrusion onto her territory for centuries past. This fact had played an important part in shaping her political, economic, and social development, breeding a debate amongst British statesmen over the extent to which the United Kingdom should steer a course apart from the patchwork of tensions and agreements which criss-crossed the political map of Europe.[1] The reserve with which British politicians could regard Continental affairs was, of course, the consequence of the 'silver streak' of water which separated the United Kingdom from the remainder of Europe: an accident of providence which appeared to insulate Britain from events overseas. Her island status was widely appreciated and celebrated: the importance of geography in determining national fortunes and character gained particular credence in Britain around the turn of the twentieth century.[2] As the influential Oxford geographer Halford Mackinder argued in 1902, 'geographical position has thus given to Britain a unique part in the world's drama'.[3]

Yet if Britain's detachment from Europe had shielded her from the maelstrom of Continental affairs and enabled her to accrue wealth and empire beyond that of any other Great Power, a lingering fear existed that it might have left her vulnerable. Was Britain indeed a 'weary titan', her avarice having incurred commitments she was unable or unwilling to sustain? Had the British people become fat upon the fruits of their success and begun to fall behind in terms of international competitiveness and 'efficiency'?[4] The notion that an envious Continental power might exploit an opportune moment to strike across the seas with all of her military might, tearing asunder the foundations upon which British prosperity was built, came to exercise a persistent dread in British minds. This fear played upon

[1] K. Robbins, *Britain and Europe, 1789–2005*, London: Hodder Arnold, 2005, pp. 160–1.
[2] R. Colls, *Identity of England*, Oxford: Oxford University Press, 2002, pp. 238–40.
[3] H. Mackinder, *Britain and the British Seas*, Oxford: Oxford University Press, 1902, p. 358.
[4] P. Kennedy, *The Rise and Fall of the Great Powers*, New York, 1987, Ch. 5; A. L. Friedberg, *The Weary Titan: Britain and the Experience of Relative Decline*, Princeton, NY: Princeton University Press, 1988; G. R. Searle, *A New England? Peace and War, 1886–1918*, Oxford: Clarendon, 2004, pp. 243–52 and 372–86.

traditional suspicions and tropes about Continental militarists, despots, and papists, and could easily be aroused during times of international tension or economic hardship.[5] Despite the growth of overseas travel, immigration, and international trade, the world beyond the English Channel remained 'foreign' to most of the population of Britain. In an age before massed aerial warfare, the most obvious means by which the Continental powers might intrude into the lives of the average Briton remained an invading army. For this reason, lurid tales of French or German troops mounting a surprise descent on London provoked great interest amongst the public, far more so than sober missives regarding pressing strategic issues such as the defence of India. This was precisely because the prospect of an invasion made abstract discussions about military and international affairs accessible to a general audience. Invasion became a prism through which concerns about imperial, economic, political, and social issues were expressed: almost no matter the cause, an invading army could serve to illustrate it.[6]

The panics over an impending *coup de main* are well known, not least due to popular works by writers such as Erskine Childers and P. G. Wodehouse, who graced the genre of invasion literature with contributions of enduring quality. Yet scholars studying British strategy in this period have seldom viewed the threat of invasion as more than a figment of the Edwardian imagination.[7] The prospect of a foreign army reaching Britain was a 'bogey, an imagined evil',[8] viewed by most historians as being 'entirely divorced from strategic reality'.[9] If the threat of invasion did exert any influence on policy, it is held, it did so only as a means of exciting public and political interest in defence matters. In Lord Esher's oft-quoted words, 'an invasion scare is the mill of the Gods which grinds you out a Navy of Dreadnoughts, and keeps the British people war-like in spirit'.[10] In other words, invasion was a shibboleth, which exerted only an indirect influence on the affairs of state. The notion that home defence might have played a significant part in shaping British strategy has thus yet to be the subject of serious historical enquiry.

This book places the defence of the United Kingdom at the heart of its assessment of British preparations for war before 1914. It argues that, even at the apogee of her imperial might, the imperative to protect the home islands was an immovable constant in British strategy: home defence had a direct bearing on the distribution and size of the Army, the strength and location of the Fleet, and the resources available for offensive action in wartime. Securing London, the heart of

    [5] P. Panayi, *Immigration, Ethnicity and Racism in Britain, 1815–1945*, Manchester: Manchester University Press, 1994, Ch. 5.
    [6] I. F. W. Clarke, *Voices Prophesying War: Future Wars, 1763–3749*, Oxford: Oxford University Press, 1992 edn, Ch. 4.
    [7] The exception being Howard Moon's unpublished Ph.D., thesis, although even he is doubtful that the invasion threat continued to be viewed as genuine by 1914: H. R. Moon, 'The Invasion of the United Kingdom: Public Controversy and Official Planning, 1888–1918', unpublished Ph.D., University of London, 1968.
    [8] A. J. Marder, *[F]rom the [D]readnought to [S]capa [F]low: The Royal Navy in the Fisher Era, 1904–1919*, Oxford: Oxford University Press, five volumes, 1961–70, Vol. I, p. 358.
    [9] N. Ferguson, *The Pity of War*, London: Allen Lane, 1998, p. 8.
    [10] Esher to Fisher, 1 October 1907 in M. V. Brett ed., *Journals and Letters of Reginald Viscount Esher*, London: Ivor Nicholson & Watson, 1934, Vol. II, p. 249.

the Empire and of the British 'World System',[11] was the fundamental starting point for all those considering how to defend the Empire in the decades prior to the First World War. How Britain planned to repel an invasion exercised a considerable influence over virtually every other aspect of her military and naval preparations before 1914 and must be understood in order fully to appreciate her position at the outbreak of the war.

If little heed has been paid to how the threat of invasion itself affected strategy, there is a well-developed and highly sophisticated body of scholarship on the issue of war planning in Britain prior to 1914. How, then, has such an important issue escaped the attention of previous scholars? The lack of any evidence of a credible invasion attempt or even a realistic plan for one in the archives of France or Germany makes British preoccupations with the threat 'difficult to understand, let alone justify'.[12] Yet the absence of such schemes is not adequate rationale for ignoring British perceptions of impending danger. That senior British officials appeared preoccupied by the prospect of an invasion reveals much about their own modes of thought, but their concerns were no less legitimate for their lack of foundation. Many influential figures, particularly within the Navy, did hold such fears and were motivated to act upon them, with far-reaching consequences for British strategy in 1914.

More important than the lack of credible planning for an invasion has been the long shadow the First World War has cast back onto the period before 1914. The experience of the Western Front and the inconclusive Battle of Jutland have created a natural tendency for scholars to cast back to discover the origins of British thinking about Continental warfare or a decisive naval battle.[13] On the military side scholars have long debated the precise origins of the so-called 'continental commitment',[14] although this thesis has been overtaken in recent years by a more measured approach.[15] For the Navy, the imperative to explain the inconclusive

---

[11] To use the phrase coined by J. Darwin, *The Empire Project: The Rise and Fall of the British World-System, 1830–1970*, Cambridge: Cambridge University Press, 2009.

[12] Marder, *FDSF* V, p. 164. For foreign plans see Moon, 'Invasion', Appendix A, pp. 653–77; Marder, *FDSF* I, p. 358; P. M. Kennedy, 'The Development of German Naval Operations Plans Against England, 1896–1914', *English Historical Review*, Vol. 89, No. 350, Jan., 1974, pp. 52–60; I. Lambi, *The Navy and German Power Politics, 1862–1914*, Boston, MA: Allen & Unwin, 1984, pp. 215–18.

[13] An excellent summary of the literature on the military side can be found in H. Strachan, 'The British Army, its General Staff and the Continental Commitment, 1904–14' in D. French and B. Holden Reid eds, *The British General Staff: Reform and Innovation c.1890–1939*, London: Frank Cass, 2002, pp. 75–94. For the Navy, see Marder, *FDSF* I, pp. 3–13 and 367–77, and A. Gordon, *The Rules of the Game: Jutland and British Naval Command*, London: John Murray, 1996.

[14] R. B. Haldane, *Before the War*, London and New York: Funk & Cagnalls, 1920, pp. 177–206, and *Richard Burdon Haldane: An Autobiography*, London: Hodder & Stoughton, 1928, pp. 188–92; H. Richmond, *National Policy and Naval Strength and Other Essays*, London: Longmans, Green, & Co., 1928, pp. 54–5; B. Liddell Hart, *The Real War, 1914–1918*, London: Faber & Faber, 1930, p. 65; N. d'Ombrain, *War Machinery and High Policy: Defence Administration in Peacetime Britain, 1902–1914*, Oxford: Oxford University Press, 1973; J. McDermott, 'The Revolution in British Military Thinking from the Boer War to the Moroccan Crisis', *Canadian Journal of History*, Vol. 9, No. 2, 1974, pp. 159–77.

[15] J. Gooch, *The Plans of War: The General Staff and British Military Strategy c.1900–1916*, New York: John Wiley & Sons, 1974; *The Prospect of War: Studies in British Defence Policy 1847–1942*,

Battle of Jutland has produced similar studies of service culture and thought in the late Victorian and Edwardian periods.[16] Such enquiries are certainly merited and have done much to further our understanding of naval and military thought before the war, yet with a handful of exceptions they have been overwhelmingly single-service in their focus.[17] This has created a false dichotomy between 'Continental' and 'blue water' schools and painted the period after 1900 as a zero-sum competition between the War Office General Staff and the Admiralty for control of British strategy. Reality was far less clear-cut than this depiction would suggest.

The General Staff had not succeeded in convincing the entire Army, let alone the government, that large-scale involvement on the Continent was in Britain's best interests by 1914, as was demonstrated by the debates held in Cabinet in the opening days of the conflict.[18] Moreover, viewing naval and military strategy as opposites—rather than as part of a larger whole—limits the scope for appreciating the dynamic and on-going interaction between the two. This is particularly problematic in the case of Britain where, due to the global scope of her interests, the relationship between Army and Navy was necessarily more interdependent than in any other Great Power. Each service had to plan based upon the capabilities and intentions of the other, because each depended on its counterpart to support its own activity—a fact reflected in a growing body of literature on the complementary

Abingdon: Frank Cass, 1981, *vii–viii*, and 'The Weary Titan: Strategy and Policy in Great Britain, 1890–1918' in W. Murray, M. Knox, and A. Bernstein eds, *The Making of Strategy: Rulers, States, and War*, Cambridge: Cambridge University Press, 1994, pp. 278–306; J. W. Coogan and P. F. Coogan, 'The British Cabinet and the Anglo-French Staff Talks, 1905–1914: Who Knew What and When Did He Know it?', *Journal of British Studies*, Vol. 24, No. 1, Jan., 1985, pp. 110–31; T. Wilson, 'Britain's "Moral Commitment" to France in August 1914', *History*, Vol. 62, No. 212, 1979, pp. 380–90; H. Strachan, *The First World War*, Vol. I: *To Arms*, Oxford: Oxford University Press, 2001, pp. 198–205; T. G. Otte, '"The Method by which we were schooled by Experience": British Strategy and a Continental Commitment before 1914' in K. Neilson and G. Kennedy eds, *The British Way in Warfare: Power and the International System, 1856–1956*, Farnham: Ashgate, 2010, pp. 301–24; K. Neilson, 'Great Britain' in R. F. Hamilton and H. H. Herwig eds, *War Planning 1914*, Cambridge: Cambridge University Press, 2010, pp. 175–97.

[16] See Marder, *FDSF*, J. T. Sumida, *[I]n [D]efence of [N]aval [S]upremacy: Finance, Technology, and British Naval Policy, 1889–1914*, London: Unwin Hyman, 1989; Gordon, *Rules of the Game*; N. A. Lambert, *Sir John [F]isher's [N]aval [R]evolution*, Columbia, SC: University of South Carolina Press, 1999; J. Brooks, *Dreadnought Gunnery and the Battle of Jutland: The Question of Fire Control*, Abingdon: Routledge, 2006; S. T. Grimes, *Strategy and [War Planning] in the British Navy, 1887–1918*, Woodbridge: The Boydell Press, 2012.

[17] Exceptions include J. P. MacKintosh, 'The Role of the Committee of Imperial Defence before 1914', *English Historical Review*, Vol. 77, No. 304, Jul. 1962, pp. 490–509; S. R. Williamson Jr, *The Politics of Grand Strategy: Britain and France Prepare for War, 1904–1914*, Cambridge, MA: Harvard University Press, 1969; d'Ombrain, *War Machinery*; D. French, *British Economic and Strategic Planning, 1905–1915*, London: George Allen & Unwin, 1982; R. Williams, *Defending the Empire: The Conservative Party and British Defence Policy 1899–1915*, London: Yale University Press, 1991; Strachan, *To Arms*, pp. 198–204.

[18] J. E. Tyler, *The British Army and the Continent, 1904–1914*, London, 1938; K. M. Wilson, 'To the Western Front: British War Plans and the "Military Entente" with France before the First World War', *British Journal of International Studies*, Vol. 3, No. 2, Jul., 1977, pp. 151–69, and 'The War Office, Churchill and the Belgian Option—August to December 1911' in his *Empire and Continent: Studies in British Foreign Policy from the 1880s to the First World War*, London and New York: Mansell, 1987, pp. 126–40; Strachan, 'The Continental Commitment, 1904–14'.

nature of naval and military strategy which began to emerge in this period.[19] As Major-General Douglas Haig argued in a paper outlining his vision for imperial defence, 'to be successful in any war we must as our first objective win command of the sea...in order to reap the fruits of sea power we must apply military force at some decisive point on land. Thus command of the sea and control of the shore are closely connected.'[20] By favouring a primarily 'naval' or 'military' approach to a particular problem, the government inevitably affected *both* services. For this reason the tacit support it gave to the policy of providing military assistance to France after 1906 had more far-reaching consequences for the course of naval strategic planning and thus the balance of British strategy as a whole than has been appreciated hitherto.

Viewing military and naval strategy as independent forces competing for political endorsement also downplays the agency of politicians in shaping the plans of the two services. Army and Navy undoubtedly vied for favour in the eyes of the government, but this process was reciprocal and political direction had a considerable influence over the focus of both departments.[21] Viewed from this perspective, it was the Unionist government of Arthur Balfour—rather than the General Staff—which fixed the attention of the War Office on expeditionary warfare against another Great Power. The military thus did not subvert British strategy and direct it towards Europe; Britain's political leaders instructed them to do so in reaction to changed international conditions.

A final difficulty stemming from the tendency to project the experience of the war back onto the period before 1914 is that it has produced an overt focus on offensive planning. Much has been written on the abortive attempts to formulate plans for combined action—probably in the form of an amphibious assault,[22] the General Staff's 'With France' (WF) plan,[23] and the Admiralty's secretive planning process.[24] Judging from the extent of this literature, one might assume that Britain gave detailed consideration to plans for how to bring a major war to a successful

[19] See, for instance S. Wilkinson, *The Command of the Sea*, London, 1894; C. E. Callwell, *The Effect of Maritime Command on Land Campaigns since Waterloo*, Edinburgh and London, 1897, and *Military Operations and Maritime Preponderance: Their Relations and Interdependence*, Edinburgh and London, 1905; L. S. Amery, 'Imperial Defence and National Policy' in C. S. Goldman ed., *The Empire and the Century*, London: John Murray, 1905, pp. 174–96; J. S. Corbett, *Some Principles of Maritime Strategy*, London, 1911.

[20] D. Haig, 'National Defence', 20 May 1906, pp. 1–2, Haig Papers, [N]ational [L]ibrary of [S]cotland, ACC 3155/40P.

[21] J. Gooch, 'Adversarial Attitudes: Servicemen, Politicians and Strategic Policy in Edwardian England, 1899–1914' in P. Smith ed., *Government and the Armed Forces in Britain 1856–1990*, London: Hambledon, 1996, esp. pp. 53–60.

[22] P. Haggie, 'The Royal Navy and War Planning in the Fisher Era', *Journal of Contemporary History*, Vol. 8, No. 3, Jul., 1973, pp. 113–31; d'Ombrain, *War Machinery*, pp. 68–81; P. Hayes, 'Britain, Germany and the Admiralty's Plans for Attacking German Territory, 1906–1915' in L. Freedman ed., *War Strategy and Intentional Politics: Essays in Honour of Michael Howard*, Oxford: Clarendon, 1992, pp. 95–116; S. T. Grimes, 'Combined Operations and British Strategy, 1900–09', *Historical Research*, Vol. 89, No. 246, 2016, pp. 866–84.

[23] See notes 14, 15 and 17.

[24] N. A. Lambert, 'Strategic Command and Control for Maneuver Warfare: Creation of the Royal Navy's "War Room" System, 1905–1915', *Journal of Military History*, Vol. 69, No. 2, Apr., 2005, pp. 361–410; Grimes, *War Planning*.

issue before 1914. She did not. By far the greatest imperial power, she had no grand territorial ambitions or revisionist agenda. Rather, she was more concerned to protect a status quo which worked largely to her benefit. As Maurice Hankey, Secretary of the Committee of Imperial Defence, later noted, 'the keynote of Asquith's and Grey's policy was peace.'[25] This attitude defined the primarily defensive mindset with which the government approached military affairs and preparation for war before 1914.

Britain's political leadership did not articulate or endorse a coherent vision for how it envisaged bringing a future Great Power conflict to a conclusion before the outbreak of the First World War.[26] The Liberal government's commitment to laissez-faire economics precluded the level of interference in the areas of economic and social policy necessary to produce a true 'grand' strategy in the modern sense. Moreover, offensive war plans were anathema to the strong Radical wing of a Liberal Cabinet focused on social reform and welfare, and which was unwilling to confront the awkward political implications which might flow from the discussion of the requirements of a major war—such as compulsory military service.[27] The Campbell-Bannerman and Asquith governments were by no means pacifist—as the escalation of the Navy Estimates after 1907 demonstrated—but their focus was always on defending British interests, rather than how to achieve victory in a war with a fellow Great Power. What little thought was spent in this direction produced no more than a series of vague assumptions. The general belief was that sea power, financial strength, and geographical isolation would insulate Britain from the most immediate effects of a European conflict. This meant that when Britain did enter a European war in 1914, she did so not with a maritime equivalent to the German 'Schlieffen' plan, but with a loosely formed military-naval strategy intended to ensure the defence of the United Kingdom, her colonial possessions, and British seaborne trade.[28] Thus, it was through decisions taken on how best to *defend* Britain and her Empire that governments shaped British strategy before 1914, and only by examining this process can we gain a full understanding of the country's position at the outbreak of the First World War.

* * *

Politicians had only begun systematically to consider the complex and contradictory requirements of defending the Empire in the mid-1870s.[29] Discussions of

---

[25] M. Hankey, *The Supreme Command, 1914–1918*, London: Unwin Brothers, 1961, Vol. I, p. 136.

[26] For a recent highly controversial attempt to suggest otherwise, see N. A. Lambert, *Planning Armageddon: British Economic Warfare and the First World War*, Cambridge, MA, and London: Harvard University Press, 2012.

[27] French, *British Economic and Strategic Planning*, Ch. 2.

[28] For the defence of trade, see Marder, *FDSF* I, pp. 358–66; B. Ranft, 'The Protection of British Seaborne Trade and the Development of Systematic Planning for War, 1860–1906' in his *Technical Change and British Naval Policy, 1860–1939*, London: Hodder & Stoughton, 1977, pp. 1–22; M. S. Seligmann, *The [R]oyal [N]avy and the [G]erman [T]hreat, 1901–1914: Admiralty Plans to Protect British Trade in a War Against Germany*, Oxford: Oxford University Press, 2012. See also M.S. Seligmann, 'Failing to Prepare for the Great War? The Absence of Grand Strategy in British War Planning before 1914', *War in History*, published online April 2017.

[29] D. M. Schurman, *Imperial Defence, 1868–1887*, J. Beeler ed., London: Frank Cass, 2000.

military matters were politically charged and highly contentious, touching on emotive topics like national service and threatening to impinge upon Britain's liberal style of government. This produced a disinclination on the part of successive administrations to make definitive decisions on key issues such as the size of the Army and inter-service co-operation. Yet despite the charges of some critics after the armistice,[30] Britain did possess a strategy to defend herself and her empire before 1914, the contours of which are relatively easily to delineate. The Royal Navy would control global sea communications, ensuring the continuation of Britain's lifeblood of trade, contact with her colonies, and the security of the home islands. The Army would provide garrisons for vital naval installations and the most valuable colonies and also constitute a modest 'striking force'. Control of the sea would enable this army to be delivered at the vital point, magnifying its effect. After the Boer War, this framework was augmented by diplomatic agreements with Japan, France, and Russia. These alliances and understandings enabled Britain to concentrate her resources in Europe and provided powerful Continental counterweights against German aggression after 1904. This state of affairs was no accident, as successive governments had taken a more active role in overseeing military and naval affairs since 1902.[31]

The Army and Navy played complementary roles within this loose strategic framework. Without the Army the security of the colonies would be threatened, vital naval bases would be vulnerable to attack, and Britain would lack the capacity to threaten enemy territory. The Navy safeguarded the global trading system upon which British prosperity was based, ensured the ability to move troops by sea, and enabled London to isolate enemies from the benefits of seaborne commerce in wartime. In all of these endeavours the two services supported each other, even if in some of their roles they acted independently. As the Director of Naval Intelligence pointed out in 1903, 'although there are many cases in which the services have to render mutual assistance, each has, in addition, a sphere of its own into which the other can never enter'.[32]

The realm where the two services shared the greatest degree of responsibility was the defence of the British Isles. Most reasonable commentators accepted the primacy of the Navy in preventing an invasion, but the correct balance of naval and military force necessary to ensure British security had been a matter of intense

---

[30] G. Aston, *The Problem of Defence: Reminiscences and Deductions*, London: Philip Allan & Co., 1925, p. 32, and 'The Committee of Imperial Defence: Its Evolution and Prospects', *RUSI*, Vol. 71, No. 483, 1926, pp. 456–63; C. R. M. F. Cruttwell, *The Role of British Strategy in the Great War*, Cambridge: Cambridge University Press, 1936, p. 20.

[31] M. Hankey, *Government Control in War*, Cambridge: Cambridge University Press, 1945, and *Supreme Command*; N. H. Gibbs, 'The Origins of Imperial Defence', Inaugural Lecture of the Chichele Chair, 1955, reproduced in J. B. Hattendorf and R. S. Jordan eds, *Maritime Strategy and the Balance of Power: Britain and America in the Twentieth Century*, Basingstoke: Macmillan, 1989, pp. 23–36; J. Ehrman, *Cabinet Government and War*, Cambridge: Cambridge University Press, 1957; F. R. Johnson, *Defence by Committee: The British Committee of Imperial Defence, 1885–1959*, London: Oxford University Press, 1960.

[32] Battenberg, 'Remarks on MID Papers 13a', 14 July 1903, CAB 3/1/16A.

debate from the 1860s onwards.[33] Could a larger Home Army free the Fleet for operations across the Empire? Might a would-be invader evade the Royal Navy? Could fortifications provide a more efficient means of defence than troops or ships? These issues had significant ramifications for imperial strategy as a whole. How many men were needed at home would dictate what proportion of the Regular Army was free for operations abroad and the size and cost of the auxiliary forces. It would also have a bearing on the location and freedom of action of the Fleet. Thus, when Arthur Balfour's government attempted to settle the number of men that could be dispatched to India in the event of war with Russia in 1903–4, it was obliged to establish the irreducible minimum required for home defence at the same time.

Ultimately, then, imperial concerns necessitated a resolution to the on-going saga of how best to protect Britain herself. Russian encroachment towards India combined with the embarrassments of the Boer War to underline to the government that a more rigorous approach to imperial strategy was required after 1902–3. Fiscal pressures meant that improvements in capability would have to be the product of increased efficiency rather than additional expenditure, and home defence was quickly identified as an area where a more effective division of labour between the services could be achieved to serve this end. The existing military system had proven unequal to the task of supplying an expeditionary force for South Africa and the defensive forces of the auxiliary establishment were also widely considered inefficient and wasteful, fit for neither home defence nor service overseas. Balfour's solution was to absolve the Army from the responsibility of dealing with an invasion, freeing it to perform its role as a reserve to India in the event of war with Russia. This policy would be predicated upon the strength of the Royal Navy, which would secure British coasts, backed by a reformed auxiliary military establishment. This streamlining of naval and military effort was not a dramatic departure from existing policy, but by codifying the relative roles of each service for the first time the government marked a new stage in the evolution of British strategy. A political decision on the defence of the United Kingdom had contributed to a major shift in military policy and British strategy: the Army would now focus more explicitly on expeditionary warfare and rely on the Navy to protect the country. This proved to be a decision with far-reaching consequences.

As Britain's position within the constellation of Great Powers shifted after the conclusion of the Entente Cordiale in 1904, the durability of this precise division of naval and military labour came under strain. As the first decade of the new century wore on, the Navy became less and less confident in its ability to fulfil the defensive function it had fought with the Army to secure with ironclad reliability. As British military planning assumed an ever-more Continental focus and the government encouraged limited contact between the British and French military

[33] J. Gooch, 'The Bolt from the Blue' in his *The Prospect of War*, pp. 1–9; M. S. Partridge, *Military Planning for the Defense of the United Kingdom, 1814–1870*, Westport, CT: Greenwood Press, 1989, *passim*; K. M. Wilson, *Channel Tunnel Visions, 1850–1945: Dreams and Nightmares*, London: Hambledon Press, 1994, Chs I–III.

staffs, the Admiralty became preoccupied with the security of the east coast. By 1914, the General Staff's plans to dispatch as much of the Regular Army as possible to the Continent at the outbreak of war had obliged the naval leadership to prioritize resisting a German landing over virtually all other strategic considerations in the North Sea. In this manner, a strategy predicated upon exploiting British sea power to enable the Army to reinforce India evolved into one which unintentionally constrained the Fleet in order to dispatch an expeditionary force to France's aid. The threat of invasion was central to this process, and thus to understanding the shortcomings in British strategy in 1914.

1

The Command of the Sea

Politicians came to play an increasingly significant role in shaping British strategy from the 1880s onwards. The growth of their involvement was born of necessity, as a more confrontational phase of international politics necessitated a more precise allocation of finite British naval and military resources. Whereas between 1815 and 1870 a largely permissive international environment had allowed Britain to rely upon a loose set of general assumptions about the use of military power, a newfound requirement to adopt a systematic approach to the size, distribution, and potential employment of the Empire's armed forces emerged as the century drew to a close. The laissez-faire approach to military and naval planning prevalent for much of the century had hampered inter-service co-ordination and encouraged short-termism. However, a series of priorities were discernable from the British state's allocation of money and attention. The protection of the United Kingdom itself was at the pinnacle of this hierarchy. Along with the defence of British seaborne commerce, it formed one of the twin priorities of British strategists. Home defence was a recurrent focus for the public, the armed services, and their political masters. Due to the maritime and imperial nature of British world power, it was also an immovable constant within emergent debates about the security and desirability of the Empire as a whole and the distribution of military power necessary to defend it.

Historians have demonstrated the manner in which the demands of colonial defence contributed to the development of the systematic consideration of strategy in Britain,[1] yet much less has been said about the manner in which home defence contributed to the development of Britain's 'war machinery'. This belies the fact that the requirements of preventing an invasion were at the heart of the development of British 'strategy' during the nineteenth century, and that they contributed to the development of the institutions and administrative structures intended to facilitate the co-ordination of military and naval effort just as much as the demands of the Empire.[2] This was for the comparatively simple reason that both services had

---

[1] Gibbs, 'The Origins of Imperial Defence'; Ehrman, *Cabinet Government and War*; W. C. B. Tunstall, 'Imperial Defence, 1897–1914' in E. A. Benians, J. Butler, and C. E. Carrington eds, *The Cambridge History of the British Empire*, Vol. III: *The Empire Commonwealth, 1870–1919*, Cambridge: Cambridge University Press, 1967, pp. 563–604; Schurman, *Imperial Defence*.

[2] The word 'strategy' itself was not in common use until the end of the century. See D. French, *The British Way in Warfare, 1688–2000*, London: Unwin Hyman, 1990, pp. 128–45; N. A. M. Rodger, 'Naval Strategy in the Eighteen and Nineteenth Centuries' in G. Till ed., *The Development of British Naval Thinking*, Abingdon: Routledge, 2006, pp. 29–30.

a role to play in preventing an invasion, and that the forces required for this vital function were a constant consideration in calculations of broader imperial strategy. The size, composition, and focus of both Army and Navy were affected by the requirements of national as much as by imperial defence. Moreover, the question of home defence contributed to the organic evolution of mechanisms for the centralised control of British strategy. As a balance of military and naval effort was required to secure Britain's coasts, political decisions on how this division of labour ought properly to be struck were a crude means through which the government (often unintentionally) began to input into what passed for British 'grand' strategy in this period. Such intervention was more common in the realm of home defence than in many aspects of imperial policy, as the spectre of invasion excited the passions of the public on a regular basis—obliging politicians to take an active, if episodic interest in the armed forces' readiness to repulse a foreign attack. This is not to say that dramatic progress towards a coherent co-ordination of naval and military effort was made during this period. Political involvement in issues of strategy remained fleeting, irregular, and nascent, and the debate regarding home defence was as live and as fiercely contested in 1900 as it had been in 1860. Indeed, to speak of a centrally directed British strategy at all in this period would be problematic. The reality was more diffuse. 'Strategy' in this sense can thus perhaps best be understood as a term used to refer to the aggregate of quasi-independent naval and military efforts which could interact in both complementary and contradictory fashions depending on the circumstances and context. Nevertheless, the point remains that political decisions became a more significant 'input' into this dynamic process towards the end of the nineteenth century, and that judgements made on the topic of home defence exerted at least an equal impact as those in the imperial sphere upon the course of British 'strategy'—in terms of both its institutional manifestations and its general tone.

The manner in which politicians exerted a greater influence over British strategy during this period and the extent to which this process occurred through discussions of home defence can best be viewed by considering the problem their intervention was intended to solve: the inefficient and ill co-ordinated nature of naval and military effort in evidence before the turn of the century. These deficiencies can best be illustrated by viewing naval and military policy during this period in parallel, thereby enabling their chaotic and unmanaged interaction to become clearly visible. By framing the discussion around the requirements of home defence, the extent to which protecting the British Isles acted as a nexus linking the activities of the Army and Navy together also becomes clear. The opening two chapters will thus consider the strategic agendas of the two services in turn, before Chapter 3 examines governmental intervention in their activities after the turn of the century.

THE BRITISH APPROACH TO 'STRATEGY' FROM WATERLOO TO THE FRANCO-PRUSSIAN WAR

Defending the British Isles was one of the few constants in what might loosely be termed British 'strategy' during the nineteenth century. Whilst debates over the desirability of acquiring and defending costly colonial possessions raged until the final quarter of the century (when the term 'imperial defence' emerged), the importance of safeguarding the United Kingdom was an objective all politicians, soldiers, and sailors agreed upon.[3]

The threat of invasion, so real in 1803–4, retreated from the forefront of the British consciousness after the defeat of Napoleon in 1815. Yet it was never far from view. The legacy of the Napoleonic Wars and the intense anti-French propaganda of the period left an enduring impression, fostering suspicions that Britain's European neighbours had little respect for property, freedom, law, or religious liberty. Thus, when the introduction of effective steam-powered ships during the 1830s and 1840s appeared to call into doubt whether the traditional bulwark against continental enemies—the Royal Navy—could still be relied upon, alarm about a hostile army landing on British shores spread rapidly. Even the taciturn Duke of Wellington was moved to predict that 'excepting immediately under the fire of Dover Castle, there is not a spot on the coast which Infantry might not be thrown on shore, with any wind and in any weather'.[4]

Developments in Europe—particularly those in France, Britain's nearest neighbour and traditional rival—exercised a particularly marked effect over impressions of her security throughout the century. The election of Louis Napoleon to the office of President of the Republic in December 1848 and his subsequent *coup d'état* and elevation to the position of Emperor as Napoleon III in 1851 drew parallels with the behaviour of his uncle and rekindled entrenched suspicions of French designs against Britain.[5] The new Emperor's unpredictability and authoritarianism stoked traditional British distrust of continental Catholicism, militarism, and Caesarism, and resulted in a persistent wariness towards the new monarch in the public imagination around the middle of the century.[6] The two countries were still able to work together effectively—particularly in the Crimean War—but tensions were never far from the surface and incidents such as the completion of the extensive new French naval base at Cherbourg and the launch of the first modern ironclad warship *La Gloire* in 1859 were construed as imminent threats to the British Isles.[7] The fear of invasion was never far from British minds during periods of discord in relations between London and Paris.

Cross-Channel tensions were exacerbated by mid-Victorian concern over the steady diffusion of British naval and military resources across a seemingly ever-expanding Empire. Worries over British naval weakness in the middle years of the

---

[3] W. C. B. Tunstall, 'Imperial Defence, 1815–1870' in J. Holland Rose, A. P. Newton, and E. A. Benians eds, *The Cambridge History of the British Empire*, Vol. II: *The Growth of the New Empire, 1783–1870*, Cambridge: Cambridge University Press, 1940, pp. 806–41; P. Burroughs, 'Defence and Imperial Disunity' in A. Porter ed., *The Oxford History of the British Empire: The Nineteenth Century*, Oxford: Oxford University Press, 1999, pp. 320–45.

[4] Wellington to Sir John Burgoyne, 9 January 1847, quoted in J. C. Ardagh, 'The Defence of London', 16 July 1888, PRO 30/40/13, fos 301.

[5] J. P. Parry, 'The Impact of Napoleon III on British Politics, 1851–1880', *Transactions of the Royal Historical Society*, 6th Series, Vol. 11, 2001, pp. 147–75.

[6] B. Porter, '"Bureau and Barrack": Early Victorian Attitudes towards the Continent', *Victorian Studies*, Vol. 27, No. 4, 1984, pp. 407–33.

[7] Gooch, 'Bolt from the Blue', pp. 3–5.

century are easily exaggerated,[8] but the impression of vulnerability was genuine. As the Board of Admiralty warned the government, 'we should now commence a war with France at a greater disadvantage than at former times'.[9]

This combination of British paranoia, poor relations with France, and the drain the Empire placed upon military resources resulted in a major invasion panic in 1858–9.[10] The episode was short lived, but prompted the government into the first of a series of isolated forays into the realm of defensive precautions. Parliament sanctioned the raising of Volunteer corps for national defence, more money was voted for the Fleet, and a Royal Commission was appointed to investigate the Defences of the United Kingdom.[11] The Commission resulted in the expenditure of £11,850,000 on fixed defences over the following four years, but its findings had little impact upon the general course of British strategy. Political reticence to discuss the topic on a regular basis soon enabled 'Treasury control' to become the guiding light of defence policy and the mid-Victorian preference for fiscal orthodoxy remained the ultimate arbiter of naval and military preparations until into the 1880s. The two decades after the report of the Royal Commission witnessed a renewed lull in British concerns about invasion, punctuated only by the reaction to Prussia's striking military victories in 1870–1.[12] Defence spending fell as successive governments refrained from significant foreign entanglements and the issue of how to defend the Empire continued to drift upon a series of broad assumptions, propelled by a general sense of British superiority and exceptionalism.

For the purposes of this investigation, the most important feature of the period between 1815 and 1870 was the lack of a systematic approach to considering the needs of defending the Empire.[13] Periodic invasion scares or minor wars prompted sporadic flashes of political interest and increased expenditure, but these were haphazard and the tendency was always to revert to prioritizing economy over military or naval necessity. Critics such as the radical MP Richard Cobden viewed this cycle of outcry and reaction as self-perpetuating: 'successive governments have rendered themselves wholly responsible for the invasion panics by making them the plea for repeated augmentations of our armaments'.[14] A more balanced judgement may be that governments did just enough to maintain British security, but that in a period of relative international calm and domestic uncertainty no more was necessary or possible. Defending the United Kingdom remained a focus of both services, but it was generally believed that British naval power would be equal to the task and that no detailed political consideration of the issue was thus required.

---

[8] J. F. Beeler, *British Naval Policy in the Gladstone–Disraeli Era, 1866–1880*, Stanford, CA: Stanford University Press, 1997, Ch. 1.

[9] Quoted in C. J. Bartlett, 'The Mid-Victorian Reappraisal of Naval Policy' in K. Bourne and D. C. Watt eds, *Studies in International History*, London, 1967, pp. 190–2.

[10] The term 'panic' was coined by Richard Cobden in his plea for calm, *The Three Panics: A Historical Episode*, London, 1862.

[11] I. F. W. Beckett, *Riflemen Form: A Study of the Rifle Volunteer Movement, 1859–1908*, Aldershot: Ogilby Trust, 1982, Ch. 1; Beeler, *British Naval Policy*, Table 6, p. 58.

[12] Clarke, *Voices Prophesying War*, Ch. 2.

[13] Gibbs, 'Origins of Imperial Defence', p. 25; Beeler, *British Naval Policy*, p. 258.

[14] Cobden, *The Three Panics*, p. 161.

BRITISH POWER UNDER PRESSURE, 1870–8

This situation began to change from 1870 onwards, however, as the growth of Prussian strength re-shaped the balance of power on the Continent and contributed to a new phase of Great Power competition in the Balkans, Near East, and central Asia. England may have been, in Disraeli's words, 'as ready and willing as ever' to intervene in the affairs of Europe, but the limits of her capacity to do so became increasingly clear.[15] General concerns about Britain's international position contributed to widespread criticism at the lack of investment in the Army and Navy and doubts over their capacity to defend British trade and interests. Evidence of Britain's seemingly perilous position was plentiful. Between 1878 and 1885 a succession of incidents and international crises combined to illustrate the limitations of British military strength, all of which augured poorly for her prospects in the event of war against a fellow Great Power.

The first Anglo-Afghan War of 1878–80 and the subsequent debates over the desirability of retaining British possession of Kandahar revealed that imperial military operations could prove prohibitively expensive, even to the world's wealthiest power.[16] A year after the eventual British withdrawal from Afghanistan in April 1881, the occupation of Egypt tested the Army's capacity still further. Whilst operationally successful, the campaign proved a major drain upon War Office resources and a considerable proportion of the department's administrative functions were paralysed by the departure of senior staff to take part in the expedition.[17] More worryingly, the campaign exposed serious shortcomings in the British Empire's military system as a whole. Despite the fact that half of the force of 35,000 men sent to Egypt arrived from India, the dispatch of a comparatively modest expeditionary force from Britain had required the mobilization of the first-class reserve, intended for use only in times of national emergency.[18] Moreover, the need to draw so extensively upon resources from India exposed Britain's position there to Tsarist aggression along the North-West Frontier. Russian expansion southward towards the Raj had been a source of concern for officials in London and Calcutta since the 1860s, but the threat had solidified into an impending danger with the Russian occupation of the frontier town of Merv in late 1882. Coming whilst a significant proportion of the British garrison of India was in Egypt, the implication was clear: with India's borders under growing pressure, her

---

[15] Quoted in K. T. Hoppen, *The Mid-Victorian Generation, 1846–1886*, Oxford: Clarendon, 1998, p. 236; T. G. Otte, *Foreign Office Mind: The Making of British Foreign Policy, 1865–1914*, Cambridge: Cambridge University Press, 2011, Chs 1–2.

[16] I. F. W. Beckett, 'The Road from Kandahar: The Politics of Retention and Withdrawal in Afghanistan, 1880–81', *Journal of Military History*, Vol. 78, Oct., 2014, pp. 1263–94.

[17] H. Kochanski, *Sir Garnett Wolseley: Victorian Hero*, London and Rio Grande: Hambledon Press, 1999, p. 136.

[18] M. J. Williams, 'The Egyptian Campaign of 1882' in B. Bond ed., *Victorian Military Campaigns*, London: Hutchinson & Co., 1967, pp. 249–53; F. Maurice and G. Arthur, *Life of Lord Wolseley*, London: William Heinemann, 1924, p. 145.

military resources could not necessarily be relied upon elsewhere in the Empire without exposing the security of the Raj.[19]

The limits of British power were rendered apparent again in 1884–5, as the threat of war with Russia over the status of the Afghan border town of Pendjeh made the rapid withdrawal of troops from the ongoing occupation of Egypt and the Sudan a matter for serious consideration in London.[20] Mobilization schemes prepared in April confirm that the majority of British forces in Egypt would have been transferred to India at the outbreak of war against Russia.[21] These episodes showed that shortages in military manpower made sustaining multiple concurrent operations on any significant scale problematic.[22] As the Adjutant General, Sir Garnet Wolseley, explained in February 1883: 'these small detached forces are, I think, always a source of danger to a nation like ours whose army is so very small.'[23]

The Navy, too, appeared ill prepared during the Pendjeh Crisis. The mobilization of the Fleet was inefficient and remained incomplete as the threat of war receded in May 1885.[24] Admiral Sir Arthur Hood, who was appointed Senior Naval Lord at the height of the crisis, subsequently acknowledged that 'when the last scare occurred the Navy was not prepared for war'.[25] Whilst Russia presented no serious challenge to Britain's position at sea, the pedestrian pace of the Navy's mobilization raised questions about the security of Britain's vital food supply during war against a more formidable maritime power.[26] Britain was undoubtedly preeminent at sea,[27] but contemporaries worried that the vast extent of her maritime trading network and her dependence upon imported foodstuffs would strain the Navy's resources to their utmost in the event of war with a naval power such as France. By 1886 Britain imported two-thirds of its domestic grain consumption as low prices, declining domestic production, and rapid population

---

[19] A. Preston ed., *In Relief of Gordon: Lord Wolseley's Campaign Journal of the Khartoum Relief Expedition, 1884–1885*, London: Hutchinson, 1967, *xxiv–xxv*.

[20] Gladstone to Queen Victoria, 13 April 1885, in G. E. Buckle ed., *The Letters of Queen Victoria*, 2nd series, Vol. III, New York: Longmans, Green, & Co., 1928, pp. 634–5; Maurice and Arthur, *Wolseley*, pp. 207–10.

[21] A. Alison, 'Preparations for Mobilization, April 1885', 25 September 1885, p. 11, W/MEM/2.20, Wolseley Papers, Brighton and Hove Archives Centre.

[22] P. Burroughs, 'Defence and Imperial Disunity', p. 342; W. S. Hamer, *The British Army: Civil Military Relations, 1885–1905*, Oxford: Clarendon, 1970, p. 106. For the Army's manpower problems see E. M. Spiers, *The Late Victorian Army 1868–1902*, Manchester: Manchester University Press, 1992, pp. 59–67.

[23] Wolseley to Hartington, 20 February 1883, CS2/340/1334, Devonshire Papers, Chatsworth House.

[24] A. J. Marder, *The [Anatomy] of British Sea Power: A History of British Naval Policy in the Pre-Dreadnought Era, 1880–1905*, Hamden, CT: Archon, 1964 edn, pp. 132–3; M. Allen, 'The Foreign Intelligence Committee and the Origins of the Naval Intelligence Department of the Admiralty', *The Mariner's Mirror*, Vol. 81, No. 1, Feb., 1995, pp. 70–1.

[25] See Hood's evidence to the Committee on the Navy Estimates, 'Fourth Report from the Select Committee on Navy Estimates', 6 August 1888, p. 37, Hansard c. 328.

[26] Marder, *Anatomy*, pp. 84–93; Ranft, 'The Protection of British seaborne trade'; A. Offer, *The First World War: An Agrarian Interpretation*, Oxford: Clarendon, 1989, pp. 217–32.

[27] Beeler, *British Naval Policy*, pp. 210–36, 264–6, and 271–8 and 'In the Shadow of Briggs: A New Perspective on British Naval Administration and W. T. Stead's 1884 "Truth about the Navy" Campaign', *International Journal of Naval History*, Vol. 1, No. 1, Apr., 2002.

growth saw foreign foodstuffs flood the British market.[28] The vulnerability this situation entailed had been recognized by the Carnarvon Commission in 1879. The body had recommended an extension of Britain's system of global coaling stations to improve the Navy's ability to operate across the breadth of the maritime trading system without restriction, yet decisive action to mitigate the danger had been put off by the Gladstone government on the grounds of cost.[29]

Beyond the threat it posed to British trade and imports, French naval power also had the potential to restrict Britain's ability to move troops by sea. This was a fundamental tenet of British imperial strategy. It enabled relatively modest concentrations of troops in Britain and India to respond to threats across the Empire, reducing the need to maintain costly garrisons in far-flung possessions and allowing London to assume the costs of local defence from colonial governments. Yet if the Navy was fully occupied defending British trade against French raiders, it might prove impossible to provide the escorts necessary to ship troops to threatened points in a timely manner. The Empire's military weakness might thus leave swathes of territory vulnerable to the machinations of rival powers or local rebels. Such a danger was far from illusory; Britain's international isolation had worried many diplomats since the 1870s. It raised the prospect of other powers co-ordinating their actions against her, either in concert or during times of unrest in the Empire— as Russia had done during her Egyptian entanglement in 1882 and 1884–5. The position in the Near East was particularly worrisome, as British agents at Constantinople returned reports of Franco-Russian collusion against British influence in Egypt during 1886–7.[30] Anglo-French relations in the region had been strained since British intervention in Egypt in 1882, after which the government in Paris assumed a belligerent stance over the territory for the subsequent two decades. Simmering colonial tensions were worsened by domestic developments in France, where a resurgence of anti-republicanism and hyper-nationalism, personified in the rise of General Georges Boulanger to political prominence, fostered antagonism towards Britain.[31] The concern in London was that popular feeling threatened to motivate the authorities to pursue a policy of foreign adventurism, a prospect which appeared imminent in February 1887 when the French Chamber acceded to Boulanger's requests massively to expand the military budget, citing 'extra war expenses' as justification for the measure.[32] Similarly threatening developments were evident in the French Ministry of Marine, where the radical Admiral Hyacinthe Aube advocated the bombardment of coastal towns and the indiscriminate sinking of enemy commerce by torpedo boats as legitimate methods of warfare. Aube was particularly bellicose in the stance he adopted towards Britain, a fact widely remarked upon in the press in both countries.[33] Persistent friction

---

[28] Marder, *Anatomy*, p. 84–5; Offer, *Agrarian Interpretation*, pp. 219–21.

[29] Schurman, *Imperial Defence*, pp. 100–25.   [30] Otte, *Foreign Office Mind*, p. 160.

[31] Otte, 'From "War in Sight" to Nearly War: Anglo-French Relations in the Age of High Imperialism, 1875–1898', *Diplomacy & Statecraft*, Vol. 17, No. 4, 2006, p. 701; *Foreign Office Mind*, pp. 174–5.

[32] Otte, *Foreign Office Mind*, p. 175.

[33] T. Ropp, *Development of a Modern Navy: French Naval Policy, 1871–1904*; S. S. Roberts ed., Annapolis, MA: Naval Institute Press, 1987, pp. 162–71; Marder, *Anatomy*, pp. 89–100.

with Russia and growing animosity from Paris meant that the British had to think in more detail about how to defend their interests in the event of war.

THE CHALLENGE AT SEA

The prospect of war with France presented a peculiar challenge for the Royal Navy. How the naval authorities proposed to meet the threat—and how these plans altered—illustrate the fundamental pillars of contemporary naval thought which were to animate discussions about war with Germany down to 1914. Since 1886 the main French battle fleet had been concentrated at Toulon in the Mediterranean as the result of escalating Franco-Italian tensions in the region.[34] From London's perspective, this reduced the danger in the Channel and Western Approaches— where Britain's vital interests lay. The developing French torpedo boat establish-ment along her northern coasts remained a source of difficulty for the Royal Navy, but the departure of her battle fleet was undoubtedly a development to be welcomed. Yet, the newly strengthened Toulon squadron was now far stronger than the peacetime establishment of the British Mediterranean Fleet. In the event of war, France would be in a commanding position in the Mediterranean. This had commercial, strategic, and diplomatic implications for Britain. The Mediterranean and Near East were crucial to British world power, forming part of the vital 'strategic corridor' through which her European and Anglo-Indian spheres of interest were linked.[35] If France commanded the Mediterranean, British seaborne trade with the Near East was likely to cease during wartime, and communications with India, China, and Australasia would have to sail via the longer Cape route. Similarly, Britain would be unable to reinforce her Egyptian or Indian garrisons via the Mediterranean route, and Malta, a vital base of supply for the fleet, would be cut off. Such eventualities would imperil the stabilizing diplomatic agreements London had concluded with Italy and Austria-Hungary in 1887 (and thereby pos-sibly undo the concomitant improvement in relations with their partner in the Triple Alliance—Germany) and have negative consequences for British prestige in the Islamic Ottoman world, with the attendant problems for her position in India.[36] How the Admiralty intended to solve the competing demands of the Mediterranean and home waters exposed the essence of how the Royal Navy thought about strategy in the late Victorian period.

Initially, the Admiralty did not alter its peacetime dispositions in response to the French re-deployment. The sixteen battleships of the Channel Fleet remained stationed in home waters, despite the fact that they faced only a single French

[34] Ropp, *Development of a Modern Navy*, p. 171.

[35] J. Darwin, 'Imperialism and the Victorians: The Dynamics of Territorial Expansion', *English Historical Review*, CXII, 447, Jun., 1997, p. 622.

[36] Otte, ' "Floating Downstream"? Lord Salisbury and British Foreign Policy, 1878–1902' in T. G. Otte ed., *The Makers of British Foreign Policy: From Pitt to Thatcher*, Basingstoke: Palgrave, 2002, p. 111.

equivalent there.[37] This reflected the traditional primacy which securing home waters occupied within British naval thought. Appearing before a parliamentary committee on the defences of the Thames Estuary in April 1887 Captain William Hall, the Director of Naval Intelligence (DNI), explained that 'our fleet in home waters will always be large, as our interests are greatest there'. 'I look upon it as an absolute necessity in a War with France', he continued, 'to keep a strong force in home waters at all times.'[38] Yet, the DNI was forced to admit that this would render the British position in the Mediterranean an uncertain one. Hall informed the assembled MPs that 'on every foreign station, with the exception of the Mediterranean, we have at the present moment...a squadron superior to that of the French, and in most cases to that of the French and Russians combined'. The DNI speculated that the current situation rendered the defeat in detail of the Mediterranean Fleet a realistic possibility.[39] Such a reverse would be rendered more likely if, as had often been the case since the 1870s, British interests in the east of the basin required the fleet to be deployed to the Levant. In this eventuality, their position at Toulon would enable the French to establish themselves between the Mediterranean Fleet and reinforcements arriving from the England. If an isolated British squadron were cut off and defeated, the losses could erode Britain's overall numerical advantage, raising the possibility that ships would have to be recalled from other theatres to bolster her fleets in European waters—a move likely to be create vulnerabilities elsewhere. The danger of the position was underlined by the C-in-C of the Mediterranean Fleet, the Duke of Edinburgh, the following year. In a letter to the Queen, the Duke stated bluntly that 'the normal strength of the squadron in the Mediterranean is insufficient in case of a sudden attack or outbreak of war'.[40] A growing awareness of the unsatisfactory nature of this situation helped to prompt a systematic review of British naval strategy during the autumn and winter of 1887–8. Conducted primarily by Captain Hall and the recently formed Naval Intelligence Department (NID), the process was predicated upon a detailed comparison between the Navy's available resources and the requirements likely to be placed upon it in the event of a war against France and Russia.[41]

Before Hall could complete his study, a war-scare swept across Europe. Relations between Paris and Berlin soured as Bismarck attempted to restrain the resurgence of French ambition and strength through a series of diplomatic manoeuvres. The bellicose attitude of the French public led to a groundswell of concern in Britain at the prospect of the country being drawn into a European war precipitated by French *revanchism*.[42] In some quarters these worries solidified into fears of a

---

[37] Evidence by Hall to the Secret Consultative Committee on Defences, 28 April 1887, Q. 2727, WO 33/47, fo. 1012.

[38] Evidence by Hall, Q. 2881, WO 33/47, fo. 1016.

[39] Evidence by Hall, Q. 2727 and Q. 2967, WO 33/47, fos 1012 and 1018.

[40] Duke of Edinburgh to Henry Ponsonby, 21 April 1888 in Buckle ed., *Letters of Queen Victoria* III: I, p. 399.

[41] R. E. Mullins, 'Sharpening the Trident: The Decisions of 1889 and the Creation of Modern Seapower', unpublished Ph.D. thesis, King's College, London, 2000, pp. 87–8, 118–20.

[42] 'The Result of General Boulanger's Success', *The Economist*, 21 April 1888, pp. 494–5.

pre-emptive French invasion of Britain.[43] The popularity of a French pamphlet depicting such an operation led *The Star* to infer that Frenchmen 'fully anticipate that the dream and predictions of the author of said pamphlet will be duly realised'.[44] The Admiralty and Foreign Office kept a close eye upon French ports and the movements of French vessels around the turn of the year.[45]

As had often been the case during the nineteenth century, the scare offered an opportunity to focus political attention on issues of defence. Perturbed by the lack of meaningful reform since the Pendjeh Crisis of 1884–5, an increasingly vociferous military and naval lobby sought to exploit Anglo-French tensions to pressurize the government to invest in the armed forces.[46] A National Defence Bill, intended to speed the mobilization of the auxiliary forces in time of emergency, was introduced to Parliament on 3 May, and a deputation of MPs called upon the Secretary of State for War anxious that additional steps be taken for the defence of London.[47] No less of a figure than the Adjutant General, Lord Wolseley, attempted to capitalize on the febrile atmosphere by adding official credibility to the danger of invasion. Wolseley was already engaged in a crusade against the system of government by party—'that curse of modern England'[48]—which he felt was undermining military effectiveness due to its inherent short-termism. He was thus quick to seize the opportunity to place the government in an awkward position and went public with a series of allegations about the vulnerability of London he had previously made before the Stephen Commission on Warlike Stores in December 1886.[49] In a speech to the House of Lords, Wolseley stated that 'as long as the Navy is as weak as it is at this moment, Her Majesty's Army cannot hold its own all over the world, dispersed as it is...our military forces are not organized or equipped as they should be to guarantee the safety of the Capital in which we are at the present moment'. His qualification that 'there is no imminent danger impending over this country' went largely overlooked.[50]

Much as more scrupulous observers decried the manner in which he called attention to his cause, Wolseley articulated the realities of the strategic situation Britain faced. Against a backdrop of growing Great Power tension it was vital for the Army and Navy to co-operate effectively to defend the Empire, the correct distribution of forces between Europe and the imperial periphery was a source of unresolved debate, and it appeared uncertain whether the naval power which guaranteed the functioning of the system of imperial defence as a whole was equal to the task before it. Wolseley's intervention received the attention he craved. His words were

[43] Marder, *Anatomy*, pp. 126–7.

[44] 'England to be Conquered by France', *The Star*, 31 March 1888.

[45] G. Aston, *Secret Service*, London: Faber & Faber, 1930, pp. 35–6; Marder, *Anatomy*, pp. 126–8.

[46] J. Sweetman, 'Towards a Ministry of Defence: First Faltering Steps, 1890–1923', in French and Holden Reid eds, *The British General Staff*, p. 29.

[47] 'Reply by the Right Hon. E. Stanhope to a Deputation of Members of Parliament on the subject of National Defence, 9th May 1888', WO 33/49, fos 216–9; Moon, 'Invasion', pp. 23–5.

[48] Quoted in Hamer, *The British Army*, p. 135.

[49] Brackenbury to Stanhope, 28 June 1888, Add. MS. 88906/16/19, Bowood Papers, [B]ritish [L]ibrary.

[50] Lords Sitting of 14 May 1888, Hansard, 3rd Series, Vol. 326, Cols 100–1.

widely reported in the press and provoked an explicit rejoinder from the government.[51] In a defiant speech to an audience in Derby the following day, the First Lord of the Admiralty, Lord George Hamilton, maintained that 'at no period in our history was the invasion of England less likely than it was at the present moment'.[52] He repeated this stance in the Commons a week later.[53] France lacked sufficient merchant tonnage in her Channel ports to mount a surprise invasion, Hamilton charged, and the dislocation of her seaborne commerce necessary to gather an invasion armada would be so obvious as to provide ample time for the Navy to counter any danger. With the relocation of French naval power to the Mediterranean, these claims had some validity. The Prime Minister did not share Hamilton's confidence, however.

Salisbury responded to the furore caused by Wolseley's speech by announcing the appointment of a Royal Commission to investigate 'the extent to which our Naval and Military systems, as at present organised and administered, are adapted to the national wants'.[54] Chaired by the Marquess of Hartington, a Liberal grandee who had served variously as First Lord of the Admiralty, Secretary of State for India, and most recently Secretary of State for War, this body had a wider-ranging and more comprehensive remit than the earlier Carnarvon Commission—marking a step towards a more thoroughgoing consideration of the defensive requirements of the Empire.[55] The Prime Minister supplemented this general investigation with a specific consideration of home defence by the Cabinet. An enquiry into the 'alleged inability of our military organisation to protect us from the invasion of London' began on 6 June.[56] It was to be in this setting that the Admiralty tentatively began to reveal the strategy it intended to pursue in the event of war with France.

Salisbury largely accepted Hamilton's arguments that the logistical and practical barriers to the French concentrating enough shipping in the Channel to conduct an invasion were insurmountable.[57] However, unlike during previous invasion scares, broader strategic calculations came to form a part of the ensuing discussions. Hinting at the direction of thought at the Admiralty, during the debate the First Lord reasoned that home waters and the Mediterranean would need to be considered as one for the purposes of conducting a naval war against France. 'The annihilation of our fleet in the Channel *and* Mediterranean', he contended, was the 'necessary preliminary' to a successful descent on British shores.[58] The French would need to muster merchant tonnage and warships from the Mediterranean

[51] 'Mercantile Marine Defence', *The Times*, 29 May 1888, pp. 11–12.

[52] 'Lord George Hamilton at Derby', *The Times*, 29 May 1888, p. 10.

[53] Commons Sitting of Monday, 4 June 1888, Hansard, 3rd Series, Vol. 326, Col. 1069.

[54] Smith to Queen Victoria, 1 June 1888, in Buckle ed., *Letters of Queen Victoria* III: I, p. 413; Hamer, *The British Army*, p. 136.

[55] 'Preliminary Report of the Royal Commissions appointed to enquire into the Civil and Professional Administration of the Naval and Military Departments', 1890, c. 5979, fo. 3. Hartington signed the terms of 7 June: see Sweetman, 'Towards a Ministry of Defence', n. 8.

[56] Salisbury note of 6 June 1888, CAB 37/21/14, fo. 179.

[57] Salisbury note of 6 June 1888, CAB 37/21/14. For criticism of Salisbury's views on strategy, see Marder, *Anatomy*, p. 77.

[58] Hamilton, 'A French Invasion', 22 June 1888, CAB 37/21/17. Emphasis added.

and move them into the Channel if they were to conduct a landing in the British Isles. The home islands might, it followed, be rendered secure from invasion by operations further afield than the Channel. A discussion of home defence thus began to spill over into broader questions of British imperial strategy as a whole. Moreover, it had also become intertwined with the current and future strength of the Fleet, and the extent to which it was able to fulfil the Admiralty's plans.

NAVAL STRATEGY FOR WAR AGAINST FRANCE

The statements Hamilton made to the Cabinet inquiry were based upon the work that Captain Hall and the Naval Intelligence Department had done over the winter of 1887–8. Hall's work represented the latest stage in the emergence of a coherent school of naval strategic thought in Britain.[59] This discourse produced a broad consensus of opinion about the exercise of naval power and its integral importance to the defence of Britain and her Empire. Captain Hall was at the forefront of this movement, a fact reflected in the sophisticated strategic appreciations he oversaw during his tenure as DNI. Since the early 1880s Hall had stressed the principle that restricting enemy access to the open seas represented the most effective means of protecting British trade and possessions. Confining enemy forces to port whenever possible would be the most economical way of preventing invasion and assuring a reasonable degree of security to British commerce. During the Pendjeh Crisis he had forwarded proposals to 'lock up' Russian vessels in the Baltic and Black Sea. By commanding the narrow entrances to these waterways, rather than try to guard what he estimated to be 92,000 miles of oceanic communications, Hall considered that British naval power could be made more effective than mere numbers might suggest. Exploiting geography in this manner would also mitigate some of the operational difficulties associated with maintaining a tight blockade of enemy ports in the absence of appropriate local infrastructure and coaling facilities.[60] The DNI advocated a similar approach to a war against France in 1888.

In the event of war the main danger, Hall assessed, was that the diffusion of British strength across the globe would leave the Navy vulnerable in European waters at the outset of war with France if the enemy adopted a vigorous offensive. Of particular concern was the prospect of the French Toulon and Brest squadrons

[59] For more on the development of strategic thought see D. M. Schurman, *The Education of a Navy: The Development of British Naval Thought, 1867–1914*, London: Cassell, 1965; A. Lambert, *The Foundations of Naval History: John Knox Laughton, the Royal Navy and the Historical Profession*, London: Chatham, 1998, 'The Development of Education in the Royal Navy: 1854–1914' in G. Till ed., *The Development of British Naval Thinking: Essays in Memory of Bryan Ranft*, Abingdon: Routledge, 2006, pp. 34–56; and A. Lambert, 'The Naval War Course, *Some Principles of Maritime Strategy* and the Origins of "The British Way in Warfare"' in K. Neilson and G. Kennedy eds, *The British Way in Warfare: Power and the International System, 1856–1956: Essays in Honour of David French*, Farnham: Ashgate, 2010, pp. 219–56; Rodger, 'The Idea of Naval Strategy' in Till ed., *Development*, pp. 30–1; Grimes, *War Planning*, pp. 14–21.

[60] W. H. Hall, 'General Outline of Possible Naval Operations Against Russia', 1 March 1885, ADM 231/6/64.

combining, against either the British Mediterranean or Channel Fleet. 'If the French defeat one of our Home Squadrons', he warned, 'they would at once obtain command of home waters... and it is needless to point out what disasters this may involve.'[61] This did not mean that the Admiralty advocated concentrating naval resources in the Channel, however. Rather, the steady shift of French naval resources and attention to the Mediterranean between 1886 and 1889 enabled Hall to reprise his earlier method of exploiting geography to Britain's advantage. By concentrating a superior British force at Gibraltar, Hall reasoned that the Navy could confine France's most powerful warships within the Mediterranean. By commanding the Strait in the west and the Suez Canal in the east, Britain could isolate the basin from the remainder of the globe, containing the worst effects of what would inevitably be an extremely expensive and troublesome conflict, and enabling the continuation of the majority of British worldwide trade. This principle defined the strategy the Admiralty grudgingly outlined to the Cabinet during the summer of 1888.

At the same time as Salisbury's foray into the feasibility of a French invasion, the Cabinet was conducting an ongoing discussion over the *matériel* material needs of the Navy. Under growing pressure from commercial and financial interests (which depended upon the security of British trade for their livelihood) to strengthen the Fleet, the government had been negotiating with the Admiralty as to the number of vessels required to protect British interests whilst Hall had been working on his strategic appreciation.[62] The naval leadership had initially been reluctant to commit to precise figures, citing uncertainty arising from the rapid pace of technological change as justification for their reticence, much to the chagrin of the government.[63] Armed with Hall's assessment of how the Navy would conduct a war against France and Russia, the naval authorities finally relented in mid-June. In the days before Hamilton presented his views on invasion to the Prime Minister, the Admiralty belatedly furnished the Cabinet with a broad outline of British naval strategy and the number of ships required to prosecute it. Most commonly cited as the basis for the programme of naval expansion provided for by the Naval Defence Act, this document was arguably more significant as one of the first explicit linkages of future procurement plans with an outline of how the Admiralty intended to fight a war. Hall and the NID had produced a strategy linking resources, a method of co-ordinating operations, and the broader aims of imperial defence.[64] In doing so they revealed that the Admiralty's intentions had changed considerably in the previous eighteen months.

---

[61] Hall, 'Comparison of the Fleets of England, France and Russia in 1890', May 1888, ADM 231/12/149A.

[62] S. R. B. Smith, 'Public Opinion, the Navy and the City of London: The Drive for British Naval Expansion in the Late Nineteenth Century', *War & Society*, Vol. 9, No. 1, May, 1991, pp. 29–50.

[63] Marder, *Anatomy*, pp. 107–10. Hood had argued that 'I am satisfied with the relative number of armoured-clad ships as compared to those of other powers' as recently as 13 June. See Hood's evidence to the Committee on the Navy Estimates, 'Fourth Report from the Select Committee on Navy Estimates', 6 August 1888, p. 28, Hansard c. 328.

[64] Mullins, 'Sharpening the Trident', pp. 87–8, 118–20.

Whereas the previous April Hall had stated that the Admiralty anticipated maintaining a strong force in home waters and accepting a margin of inferiority in the Mediterranean, the Naval Lords now proposed to shift the point of British concentration to Gibraltar. The paper stated the Admiralty's intention:

1. To assemble a strong force at Gibraltar superior to that of the French at Toulon.
2. To assemble a strong force at Portland superior of that to the French at Cherbourg and Brest.
3. To assemble a small force of fast cruizers at Queenstown for the protection of our trade off the west coast of Ireland and the entrance to the Channel.[65]

As the main French battle fleet remained at Toulon, these conditions would make the force assembled at Gibraltar the strongest of the three British contingents: the fleet based there would comprise fourteen battleships and two armoured cruisers. The five battleships of the Mediterranean Fleet would be deployed in an advanced position at Malta, ready to interfere with hostile forces approaching Egypt, the Suez Canal, or Constantinople. Nineteen of the Navy's twenty-seven available battleships would thus be deployed in the Mediterranean in the event of war with France. This would leave only eight battleships and one armoured cruiser at Portland; half the number of vessels Hall had envisaged maintaining in home waters the previous April. This shift in strategic focus was also evident in Hood's forecast of future dispositions. The Senior Naval Lord explained that, due to new vessels entering service and some overseas detachments returning to European waters, by April 1889 it would be possible to add two further battleships and armoured cruisers to the force at Gibraltar. When these reinforcements had been completed, the Mediterranean would host twenty-one battleships, compared to only nine in the Channel.[66]

The Admiralty's plans reflected the prevailing understanding of strategy embodied by the doctrine of 'command of the sea'. The naval leadership did not view the retention of a crushing preponderance of armoured warships in home waters as necessary at all times for the purposes of preventing an invasion.[67] Admiral Hood was explicit on this point. Responding to a suggestion that a reserve fleet should be confined to home waters on a permanent basis to defend British coasts, the Senior Naval Lord countered that 'it would be impossible to lay down as a rule not to be departed from, that a reserve squadron should be absolutely confined to home waters, in addition to our Coast Defence vessels'.[68] Positioning the main British force between the enemy fleet and the coasts of the United Kingdom was the crucial factor in ensuring national security, whether this required the Fleet to depart from home waters or not. With the fleet at Gibraltar effectively restricting the French Toulon squadron to the Mediterranean, the Admiralty was content that no power would risk embarking an army in the Channel in the

---

[65] Admiralty, 'The Requirements of the British Navy', 19 June 1888, p. 1, CAB 37/22/24.

[66] Ibid., pp. 2–3.

[67] For the suggestion that they did see N. A. Lambert, 'Admiral Sir John Fisher and the Concept of Flotilla Defence, 1904–1909', *Journal of Military History*, Vol. 59, No. 4, Oct., 1995, p. 649.

[68] 'Extracts from the Report of the Committee on the Naval Manoeuvres', 1889, p. 29, C. 5632.

absence of an escorting force of capital ships. The vulnerability of lightly defended transports to the action of cruisers and smaller craft made the Navy's flotilla forces too powerful a deterrent to any such enterprise. Hood stressed this point, explaining the importance of the Navy's 'armoured coast defence vessels, the 33 gunboats, and the 30 reserve torpedo boats' to his defensive strategy.[69] The defensive power of the flotilla appeared likely only to grow as the century drew to a close, due to the introduction of more effective locomotive torpedoes. By May 1890 Admiral Richard Vesey-Hamilton noted pointedly that battleships might soon offer scant defence to an invasion armada after dark, unable as they would be to shield transports 'against the number of light craft of various sorts we could send amongst them at night'.[70] The Channel was thus only likely to become more hazardous for the transports of an invading army as time wore on. The Navy would still be obliged to combat the danger posed by French cruisers raiding the Atlantic trade routes and of torpedo boats disrupting traffic in the Channel, but in the opinion of Their Lordships of the Admiralty, the danger of invasion could be forestalled at Gibraltar.

The efficacy of the dispositions Hood outlined to the Cabinet was put to the test in an extensive series of manoeuvres conducted during July and August. Planned as part of the strategic review Hall completed during the spring, the exercises involved a full mobilization of the reserve fleet and included virtually every seaworthy vessel in home waters.[71] The outcome of the exercises re-affirmed the difficulties Hall had predicted in maintaining a blockade of an enemy port with the objective of 'sealing in' enemy vessels. The blockaded 'French' fleet escaped on several occasions and raided a number of cities on the north-west coast, including the key port of Liverpool.[72] The success of the enemy squadron appeared to contradict the Admiralty's claims that the current margin of naval superiority was sufficient to protect British interests in the event of war with France and that emergency construction was unnecessary.[73] This was certainly the impression conveyed in the 'Three Admirals' report on the exercises, in which a group of senior flag officers produced a damning assessment of the Fleet's current ability to bring a war with France to a swift conclusion. 'The main lesson', they charged, 'is that Great Britain, whose maritime supremacy is her life, is very far from being as strong as she should be at sea.'[74] Yet, in many ways the lessons of the manoeuvres confirmed the validity of the strategy Hood had outlined to the Cabinet in July. The difficulties experienced in sustaining an effective blockade in the narrow confines of the Channel augured poorly for the practicality of mounting similar operations against the French base at Toulon, at the extremity of a long line of communications and supply. Hall's plan to exploit the British position at Gibraltar to seal the French

---

[69] Ibid.

[70] 'Minute of Sir Vesey Hamilton', 9 May 1890, inside folder, 'Invasion Subject, Conference with War Office', ADM 1/7046.

[71] Salisbury to the Queen, 4 May 1888 in Buckle ed., *Letters* III: I, p. 409.

[72] NID No. 179, 'Report on the Naval Manoeuvres of 1888', October 1888, ADM 231/14.

[73] Marder, *Anatomy*, pp. 107–10.

[74] 'Extracts from the Report of the Committee on the Naval Manoeuvres', 1889, p. 29, C. 5632.

fleet within the Mediterranean without recourse to such problematic tactics appeared a sound organizing principal under existing technological conditions and given the current levels of relative strength. Admiral Hood had rejected the Duke of Edinburgh's calls to mount a blockade of Toulon as unrealistic for precisely these reasons in April.[75] With the Strait of Gibraltar sealed, the detached squadron at Malta would enable the British to monitor the movements of French forces and to bring them to action if required without eroding their own strength by attempting to blockade Toulon. As to the position in home waters, the scheme of the manoeuvres had counted older, less capable French coastal defence ironclads as seagoing battleships whilst omitting their more numerous British counterparts. By amplifying French strength and exaggerating British weakness in this manner, the exercises had presented a worst-case scenario.[76] A more realistic classification of these vessels would allow the dispatch of forces to the Mediterranean without endangering vital British interests, as would the commissioning of a number of new ironclads during 1890–1. Even the partisan 'Three Admirals' were obliged to acknowledge that these factors 'will considerably improve the position'.[77]

Eighteen months after outlining its plans to the Cabinet, the Board of Admiralty met to formalize its decision to concentrate British forces at Gibraltar as official policy. On 4 December 1889 the Board agreed that:

> The existing so-called Channel Squadron... shall be considered as an adjunct to the Mediterranean Fleet in case of threatened War with France... In the event of relations becoming strained the Channel Squadron to be dispatched to Gibraltar as Head Quarters... The Mediterranean and Channel Squadrons combined should be kept up so as to be superior the total French naval force in commission, and in reserve ready for commission at Toulon and in the Mediterranean.[78]

Hamilton explained the changes to Parliament in March 1890, announcing that 'the Channel Squadron is... no longer specially required for the purposes implied by its name'. 'This name it is not proposed to alter', he continued, but 'the Channel squadron will, however, be available for other services if so required'.[79] These changes were underwritten by alterations to the composition of the Channel and Mediterranean Fleets. The Mediterranean squadron received two additional battleships, raising its strength to ten ironclads and two armoured cruisers. Changes to the Channel squadron were more extensive. Being based adjacent to the Navy's training and recruiting establishments in Britain, hitherto the fleet had served a dual purpose as a training establishment. This function meant that during peacetime the squadron had been comprised of older, larger vessels, in order to provide

---

[75] Duke of Edinburgh to Henry Ponsonby, 21 April 1888, in Buckle ed., *Letters* III: I, p. 399; memorandum by Hood quoted in Marder, *Anatomy*, p. 130.

[76] Hamilton, 'Naval Estimates, 1889–90', 1 December 1888, p. 12, CAB 37/22/40; 'Extracts from the Report of the Committee on the Naval Manoeuvres', 1889, p. 33, C. 5632.

[77] 'Extracts from the Report of the Committee on the Naval Manoeuvres', 1889, p. 30, C. 5632.

[78] 'At a Meeting in the First Lord's Room on 4th December 1889', pp. 1–2, inside docket, 'Channel Squadron', 15 July 1890, ADM 1/7027.

[79] 'Statement of First Lord of the Admiralty Explanatory of The Navy Estimates, 1890–91', 4 March 1890, p. 17, C. 5958.

instructional opportunities for the largest number of men possible. In the event of war the crews would transfer to more modern ironclads held in readiness in the steam reserve. Under the arrangements agreed in December 1889, this arrangement would be reversed, with the most modern vessels being transferred into full commission.[80] This switch was intended to address one of the potential shortcomings in the Admiralty's plans: the time it would take to dispatch the Channel Fleet to Gibraltar in the event of strained relations with France. As had been demonstrated in 1885, mobilizing ships from the reserve could prove time consuming and would be a visible sign of escalation during a diplomatic crisis. The ability rapidly and discreetly to dispatch the Channel Fleet to Gibraltar was thus of extreme strategic and diplomatic importance. The newly constituted Channel Fleet would possess some of the Navy's swiftest ironclad battleships, making it ideally suited to its reinforcing role.[81]

Concentrating the Navy's forces at Gibraltar would form the basis of British naval strategy in a war against France for the following fifteen years. Yet, the balance of British interests in the Mediterranean was such that there were on-going discussions as to the advisability of concentrating further to the east, within the basin itself. The Admiralty adopted a consistent position in this debate, revealing the powerful influence that interests in home waters continued to exercise upon naval thought and the limits of the risks deemed prudent to run there.

THE STRATEGIC ASPECTS OF
THE FRANCO-RUSSIAN ALLIANCE

Whilst the measures adopted in 1889–90 had strengthened Britain's naval presence in the Mediterranean, a fleet at Gibraltar would be impotent to affect events in the Near East. This became increasingly problematic from 1890–1 onwards, as shifting diplomatic arrangements and international conditions threatened British interests in the region, making it necessary to prepare for naval operations in the Levant. In the aftermath of the Crimean War Britain and France had sought to curtail Russian naval ambitions in the Black Sea and Mediterranean through neutrality clauses in the Treaty of Paris in 1856. Russia had taken advantage of France's defeat in 1870 to abrogate these measures and during the 'great eastern crisis' of 1875–8 had displayed a renewed determination to extend the Tsar's influence into the Balkans and towards the Straits. Russian encroachment towards Constantinople and Persia was viewed as particularly threatening in Britain, as it threatened the 'strategic corridor' to India.[82] Russian efforts to develop a credible naval presence in the Black Sea thus became the object of close attention in London, as Russian penetration

---

[80] Ibid.

[81] Hamilton, 'English and French Fleets in the Mediterranean', January 1892, ADM 121/75.

[82] J. Darwin, 'Imperialism and the Victorians', p. 622. See also K. M. Wilson, 'Constantinople or Cairo: Lord Salisbury and the Partition of the Ottoman Empire 1886–97' in his *Empire and Continent*, pp. 1–31.

into the eastern Mediterranean threatened to disrupt the delicate naval equilibrium in the basin.

These conditions produced two competing requirements on British naval power: controlling the Strait of Gibraltar and thereby securing home waters, and project-ing power to the east.[83] Planners feared that Russian action against Constantinople or the Dardanelles might occupy the British squadron at Malta, thereby reducing the number of vessels available for operations against the French.[84] Britain simply lacked the ships necessary to provide an adequate margin of superiority over the French whilst simultaneously monitoring the Dardanelles, Constantinople, Egypt, and the Suez Canal. The situation was complicated still further by rumours of French plans to fortify and expand the port of Bizerta, which reached the Foreign Office in November 1888. Situated on the southern side of the Strait of Sicily, Bizerta would provide a refuge for French torpedo boats and commerce raiders, and potentially act as a forward base for operations against Egypt and Suez Canal.[85] The threat a base so positioned could pose to British interests was articulated in several French service publications, which openly speculated that a commanding position in the central Mediterranean might enable the French fleet to isolate and destroy a detached British squadron in the Levant before it had the opportunity to rendezvous with reinforcements.[86]

The difficulties posed by the competing demands of the eastern Mediterranean and home waters were highlighted in early 1890. Russia had pursued a proactive policy in the Balkans since the turn of the year, attempting to pressure Bulgaria into acceding to Tsarist designs on Constantinople. As any such increase in Russian power would threaten the apparently precarious Ottoman presence in Europe, Britain and Austria provided diplomatic support to the Bulgarians in an attempt to preserve their independence.[87] Unwilling to surrender its position in the Balkans, Constantinople pursued a parallel series of intrigues intended to topple King Ferdinand and replace him with a ruler more sympathetic to Ottoman rule. Relations between St Petersburg and Constantinople, strained at the best of times, worsened as the Eastern Question 'burst into activity' once more. Weeks after Hamilton had publicly announced the Admiralty's policy of using the Channel Fleet in the Mediterranean in the event of war with France, rumours of a Russian attempt to seize Constantinople reached London.[88] The Cabinet instructed the Admiralty to maintain the Mediterranean Fleet within two days' steaming of Besika Bay, in anticipation of dispatching a force through the Dardanelles to disrupt a Russian seaborne assault on the Sublime Porte. Vice-Admiral Sir Anthony Hoskins, the 'able...adaptable and versatile' C-in-C of the squadron, was quick

[83] Marder, *Anatomy*, pp. 152–4; Otte, 'War in Sight', pp. 702–3.

[84] Ropp, *Development of a Modern Navy*, pp. 239–40 and 242.

[85] Marder, *Anatomy*, pp. 149–52.

[86] H. Garbett, 'The Strategic Position in the Mediterranean', *Royal United Services Institution Journal*, Vol. 36, No. 178, 1892, p. 1305.

[87] D. Gillard, *The Struggle for Asia 1828–1914: A Study in British and Russian Imperialism*, London: Methuen, 1977, p. 148.

[88] *The Times*, 26 June 1890, p. 9.

to highlight the 'extreme danger' which would result from such a dispersion of British forces, especially in light of the troublesome relationship with France.[89] He warned London that 'the gravest consequences to the country might ensue if there was any miscalculation as to the dependence to be placed upon the neutrality of France'. Hoskins calculated that dispatching a squadron through the Dardanelles would reduce the forces under his command 'to the position in which we were before the appropriation of the revised Channel Squadron as a support for the Med[iterranean] Fleet'.[90] Under such circumstances, the remaining British forces in the Mediterranean would be in a distinctly unfavourable position to meet the French Toulon squadron, being at the far end of the basin and having been reduced to rough numerical parity with their potential opponents. The Admiralty was alive to Hoskins' predicament and to the potential implications operations against Constantinople might have for the defence of the British Isles. Hamilton replied to the C-in-C, agreeing that 'the naval supremacy of England in the Channel might be endangered' if France were to declare war while the British Channel and Mediterranean Fleets were concentrated near Besika Bay. The First Lord recounted that he had warned the Cabinet of these dangers, but that his colleagues had been prepared to countenance the risk, such was the vital necessity of preventing a Russian descent on the Ottoman capital.[91]

The Cabinet's adventurous stance proved unsustainable, however. The danger of the situation facing the Mediterranean Fleet grew with each passing month due to the increasingly close co-operation evident between the French and Russians at Constantinople.[92] Co-ordination between the Russians in the east and the French in the west was foremost in Vice-Admiral Hoskins' mind as he doubted whether Paris would long be able to 'resist the temptation which would be set before her if Russia made the anticipated descent upon Constantinople'.[93] As if to illustrate the veracity of the C-in-C's concerns, the French Foreign Minister made a series of inflammatory remarks about the British occupation of Egypt as Anglo-Russian tensions remained high during June. Speaking in the French Chamber, Minister Ribot threatened that 'we cannot without protest let England seize upon the valley of the Nile and on the Suez Canal' and committed to showing 'much tenacity in reminding her of it'.[94] These ominous remarks were accompanied by calls for an expansion to the French naval construction programme.[95] The prospect of concerted Franco-Russian action increased during 1891, as relations between Paris and St Petersburg grew closer in the wake of Bismarck's resignation and the lapse

---

[89] G. F. Hamilton, *Parliamentary Reminiscences and Reflections, 1886–1906*, London: John Murray, 1922, p. 87.

[90] A. Hoskins, 'Sir A. Hoskins Memo on the Secret Orders of 24th May 1890', ADM 121/75.

[91] Hamilton, 'Secret Memorandum from First Lord to Commander in Chief Mediterranean', 10 June 1890, ADM 121/75.

[92] Otte, *Foreign Office Mind*, pp. 180–5.

[93] A. Hoskins, 'Sir A. Hoskins Memo on the Secret Orders of 24th May 1890', ADM 121/75. For British diplomats' awareness of the growing closeness of Anglo-French relations, see Otte, *Foreign Office Mind*, pp. 180–2.

[94] 'England and France in Egypt', *The Economist*, 14 June 1890, pp. 750–1.

[95] 'The French Naval Scare', *The Times*, 7 June 1890, p. 6.

of the Reinsurance Treaty between St Petersburg and Berlin. In a symbolic gesture of friendship, the French fleet visited the Russian capital that summer, after which the Secretary to the British Legation advised London that whilst a formal treaty had yet to be signed, 'it would be a mistake, in my opinion, to minimize the political effect of that visit and of the Francophile demonstration which it gave rise to'.[96] These developments intensified Britain's difficulties in the Mediterranean and rendered her evermore vulnerable to concerted Franco-Russian diplomatic pressure, a fact that was made plain in early 1892.

Since rumours of a Russian *coup de main* against Constantinople had reached London, the War Office Intelligence Department had monitored Russian military preparations in the Black Sea closely.[97] By January 1892 both the War Office and Admiralty accepted as 'certain' that plans to seize both the city and the Straits were under preparation in Russia.[98] The Cabinet Defence Committee considered the question in early March and the Directors of Military and Naval Intelligence were commissioned to assess Britain's ability to respond to a hostile move against Constantinople soon thereafter.[99] The respective intelligence departments produced a joint report in which they rehearsed arguments similar to those Hoskins and Hamilton had made two years earlier. Their central thrust was that naval operations in defence of Constantinople were too dangerous in light of the risks they would entail running in home waters. Detaching a British squadron into the Sea of Marmora would mean that the 'Atlantic, and even the English Channel, might be open to a naval combination which would be a grave menace to this country'. On this basis, the paper concluded that 'Great Britain, unsupported, cannot prevent the *coup de main* without endangering her general naval position'.[100] As had been the case when Hood refused to contemplate operations against Toulon in 1888, the Admiralty remained opposed to any operations that might risk allowing the French to force the Strait of Gibraltar. The naval leadership received consistent support on this point from Hoskins, who considered that 'the primary use of the [Mediterranean] Fleet is to prevent combinations of the French fleet'.[101] Protecting British trade in the eastern Atlantic and forestalling the threat of a French invasion thus curtailed the Admiralty's willingness to take offensive action in the eastern Mediterranean.

The report's conclusion that Britain was impotent to prevent the seizure of Constantinople infuriated Salisbury. Frustrated at Britain's manifest inability to protect its interests in the Near East by force, the Prime Minister remarked acidly that 'it is a question whether any advantage arises from keeping a fleet in the Mediterranean at all'. Betraying a fundamental misconception as to why the

[96] Howard to Salisbury, 19 August 1891, CAB 37/30/34.

[97] Marder, *Anatomy*, pp. 154–9.

[98] See folder, 'Constantinople', January 1892, ADM 1/7135.

[99] Devonshire to Salisbury, 2 March 1896, and Salisbury to Devonshire of the same date, CS2/340/2684–85, Chatsworth.

[100] Bridge and Chapman, 'Joint Report of the DMI and DNI', 18 March 1892, in C. J. Lowe ed., *The Reluctant Imperialists*, Vol. II: *The Documents*, London: Routledge, 1967, p. 90.

[101] Enclosure No. 1 to Mediterranean Letter of 5 January 1891: Proceedings of a Conference, 17 May 1890, ADM 121/75.

Admiralty deemed it preferable to send the Channel Fleet to Gibraltar rather than keep it in home waters, he continued: 'if its main duty is to protect the Atlantic and Channel, it had better go there'.[102] Such thinking ignored the benefits of exploiting the geography of the Mediterranean to Britain's advantage. Yet it also hinted at one of the major problems with the Admiralty's new strategy: the potential for public and political misapprehension of the link between the position in the Mediterranean and defence of the British Isles. The Prime Minister himself confessed that 'what our fleet is doing or expected to do in the Mediterranean is one of the mysteries of official strategy', suggesting that the Admiralty had failed to make the linkage it drew between the two theatres sufficiently clear to the Cabinet.[103] If the political leadership did not understand the rationale behind sending the Channel Fleet to Gibraltar, the chances of the public reacting favourably to such a counter-intuitive strategy appeared slim. Captain Lord Charles Beresford, an officer in the Mediterranean Fleet who had until recently served on the Board of Admiralty, encapsulated this difficulty in a letter to Salisbury's nephew, Arthur Balfour:

> It is a great question whether the people of England who are always trembling over the bug-bear of invasion would allow a force which should be able to cope with the French Battleships to leave England.[104]

Paradoxically, in the Admiralty's assessment such a refusal would actually pose a greater danger to the British Isles than deploying the fleet to Gibraltar.

The question of how to defend British European and imperial interests at either end of the Mediterranean continued to exercise the Admiralty throughout the 1890s. A debate was waged between more conservative officers who preferred to confine the French fleet to the Mediterranean and thereby secure command of the eastern Atlantic and Channel as the best course, and those who advocated a more equitable balance between British interests at home and in the east. Officers of the Mediterranean squadron, such as Vice-Admiral Sir George Tryon, equated plans to operate primarily from Gibraltar with the abdication of Britain's position in the Near East. Tryon argued that 'to abandon the basin of the Med[iterranean] and to hold the Strait of Gibraltar strongly with a large fleet would be to abandon possible future allies, to leave the Med[iterranean] open to French enterprise, to condemn the Fleet to a policy of inactivity with all the consequences'. He therefore proposed deploying a strengthened 'fast' squadron of battleships to Malta to deter enemy activity in the eastern Sea, against the Suez Canal or Egypt. Should the French fleet succeed in forcing its way past the slower battleships left to guard the Strait of Gibraltar, the Malta force's speed would enable it to return to home waters with the utmost dispatch, he reasoned. Tryon thus advocated attempting to operate in the east of the basin and hold the Strait simultaneously by dividing his fleet according to its capabilities.[105]

---

[102] Salisbury, 'Memorandum', 4 June 1892, in Lowe ed., *Reluctant Imperialists* II, p. 87.
[103] Salisbury to Devonshire, 7 October 1896, CS2/340/2697, Chatsworth.
[104] Beresford to Balfour, 1891, Add. MS. 49713, fos 30–2.
[105] Tryon, 'Memorandum in Reply', 4 December 1891, ADM 121/75.

After Tryon's untimely demise in the collision of HMS *Victoria* and HMS *Camperdown* in June 1893, his successor Vice-Admiral Michael Culme-Seymour endorsed an even more adventurous approach. Described by one contemporary as 'blustering, assertive and litigious',[106] Culme-Seymour arrived in command determined to make his own calculations as to the best dispositions of his force. During the autumn his Flag Captain, Arthur Wilson VC, prepared a paper arguing for the concentration of the main British force at Malta—loosening the hold on Gibraltar. Anticipating questions as to the risks involved in leaving the Strait so weakly defended, Wilson reasoned that the Mediterranean Fleet could simply pursue the French if the latter made way for the Atlantic:

> As the whole of our battleships not belonging to the Channel and Mediterranean squadrons will be in English waters they ought to be sufficient when mobilized to prevent the possibility of invasion for five days even against the whole French fleet combined, and in five days our whole fleet from the Mediterranean would arrive...[107]

Under Wilson's plans the reserve fleet in home waters would thus act as a 'fleet in being'; too weak to seek battle with the French but sufficiently dangerous to deny the undisputed control of the Channel necessary to conduct a landing in Britain. Culme-Seymour endorsed Wilson's views to the Admiralty.[108] These leading commanders all considered that the French Toulon squadron would have to hold the Channel for a prolonged period if a major landing was to be attempted and that to forestall such a disaster they needed only to maintain close enough touch with the French to chase them should they make for the Strait.

Whilst it shared the view that undisputed command of the Channel would be extremely difficult for the French to establish under virtually any reasonable combination of circumstances, the Admiralty remained unwilling to risk even a temporary French superiority in home waters. British trade in the Atlantic and Channel outweighed the volume of traffic in the Mediterranean by a value of four to one and much of the latter could be re-directed around the Cape of Good Hope in wartime.[109] The route to North America had already become Britain's single most significant economic 'lifeline' and was becoming more so with each passing year.[110] Ensuring the continuance of this trade was vital both to the economy and to feed the population, who relied upon imports for the majority of its wheat and over 60 per cent of its total calorific intake.[111] French interference with this crucial trade, or an attempt to rush troops across the Channel, exercised a consistent and powerful influence on decision makers in London. When he received Culme-Seymour's letter

---

[106] Spencer Ewart diary, 15 October 1896, GD527/1/1/135/5, [N]ational [R]ecords of [S]cotland, Edinburgh.

[107] A. K. Wilson, 'Remarks on Sir A. Hoskins' minute', 1893, pp. 1–5, ADM 121/75.

[108] M. Culme Seymour, 'Memorandum on what will be required in the Mediterranean in the event of war with France', 27 September 1893, p. 2, ADM 121/75. For Culme-Seymour's disposition see diary of Spencer Ewart, extended entry of 15 October 1896, GD527/1/1/135/5, NRS.

[109] 'Remarks by Capt. W. H. May', March 1896, p. 7, ADM 121/75.

[110] Ropp, *Development of a Modern Navy*, pp. 249–50.

[111] Ropp, *Development of a Modern Navy*, p. 213; Marder, *Anatomy*, pp. 84–104; Offer, *Agrarian Interpretation*, pp. 218–19.

explaining his intention to concentrate his forces at Malta, the new Senior Naval Lord, Admiral Sir Frederick Richards, criticized the C-in-C for underestimating the threat of invasion. An officer of 'unerring judgments', Richards displayed a keen awareness of the military threat to the British Isles when he noted that the escape of the Toulon Fleet into the Atlantic might enable France to secure the command of the Channel, 'the consequences of which to this Empire would be absolute ruin'.[112]

The disagreements between the Admiralty and successive C-in-Cs in the Mediterranean over where to concentrate the British fleet were matters of emphasis, rather than of fundamental strategic conception. Both parties agreed that command of the sea sufficient to guarantee the uninterrupted passage and disembarkation of troops was the necessary precursor to the transport of an army by sea. Advocates of basing naval operations at Malta considered that the reserve fleet would be sufficient to deny the French such a degree of control of the Channel, whereas the Admiralty felt that a detached squadron at Malta would provide similar insurance to Egypt. In either instance, the presence of an equal or superior force of battleships in the direct vicinity of the area to be defended was not necessary to render a landing impractical. This was not to diminish the defensive role of the fleet, but rather to qualify it. Armoured warships remained vital to contemporary conceptions of strategy, which were essentially symmetrical in nature. Their role was to confront, contain, or deter enemy ironclads. These functions could be fulfilled by forces deployed outside home waters, provided the enemy did not possess higher-value units of their own close to the British Isles. British coasts could be secured by focusing the Navy's power against the main fleet of the enemy; a large fleet in home waters was not necessary to achieve this aim. Committed to its Gibraltar strategy, the Admiralty had to pursue alternative avenues in order to improve the 'strategically vicious' position in the Mediterranean.[113]

BALANCE IN THE MEDITERRANEAN

The conclusion of the Franco-Russian alliance in 1894 exacerbated the quandary facing naval planners. Despite the visit of a Russian squadron to Toulon in 1893, a combination of the two fleets against the British was never likely to be feasible for logistical, operational, and tactical reasons. Rather it was the prospect of co-ordinated action at either end of the Mediterranean and the consequent need for Britain to divide its forces that preoccupied the Navy.[114] This threat was particularly acute between 1890 and 1895, after which the expansion of British naval power provided for by the Naval Defence Act began to improve the Navy's ability to balance its commitments more effectively.[115] By March 1896 William May, Flag Captain

---

[112] J. A. Fisher, *Records*, London: Hodder & Stoughton, 1919, p. 50; 'Memorandum by Admiral Sir F. Richards', 13 December 1893, p. 1, ADM 121/75.

[113] 'Memorandum by Admiral Sir A. Hoskins', 25 October 1893, p. 2, ADM 121/75.

[114] Ropp, *Development of a Modern Navy*, pp. 239–40 and 242.

[115] 'Minute for the Board of Admiralty by Admiral Sir Frederick Richards, First Naval Lord, August 1893' in J. Hattendorf et al. eds, *British Naval Documents 1204–1960*, Aldershot: Ashgate, 1993, p. 620; Marder, *Anatomy*, pp. 175–6.

of the Mediterranean squadron, noted with a degree of satisfaction that Britain was now in a 'superior position so far as strength goes to the French + Russian combined'.[116] Nevertheless, Admiral Richards never lost sight of the intimate relationship between the Mediterranean and national security. In a memorandum produced in November 1896 he re-iterated his view that 'the Mediterranean Fleet is in the Mediterranean for the protection equally of the Coasts of the United Kingdom, as to maintain the position and prestige of England as a leading European (& also Asiatic) Power'.[117] Even as Britain's lead in the construction of new vessels over France and Russia extended towards the turn of the century, he would not contemplate surrendering the Strait of Gibraltar. Rather, the Senior Naval Lord worked towards the more ambitious goal of forming two independent fleets in the Mediterranean, each of which would be strong enough to meet the Toulon squadron on favourable terms. This goal was achieved fleetingly towards the end of 1898. At this point, new orders were issued which explained how the 'large accession in recent years to the strength of the Channel Squadron' had been made with the expressed intention of obviating the debate over whether to prioritize British interests in the east or west of the basin. Recent additions to both fleets would enable the Mediterranean squadron to remain at Malta and the Channel force to hold Gibraltar without risking either fleet being overwhelmed by the French.[118] British interests at both ends of the basin could now be secured simultaneously, ensuring the command of the English Channel, the defence of Egypt, and the protection of the Suez Canal.[119] French perceptions of Britain's commanding position at sea were confirmed as tensions over the Nile basin precipitated a war-scare between the two countries in late 1898.

The headwaters of the Nile had long been appreciated as vital to the security of Egypt and successive governments had pursued a firm line in countering French designs on the region. In August Salisbury instructed the commander of the Egyptian Army, Major-General Horatio Kitchener, to proceed south into the Sudan in order to forestall French attempts to claim territory there.[120] After victory over the Khalifa's forces at Omdurman on 2 September, the British encountered a small French military detachment at the town of Fashoda. When the French attempted to claim the surrounding area, the government in Whitehall demanded that Paris evacuated the region immediately. This latest instalment in the long-running Anglo-French competition in the Middle East rapidly escalated into an issue of national pride and both sides threatened to resort to war. Tensions peaked in mid-October, as both sides mobilized their fleets. In anticipation of hostilities, the Channel Fleet left home waters, arriving at Arosa Bay on the Spanish coast on 15 October.[121]

---

[116] 'Remarks by Capt. W. H. May', March 1896, p. 1, ADM 121/75.
[117] Richards, 'Note Relative to Malta', 25 November 1896, ADM 116/3089.
[118] Admiralty to C-in-C Mediterranean, 26 October 1898, pp. 1–6, ADM 1/7379B.
[119] See 'DMI memorandum on Naval Policy, October 13th, 1896' and 'DNI Memorandum on Naval Policy, October 28th, 1896' in Appendix III and IV of Marder, *Anatomy*, pp. 569–88; Admiralty to C-in-C Mediterranean, 26 October 1898, ADM 121/75.
[120] Otte, *Foreign Office Mind*, pp. 229–30.   [121] Marder, *Anatomy*, p. 322.

The Fashoda Crisis is generally regarded as having been a decisive victory for British sea power.[122] With Russia pre-occupied in the Far East and unwilling to risk her already precarious financial position by supporting French imperial ambitions in Africa, Paris was left diplomatically isolated. Combined with her inferiority at sea, this obliged the French to back down and withdraw from the Sudan in early November.[123] However, British success belies the fact that the episode revealed the potential shortcomings of concentrating British naval strength outside home waters. At the height of the crisis, serious concerns regarding the position at home were evident at the Admiralty. The French had reinforced their northern squadron of battleships in October, bringing the strength of the force to six 'good' vessels. Usually held separately at Brest and Cherbourg, the French Channel and Atlantic divisions had also been concentrated at Brest for the winter.[124] This threatened to circumvent the pivot of British strategy: denying France command of the Channel by confining the Toulon squadron to the Mediterranean. The French force in the Channel was numerically only slightly weaker than the seven seaworthy battleships of the British reserve;[125] the only force of armoured warships still in home waters after the departure of the Channel Fleet. Besides the obvious threat posed by the force at Brest, this series of events also had broader implications. With the naval balance so delicate, the involvement of another power on the French side might allow an allied force to outnumber the British Home Fleet. Whilst the Russian Baltic Fleet was judged incapable of sustaining operations outside of the Kattegat, the nascent German navy might provide Berlin with a powerful diplomatic lever with which to exert pressure on Britain in the event of an Anglo-French conflict. The Germans possessed four modern battleships in late-1898, with five more completing trials.[126] Relations between London and Berlin had been sour for some time and German policy had proven especially troublesome for Britain in the east, where her agents appeared eager to cause difficulties both at Constantinople and in Egypt. The prospect of a German attempt to exploit Anglo-French tensions by siding with Paris was thus by no means out of the question.[127] Captain George Ballard, an assistant in the Naval Intelligence Department at the time, recalled that the situation had caused 'some apprehension' at the Admiralty, due to 'the conditions which would arise should the *Germans* adopt an aggressive attitude at a time when Great Britain was already fully occupied in a war with France and Russia'.[128]

The detail of the British position in home waters renders the Admiralty's concerns entirely understandable. Not only was the British Home Fleet (the name

---

[122] Ropp, *Development of a Modern Navy*, pp. 306–23; Marder, *Anatomy*, pp. 320–40.

[123] Marder, *Anatomy*, pp. 320–40; Otte, *Foreign Office Mind*, pp. 230–1.

[124] Marder, *Anatomy*, pp. 322 and 328.

[125] For the composition of the Home Fleet, see 'Battle Fleets', 28 October 1898, in folder, 'Threatened War with France, 1898, Fashoda, Preparations for Mobilisation', ADM 1/7379B.

[126] T. A. Brassey, *The Naval Annual, 1898*, Portsmouth, 1898, pp. 299–301; H. H. Herwig, 'Luxury' Fleet: The Imperial German Navy, 1888–1918, London: Allen & Unwin, 1980, pp. 33–6.

[127] Otte, *Foreign Office Mind*, pp. 215–17.

[128] Ballard, 'Remarks on the Framing of Certain Plans for War with Germany Now at the Admiralty', 3 May 1909, p. 3, ADM 1/8997. Emphasis added.

given to the forces held in reserve once mobilized) numerically only just superior to the French Northern squadron, but its key vessels, the armoured Coast Guard Ships, remained scattered around the coastline performing their peacetime administrative functions as the crisis reached its peak. In order to form an effective fighting force, these vessels required to be collected and to be bought up to full efficiency, allowing their part-time crews time to re-accustom themselves to their duties. In late 1898, this process had been put off for fear that such a sign of aggressive intent might escalate the delicate diplomatic situation.[129] The constituent parts of the Home squadron were thus left vulnerable to being defeated in detail or before they had achieved their full fighting efficiency. Richards explained the danger to the First Lord, Lord Goschen, warning that 'serious insult to our coasts and possibly the loss of the scattered units of our unformed Home Fleet' might occur if war broke out before the squadron was collected.[130] The Naval Lords' concerns were heeded and an emergency squadron duly assembled at Plymouth before the French decision to withdraw from Fashoda was announced at the end of the month. Britain's firm stance had resulted in a diplomatic success, relieving the Admiralty's concerns about the situation in home waters of their immediacy. Nevertheless, increases in the number of foreign armoured warships in the Channel and North Sea continued to command the naval leadership's attention, resulting in a comprehensive reconsideration of British naval strategy over the following eighteen months.

'CIRCUMSTANCES HAVE ALTERED'

Whilst the imminent threat of war over Fashoda receded towards the end of 1898, considerable tensions in Anglo-French relations persisted into the following year. Indeed, Britain became increasingly isolated in diplomatic terms as 1899 wore on. London had been estranged from France's partner in the Dual Alliance for some time due to disagreements in central Asia, and Russian ambitions in China ensured little prospect of an imminent rapprochement between London and St Petersburg. Relations with Germany were similarly problematic, as Berlin's opportunistic diplomacy provoked frustration and suspicion in Britain.[131] The European reaction to events in South Africa caused further concern for the Foreign Office, which began to fear a potential Russo-German accord aimed at forcing Britain to accept a negotiated settlement with the Boers.[132]

After the outbreak of open hostilities in the Cape Colony in late 1899, these worrying diplomatic developments were compounded by a series of catastrophic military failures, culminating in 'black week' of 9–15 December during which the British Army suffered three major reversals at the hands of Boer militia. With the

---

[129] Marder, *Anatomy*, p. 374.
[130] Richards to Goschen, 27 October 1898, quoted in Marder, *Anatomy*, p. 322.
[131] A. J. A. Morris, *The Scaremongers: The Advocacy of War and Rearmament, 1896–1914*, London: Routledge & Kegan Paul, 1984, pp. 15–23.
[132] Otte, *Foreign Office Mind*, pp. 223–8, 233–5.

majority of the Army deployed to South Africa and the French still smarting over Fashoda,[133] concerns that France might attempt a swift invasion of Britain waxed as 1899 drew to a close.[134] The situation reached a head in March 1900, when only 17,000 organized regular troops remained in the country and sensationalist stories of an imminent French invasion abounded in the popular press.[135] These concerns were sufficiently pervasive for Lord Salisbury to deliver an alarmist speech to the Primrose League on the virtues of rifle clubs for the population's ability to resist the advance of an invading army.[136] There appeared to be at least some military basis for these worries; French troops had been collected near the Channel ports and unusual manoeuvre arrangements of the French fleets had been observed.[137] In ominous tones, Lord Wolseley warned the Cabinet that 'France owes us a deep grudge, and may endeavour to pay it off in the autumn of 1900, or even earlier...'[138]

It has been argued that the effect of this scare upon the Admiralty was 'practically nil'; however, a series of decisions taken in early 1900 suggests otherwise.[139] In September 1899 the dynamic and ambitious Vice-Admiral Sir John Fisher had assumed command of the Mediterranean Fleet. Soon after arriving on station, Fisher challenged Richards' intention to operate the Mediterranean and Channel Fleets independently in the event of an Anglo-French war. 'Whether we are comparatively weak or strong', Fisher wrote, 'Gibraltar is the best position for assembling our Battle Fleet.'[140] The C-in-C argued that 'an immediate re-inforcement... of 8 or 9 Battleships from England would be necessary to save Egypt'. These '8 or 9' vessels would be required in *addition* to sending the Channel Fleet to Gibraltar. Sending units held in reserve to the Mediterranean during the course of a war with France had formed a part of Admiralty planning since 1888; however, Fisher stressed the urgency of reinforcing his command immediately upon the outbreak of hostilities.[141] Acceding to these proposals would involve a concomitant reduction in the forces in home waters during the crucial opening moves of a war against the Dual Alliance. The Admiralty was thus faced with two competing demands: Fisher's requests for more ships in the Mediterranean and the need to strengthen the position in home waters in the wake of the problems experienced during the Fashoda Crisis. Further alterations to French dispositions had permanently strengthened the Brest squadron to five first-class and one second-class battleship and two modern armoured cruisers, making the squadron only marginally weaker

[133] F. R. Plunkett to the Marquess of Salisbury, 23 December 1899, CAB 37/51/101.

[134] Marder, *Anatomy*, pp. 372–3; Moon, 'Invasion', pp. 129–83.

[135] War Office, 'Liability of the United Kingdom to French Invasion during the South African War', 28 February 1903, p. 1, CAB 3/1/7A.

[136] Moon, 'Invasion', pp. 134–42; Morris, *Scaremongers*, p. 102.

[137] Ropp, *Development of a Modern Navy*, pp. 344–7.

[138] Wolseley to Lansdowne, 29 December 1899, p. 1, CAB 37/51/105.

[139] Marder, *Anatomy*, p. 378.

[140] Fisher, 'Strategic Position of the Mediterranean Fleet in War', 1 November 1899, p. 2, ADM 1/7417. Emphasis in the original.

[141] Hamilton, 'English and French Fleets in the Mediterranean', January 1892, p. 2, ADM 121/75; Fisher, 'Strategic Position of the Mediterranean Fleet in War', 1 November 1899, p. 6, ADM 1/7417.

in numerical terms than the French Mediterranean Fleet at Toulon.[142] Moreover, two of the Northern squadron's oldest ships had been replaced with the larger, faster, and more modern *Masséna* and *Carnot* from the Mediterranean.[143] French forces in the Channel and Atlantic were thus both more powerful and more numerous than had been the case for much of the previous decade. The authorities in London were kept well informed of these changes by the British naval attaché to France, Captain Henry Jackson, an able officer and future First Sea Lord, who filed numerous and detailed reports on the topic.

The new Senior Naval Lord, Vice-Admiral Sir Walter Kerr, felt that the alterations in French dispositions necessitated a fundamental revision of the strategy developed prior to 1898. After discussing the situation with the Board of Admiralty in January 1900 he informed Lord Goschen that:

> Circumstances have however altered and the increase in strength in the French Northern Squadron calls for some corresponding move on our part. The probability, owing to the retardation of the date of completion of ships under construction, of not being able to send the whole of the Channel Squadron with the re-inforcements hitherto contemplated to Gibraltar, makes the concentration proposed by the C-in-C at that port in the first instance, a greater necessity than when the Board decision above referred to was arrived at.[144]

Far from providing the *additional* force of '8 or 9' battleships contemplated by Fisher, the Admiralty no longer felt able to offer an unconditional guarantee that the entire Channel Fleet would be dispatched to Fisher's aid, even if that meant prejudicing the C-in-C's ability to act against Russian movements in the eastern Mediterranean. This shift in policy was also reflected in the composition of the forces to be dispatched to Gibraltar. Captain Reginald Custance, the DNI, pointed out that whilst existing arrangements would ensure a numerical superiority in home waters, at present the British force there would 'be composed of ships individually inferior to those composing the French Northern Squadron'. On these grounds he recommended withholding 'a proportion of the newer ships in Home waters' and substituting 'a portion of the older vessels in the Mediterranean'.[145] The Admiralty's attitude may have been influenced by a downgrading of its assessments of Russian capability in the Black Sea,[146] yet this remained a significant shift

---

[142] H. Jackson, 'France. Naval Policy and Estimates, 1899', 30 March 1899, pp. 6 and 10, ADM 231/29/537.

[143] NID, 'Naval Estimates and Remarks on Naval Progress of the Principal European Countries, the United States, and Japan', August 1900, p. 27, ADM 231/32/585. For the details of the ships, see NID, 'Return Showing the Battleships and Cruisers Built, Building or Preparing to Build, and Projected for England, France, Russia, Germany, Italy, Austria, United States, and Japan', November 1899, p. 4, ADM 231/30/560.

[144] Note by Kerr to Goschen, 30 January 1900, inside docket 'Strategic Position of the Mediterranean Fleet', ADM 1/7417.

[145] Custance, Minute of 29 January 1900, pp. 4–5, inside docket 'Strategic Position of the Mediterranean Fleet', ADM 1/7417.

[146] N. Papastratigakis, 'British Naval Strategy: The Russian Black Sea Fleet and the Turkish Straits, 1890–1904', *International History Review*, No. 32, Vol. 4, 2010, pp. 647–53; M. S. Seligmann, 'Britain's Great Security Mirage: The Royal Navy and the Franco-Russian Naval Threat, 1898–1906', *Journal of Strategic Studies*, Vol. 35, No. 6, 2012, pp. 866–8.

in policy. Concentrating the British fleets at Gibraltar may have been viewed as an effective means of securing the Channel when France mustered the majority of her strength at Toulon, but the strengthening of her Northern squadron required the presence of a stronger force of armoured warships in home waters.

This change of policy was communicated to Fisher in February. 'Owing to the constant changes in the dispositions of the French fleet', Their Lordships reasoned, 'the number of battle ships which will be sent to the Mediterranean in the event of war must depend upon the conditions at the moment and cannot now be determined.'[147] The longstanding precedent for the Channel Fleet acting as reinforcement to the Mediterranean led Fisher to assume that the Admiralty communication referred to the extra '8 or 9' battleships he had deemed necessary for the defence of Egypt.[148] When this misunderstanding was revealed in October, Fisher complained bitterly that the Admiralty ought to build more ships in order to enable him adequately defend both the Strait and Egypt.[149] Selborne took the unprecedented step of bringing the Senior Naval Lord and DNI out to Malta with him to confer with Fisher directly on the issue in April 1901.[150] The result of these meetings was that the Mediterranean received two new battleships in place of the fleet's oldest two vessels, as well as three additional cruisers, ten more torpedo gunboats, and eight further destroyers permanently on station. However, the Admiralty refused to meet Fisher's much more extensive requests, citing the strength of the French forces in the Channel as justification for its stance. 'No reduction in the British force at home is permissible', Custance insisted, 'in view of the fact that it must be capable of "containing" the largest force which France can concentrate in the Channel.'[151] Kerr endorsed this assessment, noting that 'I am unable to share the view that the Mediterranean Squadron is of more importance than the Reserve Squadron' and that 'to fall in with the views of the Commander-in-Chief [Fisher] and strengthen his Squadron to the extent he asks would paralyse our Home Fleet'.[152] Fisher did succeed in extracting a tentative return to the earlier arrangement regarding the Channel Fleet, but this was only facilitated by an acceleration of reforms already under way to the forces in home waters.[153]

The process of increasing the efficiency of the reserve had begun the previous year, when the readiness of the Coast Guard Ships had been improved by providing them with their full crews all year round. Similar reforms were pursued with greater vigour from 1901 onwards.[154] However, additional crews and sea time

[147] Admiralty to Fisher, 19 February 1900, pp. 2 and 5–6, ADM 1/7417.

[148] Fisher to Admiralty, 28 April 1900, p. 2, in docket, 'Reply to Admiralty Secret Letters of Feb.19. 1900 M.193 and March 20th 1900. M. 303', ADM 1/7462.

[149] Fisher to Admiralty, 16 January 1901, FISR 5/2, [C]hurchill College [A]rchives [C]entre, Cambridge.

[150] Marder, *Anatomy*, p. 403.

[151] Custance, 'Mediterranean Fleet Reinforcements in War (Malta Conference)', 29 May 1901, p. 10, ADM 116/900B.

[152] Kerr to Selborne, 7 May 1901, in D. G. Boyce ed., *The Crisis of British Power: The Imperial and Naval Papers of the Second Early Selborne, 1895–1910*, London: Historians Press, 1990, p. 121.

[153] Admiralty to Fisher, 1 July 1901, ADM 1/7379B.

[154] M. S. Seligmann, 'A Prelude to the Reforms of Admiral Sir John Fisher: The Creation of the Home Fleet, 1902–03', *Historical Research*, vol. 83, no. 221, Aug., 2010, pp. 509–19.

were only a temporary solution to the broader shifts in the distribution of foreign of naval power. As Custance noted:

> While the policy of sending the Channel squadron to the Mediterranean as the reinforcement will give that fleet a superiority which will remove cause for anxiety in that quarter, the same cannot be said of the situation at home. The defence of the country will be left to a fleet composed of ships of inferior quality, manned by crews not hitherto kept in the same high state of efficiency as are those of the Mediterranean and Channel ships.
>
> It is submitted that under the proposed arrangements it is the Home Fleet which will require most attention, and that any demands which come from the Mediterranean should be carefully considered and weighed against the requirements of the Home Fleet.[155]

Whilst the DNI's personal enmity towards Fisher, whom he described as a 'hobgoblin', doubtless made the prospect of acceding to his requests unpalatable, Custance's logic in refusing to do so was sound.[156] The reforms already initiated were a step in the right direction, but foreign developments rendered further action an urgent necessity. The pace of German construction meant that she was projected to overhaul Russia as the third ranked naval power by 1906.[157] With her fleet concentrated in the North Sea and widely viewed as more capable than the Tsar's Baltic squadron, Germany would have a more significant effect upon the balance of naval power in northern waters than Russia ever had.[158] The revival of the French battleships construction programme after a hiatus of several years also presaged more intense competition in the Channel and Atlantic.[159] Against this threatening backdrop, the efficiency of the British Home squadron remained dubious. The force performed poorly in the 1901 manoeuvres, leading Custance to stress the 'necessity of practice and frequent exercise... if it is to be on a par with the formidable German force which is being rapidly developed in the North Sea.'[160] Additions to the strength of the fleet were also required. The umpire's report on the manoeuvres had deemed the 'fighting strength' of the Home Fleet as 'insufficient' to combat Sir Arthur Wilson's well-drilled Channel squadron.[161]

---

[155] Custance, 'Mediterranean Fleet Reinforcements in War (Malta Conference)', 29 May 1901, p. 10, ADM 116/900B.

[156] Quoted in Marder, *Anatomy*, p. 389.

[157] Note by Custance, 'In compliance with directions, the attached statement relative to the number of ships required to be built as been prepared', 19 December 1900, MS 158, Selborne Papers, [Bod]leian Library.

[158] For the distribution of Russian vessels see Selborne, 'The Navy Estimates and the Chancellor of the Exchequer's Memorandum on the Growth of Expenditure', 16 November 1901, p. 10, CAB 37/59/118. Also see Marder, *Anatomy*, pp. 462–7; M. S. Seligmann, 'Switching Horses: The Admiralty's Recognition of the Threat from Germany, 1900–1905', *International History Review*, Vol. 30, No. 2, 2008, pp. 239–58.

[159] Note by Custance, 19 December 1900, MS 158, Bod.

[160] Minute by Custance, 14 September 1901, quoted in Marder, *Anatomy*, p. 463; Seligmann, 'Home Fleet', p. 517.

[161] Unnamed report, August 1901, inscribed 'Unofficial Advanced Copy for 1st Lord', MS 28, Selborne Papers.

The situation was sufficiently serious that within six months of the completion of the manoeuvres the Admiralty moved to create a fully commissioned Home Fleet, which became the senior command in home waters. Administrative delays meant that this process eventually took until May 1903 to complete; however, progress on the efficiency of the force was such that by February 1902 Lord Selborne was able to boast that the Home squadron 'keeps the sea nearly as much as the [fully commissioned] French ships do'.[162] A more tangible measure of the improvements in the effectiveness achieved by the force's commander, Admiral Noel, was provided in July, when the Home Fleet avenged its embarrassment in the manoeuvres of the previous summer. Fisher, now at the Admiralty as Second Sea Lord, noted his pleasure at the fact; 'it's a good sign to see the Home Fleet so smart at evolutions as to beat the Channel and speaks well for Noel having worked them up'.[163] The incremental strengthening of the Home Fleet between January 1900 and May 1903 began a gradual re-focusing of British naval strategy away from the Mediterranean and towards the North Sea.[164] This shift was explicable in precisely the same terms which had determined the decision to concentrate at Gibraltar in 1888–90: the British Fleet required to be positioned between her key interests— the waters around the United Kingdom and the British Isles themselves—and the most threatening enemy naval force of the day which, by 1903, was Germany.

* * *

Between 1887 and 1903 two major shifts in British naval strategy occurred. Between 1887 and 1889 the policy of keeping 'a strong force in home waters at all times' was abandoned in favour of concentrating the Mediterranean and Channel Fleets at Gibraltar. Adopted as the result of the re-deployment of French strength to Toulon, this approach was adhered to throughout the 1890s. By 1898–9, however, the re-balancing of French force between the Channel and North Sea and the growth of the German navy resulted in a re-assessment of this strategy. In response, between 1899 and 1901 the Admiralty moved to strengthen the forces in home waters, a process which culminated in the formation of a fully commissioned Home Fleet in 1903. These changes had a circular aspect to them, the Home Fleet assuming the defensive role Hall had contemplated for the Channel squadron in 1887.

The shift of British naval power to the Mediterranean and back reveals several key facets of British naval thought. The presence of armoured warships in home waters was not regarded as axiomatically necessary to ensure the security of the British Isles. Rather, the ability to prevent a superior enemy force from controlling

---

[162] Selborne to Bridge, 11 February 1902, pp. 5–6, BRI/15, Bridge Papers, [N]ational [M]aritime [M]useum, Greenwich.

[163] Fisher to Selborne, 19 July 1902, in A. J. Marder ed., *[F]ear [G]od and [D]read [N]ought: The Correspondence of Admiral of the Fleet Lord Fisher of Kilverstone*, 3 volumes, London, 1952–9, I, p. 252.

[164] Marder, *Anatomy*, pp. 458–67, Seligmann, 'Switching Horses', 'Home Fleet', pp. 517–19, 'Britain's Great Security Mirage' and with F. Nägler and M. Epkenhans, *The Naval Route to the Abyss: The Anglo-German Naval Race, 1895–1914*, Farnham: Ashgate, 2015, pp. 103–54; Grimes, *War Planning*, pp. 41–51.

the Channel or North Sea was the vital requirement. This was due to the ability of flotilla craft and reserve vessels to threaten an unescorted invasion armada, a capability which grew with the introduction of increasingly effective locomotive torpedoes during the 1890s. Yet, whilst the flotilla might threaten armoured warships during the night or in conditions of poor visibility, battleships were viewed as central to home defence if an enemy could deploy ironclads of his own in the waters surrounding the British Isles. This is what contemporaries meant by 'command of the sea' ensuring British security. Yet, as we shall see, this doctrine was not adequately explained or conveyed to the War Office. Shifts in naval deployments and strategy were conducted with no consultation with either the military authorities or with the government. Beyond rendering the consideration of combined operations impractical, this also made aligning naval and military policy on a broader level a virtual impossibility. As the Admiralty grappled with how best to concentrate and distribute its forces in the Mediterranean, the War Office was left to absorb the implications of the situation at sea for the challenges it faced on land. During the 1880s and 1890s these were numerous, varied, and growing more pressing.

2

The Military Resources of the Empire

The military authorities in Britain devoted a seemingly disproportionate amount of time to the threat of invasion during the 1880s and 1890s.[1] Home defence played a prominent part in War Office policy papers, and leading military figures discussed the threat in a range of public and professional forums on a regular basis, often linking it to the need for Army reform.[2] Perhaps the most famous example of the Army's focus on its domestic function is the so-called 'Stanhope memorandum' of December 1888, which aimed definitively to establish the *raison d'être* of the British Army. Produced by the Secretary of State for War, Edward Stanhope, as part of an ongoing debate with the then Adjutant General, Lord Wolseley, over the administration of the Army, this document listed the Army's priorities as (i) providing aid to the civil power; (ii) supplying drafts to the Indian army; (iii) garrisoning the colonies and coaling stations; (iv) providing two army corps for home defence; and (v) the possible employment of one army corps for involvement in a European war.[3] The Stanhope memorandum has been the subject of widespread criticism, both at the time and since, for its overtly defensive focus. In his memoirs Field Marshal Sir William Robertson, who had served in the War Office Intelligence Division in the early 1890s, recalled how Stanhope's insular outlook had contributed to a situation in which 'the broad military plans essential for the defence of the Empire as a whole received no adequate treatment in the War Office of that period'.[4] Much of the subsequent scholarship has tended to support Robertson's claims, one writer noting how 'Stanhope's ordering of priorities...was more suited to the conditions of 1818 than 1888' and arguing that the reasoning behind them was 'still far from clear'.[5]

[1] W. Robertson, *From Private to Field Marshal*, London: Constable & Company, 1921, pp. 92 and 97; Aston, *Secret Service*, p. 20; Tyler, *The British Army and the Continent*, pp. 9–15; J. K. Dunlop, *The Development of the British Army, 1899–1914*, London: Methuen, 1938, pp. 14, 33–4; Moon, 'Invasion', *passim*; Marder, *Anatomy*, pp. 71–5; B. Bond, *The Victorian Army and the Staff College, 1854–1914*, London: Methuen, 1972, p. 126; Gooch, *Plans of War*, pp. 11–12 and 'Bolt from the Blue', pp. 6–8; Spiers, *The Late Victorian Army*, pp. 223–32; H. Kochanski, 'Planning for War in the Final Years of *Pax Britannica*, 1889–1903', in French and Holden Reid eds, *British General Staff*, pp. 10–11.

[2] Dunlop, *Development of the British Army*, pp. 12–19; Marder, *Anatomy*, pp. 71–5; Gooch, *Plans of War*, pp. 10–29; Beckett, *Riflemen Form*, pp. 185–8; Spiers, *Late-Victorian Army*, pp. 223–31.

[3] 'Minute by the Secretary of State laying down the requirement from our Army, dated 8th December, 1888' in Appendix III of DMO/6/2, BL.

[4] Robertson, *From Private to Field Marshal*, pp. 92 and 97.

[5] Gooch, *Plans of War*, p. 12. For other criticisms, see Dunlop, *Development of the British Army*, p. 14. For a more balanced perspective, see I. F. W. Beckett, 'Edward Stanhope at the War Office, 1887–1892', *Journal of Strategic Studies*, Vol. 5, No. 2, 1982, pp. 278–307 and 'The Stanhope Memorandum of 1888: A Re-interpretation', *Bulletin of the Institute of Historical Research*, LVII, 136, 1984, pp. 240–7.

Attempts to explain why the War Office devoted so much time to the question of home defence during this period have generally argued that the military authorities were attempting to sustain funding for the Army in the face of a tendency amongst politicians to prioritize expenditure on the Royal Navy.[6] It has also been suggested that figures like Wolseley sought to exploit public concerns about invasion as a vehicle with which to induce the government to reform Britain's military system[7] and that soldiers were simply intellectually ill equipped to engage in the discussion of grand strategy.[8] Whilst there seems little doubt that senior officers did seek to exploit the public's sensitivity to the threat of invasion in their ongoing struggle with the government over the administration and financing of the Army, such an interpretation does not adequately explain the amount of departmental time devoted to the topic. The War Office considered how to repel an invading army in forensic detail. Numerous queries on naval issues were directed to the Admiralty, an inter-service Committee on Landing Places sat between 1891 and 1894, and repelling an invading army featured heavily in the detailed mobilization schemes prepared during the 1880s and 1890s. This level of analysis and the consistency with which the topic was re-visited are inconsistent with a purely political agenda. Moreover, significant sums of the tight military budget were spent preparing fortifications and defensive positions, notably those around London. These facts suggest a more substantive basis for the War Office's concerns, one which went beyond inter-service competition for government money. Moreover, the leadership of the late Victorian Army was generally professional, experienced, and competent. Education was viewed seriously, the professional staff at the War Office was expanding, and a great many senior officers gave serious consideration and study to issues of strategy.[9] That the military leadership would devote so much time to exploring the minutiae of a strategic *cul-de-sac* with no regard to the broader picture, or to the strength of the Royal Navy, thus also seems somewhat unlikely.

The key to appreciating how and why the military authorities began to view preventing invasion as a central task lies in the timing with which home defence rose up the agenda at the War Office. Prior to 1887–8 preparing the Home Army for expeditionary operations against a European opponent was the military authorities' primary objective. Under the direction of the flamboyant and controversial Lord Wolseley, dispatching two army corps abroad was the focus of the War Office's attention. In the context of the expeditions to Egypt in 1882 and 1884–5 and the subsequent Pendjeh Crisis, such a policy fitted the strategic realities of the day.

  [6] Gooch, *Plans of War*, pp. 10–11 and 'Bolt from the Blue', pp. 7–8.
  [7] Spiers, *The Late Victorian Army*, pp. 223–32; Kochanski, 'Planning for War', pp. 10–11.
  [8] Moon, 'Invasion', pp. 80–2; Gooch, *The Plans of War*, p. 11.
  [9] D. S. Macdiarmid, *The Life of Lieut. General Sir James Moncrieff Grierson*; London: Constable & Company, 1923, pp. 82–112; Dunlop, *Development of the British Army*, pp. 11–12; J. Luvaas, *The Education of an Army: British Military Thought, 1815–1940*, Toronto: University of Chicago Press, 1964, pp. 169–248; Bond, *The Victorian Army and the Staff College*, pp. 116–211; Beckett, 'Stanhope at the War Office'; T. G. Ferguson, *British Military Intelligence, 1870–1914*, Fredrick, MD: University Publications of America, 1984, pp. 78–96; Spiers, *Late-Victorian Army*, pp. 110–14; C. Brice, *The Thinking Man's Solider: The Life and Career of General Sir Henry Brackenbury, 1837–1914*, Solihull: Hellion & Co., 2012, pp. 161–83.

Yet, by 1888–9 'the probability of our finding the French army on our breakfast tables with the *Times* tomorrow morning' had taken centre stage in War Office thought.[10] It was no coincidence that this shift occurred during the most acute period of doubt over the relative strength of the Royal Navy in the late Victorian era. Concerns over the strength of the Fleet shaped military policy in two ways. Firstly, the Admiralty increasingly advised that the movement of troops by sea would be impossible to guarantee for an undefined period after the outbreak of war with France, when the Navy would be fully occupied shielding British trade and locating enemy naval forces. This limited the scope for rapid offensive operations abroad, or for concentrating troops in central garrisons prior to dispatching them to their war stations. Combined with political reluctance to contemplate deploying troops to the Continent, the Admiralty's stance curtailed Wolseley's ambitions for amphibious operations in Europe or further afield, robbing the Home Army of part of the rationale envisaged for it in the early 1880s. Secondly, the Navy's focus on operations in the Mediterranean after 1888 denuded home waters of modern armoured warships. The military authorities were sceptical whether the remaining reserve units and flotilla forces could interrupt a French attempt to rush the Channel and felt obliged to make provision to resist such an invasion in their own plans. This unorchestrated, chaotic interaction between naval and military policy contributed to the demand for improved political oversight of the armed forces and presaged increased governmental intervention in defence policy in the aftermath of the Boer War.

THE DEVELOPMENT OF AN EXPEDITIONARY FORCE

Home defence may have 'filled the picture' at the War Office by 1890, but for much of the previous decade the trend in military thought had been in the opposite direction.[11] Political pressure to reduce spending on the Army, combined with the perennial manpower problems which stemmed from the unattractive prospect of prolonged and dangerous service overseas and relatively static levels of pay, prompted the War Office to reduce the proportion of British troops maintained abroad from the late 1860s onwards.[12] It was hoped that a rapid reaction force based in Britain could exploit the Navy's dominance at sea to reach threatened locations swiftly, thereby reducing the need to maintain costly garrisons across the Empire.[13] Generally associated with the reforming ministries of Secretaries of State for War Edward Cardwell (1868–74) and Hugh Childers (1880–2), these reforms aimed

[10] Fleetwood Wilson to Ardagh, 15 August 1889, PRO 30/40/13, fo. 322.

[11] G. Ellison, 'From Here and There: Reminiscences', *The Lancashire Lad*, October 1934, pp. 6–7, NAM 8704-35-818-31, National Army Museum; Dunlop, *Development of the British Army*, p. 11–19; Luvaas, *The Education of an Army*, p. 209; Ferguson, *British Military Intelligence*, p. 84.

[12] Spiers, *Late-Victorian Army*, pp. 4–5 and 9–11; Burroughs, 'Defence and Imperial Disunity', pp. 332–3.

[13] A. Lambert, 'Royal Navy and the Defence of Empire' in G. Kennedy ed., *Imperial Defence: The Old World Order, 1856–1956*, Abingdon: Routledge, 2008, pp. 115 and 121–2.

to reduce garrisoning and manpower costs, increase Britain's strategic flexibility, and encourage enlistment.[14] They also had the consequence of concentrating a larger portion of the Empire's military resources at home, where they could be put to a wider range of uses than if they were locked up in local garrisons. At the same time, military thought in Britain began to respond to the dramatic success of Prussian arms in 1866 and 1870–1 and to consider whether the Army should be prepared for operations against a European foe, rather than focus primarily upon imperial duties.[15]

The results of the Cardwell and Childers reforms were mixed, but a steady increase in the size of the forces available in the United Kingdom for operations overseas did occur. Whereas the first-class reserve had to be called out in order to mobilize the force of 16,400 men sent to Egypt in 1882,[16] by the summer of 1884 the War Office Intelligence Department appeared frustrated when it reported that 'the military force which could be dispatched from our shores cannot be estimated, under the most favourable circumstances, at more than 36,000 men of all arms'.[17] Despite this increase, the Adjutant General, General Sir Garnett Wolseley, still felt that the Home Army was inadequate to meet Britain's needs. The Empire's incapacity to sustain multiple large-scale military operations abroad had been underlined in 1884–5, when the defeat of General Gordon at Khartoum was rapidly followed by a British withdrawal in order to free troops for potential operations against Russia in Afghanistan.[18] Wolseley's failure to rescue Gordon reflected poorly upon his command and left him convinced that only a major war in Europe would enable him to salvage his tattered reputation,[19] yet it also confirmed aspects of his broader strategic vision, particularly the need to improve Britain's ability to project military power abroad at short notice.[20] Eager to repair his carefully cultivated public image, Wolseley thus set about attempting to re-shape the Army to meet the challenges of a more confrontational strategic environment. A sense of his willingness to challenge the status quo can be gained by considering his recommendation to reduce 'the number of General Officers from its present establishment of 140 to 63' as a measure of 'very large economy'.[21] Removing more than half of the Army's senior officer corps from the service was hardly the suggestion of an official beholden to tradition or hobbled by institutional inertia. The Adjutant General was equally adventurous in his strategic thinking. A fervent advocate of amphibious

[14] Luvaas, *The Education of an Army*, p. 201; Spiers, *The Late-Victorian Army*, pp. 58–60; D. French, 'The British Army and the Empire, 1856–1956' in Kennedy ed., *Imperial Defence*, p. 92.

[15] H. Bailes, 'Patterns of Thought in the Late-Victorian Army', *Journal of Strategic Studies*, Vol. 4, No. 1, 1981, pp. 29–45.

[16] Maurice and Arthur, *Life of Wolseley*, p. 145; Williams, 'The Egyptian Campaign of 1882', p. 253.

[17] J. S. Rothwell, 'England's means of Offence against Russia', 7 July 1884, p. 2, CAB 37/13/36.

[18] Earl of Rosebery to Sir Henry Ponsonby, 24 April 1885, in Buckle ed., *Letters* III: II, pp. 640–2; R. Johnson, 'The Penjdeh Incident, 1885', *Archives*, Apr., 1999, pp. 43–5.

[19] A. Preston, 'Wolseley, the Khartoum Relief Expedition and the Defence of India, 1885–1900', *Journal of Imperial and Commonwealth History*, Vol. 6, No. 3, May, 1978, p. 264.

[20] E. M. Spiers, *The Army and Society, 1815–1914*, London: Longman, 1980, pp. 206–9.

[21] Wolseley, memo, 20 August 1887, WO 33/48.

operations against Russia in the Baltic and Black Sea, he repeatedly forwarded plans for such assaults during the 1870s and 1880s.[22] These ambitious strategic conceptions were reflected in his administrative efforts to improve the Army's preparedness for operations overseas.

In early 1886 the Adjutant General commissioned the War Office Intelligence Department to conduct a detailed re-appraisal of the Army's mobilization schemes, intended to improve the speed with which troops could be dispatched abroad. Often considered evidence of the War Office's defensive attitude,[23] this planning exercise in fact proved quite the opposite—that Britain's military administration viewed overseas operations as the Army's core function.[24] The officer charged with assembling the plans, Major General Henry Brackenbury, noted that he had received instructions to prepare for six contingencies:

(a) The mobilization of only one Army-Corps...for war outside Great Britain and Ireland.

(b) The mobilization of only two Army-Corps...for the same purpose as given in (a)

(c) The mobilization of all the military 'forces of the Crown', except the Volunteers, with an intention to dispatch abroad two Army-Corps for war...This operation to be planned for:

    I. The complete mobilization of all troops left at home, when the expeditionary army had sailed.

    II. For the complete mobilization of only one or two Army-Corps at home when the expeditionary army had sailed.

(d) The mobilization of all the troops in Ireland and the dispatch of...troops from Great Britain to Ireland in the event of a serious rising taking place in that country...

(e) The mobilization of the whole military forces of the Crown in Great Britain and Ireland to resist invasion if threatened.

(f) The course that would be pursued, if, when (e) had been given effect to, it subsequently became necessary to dispatch abroad a military force of one or two Army-Corps.[25]

Wolseley advertised the rationale behind his reforms widely. Appearing before Sir James Stephen's Commission on Warlike Stores in December 1886, the Adjutant General explained how 'it would be possible to have always ready for rapid mobilisation two army corps; in other words, say 66,000 men, which 66,000 men we should be in a position...to send abroad from this country within a very

[22] Preston, 'Wolseley, the Khartoum Relief Expedition and the Defence of India, 1885–1900'; 'Frustrated Great Gamesmanship: Sir Garnett Wolseley's Plans for War against Russian, 1873–1880', *International History Review*, Vol. 2, No. 2, Apr., 1980, pp. 239–65.

[23] Moon, 'Invasion', pp. 21–2; Gooch, *Plans of War*, pp. 7–8 and 'Bolt from the Blue', p. 6; Bond, *Victorian Army and the Staff College*, pp. 122 and 126; Spiers, *Late-Victorian Army*, pp. 226–7.

[24] Dunlop, *Development of the British Army*, pp. 14–16.

[25] Brackenbury, Memorandum No. I, 14 April 1886, in War Office, 'Reports of a Committee on Army Mobilization', Part III, PRO 30/40/13, fo. 245.

short time, if not immediately as soon as the troops were mobilised'.[26] Reflecting on the work of the previous five years in 1887, he confided to the Duchess of Edinburgh that:

> I shall leave my post next year with the proud feeling that after over ten years of struggling against every species of opposition, I leave everything ready for the rapid mobilisation of two Army Corps—about 65,000 men, or twice the force we landed in the Crimea in 1854. If we have, by any mischance, to fight this year, we can land this little army in a very perfect condition as soon as ships for their conveyance can be obtained.[27]

Wolseley was quite explicit in his opposition to any form of reactive defence. 'It would be the worst of folly', he wrote, to make no provision for services overseas: 'no scheme for [the] defence would be worth much, in which no provision had been made for striking an offensive blow abroad at our enemy.' Wolseley considered his 'little army' of two army corps and a cavalry division an 'essential' organization, one which 'we should always have ready to strike a counter blow with abroad'.[28] Whilst the prospect of the force conducting operations in mainland Europe may have been open to doubt for political reasons,[29] Wolseley's commitment to preparing a striking force seems clear. Moreover, as was his habit, he went to considerable lengths to make his views known, both to the public and to the Admiralty.

The War Office advertised its newfound capacity to mobilize two army corps during the celebrations held to mark the celebration of the Queen's Golden Jubilee in the spring of 1887. The press was under no illusion as to the function of the exercise, commenting on military plans 'to mobilise the 1st Army Corps for foreign service'.[30] Wolseley advertised his endeavours personally, informing the Royal United Services Institute of the 'earnest endeavour made on the part of the Army authorities, as all connected with the Army knew, to organize a force which might...have to be sent abroad—two Army corps and one cavalry division'.[31] Though the confines of high office seldom restricted Wolseley from speaking his mind in public, he also pursued more circuitous methods of disseminating his ideas. These had the twin advantages of appearing as independent endorsements of his policy and allowing him greater licence to expand upon his plans behind a veil of anonymity. During 1887 the Adjutant General entered into a prolonged correspondence with the former Liberal Cabinet member and prominent commentator on defence matters, Charles Dilke, over the state of the British Army.[32] Dilke was part of the campaign to induce the government to reform the defence establishment and initiated the discussion on these grounds. The result of this dialogue was a series of inspired articles in *The Fortnightly Review*—written by Dilke but based

---

[26] Evidence by Wolseley, 1 December 1886 in 'Report of the Royal Commission on Warlike Stores', 1887, p. 108, Q. 2775, C. 5062.

[27] Maurice and Arthur, *Life of Lord Wolseley*, p. 227.

[28] Wolseley, memorandum, 9 January 1888, p. 6, WO 33/48.

[29] Wolseley, memorandum, 20 August 1887, WO 33/48, fo. 24; Preston, 'Frustrated Great Gamesmanship', p. 243.

[30] 'The Mobilisation of the Army', *Morning Post*, 25 December 1886, p. 5.

[31] 'Lord Wolseley on Army Administration', *The Times*, 21 May 1887, p. 16.

[32] Kochanski, *Wolseley*, p. 186.

upon information from Wolseley—the first of which appeared in November. In these essays Dilke emphasized the expeditionary function of the regular army, stressing that 'in the event of invasion ... the presence of any regular troops to assist the volunteers and the remnant of the militia would be "an accident" '.[33] He spoke explicitly of 'the steps that have been taken of late to prepare two army corps as a field army for foreign service'[34] and re-iterated its proper role as being 'any purpose external to the United Kingdom'.[35]

The Admiralty, too, was keenly aware of the emphasis the military authorities placed upon dispatching expeditions abroad. As part of the re-assessment of naval strategy conducted by Captain Hall and the Naval Intelligence Department during the autumn of 1887, the naval authorities wrote to the War Office to ascertain the Army's intentions for transporting troops by sea in the event of war with a maritime power. A shared assumption that a British army would be sent abroad was implicit in the request; the naval authorities stipulated in their communication that the War Office consider the issue 'apart from the question of the dispatch of a military expedition abroad'.[36] The War Office's reply reflected the instructions that had been issued to Brackenbury in 1886. It stated that escorts for troop transports would be required:

(a) When an expedition of one Army Corps and a Cavalry Division ... is dispatched abroad ... to replace in Ireland, by troops from Great Britain, those troops which have been withdrawn to from part of the expeditionary force.

(b) When an expedition of two Army Corps and a Cavalry Division is dispatched abroad to replace similarly in Ireland the troops drawn from that country ...[37]

The requirements of 'the expeditionary force' were thus at the forefront of military planning and were widely known outside the War Office. Such was the stress placed upon dispatching troops and supplies to the relevant ports in order to speed the process of embarkation that the mobilization schemes drafted between 1886 and 1888 were even considered unsuited to readying a force for defending British shores. Before leaving his post as Assistant Adjutant General, in November 1888 Colonel John Ardagh explained how:

> The general lines on which mobilization of the 2nd Army-Corps were originally framed were these: It was supposed that the 1st Army-Corps had embarked immediately on their being mobilized, and that the 2nd Army-Corps when mobilized took the mobilization stations which had been evacuated by the 1st Army Corps. That system may be adapted for a foreign expedition, but it is not adapted for home defence; because the mobilization stations of the 1st Army-Corps might not, and in many cases would not, be evacuated by the components of that 1st Army-Corps,

[33] C. Dilke, 'The British Army', *Fortnightly Review*, CCLI, 1 November 1887, p. 617.
[34] C. Dilke, 'The British Army', *Fortnightly Review*, CCLII, 1 December 1887, p. 756.
[35] C. Dilke, 'The British Army', *Fortnightly Review*, CCLVI, 1 April 1888, p. 446.
[36] Admiralty to War Office, 26 October 1887, ADM 1/7322.
[37] War Office to Admiralty, 20 February 1888, ADM 1/7322.

and the arrangements then framed for the 2nd Army-Corps would be rendered impossible.[38]

In summing up, Ardagh re-iterated that the 'plan has evident disadvantages if the mobilization takes place for home defence'.[39]

What concerns the War Office did have for national security in the mid-1880s related to the situation at the outbreak of war. The pace of Prussian operations in 1870–1 had pointed to a dramatic increase in the rapidity with which future wars could be concluded. Several officers who were to go on to play a leading role in shaping British defence policy in subsequent decades, such as Horatio Kitchener, witnessed France's rapid defeat first hand whilst volunteering in the French army. Brackenbury, who had been a military observer in France, confessed that the experience had created a considerable effect upon him: 'it was my lot to be in France when war was declared against Germany... It was my lot to see the army of Sedan and the army of Metz made prisoners, and a great country overrun and ruined.'[40] This produced a persistent concern that an enemy might exploit surprise to circumvent Britain's naval preponderance and to undercut the War Office's preparations by landing an army in the United Kingdom before a formal declaration of hostilities had even been made.

In 1882 Wolseley had commissioned the Intelligence Department to produce an historical survey of 'Hostilities without Declaration of War' in connection with his opposition to plans to build a Channel Tunnel.[41] The report was representative of a growing consensus that future wars would begin more suddenly and be characterized by a series of bold offensive strokes, culminating in a decisive battle. To some, this appeared to render the prospect of an invasion of the British Isles an increasingly attractive one to a European military power. Brackenbury emphasized the importance of suddenness in an appreciation of the threat of invasion in March 1887: 'I scarcely contemplate in my own mind any attempt by any nation ever to invade this country for the purposes of conquest... but what I do contemplate as quite within the bounds of possibility is the dispatch of a force of, say 100,000 men, crowded together on board ship and sent at short notice across the Channel to land in this country and make a descent upon London.'[42] Ardagh summarized the general feeling within military circles the following spring:

> ... the general conviction now is, that, so far from having an interval of six weeks for preparation, after the declaration of war, the actual commencement of hostilities will be our first notice of the existence of a state of war. In the great Continental States the passage from peace to war footing can be effected now in a few days; but, apart from

[38] 'Examination of Colonel J. C. Ardagh, C.B., At the War Office, Pall Mall, Wednesday, 7th November', 1888, Q. 55, PRO 30/40/13, fos 320–1.

[39] 'Examination of Colonel J. C. Ardagh', 7 November 1888, Q. 61, PRO 30/40/13, fo. 321. This point is identified in Dunlop, *Development of the British Army*, p. 15.

[40] Brackenbury, memorandum, 14 April 1886, PRO 30/40/13, fo. 246.

[41] J. F. Maurice, 'Hostilities without Declaration of War From 1700 to 1870', HMSO, 1883, DMO/14/46, BL; Wilson, *Channel Tunnel Visions*, pp. 22–32.

[42] Evidence by Brackenbury to the Secret Consultative Committee on Defences, 10 March 1887, Q. 328, WO 33/47, fo. 897.

that, their peace establishments alone are more than adequate to furnish the personnel of an expedition destined to invade England; and it is so obviously the interest of the invader to attempt a surprise, that we may be assured that the most profound secrecy will be observed...[43]

The pervasion of such ideas into the popular consciousness was illustrated in May 1888, when the *Daily Telegraph* caused a stir by printing claims made by the Chief of the Great General Staff Count von Moltke that a surprise assault by 20,000–30,000 men might succeed in capturing London.[44]

Counter-intuitively, some viewed British naval strength as inviting such a surprise attack. The consensus that the country would be safe 'as long as we had a fleet in the neighbourhood' led to speculation that an enterprising enemy might attempt to negate Britain's predominance at sea by exploiting any temporary absence of the Navy to seize London.[45] Professional opinion agreed that, if an enemy did succeed in landing, the regular troops of the Home Army would be vital to repelling any such an assault. As Wolseley contended, 'no sane general would undertake the defence of England with the Militia and Volunteers, unaided by any smaller number of regular troops'.[46] The auxiliary forces might play a useful role defending fixed positions and garrisons, thereby freeing regular forces for field operations, but their reliability against European regular troops was doubted, certainly in the short term.[47] A contingency force of 80,000 Regulars would thus be retained in Britain, even if both army corps and a cavalry division departed the country.[48] This completed Wolseley's vision for the Army: a compact striking force for operations abroad, which would transition from the defensive to the offensive as soon as the Navy had secured control of the situation at sea. British naval superiority was fundamental to Wolseley's strategy. Without it, the troops of the expeditionary force would be unable to embark safely for operations abroad, the transfer of forces to and from Ireland would be curtailed, and the Home Army might even be obliged to adopt a defensive stance due to the auxiliary forces' unsuitability for operations against European troops. Military strategy hinged upon the Admiralty's ability to guarantee the safe movement of troops by sea. Yet the military authorities had made only the vaguest preparations with the Admiralty to co-ordinate the necessary transport or covering naval forces. Thus, a military strategy founded upon naval supremacy quickly came undone when the Admiralty proved unable to guarantee the freedom of manoeuvre Wolseley had assumed.

[43] J. C. Ardagh, 'Defence of England: Mobilization of the Regular and Auxiliary Forces for Home Defence', 17 April 1888, p. 2, PRO 30/40/13.

[44] 'England in Danger: Opinion in Germany', *Daily Telegraph*, 23 May 1888 (see ref cab 37/21/14).

[45] Evidence by Wolseley to the Secret Consultative Committee on Defences, 16 March 1887, Q. 553, Q. 580, WO 33/47, fos 909–10.

[46] Comments by Wolseley, 9 January 1888, WO 33/48, fo. 211.

[47] Beckett, *Riflemen Form*, pp. 185–8. Wolseley was optimistic that their efficiency might be improved and discussed their 'great value': see Wolseley, memorandum, 20 August 1887, WO 33/48, fo. 24.

[48] Wolseley, memorandum, 20 August 1887, WO 33/48, fo. 24.

'I DON'T WANT THE RIGHT ARM WEAK'

The importance of sea control to his vision of imperial military strategy made Wolseley an interested observer of naval developments. In early 1888 the Adjutant General had been much impressed by the surge of popular and expert opinion that the Fleet was inadequate to meet the threat of a war against France. After Captain Lord Charles Beresford resigned his position as Junior Naval Lord in January in an attempt to 'induce the authorities to reorganise and strengthen our defences', he found firm support from Wolseley.[49] The General wrote to Beresford explaining his view that 'if we had an efficient Army without an efficient Navy we should be like a man with only a left arm. Because I want the left arm strong I don't want the right arm weak.' 'If we are to be in the beggarly position of having only one arm', Wolseley continued, 'I'd rather have a right than a left, but we can neither win a war or defend ourselves without both.'[50] He repeated this argument in his controversial performance in the House of Lords on 14 May: 'as long as the Navy is as weak as it is at this moment, Her Majesty's Army cannot hold its own all over the world'.[51]

The Adjutant General's comments reflected his frustration at the government's refusal to fund the adequate garrisoning of the Empire's coaling stations and fortresses—a fact which made the transport of re-inforcements to these points vital at the outset of war. Several installations key to British naval operations were situated in regions likely to be contested by rival naval forces, particularly those in the Mediterranean. This made the transport of troops to them after the outbreak of war a dangerous proposition and one that might prejudice naval operations in the region. Problems were also anticipated dispatching troops to bases in the East and West Indies, India, and Australasia, as the presence of French and Russian squadrons in those waters meant that transports would require protection for the duration of their voyage. Without their full wartime complement, fortresses and coaling stations were considered vulnerable to a *coup de main*. Wolseley presented the situation in characteristically flamboyant terms: 'any intelligent Staff Officer could in a few hours frame a workable scheme for the capture of most of our coaling stations, and of several of our important fortresses beyond the seas'.[52] In addition to the reputational damage and military losses that might occur if such installations were stormed at the outset of war, their loss could have major implications for British naval operations and seriously prejudice Britain's ability to project power around the globe. As General Sir John Lintorn Simmons, the military C-in-C of Malta, summarized in March 1887, 'a British fleet could not exist in the Mediterranean during war without the port of Malta. It is…the centre and depot

---

[49] C. Beresford, *The Memoirs of Lord Charles Beresford: Written by Himself,* Boston: Little, Brown & Company, 1914, II, pp. 353–63.

[50] Quoted in Maurice and Arthur, *Life of Wolseley,* p. 238.

[51] Lords Sitting of 14 May 1888, Hansard, 3rd Series, Vol. 326, Col. 100.

[52] Wolseley, memorandum, 8 January 1888, WO 33/48, fo. 210.

for all our expeditions in the east.'[53] The Colonial Defence Committee had underlined the sensitivity of such strategically significant infrastructure in a report published in April 1887, in which it recommended that 'no permission should be granted under any circumstances [for other powers] to land *armed* bodies of men for any purpose' during peacetime. The recent experience of two French troop transports, thought to be conveying between 2,000 and 3,000 men, berthing adjacent to each other in Singapore harbour also led to the consideration of recommendations to restrict the number of foreign transports allowed into British ports at any given time.[54]

Yet, budgetary pressures, the costs associated with maintaining troops overseas, and the problems of attracting recruits for prolonged service abroad meant that the War Office was unable to sustain the majority of Britain's garrisons at anything approaching a full war footing. The military authorities therefore continued to rely upon a policy of dispatching troops from Britain or India to bring local defences up to their wartime complement. The increasingly problematic nature of this approach was highlighted during the proceedings of a parliamentary investigation into the level of fixed defences at British military and mercantile ports.[55] When called to give evidence before this body on 28 April 1887, Captain Hall of the Naval Intelligence Department had lost no time in stating his objections to the current system:

> ... the garrisons of Malta and Gibraltar require to be more than doubled. I believe it would be impossible to reinforce the garrison of Malta after war had broken out with France. The difficulty of sending troops through the Mediterranean to Malta, past the French Algerian coast, 600 miles in length, in which there are 12 harbours capable of sheltering torpedo boats, will, I believe, render it quite impossible to send troops into the Mediterranean after war has broken out with France.[56]

Wolseley, Brackenbury, and Simmons all expressed similar views in their evidence.[57] Hall was sufficiently perturbed by the prospect of having to factor escorting such a large number of troops into the Navy's strategic calculations that he recommended his superiors at the Admiralty write to the War Office and ascertain the precise extent of the troop movements the military authorities contemplated. A request for 'what re-inforcements will be dispatched to raise our Colonial garrisons to war strength at a time when war with a maritime power is imminent or anticipated' was duly sent to Horse Guards Parade on 14 September.[58] The War Office's response, which indicated that some 15,901 men would require transportation to

---

[53] Evidence by Simmons to the Secret Consultative Committee on Defences, 10 March 1887, Q. 408, WO 33/47, fo. 901.

[54] 'Measures of Precaution required for the Security of British Ports Abroad', 20 April 1887, pp. 2–3, CO 537/522.

[55] Beckett, 'Stanhope at the War Office', p. 287.

[56] Evidence by Hall, 28 April 1887, Q. 2732, WO 33/47, fo. 1009.

[57] Evidence by Brackenbury, 10 March 1887, Q. 284 and Wolseley, 16 March 1887, Q. 531, WO 33/47, fos 895 and 907 respectively.

[58] See docket 'Reinforcements for Colonial Garrisons in time of anticipated War', 7 September 1887, ADM 1/7322.

locations as diverse as Malta, Jamaica, and Halifax, illustrated the extent of the demands the existing arrangements would make upon the Navy. To make matters worse, 12,253 of these troops would require passage to either Gibraltar or Malta, both vital locations during an Anglo-French war, exposing them to attack from the numerous French bases they would pass en route.[59]

The War Office was well aware of the Admiralty's concerns about the transport of reinforcements abroad. Brackenbury acknowledged that 'it is…an accepted fact by our naval authorities that, in the event of war with France, the Mediterranean would be closed to our troopships and to our commerce'.[60] The military leadership also accepted that the Navy's responsibilities would be at their greatest at the outset of a conflict. 'With war threatening, or war having just broken out, there would be…a great desire on the part of our naval authorities, and I think very properly so, to concentrate our fleets in certain important places', Wolseley noted, adding that this imperative 'would prevent you from having the protection of naval escort for your transports during the voyage between Gibraltar and Malta'.[61] The two services were thus in agreement that the defences and garrisons of Britain's colonial possessions were inadequate and represented a source of vulnerability in wartime. Yet, political pressure on Stanhope to keep the Army Estimates low precluded large increases in the permanent garrisons of Britain's coaling stations and overseas bases.[62] The Duke of Cambridge, C-in-C of the Army, recalled how Stanhope had informed him that 'you must not ask for more men, because the Chancellor of the Exchequer will not give them'.[63] An impasse thus emerged between the Admiralty, the War Office, and the government, with neither department able to fulfil the requirements made upon it by the other under existing conditions.

This unsatisfactory situation persisted throughout 1888. In the wake of the Cabinet meeting convened to examine Wolseley's claims about the defence of London, on 12 June the Prime Minister informed the Queen that 'the provision of troops for the defence of coaling stations and dependencies abroad' was receiving his personal attention.[64] The question may even have played a role in precipitating the appointment of the Hartington Commission to investigate co-operation between the two services. The military authorities made a renewed effort to resolve the situation the following spring, mirroring previous attempts to extract a commitment to escort reinforcements from the Admiralty. The new DNI, Captain Cyprian Bridge, lost no time in sharing his view that agreeing to such an arrangement would be 'absurd' and 'altogether inadmissable'.[65] The War Office conceded that the Navy could not be expected to commit to escorting reinforcements to

[59] War Office to Admiralty, 11 October 1887, ADM 1/7322.
[60] Evidence by Brackenbury, 10 March 1887, Q. 308, WO 33/47, fo. 897.
[61] Evidence by Wolseley, 16 March 1887, Q. 533, WO 33/47, fo. 909.
[62] For the financial situation, see Beckett, 'Edward Stanhope at the War Office', pp. 285–6.
[63] Quoted in Beckett, 'Stanhope at the War Office', p. 288.
[64] Salisbury to the Queen, 12 June 1888, in Buckle ed., *Letters* III: I, p. 415.
[65] Bridge minute to Hood, 5 April 1889, ADM 1/7322.

coaling stations at a joint conference at the Colonial Office in December 1889.[66] Possibly an attempt to underline the seriousness of the situation to the government through a demonstration of inter-service consensus, the agreement had little political effect and the problem of garrisoning coaling stations remained unresolved for the subsequent decade.[67]

In the absence of a concession of funds from the Treasury, the thorny issue of garrisoning imperial bases threatened to undermine Wolseley's efforts to develop and maintain a robust striking force in Britain by draining valuable manpower away to various overseas bases. He thus found the government's refusal to countenance paying for additional garrison troops a source of continual frustration, as it threatened to impinge upon his military policy in the round. Yet if the defence of naval installations was an irritant to Wolseley, the Admiralty's attitude to the movement of men by sea had more profound implications for the amphibious strategy he cherished.

The naval authorities' appreciation of the situation at sea in the event of an Anglo-French war introduced a new factor into an ongoing wrangle between Calcutta and London over the strength of the Army in India. Whilst a formal Franco-Russian convention remained several years away, Russia's recent history of expansionism in central Asia and her tendency to exploit periods of British weakness—such as those resulting from military commitments in Egypt in 1882 and the Sudan in 1884–5—made it unlikely that she would not seek to take advantage of an Anglo-French conflict to improve her position in Persia, the Caucuses, and Afghanistan. Salisbury's negotiation of the Mediterranean agreements with Italy and Austria-Hungary in the spring of 1887 provided some counter-weight against France, but as Brackenbury had noted the previous year 'in a contest with Russia in Asia we can hope for no European ally'.[68] Reinforcing the garrison of the sub-continent therefore became an issue of growing strategic importance. Nowhere was this viewpoint more strongly held than within the Indian administration itself. Since the early 1880s the government of India, supported by the military hierarchy, had consistently warned of the need to strengthen the European garrison. General Frederick Roberts, the C-in-C India, was particularly active in campaigning for either a permanent increase to the forces at his disposal, or at least a firm commitment to dispatch reinforcements to India at the earliest possible moment in the event of Anglo-Russian hostilities. To Roberts' mind, such forces would be necessary in order to conduct an active defence of the sub-continent. Referred to as the 'forward' policy, this strategy was predicated upon the belief that Russian aggression could best be dealt with beyond India's frontiers, in order to reduce the

---

[66] 'Report of a Conference, held at the Colonial Office, to discuss the Conveyance of Reinforcements to our Colonial Garrisons in the event of war with a maritime power becoming probable, or actually having broken out, as treated in War Office printed paper "Colonial Defence—Reinforcements for War"', 19 December 1889, ADM 1/7322.

[67] Bridge to Hood, 5 April 1889, ADM 1/7322.

[68] Brackenbury, 'General Sketch', p. 12, WO 147/32.

chances of discontent being spread throughout the Raj itself.[69] The urgency of undertaking swift offensive measures to secure the strategic initiative became more acute as Russian influence expanded into northern Afghanistan after the Pendjeh incident of 1885.[70] Roberts argued later that year that:

> if we propose to send such a force against her [Russia] as will drive her back across the Afghan frontier as it now exists, and at the same time inflict upon her a blow that will paralyse her movements in Central Asia for many years to come, we must be prepared to put a very much larger Anglo-India Army in the field than has yet been contemplated.[71]

After gaining promotion to the post of C-in-C in July 1885, Roberts proceeded to advocate his strategy with considerable vigour and through a variety of official and unofficial channels. The following year he set out his views in one of a series of lengthy memoranda, 'The Defence of the North-West Frontier of India',[72] which accompanied a new mobilization scheme. These plans, which provided for two army corps and a reserve division for service beyond the frontier, required the immediate dispatch of 700 officers and 13,000 men from England to enact.[73] Roberts' submission thus represented the first formal request for a commitment to dispatch a specific number of reinforcements to India at the outbreak of an Anglo-Russian war. It heralded an important point in the evolution of a protracted and acrimonious debate between London and Calcutta which was to remain unresolved for the next two decades.[74]

Stanhope proved resolute in his refusal to satisfy the Indian requests, replying that 'any scheme for the mobilization of the Army in India should be based on existing conditions'. Reflecting the emphasis his professional advisers placed upon expeditionary warfare, the Secretary of State justified his stance on the grounds that 'it would... be dangerous to ignore the contingency that the circumstances of the moment might render it desirable or necessary to make considerable military preparations in this country'.[75] Similar reasoning was used to repel a second proposal early the following year; 'it is evidently far from improbable', Stanhope wrote on that occasion, 'that the same circumstances which necessitated a mobilization in India might also render it impossible for this country to part with any considerable portion of the small number of regular troops in the United Kingdom'.[76]

[69] R. Johnson, '"Russians at the Gates of India"? Planning the Defence of India, 1885–1900', *Journal of Military History*, Vol. 67, No. 3, Jul., 2003, p. 711.

[70] Ibid., p. 717.

[71] Roberts, 'What are Russia's Vulnerable Points? And How Have Recent Events Affected our Afghan Policy?' 22 May 1885, p. 4, NAM 7101-23-162-14.

[72] Roberts, 'The Defence of the North-West Frontier of India', 1 June 1886, NAM 7101-23-162-14.

[73] Newmarch, 'Action to be taken in the event of Russia invading Afghanistan, and Reinforcements required from England for the Army in India', November 1891, WO 32/6349.

[74] Beckett, 'Stanhope Memorandum', pp. 245–6.

[75] Stanhope note, 5 April 1887, quoted in Newmarch, 'Action to be taken', p. 1, WO 32/6349.

[76] Stanhope note, 14 February 1888, quoted in Newmarch, 'Action to be taken', p. 1, WO 32/6349.

The War Office objected to the government of India's requests on both strategic and logistical grounds. Entering into a formal commitment to make the Home Army the first reinforcement of the sub-continent would deprive Britain of the opportunity to use its only striking force elsewhere, curtailing the scope for amphibious descents of the nature Wolseley favoured. The Admiralty's position regarding the transport of troops also factored into War Office thought. The military authorities in London advised the India Office of the problems the Admiralty anticipated in January 1889: 'should this country be involved in a war with a for-midable naval Power, difficulties as to the safe conduct of any troops sent to India might arise'.[77] On these grounds, the War Office advised that 'the Government of India should clearly understand that for any operations, short of the actual inva-sion of her frontiers by Russia, it must rely entirely upon India resources, and that no reserve for India…is maintained in this country'.[78] Deemed 'cowardly' by Roberts, this advice did little to resolve the fundamental difference of perspective between the War Office and the Indian authorities.[79] Nevertheless, the War Office maintained its stance for much of the 1890s, re-iterating to the government of India that 'no troops in relief, or reinforcements for India, other than a force accompanied by a strong naval escort could be moved at all, until the Navy had cleared the seas'.[80] Yet, if the situation at sea was a convenient means of frustrating India's demands for men, it also contributed to the defeat of Wolseley's vision for amphibious operations in Europe. The growing disparity between British military strength and the mass armies of the Continent, improving land-based communi-cations, and the erosion of Wolseley's personal influence in London all contributed to this trend.[81] However, it was the evolution of Admiralty strategy that obliged Wolseley himself to accept a shift in the emphasis of military policy.

THE 'TEMPORARY ABSENCE' OF THE FLEET

The leadership of the Army equated the presence of ironclads in home waters with the security of British coasts. Wolseley encapsulated this view in an essay he con-tributed to a collection to celebrate the Queen's Golden Jubilee in 1887. 'Every extension of our commerce served and still serves to render the concentration of our fleets in the Channel for home protection all the more impossible', he wrote, 'the loss of one great naval battle there would leave our coasts open to easy

---

[77] Note of 5 December 1890, quoted in Newmarch, 'Action to be taken', p. 3, WO 32/6349.

[78] H. Brackenbury and O. R. Newmarch, memorandum, 19 August 1889, p. 17, WO 32/6349.

[79] Roberts to Brownlow, 21 August 1890, 'Correspondence with England', Vol. IX, p. 62, NAM 1971-01-23-100/3.

[80] Secretary of State for India to Government of India, 8 April 1892, quoted in 'Short Summary of Official Decisions, Opinions, Proposals & c., Relative to the Defence of India', Appendix II of War Office, 'Military Needs of the Empire in a War with France and Russia', 1901, p. 66, WO 106/48.

[81] Preston, 'Khartoum Relief Expedition', esp. pp. 261–75 and 'Frustrated Great Gamesmanship'; P. M. Kennedy, 'Mahan *versus* Mackinder: Two Interpretations of British Sea Power' in his *Strategy and Diplomacy, 1870–1945*, London: Fontana, 1989 edn, esp. pp. 50–67.

invasion.'[82] At the time Wolseley was writing, his views appeared to reflect the consensus of opinion at the Admiralty. That April, Captain Hall had informed Stanhope's parliamentary committee on port defences that he viewed the presence of 'a strong force in home waters at all times' as 'an absolute necessity in a War with France'.[83] Thus, it was perhaps not surprising that, when a war-scare brewed up during the spring of 1887, the military authorities exhibited considerable alarm at the fact that the Channel Fleet had departed home waters for a cruise of the Mediterranean.

The turn of the year saw tensions in Europe run high as the 'double crisis' over the political future of Bulgaria was complicated by a renewed Franco-German standoff in the west. A tariff war between France and Italy and on-going Anglo-French animosity over the status of Egypt prompted Salisbury to negotiate the Mediterranean agreements with Italy and Austria-Hungary in the spring.[84] As part of these agreements, the Italian government sought a commitment of British naval assistance in the event of a French attack on its coastline or fleet.[85] Salisbury avoided any binding commitment, but the Channel Fleet was dispatched on a cruise of the Mediterranean in support of British diplomacy. The fleet appeared at Genoa in a display of Anglo-Italian solidarity in February and again in March.[86] These visits produced a considerable impression in Italy; however, the departure of the fleet from home waters during a period of strained relations with France also had an impact at the War Office.[87] When Brackenbury appeared before Stanhope's committee on port defences on 10 March he noted that a force of 100,000 men might be landed on the south coast if 'our fleet were temporarily swept out of the Channel'.[88] Wolseley echoed the DMI's remarks during his appearance before the body a week later: 'the greatest danger we have is invasion of this country, the first necessity is a powerful fleet. We are so close to France that it is quite possible for a French Army to invade this country, and invade it without any warning.'[89] Admiral William Dowell, a member of the committee, asked Wolseley whether he thought France would attempt a landing 'merely in the temporary absence of our fleet unless the fleet was destroyed?' The Adjutant General replied simply, 'I think she would', continuing that 'I am supported in that opinion by what is the well known was the intention of the great Napoleon.'[90] Commentators at the time and since have been sceptical of the argument that a temporary absence of the fleet from home waters might enable a sudden invasion. Yet, the fact remains that these statements were made during one such 'temporary absence'. Brackenbury's and

[82] Wolseley, 'The Army' in T. H. Ward ed., *The Reign of Queen Victoria: A Survey of Fifty Years of Progress*, Vol. I, London: Smith, Elder & Co., 1887, p. 176.

[83] Evidence by Hall, 28 April 1887, Q. 2727 and 2881, WO 33/47, fos 1004 and 1013.

[84] Otte, '"Floating Downstream"?' pp. 110–12; *Foreign Office Mind*, pp. 173–83.

[85] Salisbury to the Queen, 2 February 1887 in Lowe ed., *The Reluctant Imperialists* II, pp. 54–5. See also Hamilton, *Parliamentary Reminiscences*, pp. 139–40.

[86] C. J. Lowe, *The Reluctant Imperialists*, London: Routledge, 1967, Vol. I, p. 149.

[87] J. G. Kennedy to Salisbury, 12 December 1888, CAB 37/22/46; Marder, *Anatomy*, pp. 142–3.

[88] Evidence by Brackenbury, 10 March 1887, Q. 342, WO 33/47, fo. 896.

[89] Evidence by Wolseley, 16 March 1887, Q. 617, WO 33/47, fo. 911.

[90] Evidence by Wolseley, 16 March 1887, Q. 626–7, WO 33/47, fo. 913.

Wolseley's warnings were far less hypothetical than is often assumed as, with the Channel Fleet in the Mediterranean, there was no formation of fully commissioned British ironclads in home waters. Worse still, the experience of the 1888 naval manoeuvres appeared to pose serious questions as to the Navy's ability to prevent the exit of enemy forces from port even if the Channel Fleet did remain closer to home. John Frederick Maurice, whom Wolseley had appointed as a lecturer at the Staff College upon returning from Egypt in 1885, observed the Navy's exercises and concluded that 'the English fleet is completely unable, with its present strength, to save our shores and commerce from even one foreign fleet'.[91]

The War Office's worries revealed a fundamental difference between the two services over the exercise of naval power. Whilst Admiral Hood argued that it would be 'impossible' permanently to confine even the reserve fleet to home waters, senior military officials were convinced that the presence of a British battle fleet in home waters was vital to preventing an attempt to rush the Channel.[92] Brackenbury made this point clear the following summer, when he argued that 'the thorough defeat of our Fleet, or its removal to other waters than the Channel is a necessary preliminary' to invasion. The DMI went on to explain his view that 'torpedo-boats, coast-defence vessels, vessels in reserve, merchant vessels and tugs...would scarcely count for much with the commander who had decided to invade England'.[93] This attitude was doubtless informed by the conflicting views of naval officers as to the efficacy of torpedo boats and the efficiency of the naval reserve. The venerable Admiral Phipps Hornby had been particularly critical of both before Stanhope's consultative committee in 1887[94] and the 'Three Admirals' report, published in early 1889, had also stated the necessity of 'an *effective* Reserve Squadron, absolutely confined to Home waters, sufficient to hold the Channel'.[95] A month after the 'Three Admirals' report, the Admiralty announced that the Channel Fleet would not be constrained to operating in the waters around Britain in the event of hostilities with France—formalizing its Gibraltar strategy. For the War Office, the naval leadership had thus made denuding home waters of frontline warships—which they deemed vital to British security—a fundamental aspect of policy.

Significant disagreements also existed as to the volume of shipping the French would require to convey an invading army across the Channel. In June, Hamilton had dismissed Wolseley's claims about the vulnerability of London on the grounds that the merchant tonnage in French Channel ports would be insufficient to convey an invading army without significant and highly visible prior preparations.[96] However, the First Lord's arguments had not convinced Stanhope, who commissioned the War Office Intelligence Department to examine the detail of his

---

[91] Maurice, 'The Naval Manoeuvres', *Fortnightly Review*, XLIV, 1888, p. 402; Luvaas, *Education of an Army*, pp. 203–5.

[92] 'Extracts from the Report of the Committee on the Naval Manoeuvres', 1889, p. 29, C. 5632.

[93] Brackenbury to Stanhope, 28 June 1888, and attached papers, Add. MS. 88906/16/19, BL.

[94] Evidence by Phipps Hornby, 27 April 1887, esp. Q. 2533–42, WO 33/47, fo. 997.

[95] 'Extracts from the Report of the Committee on the Naval Manoeuvres', 1889, p. 29, C. 5632. Emphasis added.

[96] Commons Sitting of Monday, 4 June 1888, Hansard, 3rd Series, Vol. 326, Col. 1069; Brackenbury to Stanhope, 28 June 1888, and attached papers, Add. MS. 88906/16/19, BL.

colleague's statements in preparation for the Cabinet meeting on the defence of London.[97] Brackenbury duly produced evidence which suggested that Hamilton had considerably overstated the amount of tonnage per man required to embark a force for a short sea passage,[98] although the conflation of gross and net tonnage confused the debate.[99] In the conclusion to his memorandum Brackenbury re-iterated his conviction that 'if our Channel Fleet were to be temporarily made powerless—to be removed from controlling the Channel for a period of three weeks—a strong maritime power would be able to . . . to land 100,000 to 150,000 men on these shores'.[100]

The military and naval authorities thus disagreed as to both the necessity of maintaining a fleet in home waters and the feasibility of the French launching a rapid invasion from their Channel ports. The impact this disconnect had upon military planning became evident between 1888 and 1890, as the War Office felt obliged to curtail its attempts to form the Home Army into an effective expeditionary force and to shift its focus to repelling a potential invader.

HOME DEFENCE ASCENDANT

In January 1888 Wolseley still contemplated the dispatch of his 'little army' abroad, although he did acknowledge that the force 'was never likely to be dispatched from home, as long as any invasion of these islands is seriously threatened'.[101] During the spring the military hierarchy began to use the threat of invasion as a justification for raising the level of military preparedness in Britain. In April the Assistant Adjutant General, Colonel Ardagh, was commissioned to examine mobilization arrangements for operations within the British Isles. Ardagh projected that by using every available regular solider in the country it would be possible to mobilize three army corps, a force larger than Brackenbury had considered practical for dispatch abroad.[102] Wolseley used these calculations in support of his campaign to strengthen the Home Army. He pursued this military aim concurrently with an additional, political agenda. Wolseley was deeply frustrated by the existing system of War Office administration wherein the C-in-C and Adjutant General were held responsible for the efficiency and performance of the Army but had no ability to extract additional funds for its maintenance and development from the government. Successive administrations' willingness to incur new military obligations

---

[97] Brackenbury to Stanhope, 28 June 1888, and attached papers, Add. MS. 88906/16/19, BL.

[98] Captain James Wolfe Murray, an officer in the Intelligence Department's Russian and Far Eastern Division, appears to have played an important part in supplying Brackenbury with his figures for the tonnage/man required: see J. W. Murray trans., 'The Transport of the Russian Field Army from the Ports of the Sea of Mamora and the Gulf of Burgas to the South Russian Ports in 1878 and 1879', *RUSI*, Vol. 34, No. 145, 1888, pp. 845–62.

[99] Earl Fortesque to Wolseley, 6 June 1888, Wolseley Papers.

[100] Brackenbury, 'A French Invasion', 8 June 1888, p. 5, CAB 37/21/15.

[101] Wolseley, memorandum, 8 January 1888, WO 33/48, fo. 211.

[102] Ardagh, 'Defence of England: Mobilization of the Regular and Auxiliary Forces for Home Defence', 17 April 1888, PRO 30/40/13, fo. 297.

without providing the additional resources required to fulfil them made effective planning a virtual impossibility as the department's efforts were absorbed in a constant battle to bridge a growing funding gap. As the consensus of military and naval thought appeared to be that the Army was inadequate to meet the Empire's needs, this placed Wolseley and the aging Duke of Cambridge, C-in-C since 1856, in the invidious position of potentially being held responsible for failings they had repeatedly warned the government about. As part of his effort to redress the situation, Wolseley approached Stanhope for 'a full statement of what he conceives... the military policy of England is at present'.[103] This would provide the War Office with something definite to work towards. The Adjutant General then prompted Stanhope with an outline of what he felt the best course to follow would be. His proposals centred on preparing 'to place rapidly in the field at home... three complete Army-Corps and six brigades of cavalry'. Wolseley linked this requirement explicitly to widespread doubts over the strength of the Royal Navy, explaining that 'it is not assumed that our Navy is strong enough to guarantee this country against invasion'.[104] Wolseley's point was not that the entire regular army should be confined to home defence, but rather that the absence of a fleet in the Channel meant that the 80,000 regulars not required for the 1st and 2nd Army Corps should be organized into an effective force to repel a surprise attack at the outset of war. The troops could then transition to the offensive when the naval situation permitted their dispatch overseas. His paper, which as we shall see formed the basis of the 'Stanhope Memorandum', was thus much less insular in its focus than it might appear initially. Wolseley sought to secure minor increases to the size of the Army sufficient to maintain his expeditionary posture in addition to a more efficient defensive establishment.

The impulse towards the latter objective remained significant, however. In the face of naval policy the War Office felt obliged to augment the defensive provision in the British Isles. Colonel Ardagh of the Mobilization Division duly conducted a lengthy investigation into the defences of London during the spring, after which he recommended paying for a ring of fixed fortifications around the capital intended to enable the volunteers to play a more useful role in repelling an invading army.[105] Here was an attempt to strengthen the defences of the capital without sacrificing regular troops from the mobile formations. The altogether less palatable alternative was to modify the mobilization arrangements for the two army corps intended for service abroad. Ultimately, Ardagh subscribed to the second option, albeit reluctantly. Interviewed prior to his departure for a post in India towards the end of the year, he explained his view that 'we should regard the 2nd Army-Corps primarily from the view of home defence', with embarkation for foreign service relegated to a secondary consideration. He also noted that his department had drawn up a draft 'Emergency Powers Bill', designed to provide the necessary legal

---

[103] For these disagreements, see Hamer, *The British Army*, pp. 128–34.
[104] Wolseley, memorandum, 8 June 1888, WO 33/48, fo. 413.
[105] Ardagh, 'The Defence of London', 16 July 1888, PRO 30/40/13, fos 300–307A.

powers to the military authorities in the event of an invasion.[106] As we shall see presently, the reasons for Ardagh's concession regarding the 2nd Army Corps became clear some twenty-four months later. Before doing so, it is important to note that the War Office was giving considered attention to improving the defensive provision in the British Isles long *before* the government responded to Wolseley's request for a definite statement of the nation's military policy in what would become known as the Stanhope Memorandum. The shift in military policy from expeditionary operations to a more insular focus was thus incremental, and cannot be blamed solely upon political direction. This much became clear during the summer of 1890.

As was often the case in the late Victorian Army, officers leaving the War Office regularly took up new postings in the sub-continent. This was true for both Ardagh and Brackenbury, who departed Horse Guards to become Military Member to the Viceroy's Council in April 1891. Generally considered part of the Wolseley 'ring', Brackenbury nevertheless maintained an active correspondence with the Adjutant General's main rival in the senior ranks of the Army, the C-in-C India, General Roberts.[107] Relations between the two men had cooled in the final years of Brackenbury's time as DMI, as he consistently opposed Roberts' calls for an enlargement of the garrison of India.[108] These professional differences were soon overcome after Brackenbury's arrival in India in 1891,[109] however, and Roberts took Brackenbury's arrival on the sub-continent as an opportunity to gain an insight into the prevailing currents of military and political thought in London.[110] He therefore lost no time in interviewing the former DMI after his arrival in India. After the first such meeting Roberts wrote to his long-time confidant, the recently retired General Sir Charles Brownlow, recounting their conversation in some detail. His letter encapsulated the manner in which Admiralty policy had shaped planning within the Intelligence Department during Brackenbury's tenure:

> I opened the ball by asking Brackenbury to enlighten us as to what had been decided on at home in the event of war, He said, if the war were with Russia alone, we should enter into alliance with Turkey, and as many troops as could be spared from England would be dispatched to Constantinople, Batoum, or elsewhere in Eastern Europe ...
>
> Brackenbury then went on to say that if France joined Russia against us, not a man could be spared from England, as the Intelligence Department had clearly proved that an invasion by France was possible, and every solider would be required to defend the mother country. On my enquiring where the Channel Fleet would be, he said that both the Channel and Mediterranean fleets would be employed in the Mediterranean, and that the home seas would be left unguarded. To this I replied that it was evident

[106] 'Examination of Colonel J. C. Ardagh', Q. 61 and Q. 73, PRO 30/40/13, fos 321–2.

[107] For a summary of Brackenbury's tenure in the Intelligence Department, see Brice, *Thinking Man's Soldier*, Chs 16–20.

[108] Roberts to Newmarch, 14 January 1890, 'Correspondence with England', Vol. IX, p. 3, NAM 1971-01-23-100/3.

[109] Roberts to Thomas Baker, 23 May 1891, 'Correspondence with England', Vol. IX, p. 157, NAM 1971-01-23-100/3; Preston, 'Khartoum Relief Expedition', p. 274.

[110] Roberts to Alfred Lyall, 14 April 1891, 'Correspondence with England', Vol. IX, p. 139, NAM 1971-01-23-100/3.

our navy was not strong enough; at the same time I expressed my disbelief that France would venture to embark 100,000 men on transports without men-of-war to protect them; and that if this were done, even supposing the Channel fleet were absent, there would be many smaller ships, torpedo boats, &c., which could cause serious damage to unprotected transports. I added that even if a French army under such circumstances were able to effect a landing, I could not understand how a single man would ever get away from England. The fleets would hurry back from the Mediterranean and elsewhere and would cut off all communication between the French army and France.

Brackenbury having delivered himself of the opinion he had formed from a five years' residence in Pall Mall, had but little else to say ...[111]

Roberts, who had recently read and approved of Mahan's *The Influence of Sea Power on History*, disagreed, arguing that 'England must look chiefly to her navy to secure her from invasion'.[112] Nevertheless, Brackenbury's description of the influence of naval considerations upon War Office planning appears convincing when the timing of the shift in Admiralty thought from the Channel to the Mediterranean and Wolseley's attempts to improve the standard of the Home Army for defensive purposes are considered in parallel.[113] Whether Stanhope can be blamed for enforcing a defensive focus upon Wolseley and his colleagues, as Robertson later claimed, therefore seems open to considerable doubt.[114]

When it finally came, the Cabinet's response to the Adjutant-General's memorandum occurred against a backdrop of general dissatisfaction in Parliament as to the strength and preparedness of both Army and Navy.[115] The government was widely condemned for failures of administration which encouraged a haphazard, piecemeal approach to defence planning. As Captain Lord Charles Beresford MP charged, the agitators 'did not ask for increased expenditure for itself; they wanted a better naval administration and a definite standard of defence to be laid down'.[116] The Duke of Cambridge expressed similar sentiments in the Lords, demanding that the government 'ought to lay down absolutely what they considered to be the object and duty of both the Navy and the Army'.[117] Stanhope put Wolseley's recommendations on military policy to the Cabinet in full, supporting his proposal for preparing to mobilize three army corps for home defence.[118] However, his colleagues concluded that the government was 'not able to concur in the proposed definition of the objects to be provided for' and that 'the probability of the employment of an Army-Corps in the field of any European war is sufficiently improbable to make it the primary duty of the military authorities to organise our

[111] Roberts to Brownlow, 20 June 1891, in 'Correspondence with England, While Commander-in-Chief in India, Vol. IX: 3rd March 1890 to 8th March 1893', NAM 1971-01-23-100/3.

[112] Roberts to Alfred Lyall, 14 April and 16 June 1891, in 'Correspondence with England', Vol. IX, pp. 139 and 161, NAM 1971-01-23-100/3.

[113] For a more sceptical view, see Preston, 'Khartoum Relief Expedition', p. 274.

[114] Beckett, 'The Stanhope Memorandum', p. 242.

[115] Hamer, *The British Army*, pp. 134–9.

[116] Speech by Beresford, Hansard, 4 June 1888, p. 1058.

[117] Speech by the Duke of Cambridge, Hansard, 4 June 1888, p. 1697.

[118] Stanhope, 'Proposed Increases of the Army', 7 November 1888, p. 3, CAB 37/22/34. For Stanhope's preference for using the auxiliary forces to reduce costs, see Beckett, 'Edward Stanhope at the War Office', pp. 293, 298–300; *Riflemen Form*, pp. 186–8.

forces efficiently for the defence of this country'.[119] This was a considerable blow to Wolseley and to his strategic concept of a centrally located amphibious striking force. The decision may have been influenced by political suspicions of the Adjutant General himself; Salisbury in particular doubted his judgement and was concerned that his ambition for personal glory might distort his advice.[120] Ideological and financial opposition to military expenditure and involvement in costly continental wars also doubtless played a role in the Cabinet's decision to limit the Army's ambition. Regardless, the decision had far-reaching consequences for military policy. With the Cabinet ruling that the Home Army should not be considered part of the reinforcement for India or liable to operate in Europe, home defence and colonial expeditions were the only remaining functions for a force based in Britain to fulfil. Of the two, colonial expeditions would entail an extended sea voyage, which the Admiralty advised would be impossible until the Navy had succeeded in locating and neutralizing hostile naval forces.[121] The government's decision therefore left preparing the Home Army for operations within the United Kingdom as the last remaining operational task entirely within the purview of the military authorities. The War Office was thus obliged to confine its ambitions to the only significant field of endeavour available to it. As one official wrote resignedly the following year:

> ...so long as the Country maintains large bodies of troops which can only be used against an enemy who has penetrated within the Kingdom, the military authorities feel it to be their duty to work out beforehand, as far as can be done, plans for the action of our land forces against such an enemy...[122]

'HOME DEFENCE... FILLED THE PICTURE'

After succeeding Ardagh as Assistant Adjutant General, Colonel Coleridge Grove completed the work on mobilization for home service his predecessor had commenced prior to the issue of the Stanhope Memorandum. Reflecting the new direction of travel of War Office planning, Grove wrote, 'assuming our Navy to be absent—if a disembarkation is attempted in force they will not be able to prevent it, and the duty of dealing with the invader will fall upon the field army'.[123] Stanhope's private secretary, Guy Fleetwood Wilson, provided a telling indication of Grove's perspective in a letter to Ardagh in which he described how 'Grove is

[119] 'Minute of the Secretary of State laying down the requirements from our Army, dated 8th December, 1888', p. 29, in Appendix III of Wolseley memorandum of 22 February 1896, DMO/6/2, BL. Stanhope had not proposed to include this condition when he laid his modifications to Wolseley's June memorandum before Cabinet in November: see 'Proposed Increases of the Army', 7 November 1888, p. 3, CAB 37/22/34.

[120] Preston, 'Khartoum Relief Expedition', pp. 264–5.

[121] 'Report of a Conference, held at the Colonial Office, to discuss the Conveyance of Reinforcements to our Colonial Garrisons in the event of war', ADM 1/7322.

[122] 'Draft Letter to the Under-Secretary, War Office', 23 August 1889, quoted in Moon, 'Invasion', p. 81.

[123] Grove to Wolseley, 26 July 1890, PRO 30/40/13, fo. 343.

even madder than you are on the subject of invasion.'[124] By the time Wolseley departed to become C-in-C in Ireland in the autumn of 1890 his aspiration to create the readily deployable 'little army' he had lacked in the Sudan in 1884–5 had thus foundered on the rocks of naval obduracy and political parsimony. His replacement, Major-General Redvers Buller, was a competent soldier but lacked Wolseley's vision and capacity for political manoeuvre. 'I am always inclined to think myself a better second fiddle than a leader of thought', he reflected, noting ruefully that 'Lord Wolseley I think the contrary.'[125] Reversing the constraints placed upon War Office planners by the Admiralty and government was unlikely under Buller's oversight.

The enthusiasm with which Grove took to the task of preparing new mobilization schemes for home defence was not mirrored throughout the War Office, however, and the objections of those who opposed the policy do much to reveal its steady pervasion throughout the military planning process. Brackenbury's replacement as DMI, Major-General Edward Chapman, spent much of his tenure at the War Office railing against what he perceived to be an insidious trend towards a defensive outlook within the military hierarchy.[126] An officer with considerable experience of service in India, Chapman confounds binary notions of a split between 'home' and 'Indian' schools of strategic thought.[127] In a brief summation of his views on military policy penned in the summer of 1895, he stated simply that 'the military policy of Grt Britain must be a maritime policy & must embrace a consideration of the needs of India & of the colonies, it must be in accord with naval policy & before all things, it must be offensive in character'.[128] An advocate of amphibious operations even within Europe, Chapman's strategic preferences approximated to those which had inspired Wolseley between 1886 and 1890.[129] Six months after arriving in office, he produced a memorandum which bore striking similarities to the former Adjutant General's own views:

> ...a field army, fully equipped and prepared to take the field at home or abroad at the shortest notice, not only acts directly as a safeguard against invasion, but, at the same time, it places us in a position to adopt, should the necessity arise, an offensive-defensive policy, which might render invasion impossible.
>
> Without a field army, fully prepared to take the field abroad, the defence of England becomes purely passive, and, as such, is worthless.
>
> In the event of hostilities between this country and France...the existence of a British field army...without so much as quitting our shores, would contain a very much larger French force on the French coast...

[124] Fleetwood Wilson to Ardagh, 15 August 1889, PRO 30/40/13, fo. 322.

[125] Buller to Campbell-Bannerman, 18 June 1895, quoted in Hamer, *The British Army*, p. 161; Preston, 'Khartoum Relief Expedition', p. 273.

[126] Ferguson, *British Military Intelligence*, p. 106.

[127] For a tendency towards such a depiction, see Preston, 'Khartoum Relief Expedition', pp. 273–5. For an alternative view, see Bailes, 'Patterns of Thought in the Late-Victorian Army'.

[128] Chapman, note of 24 June 1895 on the inside front cover of DMO/14, BL.

[129] Chapman, 'Memorandum', 22 December 1891, DMO/14/8; C. à Court, 'Report on Measures for Interrupting a French Mobilization on the Shores of the Channel', 28 March 1894, DMO/14/6; Chapman to Buller, 11 April 1894, DMO/14/18, BL.

Revealingly as to the state of thought at the War Office, Chapman concluded that 'I know of no single reason that justifies the abandonment of this policy.'[130] The clear inference of this line of argument was that something of a shift away from such a stance *was* under way in late 1891.

Despite Chapman's entreaties, the change in War Office priorities he sought to avert continued unabated. The following May the Secretary of State for War wrote to the Admiralty informing Their Lordships that plans for dispatching two army corps abroad had been abandoned: 'it is not now intended to carry our preparations for the dispatch of an expedition abroad at short notice, beyond those required for a force consisting of an Army-Corps, a Cavalry Division and Line of Communication Troops'.[131] The fall of the Conservative government in the autumn confirmed this trend. Henry Campbell-Bannerman, the new Liberal Secretary of State for War, was staunchly opposed to the deployment of a British army on the Continent, a view he had previously made clear by opposing the Hartington Commission's recommendation to form a general staff lest such a body 'manufacture a military policy for the country'.[132] His appointment ensured that the functions outlined in the purposefully limiting Stanhope Memorandum were preserved as War Office policy.

In December 1892 Chapman reflected upon what he viewed as this unsatisfactory trend towards the defensive in military planning in a paper submitted to Buller:

> During the past year much has been done to further elaborate and complete our system of mobilization for Home Defence... There is one point, however, which as more particularly concerning my own Division, I have lately been studying, and that is: how the present system of mobilization affects out power of assuming an active offensive on a favourable opportunity offering itself... To my mind there is no reason why our arrangements for defence should conflict with our arrangements for offence ...

The DMI concluded by returning to his appeal not to abandon the earlier emphasis upon expeditionary warfare: 'I recommend a continuity of policy, and an adherence to the two Army Corps mentioned in the report of the Committee on Army Mobilization, dated December 1886.'[133] A week later he wrote to Brackenbury lamenting the trend towards 'passive defence' in War Office thought. 'I find myself met everywhere', he bemoaned, 'with the belief, that if this Home Defence is completed we shall never require to embark an army for foreign service & need not consequently take the precautions which I deem all very necessary.' The DMI condemned the 'complete separation that has been brought about in the policy to be adopted by the Navy, & in that wh[ich] *we ourselves are being forced to accept*.'[134] Almost as confirmation of the DMI's worries, on 21 December Buller announced the abandonment of the existing nomenclature of '1st Army Corps for Service

130 Chapman, 'Memorandum', 22 December 1891, DMO/14/8, BL.
131 War Office to Admiralty, 24 May 1892, ADM 1/7135.
132 Robertson, *From Private to Field Marshal*, p. 93; Hamer, *The British Army*, pp. 149–52.
133 Chapman to Buller, 25 November 1892, DMO/14/7, BL.
134 Chapman to Brackenbury, 2 December 1892, WO 106/16, fos 224–5. Emphasis added.

Abroad' in favour of '1st Army Corps for Home Defence'. The insularity of the Army's preparations was completed by the integration of the auxiliary forces, which were entirely unsuited to rapid deployment overseas, into the mobilization arrangements of the 2nd and 3rd Army Corps. Stores, equipment, and transport hitherto reserved for service abroad were distributed more evenly between these new formations. Whilst the 1st Army Corps nominally remained 'specially consti-tuted' for rapid embarkation,[135] the integration of the reserves into the 2nd Army Corps led Chapman to concede that 'no portion of the Home Establishment is in a position to take the field without our reserves'. The force could therefore only be mobilized upon calling out the reserves, a measure reserved for times of national emergency due to the disruption it would cause.[136]

Chapman mirrored Roberts in turning to Mahan's work on naval strategy to support his arguments in favour of a more proactive military stance. In January 1893 he sent both Grove and Buller a copy of the scholar's latest work, *The Influence of Sea Power upon the French Revolution and Empire, 1793–1812*, despairingly entreating Grove to 'please read it'.[137] The DMI's efforts proved to be in vain, how-ever. At the instigation of the War Office, a joint military and naval committee was formed in 1891 to consider the feasibility of a hostile power landing troops on British shores. The Admiralty regarded the proceedings as pointless from the out-set. The First Lord, George Hamilton, summed up the consensus of naval opinion when he noted how 'the assumption that our whole naval force is absent & the whole French force present is so absurd an assumption that it would be a sheer waste of time to discuss what might under such impossible conditions occur'.[138] The military representatives were insistent that such blandishments were no guar-antee against a hostile descent on British shores, however. In an effort to diffuse the tension between the military and naval departments, the feasibility of a full-scale invasion was removed from the scope of the group's investigations, artificially confining its remit to the logistical and practical considerations of transporting and landing troops on the British coast. This did little to reconcile the opposing sides, both of whom produced separate final reports. The military section of the final report saw Colonel Grove attempt to justify the requirement to prepare for a landing on British shores once again:

> The assumption that the home fleet will always be able to offer effective interference to an attempted invasion appears to us to carry with it the assumption that it will never, under any conditions, be reduced to a condition of marked inferiority to the fleet which an enemy, or a combination of enemies, can assemble in the Channel. We do not think this is an assumption on which it would be prudent to rest our defensive arrangements. In 1882 our battle-ships in commission in the Channel were reduced

[135] Buller, 'Organization of a Force for Active Service Abroad', 21 December 1892, DMO/14/19, BL.
[136] Chapman to Buller, 18 November 1892, DMO/14/9; Chapman to Buller, 3 December 1892, DMO/14/7, BL; Chapman to White, 16 March 1893, WO 106/16, fo. 321.
[137] Chapman to Grove and Chapman to Buller, 21 January 1893, both in WO 106/16, fo. 280.
[138] Note by Hamilton, 15 May 1890, in 'Invasion Subject: Conference with War Office', ADM 1/7046.

to eight, and so recently as 1887, Admiral Hornby...stated to Mr. Stanhope's Consultative Committee that, under certain circumstances, he considered the obtaining the command of the Channel by the French as 'extremely probable'.[139]

Vice-Admiral Philip Colomb, who chaired the body, was so frustrated by the proceedings that he enlisted the support of Colonel John Frederick Maurice, recently retired as professor of military history at the Army Staff College, to produce a fictionalized account of a French invasion which stressed the centrality of the Navy to the defence of Britain.[140]

Wolseley's return to the War Office as Commander-in-Chief in 1895 did signal a gradual return to a more offensive military policy. Changes were made to the mobilization arrangements, enabling two regular army corps to be prepared for foreign service at short notice once again.[141] Captain Gerald Ellison, then serving as Staff Captain to the Assistant Adjutant General, later recalled how 'it was Lord Wolseley, and Lord Wolseley alone, who conceived the idea of an Expeditionary Force, and, when he became C-in-C, he gave effect to the idea after lesser men had done all in their power to obscure the vital point at issue'.[142] Even the long-frustrated Chapman was able to record with some pleasure in March 1896 how whilst 'our military policy at the present time is based on home defence...we have during the last few years adopted ideas that are mainly offensive'.[143] On the eve of the Boer War, Wolseley was able to boast that the Army could prepare two army corps for foreign service faster than the Admiralty could find the shipping, a claim justified by the efficiency which marked the dispatch of the Army to South Africa in 1899–1900.[144]

It would be wrong to over-emphasize the degree to which operations overseas displaced home defence in the War Office's order of priorities, however. As troops embarked for South Africa, Wolseley warned Lord Lansdowne, the Secretary of State for War, of the 'dangerous weakness of our military position in England' and advised that the militia should be embodied for 'the safety of these islands'.[145] Moreover, the policy of both the Admiralty and the government remained powerful constraints on the adoption of a more offensive strategy. Buller reminded Chapman that 'the army must wait on the Policy of the Government' and Wolseley lamented how 'we have still got to convince the Navy that they can't win a war by themselves, and that we are not trying to nab the money they ought to have, but

[139] 'Memorandum II' in 'Report of the Landing Places Committee', 1894, xxii–xxiii, WO 33/54.

[140] P. H. Colomb, J. F. Maurice, F. N. Maude, A. Forbes, C. Lowe, D. Christie Murray, and F. Scudamore, *The Great War of 189-: A Forecast*, London: William Heinemann, 1893. The text was originally published in *Black and White* magazine, December 1891–March 1892; also see Clarke, *Voices Prophesying War*, pp. 62–4; Moon, 'Invasion', pp. 101–2.

[141] Lyttelton to Wolseley, 17 December 1896, WO 32/8770; Maurice and Arthur, *Wolseley*, pp. 306–7; Dunlop, *Development of the British Army*, p. 15; Spiers, *Late Victorian Army*, p. 231.

[142] Ellison, *Lancashire Lad* xii, October 1934, p. 7; Dunlop, *Development of the British Army*, p. 16.

[143] Chapman to Buller, 10 March 1896, DMO/14/58, BL.

[144] Stopford to Wolseley, 21 February 1898, PRO 30/40/13, fo. 379; Beckett, 'Stanhope at the War Office', p. 299.

[145] Wolseley to Lansdowne, 30 September 1899 and 30 October 1899, in docket 266, WO 32/6359; Tunstall, 'Imperial Defence, 1897–1914', p. 571.

want to make our power, what it must be to be effective, amphibious'.[146] 'What is the use', the C-in-C questioned, 'of our being able to mobilise in a fortnight...if the Navy are going to take a month to find the ships.'[147] Ultimately it took the failings the Army exhibited in South Africa to reveal the dangers of failing to prepare for major combat operations abroad.

* * *

Between 1888 and 1895 uncertainty as to the naval position in a war against France and political reluctance to finance a military policy capable of meeting the challenges facing the Empire combined to restrict the War Office to an insular focus on national defence. The Navy's focus on the Mediterranean and its argument that armoured warships need not be shackled to the defence of home waters convinced the military hierarchy that a French attempt to rush the Channel had to be provided against. The resulting defensive focus was reinforced by the War Office's inability to secure reliable commitments to move troops by sea and by an unwillingness to subordinate the Home Army to the defence of India. The majority of the Home Army was thus confined to the British Isles, beholden to the Admiralty to decide when it might be safe to adopt a more aggressive strategy. Politicians were content to allow the situation to persist as it justified suppressing military spending. The money thus saved could be invested more profitably and to greater political effect by building more warships, the regular appearance of which satisfied the powerful commercial interests of the City of London. Yet by the close of the century, the sustainability of this approach was open to doubt. Steady Russian encroachment into central Asia presaged a growing threat to the Indian frontier and the military and financial shock of the Boer War challenged the assumption that the British could afford not to possess an Army capable of operating against a European opponent. As students of 'imperial defence' had demanded since the 1880s, the government needed to define the purpose for which the armed forces of the Empire were constituted.

---

[146] Buller to Chapman, 10 March 1896, DMO/14/58, BL.
[147] Quoted in Maurice and Arthur, *Wolseley*, pp. 285–6.

3

'Practical Politics'

Wolseley's return to Horse Guards Parade in 1895 presaged a revival of earlier attempts to prepare the Army for operations overseas. However, the context in which he was operating had altered significantly during the five years of his absence. The conclusion of the Franco-Russian alliance and the spread of Russian power southward towards the Straits, Persia, and Afghanistan threatened to render Wolseley's strategic conception of a centrally based amphibious striking force an anachronism. Accepting that 'nothing much can be done till the Navy has asserted its superiority' would not safeguard India from Russian activity on her borders and the new Commander-in-Chief's preference for amphibious operations in the Baltic or Black Sea seemed increasingly unlikely to have a meaningful impact upon St Petersburg's ability to deploy military force in central Asia.[1] Equally concerning were the extent of the difficulties the British Army encountered in subduing the Boer militiamen in South Africa. The experience of 1899–1902 proved to be a military challenge without precedent in the recent history of the Army, revealing concerning tactical and operational shortcomings as well as the limited ability of the British military system to sustain a major deployment overseas. These failings augured poorly for the Army's chances against the mass conscript forces of the European Great Powers, whether on the Indian Frontier or on the Continent.

The war in South Africa lasted almost three years, required the deployment of 448,000 British and Imperial troops, and cost the Exchequer in excess of £230 million.[2] Embarrassing and costly defeats at Stormberg, Magersfontein, and Colenso, and the disaster at Spion Kop in January 1900 all cast doubt over the Army's fighting effectiveness. Arguably more significant than these operational setbacks, however, were the limitations the conflict exposed in the Empire's military capacity.[3] As Leo Amery, *The Times*' official correspondent in South Africa noted, the conflict revealed 'how slight and uncertain was the reserve of military manpower of the British Empire'.[4] As had been the case in the Sudan in 1884–5, with the majority of the Army committed in one theatre, other reaches of the Empire were rendered vulnerable.

---

[1] Unsigned memorandum, 'Offensive Movements', 1899–1900, Add MS 88906/16/19, BL.
[2] E. Spiers, 'Between the South African War and the First World War, 1902–1914' in H. Strachan ed., *Big Wars and Small Wars: The British Army and the Lessons of the 20th Century*, Abingdon: Routledge, 2006, p. 21.
[3] Dunlop, *Development of the British Army*, pp. 121–6.
[4] Quoted in Spiers, *Army and Society*, p. 236.

A steady decline in Britain's ability to defend her interests by force alone had been in evidence since the 1870s. The Mediterranean agreements with Italy and Austria in 1887 were concrete evidence of this fact, as was the grudging acknowledgement of Britain's reduced ability to coerce the Sultan by threatening naval action against the Dardanelles after 1890.[5] By the close of the century, the power against which British strength seemed least likely to be effective was Russia. Developments in her railway infrastructure, the fortification of her Baltic and Pacific ports, and the diplomatic and practical difficulties in accessing the Black Sea all insulated Russia from the effects of British sea power.[6] This would have counted for little, were it not for the fact that as Britain's ability to coerce Russia militarily waned, the degree to which the Tsar appeared able to threaten British interests appeared to increase with each passing year. Russian expansion in Asia brought her into contact with British spheres of influence in China, Persia, and India. The geographical distance which had enabled India to be defended 'without those huge standing armies found necessary by continental nations whose boundaries are coterminous', in John Bright's memorable formulation, had shrunk precipitously by 1900.[7] The prospect of a physical invasion remained remote due to the formidable logistical barriers involved, but the legacy of the Indian Mutiny and the costs and political difficulties involved in maintaining a large garrison of European troops on the sub-continent combined to create a major problem for planners in London. Even a relatively modest increase in the amount necessary to fund the defence of India might prove beyond the tolerance of the British (or Indian) taxpayer. Russia's willingness to exploit British anxieties over Indian security were made all too clear in February 1900, when she began agitating over the status of the Afghan border whilst British forces (including a portion of the Indian garrison) were fully engaged in the Boer War. British diplomats were keenly aware that no other European power would risk antagonizing Russia for the sake of British interests in Asia, and London's increasing isolation from both France and Germany limited the scope to mobilize the support of either power as a counterweight to balance Russian ambition. Lacking either military or diplomatic leverage, how to halt the seemingly inexorable encroachment of Russia towards the Raj was unclear.

Against this backdrop, the Army's travails in South Africa and the cost of the war there obliged the government to take a more active role in addressing Britain's preparedness for war. The subsequent political intervention produced the definitive statement of 'what they considered to be the object and duty of both the Navy and the Army' which service leaders had been agitating for since the 1880s. Between 1902 and 1904 Balfour's Unionist administration constructed the framework within which all subsequent considerations of strategy in Britain prior to 1914 were conducted. This was done in both institutional and conceptual terms. The

    [5] Wilson, 'Constantinople or Cairo'; Otte, *Foreign Office Mind*, pp. 150–85.
    [6] J. S. Rothwell, 'England's Means of Offence Against Russia', 7 July 1884, CAB 37/13/36; K. Neilson, 'The British Way in War and Russia' in Neilson and Kennedy eds, *The British Way in Warfare*, pp. 12–13.
    [7] Quoted in Johnson, 'Russians at the Gates of India', p. 714.

newly formed Committee of Imperial Defence (CID) became the primary instrument for political oversight of military and naval policy. More significantly, the politicians also clearly set out the responsibilities of the two services and the demarcation between them. In doing so, they made a fundamental break with previous British strategy by explicitly divorcing the Regular Army from the defence of the United Kingdom. This had far-reaching consequences for both services, concentrating the Army on operations overseas and the Navy on facilitating the rapid departure of a military striking force. In many respects complementary, these changes were soon to come into conflict after 1905.

* * *

The period between 1899 and 1902 saw Britain confronted both by the acute challenge of a major military campaign in South Africa and by an intensification of the longer-term problem of defending India. The scale of mobilization required to subdue the Boers and the operational shortcomings revealed during the campaign represented a stark warning as to the state of British military preparedness.[8] The problems encountered were particularly troubling when the British military effort was compared to the size, efficiency, and capacity of Continental armies. Even as troops set sail for South Africa, Wolseley cautioned the Secretary of State for War that the decision to commit the majority of the Regular Army to the campaign left Britain and the remainder of the Empire vulnerable, stressing 'the dangerous weakness of our military position in England'.[9] The C-in-C's warnings were doubtless calculated to induce the government to embody the Reserve and Militia battalions, thereby facilitating the dispatch of additional forces to South Africa if required. Nevertheless, his point remained a legitimate one: the Army could not simultaneously prosecute the campaign in South Africa and sustain the two army corps of troops for operations in Britain laid down in the Stanhope Memorandum.

In some respects the Boer War conformed to the model of the numerous colonial campaigns Britain had prosecuted during the nineteenth century. The area of operations was remote and the enemy was landlocked and poorly resourced compared to the might of the British Empire. These conditions meant that the Admiralty's objections to the dispatch of troops during war with a maritime power did not apply, enabling the rapid embarkation of men and supplies for South Africa. Yet, by January 1900 it was apparent that the Boers were more formidable than the indigenous peoples the Army had confronted in Egypt or Asia. The defeats of 'black week' in December 1899 created a powerful impulse to commit additional military resources in order to maintain British prestige. As the Secretary of State for War, Lord Lansdowne, noted: 'troops equivalent to more than two Army-Corps' had been dispatched by the turn of the New Year.[10] This was a logistical triumph for the War Office, which had laboured to prepare such a force for rapid deployment since

---

[8] Dunlop, *Development of the British Army*, pp. 121–6.
[9] Wolseley to Lansdowne, 30 September 1899, WO 32/6359.
[10] Lansdowne, 'Army Proposals', 8 February 1900, pp. 1–2, CAB 37/52/14; Minute by Lansdowne, 18 October 1899, WO 32/6359.

the mid-1880s. However, it also posed fundamental questions about British imperial strategy. The dispatch of so large a portion of the Regular Army would not have been contemplated in the event of war with a major maritime power until the threat of invasion had receded. The departure of so large a proportion of the Army's trained manpower meant that speculation abounded that an opportunistic European power might take advantage of the situation to strike a blow against the exposed heart of the Empire.[11] Widespread pro-Boer demonstrations in Paris led Britain's ambassador to caution that such sentiment 'might excite into practical mischief'[12] and Wolseley warned prophetically that 'France owes us a deep grudge, and may endeavour to pay it off in the autumn of 1900, or even earlier, being encouraged to do this by the fact that the greater portion of the small army on which we are content to rely for the defence of our shores, is no longer in this country, but committed to a difficult war 6,000 miles away.'[13]

It seemed that, whilst Britain could dispatch her Army overseas reasonably efficiently, she could only do so by imperilling the home islands. Major-General John Ardagh, returned to the War Office as Director of Military Intelligence, described how 'the general fabric of our Home Defence Force has been seriously impaired—to such a degree indeed as to render an invasion of Britain more tempting than it has been for the last century'. 'It is evident to all the world', he continued, 'that the entire absence of an organization for providing for automatic expansion of our armed forces in war has brought us into a position which it is no exaggeration to call perilous'.[14] These failings left Britain singularly ill-equipped to face the most serious and plausible military threat of the day: war with Russia in Asia, in the context of the Franco-Russian alliance. Were the forces deployed to South Africa in 1899–1900 to have been sent to defend the North-West Frontier during an Anglo-Russian war, the threat of a French strike against Britain, timed to occur after the troops had sailed, would have assumed an altogether more threatening aspect than the rumours which circulated in January 1900. Even in the absence of direct Russian action, civil unrest in India extensive enough to require the dispatch of troops from England might have similar consequences.

The military authorities were understandably perturbed by the situation and what it revealed. Displaying their traditional scepticism of the Navy's ability to guarantee the inviolability of British shores, the War Office continued to regard the shortage of trained manpower in the country as a cause for concern throughout the conflict in South Africa.[15] Some 400,000 troops were nominally with the colours in the United Kingdom in February 1900, but the Army lacked sufficient specialist troops and experienced regulars to form them into the two mobile army corps that the government had deemed necessary to repel an invasion in 1888.[16]

[11] The best summary of the invasion panic is in Moon, 'Invasion', Ch. III.

[12] Monson to Salisbury, 7 September 1900 quoted in Otte, *Foreign Office Mind*, p. 234.

[13] Wolseley to Lansdowne, 29 December 1899, CAB 37/51/105; Wolseley to Lansdowne, 23 January 1900, WO 32/6360.

[14] Ardagh, 'Organization of Provisional Battalions of Infantry for Keeping up the Home Defence Force', 29 May 1900, PRO 30/40/13, fos 747–8.

[15] Ardagh to Wolseley, 11 July 1900, PRO 30/40/14, fos 217–19.

[16] Wolseley to Lansdowne, 23 January 1900, WO 32/6360.

Reflecting on the experience of the war in 1903, Wolseley re-stated his conviction that sending the Regular Army abroad before any threat of invasion had been removed would be inadvisable: 'I do not think any soldier would recommend sending three Army Corps abroad to any part of the World unless he felt that the country was absolutely secure against invasion.'[17] Yet, even as the experience of South Africa underlined the difficulties involved in balancing the demands of a major combat operation overseas with defensive requirements at home, the prospect of needing to dispatch a large number of trained troops abroad appeared to be growing.

The spectre of Russian encroachment into central Asia had troubled British officials since the 1830s; however, the final decades of the nineteenth century saw these worries solidify into a consistent sense of threat. The logistical and practical difficulties of concentrating troops near the Afghan border, particularly with Russia's inefficient transportation infrastructure, rendered the prospect of a direct attack upon India remote. However, the British remained acutely sensitive to the lessons of the mutiny. Maintaining internal order was vital to Indian security and the encroachment of a hostile power had the potential to sow discord amongst the unruly border tribes and to de-stabilize the frontier. Such eventualities might require significant, costly additions to the European garrison and the Indian military budget, measures likely to prove unpopular with the British public and unsustainable to the Treasury.[18] Concerns over domestic stability prompted the authorities in Calcutta to advocate defending India beyond her borders. Opinion was divided between the desirability of supporting a buffer state in Afghanistan and adopting a so-called 'forward policy' of advancing north at the outbreak of war to establish a defensive position along a supposed 'scientific frontier', hinging about Herat on its western flank.[19] Establishing an Afghan government reliable enough to resist Russian overtures and sufficiently sympathetic to British interests proved problematic. As Russia encroached southwards during the late 1880s, the 'forward policy' thus became the preferred option in Calcutta.[20] Military operations beyond the frontier would, however, require additional resources from Britain—in terms of both men and infrastructure to transport them to the border and beyond.

London had rebuffed the Government of India's requests for a commitment to dispatch a specified number of reinforcements in the event of war with Russia throughout the 1890s. Yet the War Office's reluctance did nothing to alter the reality of the Russian threat to the stability of the Raj. Indeed, the danger only grew as the decade progressed and Russia asserted herself with greater authority on

[17] Evidence by Wolseley to the Royal Commission on the Militia and Volunteers, 9 June 1903, Minutes of Evidence I, p. 62, Q. 1624, Cd. 2062.

[18] M. Yapp, 'British Perceptions of the Russian Threat to India', *Modern Asian Studies*, Vol. 21, No. 4, 1987, p. 650; Johnson, 'Russians at the Gates of India', pp. 734–5; Otte, *Foreign Office Mind*, pp. 204–5.

[19] Yapp, 'Russian Threat to India'; Johnson, 'Russians at the Gates'; Neilson, 'The British Way in Warfare and Russia', pp. 11–12.

[20] A. Preston, 'Sir Charles Macgregor and the Defence of India, 1857–1887', *Historical Journal*, Vol. 12, No. 1, 1969, pp. 58–77.

the northern border of Afghanistan and in the mountainous terrain above the Hindu Kush.[21] The potential military implications of the situation were brought home with considerable force in February 1900 when the Secretary at the Russian Embassy in London informed Lord Salisbury of his government's intention to establish direct relations with the Amir of Afghanistan in order to resolve 'frontier matters'. Coming within weeks of the humiliating British defeat at the Battle of Spion Kop on 24 January, this communication was accompanied by widespread rumours of major Russian troop concentrations along the border with Afghanistan. London's plaintive request for restraint only served to highlight Britain's incapacity to respond militarily.[22] Calcutta was sufficiently concerned for the Secretary of State for India, Lord George Hamilton, to re-open the thorny issue of reinforcements for the sub-continent. In an attempt to deflect criticism that the Indian authorities were seeking resources to pursue an unnecessary and undesirable policy of expansion, Hamilton sought to limit the scope of the discussion by discounting operations beyond the frontier. However, the Government of India refused to accept his proviso, reiterating its view that a forward policy represented the most realistic and cost-effective means of safeguarding the Raj. The military authorities in India calculated that establishing a defensive position between Kabul and Khandahar would require 30,000 troops from Britain at the outset of an Anglo-Russian war and a further 70,000 reinforcements within the subsequent twelve months. Scepticism amongst the military authorities in London and the extent of Britain's commitments in South Africa meant that no agreement on this point proved possible throughout 1901.[23] Thereafter, the fallout from the Boer War produced a further interregnum as the government battled to re-structure the home army.

ARMY REFORM

Before any decision was possible on the best policy to adopt towards India, the government was obliged to address the more immediate implications of the Army's poor performance in South Africa. Changes within the military leadership had begun during the conflict itself when Wolseley's close friend and confident, General Buller, was removed from command of the forces in South Africa in favour of Lord Roberts in early 1900.[24] Shortly thereafter, Wolseley himself became the object of widespread criticism, despite the efficiency of the Army's initial mobilization arrangements.[25] Lord Lansdowne's transfer from Horse Guards Parade to the Foreign Office in November 1900 combined with the illness and death of Queen

---

[21] Gillard, *The Struggle for Asia*, pp. 153–5.

[22] Salisbury to C. Scott, 10 February 1900, CAB 37/52/18.

[23] Report of a Committee Appointed to Consider the Military Defence of India, 24 December 1901, pp. 1–6, WO 105/42.

[24] Spiers, *Army and Society*, p. 240.

[25] For a defence of Wolseley, see Robertson, *Private to Field Marshal*, p. 127; Beckett, 'Stanhope Memorandum', p. 247.

Victoria, a staunch supporter of the C-in-C, removed the final obstacle to Wolseley's replacement. His health failing, Wolseley resigned at the turn of the year, clearing the way for Roberts to succeed him as head of the Army. Whilst some within military circles felt that Roberts had left South Africa somewhat prematurely, his appointment was widely heralded as necessary to reform a stagnant War Office. One cartoonist captioned a depiction of his arrival with the words 'Clean it up, My Lord'.[26]

Some have viewed Roberts' appointment as emblematic of the 'Indianization' of British strategy after the turn of the century.[27] A staunch believer in the necessity of adopting a forward policy in Asia, the new C-in-C certainly arrived in London possessed of a firm conviction that the requirements of India should play an important role in determining the organizsation of the Home Army. Initially these views appeared to coincide with those of the ambitious new Secretary of State for War, St John Brodrick. The two men were in communication during Roberts' voyage home in December, at which point the General expressed his 'cordial support' for what he had seen of the minister's intentions.[28] Whilst their relationship rapidly became complicated by disagreements over the extent of civilian control of the Army,[29] Roberts and Brodrick were in accord upon one vital point of overall strategy: the need to divorce the Regular Army from the defence of the British Isles in order to enable it to fulfil its imperial responsibilities.

The experience of South Africa provided a powerful impetus to those who had argued that the Regular Army should be constituted primary for operations overseas prior to 1899. Several prominent officers even went so far as to blame the onus placed on home defence during the 1890s for the shortcomings revealed in fighting the Boers.[30] Testifying before the Norfolk Commission on the auxiliary forces in 1903, the new Director of Mobilization and Intelligence, Lieutenant General Sir William Nicholson, stated bluntly that 'the [Stanhope] Memorandum appears... to have laid somewhat undue stress on home defence, and to have made insufficient provision for the general needs of the Empire'.[31] Major Gerald Ellison captured the essence of this argument in a series of notes on military organization he penned during the second half of 1900. Ellison had served in the War Office mobilization department between 1894 and 1898 before embarking for South Africa in late 1899, where he was mentioned twice in dispatches.[32] During his time in the Mobilization Division he had won the RUSI Gold Medal for an essay in which he had advocated absolving the Regular Army of its 'double duty of home defence and of Imperial protection'.[33] An admirer of Wolseley, Ellison mirrored

[26] R. Atwood, *The Life of Field Marshal Lord Roberts*, London: Bloomsbury, 2015, pp. 218–19.

[27] Preston, 'Khartoum Relief Expedition', pp. 272–5.

[28] D. James, *Lord Roberts*, London: Hollis & Carter, 1954, p. 375.

[29] James, *Roberts*, pp. 372–4, 376–82; Hamer, *The British Army*, pp. 193–8.

[30] Robertson, *Private to Field Marshal*, p. 97.

[31] Nicholson Testimony to the Norfolk Commission, 19 May 1903, Q.6 in 'Royal Commission on the Militia and Volunteers: Minutes of Evidence (Vol. I)', 1904, p. 1, Cd. 2062.

[32] Ellison, 'Reminiscences', X, *The Lancashire Lad*, April 1934, p. 6.

[33] G. F. Ellison, 'The Relative Advantages of Voluntary and Compulsory Service, both from a Military and National point of view', *RUSI*, Vol. XLI, No. 230, Apr., 1897, p. 425.

Chapman in his wish to dissociate the Regular Army from the defensive function envisaged for it under the confines of the Stanhope Memorandum. Articulate, possessed of an intimate knowledge of the Army's mobilization arrangements, and with direct experience of the difficulties encountered in South Africa, Ellison was ideally placed expound an alternative arrangement. This he did in a series of notes produced in late 1900 in which he reflected on the experience of the past twelve months; 'if then', he wrote, 'it needed a foreign war demanding the dispatch from these shores of practically every available regular soldier, and of a large body of militiamen as well, to prove to Englishmen that the regular army and the militia cannot be counted on as instruments for home defence, this one lesson taught by the Boer War were indeed worth all the lives and treasure expended on it'. In his view, the conflict had shown the need for 'a home defence scheme which would remain operative even though every paid professional soldier of the Crown were called away to take part in some distant offensive movement'.[34] Ellison's arguments mirrored the views of Roberts and the senior advisers he appointed to key posts within the War Office.

Upon arriving in London, the new C-in-C oversaw a re-structuring of the military administration. The changes with the greatest immediate impact upon the direction of military policy were those made to the Intelligence Department, which was merged with the Mobilization Division and had its staff nearly doubled.[35] The new body was in effect a prototype general staff, albeit still a chronically under-resourced one, which conducted the majority of the Army's strategic planning until it was subsumed into the Staff proper in 1904–5.[36] Command of the division was given to Lieutenant-General Nicholson, an astute and capable officer who had served under Roberts in India. Nicholson's authority was expanded to allow him to attend meetings of the Defence Committee of the Cabinet and the War Office Council, placing him at the very heart of military strategic planning.[37] Upon assuming his brief, Nicholson made clear that he did not rank home defence as one of the most serious challenges the Army faced. In an appreciation of the prevailing strategic situation produced in May 1901, he argued that 'our weak points at present are India and Egypt'. 'In India we occupy a continental position with the disadvantage of having our ultimate reserve in England', he continued, alluding to the role he envisaged for the Home Army. Nicholson calculated that the defence of India would require 'the equivalent of two Army Corps'—in other words, the entire establishment of the Regular Army currently organized for operations abroad.[38] He was less precise in his thinking about the military requirements of the British Isles. Nicholson was equivocal as to the Admiralty's view that invasion 'hardly comes within the range of practical politics', but felt sufficiently confident in the Navy to propose relying primarily upon the

---

[34] G. Ellison, 'Some Administrative Lessons of the War', 1900, Ch. IV, pp. 3 and 5, NAM 1987-04-35-33, NAM.

[35] Ferguson, *British Military Intelligence*, pp. 116–17.

[36] Robertson, *Private to Field Marshal*, p. 130; Gooch, *Plans of War*, pp. 20 and 22–4.

[37] Robertson, *Private to Field Marshal*, p. 128; Hamer, *British Army*, p. 191.

[38] Nicholson paper of 9 May 1901, NAM 7101-23-197-1.

auxiliary establishment to provide for the military defence of Britain, 'provided measures were taken to improve the[ir] organisation and training'.[39] Roberts endorsed Nicholson's analysis, remarking that 'while the force for home defence seems in excess of our requirements, that for expeditionary action and for the reinforcement of our Indian and colonial garrisons is seriously deficient'.[40] When Brodrick informed the Commons in March 1901 that 'the War has taught us that we must be prepared at any time to send more than two army corps abroad and yet have sufficient organisation left for home defence', he was reflecting a growing consensus amongst his professional advisers.[41]

MR BRODRICK'S SCHEME

Before taking office Brodrick had opposed plans to reform the Army whilst hostilities in South Africa were still ongoing. His opinion changed soon after he arrived at the War Office, however. The extent of British military weakness, the need to respond to widespread criticism of the Army's performance, and the possibility of absorbing some of the costs associated with reform into the expanded wartime taxation yield convinced him to take action immediately.[42] The Secretary of State believed that the Army was not large or powerful enough to protect British interests and that strengthening the military forces of the Crown was an urgent necessity. Unlike many of his political colleagues, Brodrick was willing to countenance future British military intervention on the Continent and sought to prepare the Army as best he could for such an eventuality.[43] Formed in the context of widespread popular and political support for increased military expenditure, this conviction shaped his plans to reorganize the Army.

Brodrick envisaged a system of six regionally based army corps, modelled on the German approach of associating formations with specific territories for administrative and recruiting purposes. Three corps would be composed entirely of regular troops and organized with expeditionary warfare as their primary rationale. The remaining three would be a mix of regular and auxiliary forces, intended for home defence and to enable the rapid expansion of the Army in wartime. The plans would require an additional 11,500 regular troops to be added to the Army List, a rise in pay to encourage enlistment, and an increase in the efficiency of the auxiliary forces.[44] In strategic terms, his scheme had a distinctly expeditionary focus in mind, particularly when compared to proposals made during the early 1890s. Yet it made little attempt to reconcile the competing demands of overseas expeditions

[39] Nicholson to Roberts, 4 September 1901, NAM 1971-01-23-52.
[40] Roberts to Brodrick, 17 October 1901, in War Office, 'Military Needs of the Empire in a War with France and Russia', 1901, p. 5, CAB 3/1/1A.
[41] Ellison, 'Reminiscences', *The Lancashire Lad*, November 1935, p. 5.
[42] Williams, *Defending the Empire*, p. 10.
[43] L. J. Satre, 'St. John Brodrick and Army Reform', *Journal of British Studies*, Vol. 15, No. 2, 1976, p. 121.
[44] Satre, 'Brodrick and Army Reform', pp. 120–1; Williams, *Defending the Empire*, pp. 10–13.

and British security. Rather than challenging the precepts of the Stanhope Memorandum and shifting the emphasis of British military policy decisively towards expeditionary operations as his professional advisers thought necessary, Brodrick sought to maintain the level of defensive provision Stanhope had recommended whilst simultaneously increasing the size of the field force for foreign service. In essence he sought to overcome the dilemma that had afflicted War Office planning during the 1880s and 1890s by increasing the size of the Army. Whilst this would remove the need to delay the dispatch of regular troops abroad, it was hardly an imaginative solution to Britain's military requirements, threatened to offend the sensibilities of powerful interest groups in Parliament and the government, and paid scant heed to the deteriorating financial situation.[45]

The greatest obstacle to Brodrick's proposals was the inevitable costs associated with increasing the size and pay of the Army. Despite reassuring Salisbury that 'I know big schemes must be cut according to our cloth', his plans were projected to cost around 50 per cent more per annum than the establishment of the Army on the eve of the Boer War.[46] Anxious to make haste, the new Secretary of State also betrayed a lack of political judgement when he announced his plans intentions to Parliament in March 1901. Brodrick divulged too much detail to the House, limiting the scope for subsequent adjustment and compromise. As his proposals relied upon the widespread support for increased military expenditure evident during the first year of the Boer War, he had scant room for manoeuvre once this initial war enthusiasm had ebbed. Plans to expand the Army could count on backing from the large, predominantly Unionist volunteer and militia lobby in the House of Commons, which had been returned in the 'khaki' election of October 1900. However, they were also sure to stimulate equally staunch opposition from the embattled Treasury, the leadership of the Liberal Party, Unionist rebels, and pro-naval MPs.[47]

One of the most damaging criticisms levelled at the War Office during the first year of the war had been the department's failure to align the organization of the Army with a realistic calculation of the assessments of the strategic challenges facing the Empire. Hugh Oakeley Arnold Forster MP, the energetic parliamentary under-secretary to the Admiralty, charged that 'our existing military organisation is based upon no known and accepted principle' and that 'no one knows what the army is really intended to do'.[48] Publicly Brodrick appeared to acknowledge the legitimacy of these arguments. When he introduced his plans to the Commons he had stressed the importance of clearly defining 'what our Army is organised for'.[49]

[45] Satre, 'Brodrick and Army Reform', p. 125.
[46] Brodrick to Salisbury, 28 October 1900, PRO 30/67/6; E. Spiers, 'The Late Victorian Army, 1868–1914' in D. G. Chandler and I. W. F. Beckett eds, *The Oxford History of the British Army*, Oxford: Oxford University Press, 1996, p. 201.
[47] Moon, 'Invasion', pp. 174–5, d'Ombrain, *War Machinery*, p. 26, Satre, 'Brodrick and Army Reform', p. 122; Williams, *Defending the Empire*, pp. 14–15.
[48] H. O. Arnold Forster, *The War Office, the Army and the Empire*, London, 1900, quoted in J. McDermott, 'The Immediate Origins of the Committee of Imperial Defence', *Canadian Journal of History*, Vol. 7, No. 3, 1972, p. 259.
[49] Hansard, Commons, 8 March 1901, co. 1054.

Yet, whilst his scheme was matched to his own broad conception of Britain's strategic requirements, it was not based upon systematic professional analysis or upon widespread consensus within the War Office or Cabinet. Brodrick neglected to align his views with those of his professional colleagues, or to use the newly strengthened Directorate of Mobilization and Intelligence to justify his suggestions. He later unapologetically admitted that his estimation of the Army's requirements had been 'a rough guess'.[50] This may have been a deliberate attempt to deflect opponents away from points of detail that might be open to dispute; however, it had the unfortunate effect of rapidly alienating the professional staff at the War Office and undermining his position as Secretary of State.

Despite Brodrick's rhetoric about linking the organization of the Army with its likely future employment, Nicholson quickly formed the impression that Brodrick's scheme was 'based on nothing in particular'.[51] The DMI noted sarcastically that 'it might almost have been taken for granted that, before proposing the reorganisation of the Army, Mr. Brodrick would have carefully considered our military requirements... but apparently this course was not adopted'.[52] This impression was shared by a number of his colleagues in the Directorate of Mobilization and Intelligence. Lord Roberts' military secretary, Captain Henry Wilson, recorded how the plans were 'universally condemned by all of us at the office'.[53] Significantly, Nicholson was particularly scathing about what he viewed as the undue emphasis Brodrick placed upon the defensive requirements of the British Isles. Imperial, rather than domestic, security was the primary focus of the Directorate of Mobilization and Intelligence, and 'as long as we were superior at sea' a large Home Army could only detract resources more urgently required elsewhere.[54] Soldiers' opposition to what they regarded as excessive defensive provision was repeated at a local level. During a tour of Britain's coastal defences during the summer, another member of the Nicholson's staff, Lieutenant Colonel William Robertson, complained how 'at no place so far have we found the local people keeping the probable strength of the attack sufficiently in mind, and there is a consequent tendency to provide against a landing force of more than the accepted number'.[55] His colleague Lieutenant Colonel Ivor Maxse, concurred. After examining the existing home defence scheme, Maxse felt the plans to be so impractical that to all intents and purposes 'no considered scheme appears to have been put forward: perhaps none existed'.[56] As Wolseley had complained during the 1880s, the consensus in the War Office was that the department remained hampered by a lack of clear political

[50] Brodrick to Kitchener, 29 April 1904, PRO 30/57/22/4, fos 629.

[51] Nicholson to Roberts, 8 May 1901, NAM, 1971-01-23-52.

[52] Nicholson to Roberts, 10 May 1901, NAM 7101-23-197-1.

[53] Wilson diary, 11 March 1901, quoted in K. Jeffery, *Field Marshal Sir Henry Wilson: A Political Soldier*, Oxford: Oxford University Press, 2006, p. 46.

[54] Nicholson, memorandum, 9 May 1901, NAM 7101-23-197-1.

[55] W. R. Robertson, 'Notes Made During a Visit of the Committee on Garrisons to the Defended Ports of the United Kingdom, 1901', p. 4, Robertson Papers, 1/2/2, [L]iddell [H]art [C]entre for [M]ilitary [A]rchives, King's College London.

[56] I. Maxse, 'Home Defence: Notes by Lt. Colonel Maxse', 26 September 1901, p. 6, Maxse Papers, 1/1, [I]mperial [W]ar [M]useum.

direction and by a tendency to prioritize short-term expedients over attempts to prepare the Army for its likely future deployment.

Faced with the demands of protecting Egypt and India, the necessity to maintain a sizeable force in South Africa, and the ongoing issues of garrisoning bases across the world, the professional staff at the War Office were eager to overturn the confines of the Stanhope Memorandum and to distribute the Army's resources in a manner better suited to the challenges of the new century. Yet Brodrick, mindful of the public uproar at the apparent lack of troops in the country during the Boer War, remained unwilling to run such risks and appeared wedded to his unwieldy scheme of six army corps—despite the extensive re-structuring of the Army that would be required to implement his plans. In an attempt to reconcile the six army corps system to the military requirements of the day, Nicholson ordered new schemes outlining likely future offensive and defensive operations to be produced in an attempt to match Brodrick's plan to an informed calculation of the Army's requirements.[57]

The Directorate of Mobilization and Intelligence duly produced a dossier detailing the 'Military Needs of the Empire in a War with France and Russia' in early August 1901. The document embodied many of the progressive trends in military thought evident since the 1880s.[58] Prepared by Colonel E. A. Altham, it acknowledged that the current establishment for home defence, which had swelled to some 594,000 men due to large increases in the Volunteers, Militia, and Yeomanry during the Boer War, was far in excess of Britain's strategic requirements. Due to the strength of the Navy, Altham reasoned, 'it would be folly to lay upon the country the financial burden of an enormous home army, adapted only to meet a contingency which will not arise (i.e. invasion), and unavailable for the needs of the Empire'.[59] The Directorate therefore proposed reducing the forces retained for home defence to 350,000 men. By doing so, Altham adhered to the traditional assumption that until the Admiralty had secured the situation at sea, the regulars of the expeditionary force would remain in Britain to stiffen the auxiliaries detailed for home defence. This displayed an implicit acknowledgement that it was beyond the purview of the military authorities to dictate British strategy as a whole. Without co-operation from the Admiralty, discussions about how many troops to dispatch to Egypt or India at the outset of war were entirely theoretical. The tension between home and imperial defence which so occupied Nicholson and Roberts thus remained unresolved due to the absence of a forum for co-ordinating the efforts of the two services. The C-in-C described the situation to Brodrick early in the New Year:

> It may perhaps be contended that our home army is sufficient for the land defence of the United Kingdom, and such a statement would probably be correct under ordinary conditions... But it is possible that a war once begun might develop in unexpected

[57] Nicholson to Roberts, 8 May 1901, NAM 1971-01-23-52.

[58] Gooch, 'Bolt from the Blue', p. 9.

[59] E. A. Altham, 'Military Needs of the Empire in a War With France and Russia', 10 August 1901, pp. 15–17, CAB 3/1/1.

directions... For example, we might be fighting Russia in Central Asia and have sent out 60,000 or 70,000 men to India. France might then suddenly throw in her lot with Russia, and if by any chance she could acquire naval superiority in the Channel for ten days or a fortnight, there would be nothing to prevent her from attempting an invasion of England ...[60]

Separating the Regular Army from the defence of the British Isles thus appeared increasingly urgent to fulfil the defensive needs of India and Egypt, yet doing so would leave Britain militarily vulnerable. Moreover, in the absence of advice from the Admiralty on the movement of troops by sea or the Navy's defensive capabilities, precise calculations of the number of men required for the Army to meet these challenges appeared impossible. Affairs showed scant prospect of reaching a satisfactory resolution by the end of 1901, as Brodrick and his scheme came under widespread attack in the press and Parliament.

POLITICAL PRESSURE FOR DEFENCE REFORM

The opening nine months of 1902 witnessed British military policy continue to drift as Brodrick's plans became ever more divorced from the financial realities the government faced. The Treasury had been highly critical of Brodrick's proposals for much of the previous year. Its opposition stiffened during the autumn when it became clear that more recruits would be required in order to make the six army corps functional. The Chancellor, Michael Hicks-Beech, was particularly aggrieved at Brodrick's calls for separate long and short service commissions, which he viewed as inefficient, and by his attempts to increase pay in order to cover shortfalls in recruiting. The additional charges involved were thought to amount to around £1¾ million a year, suggesting that ordinary expenditure on the Army would remain above £29 million in 1902–03.[61] Hicks-Beech attempted to force Brodrick to abandon this aspect of his scheme in January, but the Secretary of State survived a vote in Cabinet on the issue by an unconvincing majority of eleven votes to eight.[62] February 1902 saw Army Estimates containing ordinary expenditure of £29,310,000 introduced to Parliament.[63] The public might have grudgingly agreed to bear such expenditure whilst hostilities in South Africa rumbled on, but the conclusion of peace in May dramatically altered the landscape within which Brodrick was operating.

The Secretary of State drew increasing criticism from both sides of the House for his inability to rein in military spending despite the cessation of hostilities. Divided since the leadership's decision to support the Boer War, the Liberal Party began to

---

[60] Roberts to Brodrick, 10 January 1902, reprinted in 'The Military Resources of France and Probable Method of Their Employment in a War Between England and France', CAB 3/1/5.

[61] 'Mr Brodrick's Experiment', *The Economist*, 8 March 1902, p. 374; 'The Budget Prospect', *The Economist*, 15 March 1902, p. 414.

[62] Satre, 'Brodrick and Army Reform', pp. 129–30 and n. 72.

[63] Brodrick, 'Memorandum of the Secretary of State relating to the Army Estimates for 1902–1903', 6 February, Cd. 887.

coalesce into an effective opposition during the summer of 1902, presenting a more consistent challenge to government policy. Equally problematic were the vociferous Tory backbenchers, who no longer felt constrained by the war in their ability to criticize the party leadership.[64] Many of these MPs had military experience or identified strongly with Army affairs, and this led them to disagree vehemently with aspects of Brodrick's plans on technical grounds, and to dislike his abrupt and irascible manner. A measure of Brodrick's waning fortunes can be gained by the fact that, upon succeeding Salisbury to the premiership in July, Arthur Balfour considered removing the Secretary of State in the subsequent Cabinet reshuffle. Whilst the new Prime Minister refrained from shifting Brodrick in the summer, by the end of the year he admitted that 'never before has his stock been so low'.[65]

The Secretary of State's aloof manner, described by one parliamentarian as 'hectoring pomposity', hampered the successful implementation of his plans, as did his inflexibility in refusing to adapt them to meet the political needs of the moment.[66] His intransigence was not without reason: the threats the Empire faced remained broadly similar to those present when he conceived his plans, and his colleagues had been happy enough to strengthen the Army accordingly in late 1900. However, Brodrick's failure to link his administrative reforms to identifiable strategic requirements left his proposals vulnerable to accusations of extravagance. Many MPs were alive to the need to prepare the Army for operations overseas; however, few shared Brodrick's view that involvement in a future European war ought to be a factor in determining its size and organisation. A young Winston Churchill MP encapsulated these doubts in a series of stinging attacks on the Secretary of State. 'We must be prepared to deal with all the little wars which occur continually on the frontiers of the Empire', Churchill charged, 'we cannot expect to meet great wars.' 'The first and main principle which should animate British statecraft in the realm of imperial defence... [should be] a steady transfer of expenditure from the military to the marine', he concluded.[67] Leo Amery, another Unionist MP, made similar arguments, denouncing the current level of provision for home defence and forwarding proposals which promised to deliver an equivalent expeditionary capability for only £23 million a year.[68]

Critics of Brodrick's profligacy argued for a more efficient division of labour between the services, rather than simply expanding the Army Estimates to cover all potential eventualities. Naval power should guarantee against invasion and preserve trade whilst a modest yet efficient Army could perform the imperial policing duties required to maintain order within the Empire. Whether this vision was adequate to face the challenges Britain faced in central Asia was a moot point.

---

[64] Satre, 'Brodrick and Army Reform'; Williams, *Defending the Empire*, pp. 16–17; Spiers, 'Late Victorian Army', pp. 201–2.

[65] Balfour to Lady Elcho, late 1902, quoted in Williams, *Defending the Empire*, p. 16 n. 57 and p. 42.

[66] Williams, *Defending the Empire*, p. 16.

[67] Quoted in Williams, *Defending the Empire*, p. 15.

[68] Satre, 'Brodrick and Army Reform', p. 132.

The War Office certainly felt that it was not. Nevertheless, the ferocity of the attacks on Brodrick and his stubborn refusal to countenance modifying his plans eroded his support within a Cabinet beset with internal strife over issues of tariff reform and struggling to address the financial legacy of the Boer War.[69] Under these circumstances expending political capital on unpopular and costly plans to increase the strength of the Army was unrealistic. A conviction emerged that, as Amery had argued, greater military efficiency could be achieved at a reduced cost—but only if Brodrick were removed. The Secretary of State's declining credibility was further damaged by Roberts, who felt alienated by Brodrick's conduct and by ongoing disagreements over the status and powers of his post as C-in-C.[70] In private the Field Marshal petitioned Balfour to form a 'council of defence' intended to improve the co-ordination of military organization during the spring, indicating his own doubts about the six army corps.[71]

THE NEED FOR A NATIONAL POLICY

For his part Brodrick felt that he had been hampered by a lack of direction and support from his colleagues. He complained bitterly about 'the apparent apathy of Lord Salisbury & A.J.B. [Balfour]'.[72] He was not alone in wishing for greater oversight. His counterpart at the Admiralty, Lord Selborne, expressed similar frustrations, lamenting the 'absence of a lead and a controlling spirit and directing mind' in the Cabinet.[73] The First Lord was in a much more secure position than Brodrick, but faced stark financial challenges of his own and by 1902 was struggling to contain the apparently inexorable rise in the Navy Estimates evident since the late 1890s.[74] Driven by the rapidly escalating costs of warship manufacture, the extended programme of defensive works along the south coast, and the demands of adhering to the 'two-power' standard of strength in the face of the Dual Alliance, naval spending had risen dramatically, increasing from £21.8 million in 1897/8 to a predicted £38.3 million in 1904/5.[75] With the Treasury mounting evermore belligerent opposition to his Estimates, Selborne became convinced that the current state of affairs was unsustainable. After an autumn and winter spent 'constantly thinking about our shipbuilding program',[76] in April 1902 the First Lord informed Balfour that 'I am not prepared to commence another period of intense labour

---

[69] Williams, *Defending the Empire*, pp. 16–17.

[70] James, *Roberts*, pp. 372–7, 386–9; Satre, 'Brodrick and Army Reform', pp. 126–8; Hamer, *The British Army*, pp. 193–8.

[71] Roberts to Balfour, 2 May 1902, quoted in R. Mackay, *Balfour: Intellectual Statesman*, Oxford: Oxford University Press, 1985, pp. 114–15.

[72] Brodrick to Curzon, 25 October 1901, quoted in Satre, 'Brodrick and Army Reform', p. 130.

[73] Selborne to Curzon, 13 July 1901, quoted in Satre, 'Brodrick and Army Reform', p. 130; Mackay, *Balfour*, p. 116.

[74] See, for instance, Kerr to Selborne, 14 February 1901, and Selborne to Kerr, 12 September 1901, both in MS 27, Selborne Papers, fos 31–3 and 146–6, respectively.

[75] Sumida, *IDNS*, pp. 18–23.

[76] Selborne to Kerr, 12 September 1901, MS 27, Selborne Papers, Bod.

next autumn in the preparation of the Navy Estimates unless I know that I am working out a policy of which the Cabinet approve.'[77]

Selborne made explicit an important message: if the government did not settle upon a definitive object towards which the service departments could work, it would be virtually impossible to reconcile the urgent requirement for retrenchment with improving the efficiency of the armed forces. Cries for greater governmental direction reached their climax during the autumn. Selborne demanded 'that the Cabinet should adopt a definite naval policy', suggesting ominously that 'I do not think that it is possible efficiently to administer such a Department... without working on a fixed policy.'[78] In support of these requests, the Admiralty circulated a paper on 'The Need for Organisation for War' to the Cabinet.[79] Drafted by Arnold-Forster, this document was soon followed by a joint War Office and Admiralty position paper on the 'Intellectual Equipment of the Services', in which Brodrick and Selborne called for the formation of a new department to resolve issues concerning both services. What was required, they argued, was a body tasked specifically to deal with 'the most difficult and important problems of all... viz. those which are neither purely naval nor purely military, nor purely naval and military combined, but which may be described as naval, military, and political'.[80]

Balfour's government had already taken a tentative step towards assuming greater control over the formation of defence policy in August, with the appointment of a Royal Commission to investigate the conduct of the war in South Africa.[81] Such an inquiry was insufficient to address the systemic shortcomings in the British system of defence administration which had become evident during the preceding decade, however. It would also do little to resolve the problem of the inexorable rise in the Army and Navy Estimates. The Boer War had created significant short-term financial difficulties, but Hicks Beach had made clear that the underlying increases in naval and military spending in evidence before 1899 were the more serious financial issue facing the government. The Chancellor explained to Joseph Chamberlain that 'I am convinced that we must seriously check the increase in our ordinary expenditure, especially on the Army and Navy.'[82] Income tax had been doubled to pay for the war in 1900/1 before being raised again the following year and Hicks-Beach had been forced to introduce further additional duties on corn, meal, and flour to offset naval and military spending early in 1902.[83] Yet, the end of hostilities in South Africa had done little to improve the financial outlook due to a growth of around £30 million in ordinary government expenditure between 1899 and 1902. An impressive £10 million of this rise was

[77] Selborne to Balfour, 4 April 1902, in Boyce ed., *The Crisis of British Power*, p. 142.

[78] Selborne, 'Navy Estimates, 1903–1904', 10 October 1902, CAB 37/63/142.

[79] H. O. Arnold-Forster, 'Memorandum on the Need for Organization for War', October 1902, CAB 37/63/145.

[80] Selborne and Brodrick, 'Memorandum on the Improvement of the Intellectual Equipment of the Services', 10 November 1902, p. 2, CAB 37/63/152; d'Ombrain, *War Machinery*, p. 27; Mackay, *Balfour*, p. 116.

[81] Dunlop, *Development of the British Army*, pp. 148–9.

[82] Hicks-Beach to Chamberlain, 10 September 1901, quoted in Friedberg, *Weary Titan*, p. 111.

[83] Friedberg, *Weary Titan*, pp. 106–7; Boyce ed., *Crisis of British Power*, p. 147 n. 49.

accounted for by the growth of non-war-related military spending.[84] C. T. Richie, who succeeded Hicks Beech at the Treasury, summed up the gravity of the situation when he warned that this scale of increase meant that 'practically the whole of the taxation imposed for the war would now be required to meet the present scale of expenditure'.[85]

After some procrastination on Balfour's part during the autumn, a new committee of the Cabinet was eventually convened in December 1902 with 'its duty to survey as a whole the strategical military needs of the Empire'.[86] The formation of this body, subsequently named the Committee of Imperial Defence, marked the climax of the series of fleeting political forays into the oversight of defence policy which had occurred since the late 1880s. Against the backdrop of a worsening financial situation, a manifestly inefficient military system, and ongoing tensions on the North-West Frontier, the CID set about its task with gusto during 1903. In so doing it established the parameters within which discussions of British military and naval policy would be conducted until after the outbreak of the First World War.

THE COMMITTEE OF IMPERIAL DEFENCE

Balfour's new committee began its work by focusing on the most pressing military strategic issue Britain faced at the turn of the century: the defence of India. Calcutta's requests for reinforcements had become ever more urgent during the Boer War in response to Russian posturing on the Afghan border. The War Office had responded by convening a committee to investigate the problem in December 1901. Chaired by Nicholson in his capacity as Director General of Mobilization and Intelligence (DGMI), the group had recommended permanent additions to the garrison of the sub-continent as the most effective guarantee of Indian security. The DGMI hoped that an additional eighteen battalions of infantry stationed permanently in the country would provide sufficient resilience to enable India to sustain a strategic defence until such time as conditions allowed for the safe dispatch of more men from Britain.[87] Ultimately Nicholson was willing to assign the defence of the frontier the highest priority within British military planning, acknowledging that 120,000 reinforcements might ultimately be necessary, but this was tempered by the demands of other theatres and the difficulties of moving troops by sea if France was also belligerent.[88] As Altham had summed up in October, 'any doubt as to . . . sea supremacy at once vitiates all our plans'.[89] Asked

---

[84] Brodrick, 'Army Estimates, 1903–04', 15 November 1903, p. 3, CAB 37/63/157.

[85] Ritchie, 'Our Financial Position', 21 February 1903, quoted in Friedberg, *Weary Titan*, p. 119.

[86] Speech by Balfour, Hansard, 5 March 1903, col. 1579.

[87] War Office, 'Report of a Committee Appointed to Consider the Military Defence of India', 24 December 1901, p. 20, WO 105/42.

[88] Nicholson, 'The Organisation of the Auxiliary Forces Considered in Relation to the Military Defence of the Empire', 11 May 1903 in Appendix A of 'Report of the Royal Commission and Volunteers', 1904, p. 71, Cd. 2061.

[89] Altham, 'Military Needs of the Empire', 1901, p. 24, CAB 3/1/1.

for their opinion on the shipping of troops, however, the Admiralty re-iterated blandly that 'they could not guarantee at any particular time the safe transport of troops to foreign stations'.[90] This ambiguous advice had been an important factor in determining Nicholson's recommendation to enlarge the permanent garrison rather than relying on men from Britain in the first instance. The fact that the Government of India would be liable bear the cost of such an increase, as the men would be stationed on the sub-continent, was doubtless viewed as a further benefit of the scheme.

Predictably, these views proved anathema to the Government of India. The military authorities in Calcutta were convinced that a forward policy represented the only realistic means of defending the frontier, particularly after the accession of the unreliable Habibullan Khan to the Afghan throne. The figure of 30,000 additional troops as the minimum required to conduct an advance to a defensible position beyond the frontier was thus re-iterated. Nicholson's proposal to add 18,500 men to the Indian garrison was dismissed as being insufficient to enact the forward strategy favoured by the Indian Army. Moreover, the authorities in Calcutta were reluctant to fund permanent increases to the garrison of India, charging that they could not be expected to bear the entire cost of fighting a land war against Russia. They therefore resolved to hold out for a firm commitment of reinforcements from Britain.[91] Representations were renewed in August 1902, in an increasingly robust tone. The War Office's claims regarding the problems of sending troops by sea were dismissed as 'greatly exaggerated', Nicholson's proposed additions to the garrison were characterized as 'excessive and uncalled for', and it was insinuated that the military authorities were attempting to use naval difficulties as a pretext with which to avoid taking action.[92] The India Office even wrote directly to the Admiralty for confirmation of its position on the movement of men by sea.[93] These suspicions were misplaced. The War Office was not unsympathetic to India's needs: Roberts had been the most vocal and proactive supporter of the 'forward' policy since the 1880s.[94] Rather, the military authorities in London were constrained by the Admiralty's advice about the transport of troops by sea, which had remained constant for two decades and seemed unlikely to change. When the War Office's Committee on the Military Defence of India was reconvened in late 1902 it sought renewed guidance from the naval authorities on this very point. The request met with an unmodified response and the impasse persisted.[95]

---

[90] 'Statement of Case and Question of Opinion', attached to India Office to Admiralty, 7 November 1902, in Appendix of 'Second Report of A Committee Appointed to Consider the Military Defence of India', 30 December 1902, p. 12, WO 105/42.

[91] Gooch, *Plans of War*, pp. 199–200.

[92] Indian Military Committee to Hamilton, 21 August 1902, CAB 6/1/2.

[93] India Office to Admiralty, 7 November 1902, in Appendix of 'Second Report of A Committee Appointed to Consider the Military Defence of India', 30 December 1902, p. 12, WO 105/42.

[94] For the recognition of the military threat to India, see Robertson, 'The Military Resources of Russia, and Probable Method of Their Employment in a War Between Russia and England', 17 January 1902, WO 106/48.

[95] Admiralty to War Office, 15 December 1902, in Appendix II of 'Second Report of A Committee Appointed to Consider the Military Defence of India', pp. 14–15, WO 105/42.

Caught between the Indian government and the Admiralty, the DGMI concluded that only the Cabinet could adjudicate on what policy to pursue.[96] He therefore referred what appeared to be an intractable problem to Balfour's newly formed Defence Committee.[97] He was inspired to do so in part by the naval authorities themselves. The Admiralty had hinted at a willingness to modify its stance on moving troops by sea should government policy deem it necessary to do so, informing Nicholson that 'the urgency for... reinforcements might justify risks that would not otherwise be contemplated'.[98] They re-iterated this stance when the CID came to discuss the matter the following spring, informing the committee that an attrition rate of 10 per cent could be anticipated if troops were sent unescorted at the outset of war, but that it would be possible to work out a transport scheme 'if... His Majesty's Government is prepared to face the possibility of these losses'.[99] The political nature of the problem was confirmed when Nicholson appeared before the Norfolk Commission a week later, when he made clear that his office would remain 'in the dark' about the issue of Indian reinforcements until the CID had made its intentions clear.[100] Here, then, was an opportunity for the new committee to display its worth.

The defence of India could not be considered in isolation, however. A decision to commit a portion of the Home Army to reinforcing the sub-continent would have important implications for other aspects of military policy. As the War Office had argued in 1901, 'our plans must aim at the defence of the Empire as a whole... if the heart of the Empire falls into the enemy's grasp, its existence must cease... Home defence, therefore, is the primary problem to the solved.'[101] The Regular Army remained linked to the defence of the British Isles and the consensus of professional opinion was that the auxiliary forces were too inefficient to provide an effective defence against invasion. The thorny issue of how best to protect the British Isles was therefore fundamental to releasing the Regular Army from its defensive responsibilities. A conclusion on Indian defence would thus necessitate a re-alignment of both naval and military policy in order to produce what amounted to a unified grand strategy which linked naval and military force structures, war plans, and objectives to the government's policy on imperial defence. Financial concerns made this requirement all the more pressing. By late 1902 the Treasury had come to view the Army Estimates as a prime target for reductions in government spending. 'I regard the increase in the Army Estimates... with dismay', the Chancellor wrote in December, and 'I feel persuaded that this rate of expenditure on our army cannot safely be continued.'[102] The need for action became urgent on

[96] 'Second Report of A Committee Appointed to Consider the Military Defence of India', p. 8, WO 105/42.

[97] Gooch, *Plans of War*, p. 202.

[98] Admiralty to War Office, 15 December 1902, in Appendix II of 'Second Report of A Committee Appointed to Consider the Military Defence of India', pp. 14–15, WO 105/42.

[99] Battenberg, 'Reinforcements for India', 12 May 1903, CAB 6/1/15.

[100] Nicholson Testimony to the Norfolk Commission, 19 May 1903, Q. 331 in 'Royal Commission on the Militia and Volunteers: Minutes of Evidence (Vol. I)', 1904, p. 14, Cd. 2062.

[101] E. A. Altham, 'Military Needs of the Empire', 1901, pp. 1 and 18, CAB 3/1/1.

[102] Ritchie, 'Public Finance', 23 December 1902, p. 5, CAB 37/63/170.

24 February 1903, when a backbench revolt broke out over Brodrick's army reform plans. The rebellion moved William Hood Waleron, Chancellor of the Duchy of Lancaster, to warn Balfour that 'if we persist in sticking to Brodrick's scheme...it will end in disaster in the House, and we shall have the country and the Press against us'.[103] Balfour staved off criticism in the House by appointing a Royal Commission to consider the condition of the auxiliary forces in an attempt to justify reductions to the costly and inefficient Volunteer force.[104] Yet this measure alone would never be adequate to address the range of issues facing the government. Thus, as the Royal Commission prepared its investigation Balfour turned the CID to the work of defining a strategy for imperial defence.

THE GOVERNMENT ADJUDICATES

During the spring the committee pursued the dual objectives of making a realistic assessment of the military requirements of India and establishing the feasibility of an invasion of the British Isles. These were the great 'naval, military, and political' problems it was hoped the CID would address. Both required judgement on the government's behalf to settle long-running disputes between the various professionals involved. India dominated the initial proceedings, partially as a result of the sense of increasing danger resulting from the imminent completion of the Russian Orenburg–Tashkent railway connection, which would speed the flow of the Tsar's forces to the Afghan border. The Indian authorities advocated construction of a British line towards the frontier and pressed their demands for troops with renewed vigour.[105] The committee therefore resolved to address the question of home defence only after 'the question of the number of troops necessary for the defence of India was settled'.[106] The implicit assumption was that the Home Army would be linked to the defence of the frontier, the only question being to what extent.

Balfour prepared the first of a pair of preliminary memoranda summarizing the course of the committee's discussions on Indian defence towards the end of April. The documents indicated the Prime Minister's intention to accept the Government of India's request for 30,000 men at the outset of war with Russia, followed by 70,000 additional troops within the first year.[107] In doing so he over-ruled both the Admiralty's advice about the movement of men by sea and those within the War Office who remained wary of binding the Army to the defence of India. He thereby injected a new imperative into British strategy.

---

[103] Hood to Balfour, 1 March 1903, quoted in Williams, *Defending the Empire*, p. 17.

[104] 'Report of the Royal Commission on the Militia and Volunteers', 1904, v, c. 2061; Williams, *Defending the Empire*, pp. 19–21.

[105] M. Howard, *The Continental Commitment: The Dilemma of British Defence Policy in the Era of Two World Wars*, Harmondsworth: Penguin, 1971, p. 17; Gooch, *Plans of War*, pp. 202–3.

[106] CID, 'Minutes of 11th Meeting, April 29th, 1903', CAB 2/1/11.

[107] 'Indian Defence. First Instalment of a draft by the Prime Minister', 28 April 1903, CAB 6/1/12; 'Second Instalment of Draft Conclusions on Indian Defence by Mr. Balfour', 20 May 1903, CAB 6/1/19; Gooch, *Plans of War*, pp. 206–7.

Whether by specific instruction or by inference, initially the War Office envisaged the entirety of the force destined for India being comprised of regular troops.[108] Naturally, the departure of so large a portion of the Home Army would result in problems elsewhere. If the entire force were made of up of regular troops, the Army's ability to respond to a second crisis elsewhere around the world would be severely curtailed. Furthermore, if Britain were drained of trained soldiers in a manner reminiscent of 1900–1, the desultory condition of the auxiliary forces would raise questions as to the security of the country. Roberts articulated his reservations on this score in May, informing the Norfolk Commission on the auxiliary forces that 'no attempt would be made at invasion of this country until we had sent all of nearly all of our regular troops abroad'. The clear inference of the C-in-C's statement was that an opposing power might contemplate launching such an operation at some point thereafter. Roberts still regarded the auxiliaries as inadequate for the defence of the country in their current condition, making the government's commitment of reinforcements to India a source of considerable vulnerability in his eyes.[109] Nevertheless, with the most likely function of the Regular Army now defined, the military authorities were at least able to make preparations for a specific course of action. Having reached a preliminary conclusion on the question of India, the CID turned to the question of military provision for home defence.

The War Office was requested to outline a system of military organization able to fulfil the government's pledge to reinforce India and to satisfy what it judged to be the defensive requirements of the country during the summer. In one sense the resulting document demonstrated the military authorities' willingness to accept a lower level of protection at home. Gone were the two army corps of regular troops deemed necessary under the confines of the Stanhope Memorandum, replaced by a much smaller contingent of 31,059 regulars—which were to form the core of a mobile field force—and 18,617 others for garrison duties. The War Office was also prepared to accept a reduction in the size of auxiliary forces, provided those remaining were made more efficient with additional training. No agreement had been reached as to the likely scale of attack this force was meant to face, however. The Directorate of Mobilization and Intelligence therefore estimated the size of a potential invasion according to its own lights, violating its own advice to plan only after having 'carefully considered our military requirements'.

Guided by Nicholson's doubts about of the Admiralty's position on invasion and the general conviction that a larger reserve of trained manpower was necessary in Britain, this led to proposals for an auxiliary establishment of 390,000 men. A considerable reduction upon the 594,000 men with the colours during the Boer War, this figure still represented a significant force—one which was quite possibly in excess of the existing strength of the auxiliary forces. A dramatic wane in enthusiasm

---

[108] War Office, Intelligence Department, 'Home Defence: Comparison of Establishments of Military Forces with War Requirements (exclusive of Native Troops)', 7 July 1903, CAB 3/1/15A.

[109] Roberts Testimony to the Norfolk Commission, 25 May 1903, Q. 1062 in 'Royal Commission on the Militia and Volunteers: Minutes of Evidence (Vol. I)', 1904, pp. 38–9, Cd. 2062.

for military service had become evident since the conclusion of the war. Ongoing disagreements over terms of enlistment and difficulties in attracting recruits meant that the War Office anticipated that reaching even the reduced figure of 390,000 men would require the addition of 104,000 troops to the current establishment of the auxiliary forces in mid-1903.[110] 1902 had been the worst year of recruiting in the history of the Volunteer force, suggesting that meeting this shortfall would be a slow and costly process and making it an altogether unappealing suggestion to the government.[111]

A second major decision was therefore required of the government. If the Army was to fulfil its role as a reinforcement to India within the confines of lower Estimates, then provision elsewhere would have to be sacrificed. It was widely acknowledged that there was little point preparing the Regular Army for dispatch abroad if sufficient manpower to sustain it was not present in Britain. The Militia functioned as precisely such a reserve of trained manpower and was integral to the efficiency of the Regular Army. It could not, therefore, easily be reduced without compromising the performance of the expeditionary force. If economies were to be achieved, the Volunteers, whose terms of enlistment precluded service outside of the United Kingdom, appeared the most suitable target. The War Office's calculations for the numbers of Volunteers required for home defence were not based upon a specific number of potential invaders and contained provision for a force of 125,000 men for the defence of London which owed more to tradition than strategic reality.[112] If, as Balfour had previously argued, 'it is impossible really to consider invasion without taking maritime affairs into account', and the Admiralty's contention that organized invasion was outside the realms of strategic reality was to be taken at face value, the Volunteers seemed ripe for rationalization.[113] With the requirement for retrenchment ever present, the CID therefore set about reprising the well-worn arguments over home defence.

The soldiers approached the discussions prepared to contemplate a significant decrease in the number of regulars assigned to home defence in order to free troops for overseas operations.[114] However, the initial exchanges between the military and naval representatives were acrimonious and have tended to obscure their willingness to countenance change.[115] Concerned that significant cuts to the Army Estimates would imperil efforts to improve the system required to provide trained replacements for the Regular Army in wartime, the military addressed the committee with an air of concern and scepticism from the outset. These suspicions

[110] War Office, Intelligence Department, 'Home Defence: Comparison of Establishments of Military Forces with War Requirements (exclusive of Native Troops)', 7 July 1903, CAB 3/1/15A.

[111] Dunlop, *Development of the British Army*, pp. 220–4; Beckett, *Riflemen Form*, pp. 221–6.

[112] War Office, Intelligence Department, 'Home Defence: Comparison of Establishments', CAB 3/1/15A; Beckett, *Riflemen Form*, pp. 186–8.

[113] 'Committee of Defence: Minute by First Lord of the Treasury', 24 August 1895, quoted in Mackay, *Balfour*, p. 67.

[114] Altham, 'Military Needs of the Empire', 1901, p. 18, Roberts to Brodrick, 17 October 1901, reproduced in 'The Military Needs of the Empire', p. 5, CAB 3/1/1; Nicholson to Roberts, 4 September 1901, NAM 1971-01-23-52.

[115] D'Ombrain, *War Machinery*, pp. 28–9.

were entirely understandable when considered in the context of the government's incessant prioritization of economy over military efficiency, which it pursued despite the shortcomings exposed in South Africa and the growing demands India would place upon the Home Army.

The War Office's sensitivity reached acute proportions in the weeks preceding the CID's first foray into home defence as a result of several parallel exchanges it shared with the Admiralty. The first of these pertained to the issue of home defence itself. Between the first and second meetings of the committee, the Secretary of State for War wrote to the Admiralty regarding the level of fixed defences required at major ports. This issue had been under investigation for several years, since an inter-departmental committee under the Treasury official Sir Francis Mowatt had identified serious deficiencies in the standard of the armament of ports in Britain in late 1899. The essence of the problem was that of calculating the level of local defence necessary to afford freedom of action to the Fleet without locking up excessive amounts of scarce manpower in garrisons or wasting money on superfluous fortifications. These deliberations could be quite narrow and technical in nature— relating to conditions at individual ports—but they also related to much broader questions of imperial strategy and the relative roles of the two services therein. Both departments thus exercised considerable care when discussing the topic, as precedents established in one location could easily be seized upon to secure concessions in another.

In 1901 the Admiralty had advised that coaling stations and bases abroad should receive top priority for consideration as they were vital to the mobility of the Fleet and their condition had been neglected for some time. This presented the hard-pressed Brodrick with an opportunity to seek concordant economies at bases in Britain, which the Navy appeared to regard as less vulnerable.[116] With the need to trim his over-ambitious military budget becoming urgent, the Secretary of State therefore asked the Admiralty for an appreciation of 'the possibility of a lightly equipped force of say 20,000 men being landed, in the temporary absence of the fleet, at any spot on our Southern coast' in January 1903.[117]

The Admiralty was keenly aware of the politically sensitive nature of any query which touched upon the feasibility of invasion—particularly one arriving whilst the CID was actively engaged in deciding issues of national strategy—and handled the request accordingly. The task of drafting a suitable response to Brodrick's query about coastal armaments fell to the DNI, Captain Prince Louis of Battenberg, himself a former secretary to the Landing Places Committee and thus well acquainted with the politicized debate over home defence. His reply, approved by Lord Selborne several weeks before the CID came to discuss home defence, re-iterated the Admiralty's previously stated position that 'in neither of the two contingencies Mr Brodrick mentions...would either "the Fleet leave the Channel

---

[116] Joint Naval and Military Committee on Defence, Report XXXIII: Order of Precedence of Provision of Approved Armaments of the Coast Defences at Home and Abroad, 18 June 1901, CAB 18/22A.

[117] War Office to Admiralty, 6 January 1903, inside folder 'Protection of Fortresses and Defended Commercial Ports. Co-operation of Navy with Military Operations', ADM 1/8880.

unguarded" or "the Fleet be temporarily absent"'.[118] The naval authorities then referred the War Office back to the findings of an inter-service conference held in 1901 at which Their Lordships had stated their view that minor raids of 5,000 men were theoretically possible, but 'not probable'.[119] Although left unstated, the logical inference was that military provision for home defence on any significant scale was superfluous so far as the Admiralty was concerned. This line of argument was likely to prove attractive to politicians determined to reduce government expenditure at the expense of the Army, and Nicholson worried that short-term fiscal concerns would again receive precedence over realistic assessments of strategic necessity.

Even more frustratingly for the military hierarchy, a parallel exchange regarding the defence of Egypt appeared to hint at inconsistencies in the Navy's arguments. At around the same time as Battenberg's reply reached the War Office, the military authorities sent another query to the Admiralty regarding the Navy's ability to prevent a French or Russian raid of up to 5,000 men reaching Egypt. The War Office was considering the issue as part of an ongoing assessment of the size of the British garrison in the region, and desired confirmation of the Navy's previously stated position that the strength of the Mediterranean Fleet would be able to prevent any such descent. When it came the Admiralty's response was superficially reassuring, describing the chances of a successful raid as 'remote'. However, Their Lordships conceded that the naval forces in the eastern Mediterranean were not sufficient to render it impossible—particularly at the outbreak of war when the British aimed to concentrate at Gibraltar.[120] From the perspective of a military planner attempting to balance the size of the Egyptian garrison with the requirements of India, South Africa, and elsewhere, the naval authorities' opacity could hardly have been greater. The question appeared to hinge on the Admiralty's ambiguous use of the phrase 'command of the sea'. Upon reading the Navy's reply, Colonel Altham of the Intelligence Department seized upon this point, remarking acidly that 'formerly that doctrine was held to be of universal application, but we have learnt from recent Admiralty letters...that this is no longer the case'.[121] Nicholson noted the same discrepancy, identifying that command of the sea sufficient to accomplish one task was seemingly not adequate to achieve another.[122] The Navy's ambiguous advice regarding affairs at sea was thus hampering the War Office's plans to reinforce India, to garrison Egypt, and to find a workable means of providing the necessary degree of insurance at home—and there appeared to be no end to this unsatisfactory situation in sight. The DGMI's initial hostility to the CID discussions on home defence must be understood within this context.

---

[118] Admiralty to War Office, inside docket, 'Defence of Home Fortresses', drafted on 24 January 1903, in 'Protection of Fortresses ...', ADM 1/8880.

[119] 'Report of a Conference between Admiralty and War Office Representatives to consider the Strategic Conditions governing the Coast Defence of the United Kingdom in War as affected by Naval Considerations', February 1901, p. 3, CAB 3/1/9, ff. 58.

[120] Admiralty to War Office, 28 February 1903, WO 106/41/C3/1B.

[121] Altham to Nicholson, 3 March 1903, WO 106/41/C3/1B.

[122] Nicholson to Roberts, 7 March 1903, WO 106/41/C3/1B.

Nicholson's first submission to the committee was written between receiving the Admiralty's two responses. It conveyed his indignation at the Navy's doctrinaire insistence that British 'command of the sea' would preclude an organized invasion. 'It is understood that the Admiralty now contend that the Navy will entirely suffice to protect the United Kingdom from any attack or invasion in considerable strength', he wrote, 'and that, therefore, it is unnecessary to provide troops for home defence'.[123] The wording of this document has led some to suppose that the Admiralty had dramatically altered its 'traditional' position on invasion in late 1902 in order to secure a political victory over the War Office in the struggle for scarce funding.[124] Yet whilst the military authorities certainly did suspect discrepancies in the Navy's arguments, they had done so for much of the preceding two decades.[125] Battenberg's letter about fixed defences had embodied arguments the Admiralty had espoused since the 1880s, albeit in a perfunctory and incomplete manner, not a radically new stance on home defence. Indeed, faced with the accusation of political manoeuvring, the DNI moved quickly to refute Nicholson's suggestion, pointing out that 'the Admiralty have never felt called upon to express an opinion as to the number of troops which should be maintained at home by the War Office'.[126] He left the members of the committee to draw their own conclusions as to the level of military provision required to defeat potential raiding parties. The Admiralty simply did not need to alter its position for financial reasons, as the consensus of political opinion was already against the embattled Brodrick and the bloated military budget. Chancellor Ritchie had made clear since the turn of the year that the Cabinet and the Treasury supported Selborne's Navy Estimates and his policy,[127] a fact confirmed by Balfour's public announcement of the government's intention to establish a costly new naval base at Rosyth during the summer.[128] When compared to that of the Army, the naval budget was secure. Nicholson's frustrations were an indication not of political manoeuvring from the Admiralty, but of the urgent requirement for a body such as the CID to resolve the growing list of intractable problems accumulating to obstruct the efficient co-ordination of British naval and military effort.

That neither service had departed from the position it had occupied for the previous two decades became clear as they laid their arguments out before the committee during the spring. Genuine differences of opinion and outlook defined the discussions, although financial, bureaucratic, and partisan considerations doubtless factored into the proceedings. Captain Battenberg presented the now familiar naval case, based upon 'command of the sea'. 'If our strength in battle-ships is kept up to a proper level,' he argued, 'it ought to be beyond the power of any combination

---

[123] War Office, 'Provision of Land Forces for the Defence of the United Kingdom', 14 February 1903, p. 2, CAB 3/1/3, ff. 40.

[124] Lambert, *FNR*, p. 56.

[125] Nicholson to Roberts, 4 September 1901, NAM 1971-01-23-52; d'Ombrain, *War Machinery*, p. 28.

[126] Battenberg, 'Naval Remarks on the Military Paper, "Provision of Land Forces for the Defence of the United Kingdom," of the 14th February, 1903', 4 March 1903, CAB 3/1/8.

[127] Williams, *Defending the Empire*, pp. 35–6.

[128] Mackay, *Balfour*, p. 129.

of enemies that can be reasonably anticipated to obtain even a temporary command of the sea in home waters.'[129] He also stressed the defensive utility of the Navy's flotilla forces. Britain had 170 torpedo craft of various types in home waters and these would pose a vital threat to weakly defended troop transports, particularly after dark. Recent manoeuvres had underlined the difficulties of detecting small torpedo boats after cover of darkness and the services had co-operated to improve the defensive arrangements at British ports during the night for the past eighteen months.[130] Based on this experience Battenberg suggested that improvements in torpedo technology may have made the flotilla an even more significant obstacle to invasion than had historically been the case, stressing how 'the convoy, with its invading army...would be compelled to accept risks of a very serious nature for some hours of darkness at least'.[131] In response the War Office held to its willingness to reduce the size of the home defence forces, but only so far as would not prejudice the training and replenishment of the Regular Army and would allow for a mobile defensive force to be formed in Britain.[132]

The key point of disagreement between the two service departments remained their differing conceptions of what both referred to as the 'command of the sea'. The War Office felt that providing an adequate military force for home defence would 'supplement naval action and thus give the navy a freer hand', by removing the need to maintain a superior fleet in home waters. Derived from entrenched scepticism of the Navy's ability to guarantee British security independently and motivated by the ulterior goal of providing an Army capable of meeting the Empire's needs, this viewpoint appeared to be strengthened by the Admiralty's insistence that the Navy could not be held responsible for the defence of coaling stations and fortresses abroad. If 'command of the sea' would safeguard Britain, then why would it not also protect Malta or Hong Kong? The tension between these two lines of argument led Nicholson to accuse the naval authorities of being 'hardly logical'.[133]

Yet these criticisms were based upon a binary understanding of the Admiralty's admittedly opaque arguments regarding 'sea command'. As was proven throughout the 1890s, the naval authorities did not view the presence of a battle fleet at home as necessary under all circumstances. Rather, the Fleet need only be positioned so as to prevent an enemy from gaining a degree of sea control sufficient safely to transport troops to British shores. In the imperial sphere, this was reflected most clearly in the Admiralty's warnings about the transport of British troops by sea: if 'command of the sea' remained disputed then embarked troops would be

---

[129] Battenberg, 'Memorandum on the Possibilities of Invasion During Temporary Loss of Command of the Sea in Home Waters', 31 March 1903, p. 1, CAB 3/1/11.

[130] Admiralty circular to all C-in-Cs, 21 January 1902, ADM 144/27, fo. 17; Grimes, *War Planning*, pp. 25–35.

[131] Battenberg, 'Memorandum on the Possibilities of Invasion', p. 2, CAB 3/1/11.

[132] War Office, 'Provision of Land Forces for the Defence of the United Kingdom', 14 February 1903, p. 4, CAB 3/1/3A.

[133] War Office Intelligence Department, 'Remarks on the Memorandum Prepared by the Naval Intelligence Department, Dated March 31st, 1903, on "The Possibilities of Invasion During Temporary Loss of Command of the Sea in Home Waters"', 27 April 1903, p. 2, CAB 3/1/13A.

acutely vulnerable to enemy action. This belief was fundamental to the Admiralty's conception of British grand strategy, namely that the Army should transition to the offensive when the naval position enabled it to do so to maximum effect. Battenberg summed up the implications of this approach for military policy during a discussion of operations against French colonies in July. 'There is no need to keep any troops specially ear-marked at home for these over-sea expeditions', the DNI advised, 'by the time they become possible, the army for home defence should be able to provide all that is needful.'[134] The naval authorities adhered to the arguments that had shaped military policy under the Wolseley regime in 1885–91: until such time as the situation at sea had been secured, the Home Army would be confined to the British Isles anyway, making the prospect of invasion all the more unlikely. Faced with such a fundamental and well-entrenched difference of opinion, how the government chose to resolve the disagreement was likely to have significant ramifications for both departments.

Presented with a familiar impasse between the Admiralty and War Office, the CID displayed its potential worth by bringing the disagreement to a rapid and reasonable conclusion. Whereas Salisbury had been unwilling to involve himself in the detail of inter-service squabbling in 1888, Balfour showed no such reticence. The Prime Minister's agile mind and perceptive instincts added clarity to the pro-ceedings and proved key to extracting the information required to make an informed decision. Identifying the crux of the disagreement, Balfour sought to establish the likely scale of a potential attack in order to frame the remainder of the discussion. He requested that the War Office provide an estimate of the smallest force with which a hostile power might attempt an invasion. This helped to move the debate from the abstract to the practical, enabling reasoned conclusions to be drawn by non-experts. Nicholson and Roberts considered that 70,000 men, with a modest amount of artillery, cavalry, and supplies would be the smallest force with which an enemy might conceivably attempt to invade Britain with the object of subjugating the country. The Admiralty was quite certain of the Navy's ability to detect and interdict a force of this size, which it believed would require around 210,000 tons of transport to convey to British shores. With the situation described in this manner, Balfour and his colleagues felt able to judge for themselves the scale of military provision necessary.

The government's intentions were hinted at on 8 July, when the CID discussed alternative means of re-structuring the Army under the assumption that 'an inva-sion in force of these islands need not be taken into account'.[135] Despite Nicholson's efforts to the contrary, Balfour had sided with the Admiralty. Accepting the naval argument that a force of 70,000 invaders would be unable to evade the attentions of the Navy meant that the military provision in the United Kingdom could now be scaled to meet a defined threat. As the War Office itself considered that an attack intended to subdue the country would not be attempted with a force smaller

---

[134] Battenberg, 'Remarks on Offensive Over-sea Expeditions suggested by the War Office as feas-ible in the Memorandum on the Military Needs of the Empire in a War with France and Russia (No. 1A, 12th August, 1901)', 1 July 1903, p. 2, CAB 3/1/14A.

[135] 'Minutes of 20th Meeting, July 8th, 1903', CAB 2/1/20, fo. 61.

than 70,000, the role of the field forces in Britain became that of dealing with smaller raiding parties of around 5,000 men which the Admiralty admitted might evade the Navy. By the time the committee adjourned for the summer recess, a provisional decision on the size of the auxiliary forces necessary to fulfil this task had been reached. Whilst no record is preserved in the minutes of the committee, correspondence between the Secretary and the Duke of Norfolk provides an indication of Balfour's thoughts on the matter. After the final CID meeting of the parliamentary session, the Duke of Devonshire wrote to his colleague, informing him that 'the Duke of Norfolk's Commission will base their recommendations on the assumption that the Mobilization Scheme for Home Defence will be met by an effective force of 100,000 Militia and 200,000 Volunteers'. Whilst not yet official policy, these numbers implied a reduction of 60,500 over the last figures the War Office had presented in July.[136]

* * *

How best to organize the auxiliary forces to fulfil their newfound role as the primary military defence of the United Kingdom proved a source of ongoing controversy which defied satisfactory resolution before the outbreak of war in 1914. Disagreements over the efficiency of the force, its capacity to provide reinforcements for the Regular Army in wartime, and the political, economic, and social questions associated with voluntary service and the auxiliary establishment as a whole proved intractable for successive governments. Nevertheless, by defining its policy on two of the longest-running controversies within British military and naval policy—the role of the Regular Army and the invasion question—Balfour's government established the contours within which all subsequent considerations of strategy prior to 1914 were conducted. The activity of the CID during 1903 was far from perfect: the size of the force designated for India was in all likelihood inadequate and scant attention was devoted to how a war against a Franco-Russian combination could be brought to a satisfactory conclusion. However, it demonstrated how the continual and effective oversight of defence matters by the political leadership could overcome inter-service issues that were otherwise impossible to resolve. The CID achieved greater clarity of vision for how the Empire ought to be defended during 1903 than had been established in the previous two decades. Unfortunately, this model was not seized upon and improved under subsequent governments. Many of the conclusions of 1903 went unrefined for too long, despite shifts in the international landscape which left many of them questionable. This neglect made one particular facet of the CID's initial investigations assume far greater importance than was attributed to it at the time. The government's decision to overrule the naval authorities' reservations about the transport of troops by sea removed a major obstacle to the development of a military policy independent of naval control. Ironically, Balfour's attempt to achieve greater co-ordination between the two services paved the way for naval and military planning to diverge after 1904–5.

---

[136] Letter to the Royal Commission on the Militia and Volunteers, giving provisionally the number of each of those Forces to be taken as the basis of their discussion, 5 August 1903, CAB 4/1/10B.

4

Preparing for War

In 1903 the government had defined the role each service would play in the defence of the Empire. Based upon the proceedings of the CID, it was settled that the Navy would be responsible for preventing the organized invasion of British territory from the sea and for securing her trade worldwide. Behind this naval shield, the auxiliary forces and a handful of regulars would ensure that minor raiding parties that might evade the Fleet would be rapidly overwhelmed if they succeeded in landing in the United Kingdom. The Regular Army would thus be absolved of any defensive function, freeing it for operations overseas. Beyond this broad outline, however, no consensus existed on how best to prosecute a war against another Great Power. Politicians and the military remained divided over the size and function of the Army and the extent to which the requirements of India should determine its organization. The Admiralty and the War Office clashed over the movement of men by sea and the desirability of conducting operations against enemy colonies. The schism between the two was such that the Director of Military Operations (DMO), Major-General James Grierson, was moved to remark that the two services disagreed on the fundamental question 'of what war means'.[1]

Balfour took what might have become a first tentative step towards translating his proposed division of labour between the services into a coherent imperial strategy during the summer of 1905, when he assented to the formation of a new sub-committee of the CID to co-ordinate and prepare combined operations. However, his lukewarm support for the initiative meant that nothing was achieved before the fall of his administration at the end of the year. The immediate prospect of a Franco-German war at the turn of 1905–6 revealed the paucity of thought within either service as to how to bring a Continental war to a successful conclusion, and the new Liberal administration's ambivalence towards military matters saw no attempt to remedy these deficiencies after 1906. This failure to give purpose to the framework established in 1903–4 by shaping an evolving combined strategy for the defence of the Empire meant that the service departments were assigned responsibility without direction. Left to interpret the roles Balfour had prescribed for them independent of effective political oversight, the Admiralty and War Office became increasingly polarized as they competed to earn the government's endorsement for their preferred method of prosecuting a war against Germany. After the relatively dynamic period of decision making between 1903–4, political irresolution

---

[1] Grierson, 'Further Memorandum on Military Policy in the Event of War with France', July 1905, p. 2, ADM 116/3111.

saw the CID cease to function as a means of co-ordinating 'naval, military, and political' problems. The result was a return to a situation analogous to that present before Balfour had de-conflicted the service's position on home defence in 1903. Competing approaches threatened to offer less than the sum of their parts as military planning marginalized the Navy and increased the defensive burden on the Admiralty, whilst the Navy became defensive and intransigent. Far from creating efficiencies through improved organization, the CID had wrested the control of what passed for British strategy from the Admiralty's grasp and then left the service departments to compete to shape how the country should conduct a future war through a lack of ongoing political engagement. The new body had not defined imperial strategy; it had merely altered the terms of the inter-service rivalry to control it.

* * *

After the CID's initial investigations during the spring of 1903, Balfour's time became dominated by the vicissitudes of party politics. The Prime Minister had been battling to control an acrimonious split in his Cabinet over the issue of tariff reform for much of the spring, but the issue reached a head as Parliament dispersed for the summer recess. Disagreements on the question of protectionism and imperial preference had been a source of tension within the Unionist Party since the Colonial Conference of 1897, when Canada had cut her tariffs by a quarter in favour of British goods. The flamboyant and popular Colonial Secretary, Joseph Chamberlain, hoped to use the Canadian example as a model for a broader system of imperial preference and believed he had secured Balfour's approval for the principle in late 1902. Whilst he was away on a trip to South Africa, however, it became clear that the remainder of the Cabinet were less amenable to Chamberlain's plans. Advocates of free trade, particularly Chancellor Ritchie, threatened resignation if the open market was abandoned in favour of a protectionist or preferential system. The division widened as the year wore on and the irreconcilable positions of Chamberlain and Ritchie hardened. The Prime Minister predicted a split in a letter to the King in August, and the seemingly inevitable occurred on 15 September with the resignations of several prominent members of the Cabinet, including the Chancellor and Chamberlain himself.[2]

Balfour took the opportunity offered by the subsequent re-shuffle to shift Brodrick, whose army corps scheme he admitted had become 'the topic of universal criticism', to the India Office.[3] After unsuccessfully attempting to convince Lord Esher to assume the responsibility, without a great deal of enthusiasm or confidence, the Prime Minister eventually handed the War Office to the ambitious and strong-minded Arnold-Forster.[4] Brodrick resented his censure sufficiently to make the first meetings of the new Cabinet frosty affairs, efforts being made to ensure that the two men did not sit next to each other.[5] This hostility was to presage

---

[2] Mackay, *Balfour*, pp. 135–51.

[3] Balfour to Devonshire, 27 August 1903, p. 3, CS2/340/2943, Chatsworth.

[4] A. Tucker, 'The Issue of Army Reform in the Unionist Government, 1903–5', *Historical Journal*, Vol. 9, No. 1, 1966, pp. 92–3.

[5] Sandars to Gerald Balfour, 9 November 1903, GC433/2/122, fo. 7, NRS.

a steady stream of criticism of Arnold-Forster's proposals from the new incumbent of the India Office. Nevertheless, with the government stabilized in the short term, the arrival of a new Secretary of State for War offered an opportunity to approach the vexed issue of Army reform afresh, an endeavour to which the Committee of Imperial Defence returned after the summer recess.

One of the committee's final acts before Parliament dispersed had been to write to the Duke of Norfolk regarding the proceedings of his commission on the auxiliary forces. Acting as Secretary to the CID, the Duke of Devonshire had instructed Norfolk to confine his enquiries to the auxiliary's efficiency and not to make recommendations as to their size or potential employment. Norfolk was warned that his commission 'was not intended to cover our [i.e. the CID's] inquiry into the numbers of either Regular or Auxiliary Forces which should be maintained for Home Defence'.[6] The rationale behind this communication was made explicit soon after the CID returned to work, whereupon Balfour circulated a lengthy memorandum on home defence, similar in principle to his earlier summations of the Indian situation. This document encapsulated the conclusions the Prime Minister had drawn from the work of the CID earlier in the year, namely that 'the chief military problem which this country has to face is that of Indian, rather than of Home, Defence'.[7] His main deduction was that the Navy should be responsible for preventing invasion in force and that Britain's predominance at sea was such that military provision to resist a landing large enough to subdue the country was an unnecessary expense. The auxiliary forces ought only to be strong and efficient enough rapidly to overwhelm lightly equipped raids of 5,000–10,000 men that might elude the Navy, and the Regular Army had little part to play in home defence.[8] Reflecting on the work of the previous year in December 1903, the Prime Minister summarized his views on military organization to General Horatio Kitchener, the C-in-C India:

> ...our Regular Army does not exist principally for the defence of Great Britain, but almost entirely (1) for the defence of India, (2) the retention of South Africa, (3) conceivably (but only barely conceivably) for the defence of Canada, and (4) for the purposes of small expeditions against the Naval stations and Colonies of other Powers.[9]

In the context of the ongoing wrangling about the number of reinforcements necessary to defend the North-West Frontier, these words were doubtless calculated to sooth tensions between the military authorities in London and Calcutta.[10] They contained the seeds of conflict closer to home, however.

As had been the case in the 1880s and 1890s, the War Office remained unwilling to bind itself slavishly to the demands of the sub-continent. Events during the Boer War had highlighted the dangers of sacrificing the organizational and strategic

---

[6] 'Memorandum for the Duke of Norfolk in reply to his letter of May 26, 1903', 22 June 1903, CAB 4/1/6B.

[7] Memorandum by Balfour, 30 November 1903, p. 1, CAB 38/3/77.

[8] Balfour, 'Draft Report on the Possibility of Serious Invasion', 11 November 1903, CAB 3/1/18A.

[9] Balfour to Kitchener, 3 December 1903, Add. Ms. 49726, fo. 4, Balfour Papers, BL.

[10] Gooch, *Plans of War*, pp. 206–8.

flexibility required to conduct operations in other parts of the Empire in favour of concentrating upon a single theatre. Russian posturing in Afghanistan, Persia, and the Black Sea in early 1900 had been perceived by many diplomats as a test of Britain's will to defend her global interests whilst sustaining her campaign against the Boers.[11] Obliged to consider a greater range of threats than their counterparts in India, the military authorities in London viewed Calcutta's incessant demands for men and resources as parochial and unrealistic. Many at the War Office doubted the veracity of Indian claims about the impact Russian railway construction might have upon the defence of the frontier, pointing to the formidable logistical barriers which remained to a physical invasion. Lieutenant Colonel Robertson, who became head of the Foreign Section of the re-organized Directorate of Mobilization and Intelligence upon returning from South Arica in 1901, later described the claims for additional troops as 'exaggerations' and as 'quite untenable'.[12] Even Roberts recognized the impossibility of acceding to Calcutta's requirements in their entirety. The C-in-C had differentiated between the requirements 'for expeditionary action and for the reinforcement of our Indian and colonial garrisons' ever since arriving in office in 1901.[13] Defending India whilst also being 'prepared for troubles that might arise in other parts of the Empire' was an important aspect of his strategic vision. Given the current manpower and organizational problems the Army was grappling with, Roberts therefore proposed limiting the initial tranche of reinforcements for India to 14,677 men, less than half the number requested. He also suggested confining the number of regular troops in the second wave (scheduled to be 70,000 men) to 33,000, thus enabling the retention of some regulars for operations elsewhere.[14] A weighty consideration in these manpower calculations was the unsatisfactory condition of the auxiliary forces. Roberts' experience in South Africa had confirmed his belief that Britain's non-professional soldiers were in no fit state to take the field against European troops.[15] If the vast majority of the Regular Army were dispatched to India, the C-in-C was doubtful whether the auxiliary forces could be relied upon to defend the British Isles. Indeed, whether the Regular Army was to be used in India or elsewhere, the ability of the auxiliary forces to guarantee British security would be fundamental to its departure. Resolving this deficiency within the boundaries of financial and political reality would be the central challenge facing the new Secretary of State, Arnold-Forster.

NOT QUALIFIED TO TAKE THE FIELD

Despite his best efforts, Brodrick had largely failed in his attempts to improve the efficiency of the auxiliary forces. Attempts to reform the organization had met with

---

[11] Otte, *Foreign Office Mind*, p. 234.   [12] Robertson, *Private to Field Marshal*, p. 136.
[13] Roberts to Brodrick, 17 October 1901, in 'Military Needs of the Empire', p. 5, CAB 3/1/1A.
[14] Roberts, 'What number of Troops could be spared for India', 23 March 1904, CAB 38/4/20.
[15] James, *Roberts*, p. 388.

staunch opposition from the vociferous Volunteer lobby in the House of Commons, the protests of which had helped to prompt the appointment of the Duke of Norfolk's commission in the spring of 1903.[16] Resistance to plans for additional training camps was accompanied by serious shortfalls in manpower which further weakened both the Militia and the Volunteers. The year 1902–3 was the worst for recruiting in the history of the Volunteer force and on 1 January 1903 the Militia was 20,596 men under its established strength.[17] Against this backdrop it was not entirely surprising that the Norfolk Commission observed bluntly that the Militia was 'unfit to take the field for the defence of this country' and that the Volunteers were similarly 'not qualified to take the field against a regular army'.[18] The body went on to warn that 'if the purpose is to produce a force which without substantial help from the Regular Army can be relied upon to defeat an invader, then improvements in the Militia and Volunteer Forces will not be sufficient'.[19] In the commissioner's view, only conscription would ensure British security in the absence of regular troops. These views reflected the make-up of the commission and its choice of witnesses, the majority of whom remained sceptical that the Navy could guarantee against an invasion and considered some form of compulsion desirable in any case. The deficiencies in the auxiliary forces it reported were very real, however.

Roberts and his colleagues at the War Office had been damning in their assessments of the efficiency of the auxiliary forces since 1901 and remained sceptical of their military value.[20] Shortly after arriving as Director of Military Operations in early 1904, Major-General James Grierson presaged the report of the Norfolk Commission, stating that 'I regard the Volunteers as a force on which it is impossible to rely for the defence of the United Kingdom once the greater part of the Regulars and Militia are withdrawn for service in India or elsewhere.'[21] Once Balfour had made clear his intention to assign the auxiliary forces a more definite strategic function and to separate the Regular Army from defensive duties as much as possible, improving the efficiency of the organization became a matter of the utmost priority for the War Office. Overseeing this unenviable task fell to the new Secretary of State for War, Arnold-Forster. Neither the government's tenuous grasp on power, nor the difficulties the previous incumbent of his seat at the Cabinet table had encountered in dealing with the issue, augured well for his prospects. Not Balfour's first candidate for the post, Arnold-Forster had to contend with the additional impediment of his two direct predecessors continuing to hold senior positions within the Cabinet. He exacerbated these difficulties by approaching his task with an inflexible set of prior assumptions and intentions, which he proved resolutely unwilling to modify to meet the realities of the situation he faced.

[16] Beckett, *Riflemen Form*, p. 231.

[17] Dunlop, *Development of the British Army*, pp. 162, 220–4; Beckett, *Riflemen Form*, p. 221–6.

[18] Report of the Royal Commission on the Militia and Volunteers, 20 May 1904, pp. 6, 9, Cd. 2061.

[19] Report of the Royal Commission on the Militia and Volunteers, p. 13, Cd. 2061.

[20] Beckett, *Riflemen Form*, pp. 233–4.

[21] Grierson to Arnold-Forster, 12 March 1904, p. 4 in War Office, 'Replies to Questions as to the existing strength and efficiency of the Military Forces of the Crown having regard to Indian and Home defence requirements', WO 106/44.

Arnold-Forster's proposals, circulated to the Cabinet during the first half of 1904, were for an entirely new system of military organization. He envisaged a dual approach of long- and short-service recruiting of nine and three years respectively. The long-service troops would man foreign garrisons and constitute a striking force ready for rapid deployment overseas, whilst short-service men would provide drafts and conduct duties within the United Kingdom. The Militia would gradually be incorporated into the Regular Army and the Volunteers were to be scaled down and divided into two classes of efficiency, depending on an individual's commitment to training.[22] Writing to Major-General Ian Hamilton, then serving as an observer to the Russo-Japanese War, the Secretary of State encapsulated his views on the auxiliary forces. 'The money spent on the Militia and Volunteers as at present constituted, is money wasted', he stated; 'the Militia...will be no good as long as it is drawn from the dregs of the people, is composed...of men rejected from the Line, is under Officered, ill Officered and untrained'.[23] Arnold-Forster's proposals threatened to be even more unpopular than Brodrick's had been. His treatment of the Militia was particularly troublesome, all the more so for the fact that several members of the Cabinet, including Lord Selborne, were staunch supporters and members of the force. An indication of the hostile reception his plans were to provoke was provided in May 1904, when a deputation of MPs called upon Balfour to register their concerns after some details of the proposals were leaked ahead of their announcement to the Commons.[24]

Arnold-Forster was firm in his view that the strength of the Navy made a hostile landing in force impractical. As Balfour wished, he made this assumption the basis for his scheme of army organization and set about trying to enforce it on his military colleagues soon after arriving in office.[25] However, despite the Prime Minister endorsing the principle that the Regular Army had no role to play in home defence in early November, the point remained a contentious one in military circles. Reform of the auxiliary forces remained inseparable from broader questions of military organization and strategy. Inefficient as the establishment may have been in its present condition, a reserve of trained manpower would form a vital support to the Regular Army in wartime—particularly if a portion of it was to be used to reinforce India. Tension therefore remained between producing an organization lean and cheap enough to satisfy the Treasury, and sufficiently large and capable to bolster the Regular Army in the event of war. The issue of invasion, through which it was possible to argue for a larger auxiliary establishment without making unpopular demands for military expansion in a more general sense, thereby assumed significance as a pretext for strengthening the military as a whole.

Nicholson and Brodrick prepared a critique of the Prime Minister's paper on home defence in December, in which they argued against the proposed reductions

---

[22] Beckett, 'H. O. Arnold Forster and the Volunteers' in Beckett and Gooch eds, *Politicians and Defence: Studies in the Formulation of British Defence Policy*, Manchester: Manchester University Press, 1981, p. 52.

[23] Arnold-Forster to Hamilton, 3 March 1905, Add MS 50345, fos 19–20, Arnold-Forster Papers, BL.

[24] Williams, *Defending the Empire*, pp. 47–51.

[25] Arnold-Forster diary, 21 November 1903, Add MS 50335, fo. 94, BL.

in the auxiliary forces to a figure sufficient to meet only minor raids, on the grounds that doing so 'might produce a serious effect on the martial spirit and physical training of the home population'.[26] Moreover, even if the Prime Minister wished the auxiliaries to play a leading role in home defence, the force was categorically not capable of fulfilling that function in the immediate future. The report of the Norfolk Commission, published in May 1904, stated bluntly that entrusting British security to the auxiliary forces risked fatal embarrassment if an enemy did succeed in evading the Fleet long enough to conduct a landing. It would thus take time to transition the regular forces out of the Army's defence schemes. Finally, resistance to slavishly committing the Home Army to the defence of India remained. Nicholson was unceremoniously unseated by the Esher Committee in the spring of 1904 and departed to observe the Russo-Japanese War, but Brodrick continued to agitate on this issue from his new position at the India Office. The Secretary of State for India referred to the views of Nicholson and Roberts (another casualty of War Office reorganization) when he noted that 'I should hesitate, in the face of the strong military opinions which have been given in the past, to reduce our regular forces at home so low.' This was doubly so, he continued, 'as we must, in the event of war with France & Russia, count on this force for striking at vulnerable points'.[27] Brodrick reasoned that the same basic conundrum that had faced Britain since the 1890s remained; if 100,000 regulars were sent to defend India, the British Isles would remain vulnerable to an opportunistic attack from France and professional troops would be required to meet any such assault.[28] Brodrick's preferred conception would require the auxiliaries to play a greater role in reinforcing India, and likely entail additions to the size and training that the forces received.

Arnold-Forster quickly formed the view that factions within the War Office, Cabinet, and Parliament were using the threat of invasion as a means to obstruct his attempts to reduce the auxiliary forces due to their own conflicting agendas. He petitioned Balfour for support in convincing the Cabinet to accept his proposals, which the Prime Minister grudgingly assented to provide.[29] Balfour adopted a dual approach to the issue, intended to mollify Arnold-Forster without placing his fragile government on a collision course with Parliament on the issue of Army reform. In the first instance, he acknowledged military advice about the danger of relying solely upon auxiliaries for home defence. The Prime Minister recommended to the CID that no fewer than two divisions of regulars, some 16,000–20,000 infantry, should be retained in Britain after the outbreak of hostilities 'until our Auxiliary troops are more effectively organised as a mobile force'.[30] This idea had originated in a General Staff paper the previous month, which had argued that an increase in

[26] Sandars to Gerald Balfour, 21 November 1903, fo. 23, GD433/2/122, NRS; Nicholson, 'Home Defence: Remarks on the "Draft Report on the Possibility of Serious Invasion"', 7 December 1903, CAB 31/1/19A.

[27] Brodrick to Clarke, 26 June 1904, Add MS 49700, fo. 40, Clarke Papers, BL.

[28] Brodrick to Clarke, 1 July 1904, CAB 17/22, fos 40–2.

[29] Arnold-Forster diary, 28 April 1904, Add MS 50337, fo. 164, BL.

[30] Balfour, 'A Note on Army Reform and the Military Needs of the Empire', 22 June 1904, p. 2, CAB 38/5/65. For the figure, see Brodrick to Clarke, 26 June 1904, Add MS 47900, fos 39–40, and Brodrick to Clarke, 1 July 1904, CAB 17/22, fo. 40.

the number of regular troops might provide for home defence more efficiently than the unwieldy auxiliary organization in the short term.[31] Adopting the measure offered the benefit of temporarily allaying the War Office's concerns about the efficiency of the home defences whilst enabling the Secretary of State to continue with his plans for the auxiliaries. Withholding a force of regulars at the outbreak of war was also compatible with Arnold-Forster's desire to maintain a 'striking force' and the conclusions the CID had reached regarding the reinforcement of India.

Such manoeuvring did not represent a major show of support for Arnold-Forster's plans or offer a solution to the broader problems of military organization, however. Brodrick, for one, was not convinced.[32] Caught between ongoing controversies over the number of men required for India and domestic opposition to shrinking the auxiliary forces, Balfour attempted to circumvent the problem by returning to the realm of strategy. In June he had George Clarke, the new Secretary to the CID, re-visit the practical aspects of a French invasion. This offered the prospect of proving that military preparations to resist a surprise assault were superfluous owing to the insuperable logistical barriers to conducting such an operation. Captain Ottley RN, the highly respected Naval Assistant Secretary to the CID, was tasked to produce an analysis of the shipping present on an average day in French ports. Ottley warmed to his task and produced a colourful memorandum in which he argued that, owing to a lack of suitable points of embarkation and available shipping, 'the writer deems the task an impossible one, even if every battleship in the British Fleet had previously been sent to the bottom'.[33] The document was circulated to the CID during the autumn.[34] By buttressing the findings of his paper on home defence in this manner the Prime Minister sought to press home the vital point that, in his view, the auxiliaries were required only to deal with raids of 5,000–10,000 men. Balfour even asked the Cabinet to consider publishing his memorandum on invasion to make the case clear to Parliament and the public. The idea came to nothing, however, perhaps indicating the depths of the divides within the Cabinet over Arnold-Forster's plans.[35]

Despite continued doubts over the advisability of relying upon the auxiliaries for home defence, the military authorities moved to translate the Prime Minister's wishes into reality. In May the General Staff had proposed to retain a field force of 80,000 men, drawn equally from the Yeomanry and the Regular Army, to defend against raids on the basis that 'the present training of the Militia and Yeomanry, and still less that of the Volunteers...is not sufficient to enable them to oppose continental troops in the field'. At that time the War Office had insisted that 'any lower estimate than the above will not provide the security demanded in such an

---

[31] General Staff, 'The Strength of the Regular Army and Auxiliary Forces, having regard to Peace and War Requirements', 1 May 1904, p. 3, CAB 3/1/22A.

[32] Brodrick to Clarke, 1 July 1904, CAB 17/22, fos 40–2.

[33] Ottley, 'The Question of Invasion', 28 June 1904; and Clarke to Balfour, 30 June 1904, Add MS 49700, fos 54–60, BL.

[34] 'Invasion. Analysis of Shipping available in French Ports on July 7th, 1904', 24 October 1904, CAB 3/1/25A.

[35] Mackay, *Balfour*, p. 209.

important scheme for national insurance' and that these men 'must...be regarded as entirely independent of any troops which either before or after declaration of war might leave the country', even if this meant a concomitant reduction in the force available for India.[36] However, by the autumn the General Staff were prepared to sacrifice this force in order to free the largest possible contingent for operations overseas. This was confirmed when a war-scare with Russia prompted a hasty series of precautionary military preparations.

Anglo-Russian tensions had simmered throughout the year due to the war in the Far East, where Britain's ally Japan was proving unexpectedly successful against the Tsar's forces. The government had been successful in preserving British neutrality thus far, but when the Russian Baltic Fleet opened fire on British fishing vessels in the North Sea whilst en route to the Far East on the night of 21 October, a major diplomatic crisis ensued. Opinion in London was divided over the best course to pursue. Demanding redress from St Petersburg risked escalating the situation into war, but diplomatic satisfaction was unlikely due to what one Cabinet member described as the Russians' 'inveterate habit of trying to take back in detail what they have concluded in the gross'.[37] The General Staff began making preparations for hostilities immediately after news of the incident in the North Sea reached London. However, the abandonment of Brodrick's army corps scheme meant that no approved arrangements for the organization or deployment of either the auxiliary forces or the reinforcements for India existed.[38] General Neville Lyttelton, the Chief of the General Staff, summed up the situation:

> Between the abandonment of the scheme for home defence, in which the Auxiliary Forces were incorporated in the IV, V and VI Army Corps, and the ultimate completion of a new scheme which cannot be elaborated until the reorganization of the Auxiliary Forces has been decided, there exists a hiatus in which the mobile defence of the United Kingdom is unprovided for, except by an unorganized mass of units which, however efficient they may or may not be, are quite unprepared to meet a disciplined and organized enemy.[39]

A provisional arrangement was hastily drafted and rushed before the next meeting of the Army Council.[40] Arnold-Forster's Military Secretary, Colonel Spencer Ewart, recorded how 'all the past week I have been going early to the War Office for I have been working hard at all my part of the mobilisation arrangements in case of war with Russia'.[41] The General Staff proceeded on the basis that the composition of the field army for home defence 'must be drawn, to the greatest extent

---

[36] General Staff, 'The Strength of the Regular Army and Auxiliary Forces, having regard to Peace and War Requirements', 1 May 1904, CAB 3/1/22a, fo. 103.

[37] Gerald Balfour to Balfour of Burleigh, 2 November 1904, GD433/2/330/80, NRS; Otte, *Foreign Office Mind*, pp. 291–2.

[38] A. H. Gordon to Lyttelton, 2 November 1904, in '"War Organisation" for Field Army for Home Defence', 1904, WO 32/6363.

[39] Lyttelton note, 2 November 1904, in '"War Organisation" for Field Army for Home Defence', WO 32/6363.

[40] A. G. Dallas to AQMG, 28 October 1904, '"War Organisation" for Field Army for Home Defence', WO 32/6363.

[41] Ewart Diary, 6 November 1904, GD527/1/1/135/8, NRS.

possible, from the Auxiliary Forces', so as 'all the regular troops on the Home Establishment, are kept available for service oversea'.[42] Eight divisions of regulars were allotted to the defence of India, although no mention was made of a time-scale for their departure. This left only fourteen organized regular battalions, equivalent to just shy of two divisions' worth of infantry, in the United Kingdom to act as a striking force and to stiffen the auxiliary forces. The General Staff had thus enacted the Prime Minister's wish to develop the maximum possible number of units for operations abroad whilst maintaining only a bare minimum of regular troops in Britain. This task had only been possible, however, by relying heavily upon the Militia, which provided the mainstay of the field force for home defence.[43] How Arnold-Forster's system of organization, with no Militia and fewer regulars and Volunteers, would have coped with the demands of mobilization was far from clear.

After the threat of war had receded, the unsatisfactory situation Arnold-Forster's reforms had produced at the War Office was laid bare before the CID. In December Lyttelton presented a paper on 'The Military Requirements of the Empire and Mr. Arnold Forster's Army Scheme compared'—the title of which made the General Staff's lack of faith in the Secretary of State's proposals clear. Their disapproval was spelled out in the memorandum, the tone of which bordered on the sarcastic:

> it is understood that the scheme of the present Secretary of State for War for the reorganisation of the army has been accepted by the Cabinet, and therefore it is presumed that the numbers provided by it are deemed sufficient for our military requirements. But as they fall short very materially of the numbers laid down in Paper 22A[44] it seems important that the shortage be shown and understood.

The CGS went on to demonstrate that Arnold-Forster's scheme appeared to deliver 100,000 fewer troops than were necessary to fulfil the requirements set out by the CID. He concluded with what amounted to an open challenge to the Secretary of State's plans: 'it is left to the Committee of Imperial Defence to say whether this shortage is accepted'.[45] The Prime Minister was quick to point out that the General Staff's proposals exceeded the number of men required to satisfy the requirements set out by the CID, particularly regarding the maintenance of a 'striking force' distinct from the Indian reinforcement.[46] Nevertheless, affairs at the War Office appeared to show no imminent signs of improving.

The disagreement over the requirements laid out by the CID combined with Arnold-Forster's manifest inability to control his professional advisers led Balfour

---

[42] Lyttelton note, 2 November 1904, '"War Organisation" for Field Army for Home Defence', WO 32/6363.

[43] 'Precis for Army Council No. 130. Provisional Organisation of Field Army for Home Defence', November 1904, '"War Organisation" for Field Army for Home Defence', WO 32/6363.

[44] The General Staff Paper, 'The Strength of the Regular Army and Auxiliary Forces, having regard to Peace and War Requirements' which had put the number of regular troops required at 322,794 on 1 May 1904, CAB 3/1/22A.

[45] Lyttelton, 'The Military Requirements of the Empire and Mr. Arnold-Forster's Army Scheme compared', 15 December 1904, CAB 3/1/27A.

[46] Balfour, 'Supplementary Note on the Military Needs of the Empire', 19 December 1904, CAB 3/1/28A.

to convene a committee to investigate the detail of the War Office's plans. Displaying an extraordinary lack of faith in the Secretary of State, the Prime Minister excluded him from the body, which consisted of Esher, Clarke, the Treasury official Sir George Murray, and Balfour himself. Predictably, this latest insult to Arnold-Forster's often-impinged-upon authority presaged a severe modifications of his plans, leaving him as little more than a lame duck.[47]

THE STRIKING FORCE

If the Regular Army were to be liberated from its defensive function in the British Isles, how it ought best to be employed elsewhere remained a topic of contention in military circles. The experiences of 1885 and 1900–1 had demonstrated the importance of being able to respond to more than one military emergency at a time. This requirement became ever more pressing as Russia encroached further into central Asia, which threatened to focus British attention on India at the expense of all else. An element of strategic flexibility was vital, a fact that had not been lost on Roberts. Yet the situation in India and the regular representations of the authorities in Calcutta threatened to envelop the entire establishment of the Home Army into the defence of the North-West Frontier. By mid-1904 General Kitchener calculated that 135,614 men would be necessary to defend the frontier in the first year of an Anglo-Russian war—a rise of 35,000 men in the previous twelve months.[48] Satisfying his demands would now absorb the majority of the regular troops in Britain.

From the outset Arnold-Forster had been committed to retaining a striking force of troops for rapid deployment distinct from the Indian reinforcement. Support for the maintenance of such as force has been viewed as evidence of the growth of 'continentalism' within the General Staff and as the ancestor of plans to send troops to France in 1914.[49] However, in many ways this 'striking force' was one of the least contentious aspects of Arnold-Forster's reform plans, receiving as it did support from the government, the CID secretariat, and senior elements within the Navy. Arguably the idea owed more to the traditional debate between those who viewed the Home Army or the defence of India as the correct focus of British military strategy than it did to any newfound push towards involvement in a future European conflict.

The new Secretary of State had laboured the necessity of providing a rapid reaction force distinct from the Indian reinforcement from the moment he took office.[50] After succeeding Brodrick in the autumn of 1903, Arnold-Forster circulated a list of issues for comment amongst the senior officer corps. In an effort to display

---

[47] Beckett, 'Arnold-Forster and the Volunteers', p. 56.

[48] Gooch, *Plans of War*, pp. 214–15.

[49] McDermott, 'The Revolution in British Military Thinking', pp. 170–2; d'Ombrain, *War Machinery*, pp. 76–89.

[50] Arnold-Forster, 'Memorandum No. 3', 8 December 1903, p. 3, AC 43/7C, Austen Chamberlain Papers, [Cad]bury Library, University of Birmingham.

the consensus of professional support his plans enjoyed, he then distributed the findings of the exercise to the cabinet. Of those he consulted, Brackenbury, Nicholson, the Duke of Connaught, Frederick Stopford, John French, and George Clarke all agreed that the lack of a force organized for swift deployment overseas was a major shortcoming in the current military system.[51] On these grounds the War Office prepared plans to provide both the number of reinforcements the CID had deemed necessary for India and troops for operations elsewhere. The Indian government's own mobilization schemes confirmed that men arriving from Britain would initially be used to replace soldiers tied to garrison duties, thereby freeing seasoned manpower for mobile operations. This presented an opportunity to use auxiliaries and drafts to form a large part of the Indian reinforcement, preserving valuable regulars for other tasks. Lord Selborne had proposed comprising the entire reinforcement for India from the Militia on these very grounds.[52]

Major-General James Grierson, head of the War Office Operations Division, advanced similar arguments. He calculated that the theoretical maximum number of units that could be sent to India was 'considerably in excess' of the Viceroy's initial requirements, meaning that the authorities had some room for discretion in selecting which troops to send. To his mind, 'it is more important to have good troops in the so-called Home Expeditionary Force than in the reinforcements to be sent to India'. On these grounds the DMO advocated prioritizing the best men for 'the expeditionary force maintained at home…which would number approximately two army corps. The regular units which remain after mobilisation of this force might be sent to India, and the balance should be made up by Militia.'[53] Arnold-Forster ensured that Grierson's views were distributed to the Cabinet as part of his 'striking force' campaign, rendering problematic the notion that the General Staff were planning in contravention of the government's intentions and without its knowledge.[54]

By including 37,000 drafts in the number of men for the sub-continent, the military department hoped to maintain a force of around 90,000 troops for 'offence' elsewhere. 'The most probable objective for such action would be French colonial bases', it was reasoned. Studies of such operations had been elaborated for the past several years under Nicholson's supervision. These had indicated that forces of 13,000–15,000 and 23,000–25,000 men would be required to capture Dakar and Martinique and Diego Suarez or Saigon, respectively. Operations in Egypt and South Africa were also contemplated. Both in scale and intent, then, the military authorities remained attached to an imperial policy reminiscent of that

---

[51] 'Remarks of various Officers to the Memorandum relating to Some Defects in the Existing System of Infantry Organization and Recruiting', February 1904, AC 43/23, Cad.

[52] Williams, *Defending the Empire*, p. 25.

[53] Grierson to Arnold-Forster, 12 March 1904, p. 6 in War Office, 'Replies to Questions …', WO 106/44.

[54] Grierson, 'Replies to Questions as to the Existing Strength and Efficiency of the Military Forces of the Crown having regard to Indian and Home Defence Requirements: Prepared for the consideration of the Committee of Imperial Defence', 12 March 1904, CAB 38/4/17. For the suggestion that the General Staff were planning surreptitiously, see McDermott, 'The Revolution in British Military Thinking', pp. 168–71.

propounded by Wolseley and the 'Home Army' school. Whilst Roberts may have advocated an Indo-centric strategy in the 1890s, after arriving as C-in-C his views equated far more closely with those of his former rival than is commonly accepted. Roberts undoubtedly remained concerned about the spread of Russian power in central Asia, but the War Office simply could not prioritize the needs of the sub-continent above those of the numerous other parts of the Empire that required defence, or sacrifice Britain's capacity to undertake offensive military operations against an enemy's vulnerable points.

Despite the claims of some scholars,[55] the Prime Minister was also sympathetic to this requirement. The Indian command's escalating demands for men meant that the CID's provisional ruling on reinforcements was not confirmed until March 1904. When a decision was finally announced, the committee purposefully declined to commit the entire regular Army to India as the War Office had originally assumed would be the case. Rather, it was resolved to adopt a proposal from Roberts to 'keep in this country the only two organised forces we possess, viz., the 1st and 3rd Army Corps, until we know what further demands would have to be met'. The government supported the War Office by decreeing that the initial reinforcement could contain as many as 15,000 militiamen as circumstances dictated. The subsequent tranche of troops would include a further 19,000 militiamen and 33,000 drafts.[56] This would enable the retention in Britain of a body of troops prepared for instant dispatch to other threatened areas or for offensive action. Balfour suggested that 'not less than two divisions, with their proper complement of cavalry and artillery' should be reserved for this role.[57] The government purposefully demurred from committing organized units of the Regular Army to the defence of India, at least in the first instance. Elements of the force would very likely be available for dispatch to India if the circumstances demanded, but by not making an official commitment to this effect, the government maintained a degree of flexibility to meet other military requirements without betraying its agreements with Calcutta. As Balfour summarized in June; 'A "striking force" … must certainly be provided; though not necessarily in addition to the Indian reinforcements, of which they might, and probably would, form a part.'[58]

The government adhered to this position throughout the autumn, despite Kitchener's rapidly escalating demands for men. Heeding the Adjutant General's warning that under present conditions satisfying the Viceroy's demands would leave 'no troops for any other Imperial purpose', the CID agreed that the War Office should not be bound to supply more men for the defence of India than was realistic. The government specifically decreed that the 1st Army Corps—the Aldershot Command which had traditionally formed the vanguard of the War Office's home 'striking force'—should not form part of the first batch of troops sent to the sub-continent.[59]

[55] McDermott, 'The Revolution in British Military Thinking', pp. 168–9.
[56] CID, 'Minutes of 36th Meeting, March 24th, 1904', CAB 2/1/36.
[57] Balfour, 'A Note on Army Reform and the Military Needs of the Empire', 22 June 1904, p. 2, CAB 38/5/65.
[58] Ibid.
[59] CID, 'Minutes of 57th Meeting, November 16th, 1904', CAB 2/1/57.

Yet, despite this fact, the 1st Army Corps was the only formation provided with the requisite stores to enable it to embark immediately for operations overseas.[60] Moreover, the force was trained and prepared specifically 'to be ready in all respects to take the field, in the most efficient condition, at the shortest possible notice'.[61] All of this indicates that, whilst Balfour was opposed to the maintenance of a high-readiness force entirely exclusive of the reinforcement of India, both he and the Cabinet remained unwilling to subjugate Britain's entire military policy to the demands of the sub-continent. He was also quite prepared to make the fact that British strategy could not be entirely predicated upon the needs of India clear to the authorities in Calcutta. At a CID meeting on 22 November it was agreed that 'the Indian Government should be informed that these numbers do not compre-hend the whole of the military forces which would be available if Imperial policy permitted their dispatch to India'.[62]

The debate over the desirability and constitution of a 'striking force' was not conducted solely between the General Staff and the government, however. Both the CID secretariat and senior elements within the Navy encouraged Balfour to develop a rapid reaction force for military operations outside the British Isles. Establishing a full-time secretariat to the CID had been one of the primary recom-mendations of Lord Esher's War Office Reconstitution Committee. It was hoped that a permanent staff would improve the committee's powers of co-ordination, empowering the body to become the nucleus of a joint staff.[63] After serving on the War Office Reconstitution Committee, Sir George Clarke was the first man appointed to the post after vociferous backing from Esher, with whom he had served on the Hartington Commission in the 1890s, and Admiral Fisher.[64] Clarke took the position intent on applying his considerable energies to influencing government policy.[65] The new Secretary's views on imperial strategy were well known. After working on the Hartington Commission he had been Secretary to the Colonial Defence Committee and had published widely on the topic, informing his readers that 'military force—the offensive weapon of the Empire—cannot be brought into play except on conditions determined by the actions of the Navy'.[66] His selection was thus a measure of the ascendance of a maritime approach within the committee and the government.

Soon after arriving at Whitehall Gardens, Clarke began peppering Balfour with ideas and suggestions on a wide range of topics. On Army reform, one of the areas where he was on the surest ground in offering advice, Clarke proposed a system of organization intended to provide for a striking force of two divisions in addition to

[60] Duckworth to Austen Chamberlain, 13 January 1905, AC 43/111b; Arnold-Forster to A. Chamberlain, 6 February 1905, AC 43/121b, Cad.

[61] J. French, 'Memorandum on the Training of the 1st Army Corps', 28 September 1904, p. 1, ESHR 16/7, Esher Papers, [C]hurchill [C]ollege [A]rchives [C]entre, Cambridge.

[62] CID, 'Minutes of 58th Meeting, November 22nd, 1904', CAB 2/1/58.

[63] D'Ombrain, *War Machinery*, pp. 5 and 39.

[64] Fisher to Sandars, 10 November 1903, Add MS 49710, fos 51–52, BL.

[65] Gooch, 'Sir George Clarke's Career at the Committee of Imperial Defence, 1904–1907' in his *The Prospect of War*, p. 74.

[66] G. S. Clarke, *Imperial Defence*, London, 1897, p. 158.

the Indian reinforcement, whilst simultaneously reducing the overall size of the Army.[67] He considered Arnold-Forster's proposed striking force of two divisions 'too small' and worked consistently to prevent the demands of India from absorbing the entirety of Britain's military resources.[68] In November 1904 he warned Balfour of the 'real danger that compliance with Lord Kitchener's demands will have the effect of making India the predominant partner in Imperial defence' and cautioned against such a course.[69] The Secretary ultimately proved impotent in affecting Balfour's views, but it is instructive to note that advocates of maintaining a powerful striking force, distinct from the requirements of India, existed outside of the War Office.

One other such figure was Admiral Fisher. Whilst working with Clarke on the Esher Committee, the Admiral had fought hard to install officers at the War Office who he felt would be sympathetic to a CID dominated by the Admiralty and to a maritime approach to imperial defence. 'Again, I say', he wrote to Esher, 'the *Regular Army* (as distinguished from the *Home* and *Indian Army*) should be regarded as a projectile fired by the Navy!'[70] A major obstacle to the achievement of this vision was the presence of Nicholson, who Fisher felt was 'so hateful to the Admiralty, and such a thorough cad' that 'the Admiralty must make Nicholson a "casus belli" and if they don't *then I must!*'[71] The Admiral impressed Balfour and, with Esher's staunch support, he was offered the chance to succeed Lord Walter Kerr as First Sea Lord shortly after the committee concluded its work.[72] Between accepting the post and arriving in office in the autumn, Fisher continued to write to the Prime Minister outlining his views on imperial strategy and Army reform. During the summer he entreated Balfour to '*instantly publish his great paper on invasion* and say the Aldershot Force all that is wanted *so reduce Home Army*'. He thought spending a combined sum of £6½ millions a year on the auxiliary forces and volunteers 'absurd' and entreated the Prime Minister to '*Get rid of Indian Bogey!*', preferring to raise the men required to reinforce the sub-continent after the outbreak of war.[73] The incoming First Sea Lord was thus another prominent proponent of shaping the Army to deliver an amphibious striking force, separate from the requirements of India.

Clarke, Fisher, and the like-minded Esher were given unprecedented (and much resented) power to decide appointments within the re-organized War Office. They exploited this influence to populate the department with officers they felt to be receptive to the 'correct' approach to imperial strategy. That the General Staff

[67] Clarke to Sandars, 18 June 1904, Add MS 49700, fos 31–7, BL; Clarke, 'Notes', June 1904, ESHR 10/34, CAC.

[68] Clarke to Balfour, 9 December 1904, Add MS 49700, fo. 240, BL.

[69] Clarke, 'Note on the Discussions of the 22nd Inst. Indian Reinforcements', 24 November 1904, Add MS 49700, fos 217–19, BL.

[70] Fisher to Esher, 19 November 1903, in Marder ed., *FGDN* I, p. 291.

[71] Fisher to Esher, 17 January 1904, in Marder ed., *FGDN* I, p. 298; Fisher to Sandars, 23 January 1904, Add MS 49710, fo. 109, BL.

[72] Fisher to Esher, 17 May 1904, in Marder ed., *FGDN* I, p. 316.

[73] Fisher to Sandars, 29 July 1904, Add MS 49710, fos 150–1, BL; Fisher to Esher, 30 July 1904, in Marder ed., *FGDN* I, pp. 320–1.

would resist attempts to make the defence of India the primary *raison d'être* of the British Army had been their intention from the outset. The notion that the Staff inaugurated a 'new' military policy of Continental involvement by supporting the creation of a striking force in preference to reinforcing India thus ignores both the continuities in military policy evident from the Wolseley era and the importance the War Office attached to imperial and colonial warfare in 1904–5.[74] If British military thought had assumed a Continental aspect at this time, it had done so in India, not London. Moreover, officers inclined to favour preparing for large-scale operations against a Great Power had decisively lost the political battle for the resources necessary to enact such a vision. If one accepted Kitchener's figures for the number of troops Russia could deploy towards the North-West Frontier, the General Staff were most likely justified in their conclusion that India could not be defended by force without a system of conscription.[75] Nevertheless, the requirements of India did make an important conceptual contribution to the future development of plans to deploy the British Army to Europe—far more directly than the desire to constitute a 'striking force'.

THE MOVEMENT OF TROOPS BY SEA

Clarke and Fisher supported the idea of a 'striking force' because they did not view it as conflicting with a primarily maritime approach to imperial defence. Indeed, amphibious operations against the weak points of an enemy were very much part of the strategy envisaged by the members of the Esher Committee. From the Navy's perspective, a military strategy focused around a compact striking force would have the additional benefit of ensuring the Admiralty's control over British strategy due to its responsibility for the transport, escort, and disembarkation of such a contingent. As had been the case under Wolseley in the 1880s and 1890s, an expeditionary force of this nature would likely remain in the British Isles until the Navy had established control of the sea lanes, at which point the flexibility of maritime communications could be exploited to deploy the Army to the greatest possible effect.

Discussing the 'striking force' with Lord Esher, Fisher enthused about how 'The Navy embarks it and lands it where it can do most mischief!' and argued that a force of this nature could tie up a disproportionately large number of enemy troops due to the uncertainty as to where it might land.[76] Advocates of amphibious operations were essentially hoping to exploit the mobility afforded by the sea and to use it as a substitute for Britain's modest military capabilities. Such combined operations, it was argued, would lend maximum effect to British sea power. Yet Fisher and Clarke's arguments were made against the backdrop of a subtle, though significant

---

[74] McDermott, 'The Revolution in British Military', pp. 169–71.

[75] Grierson to Arnold-Forster, 12 March 1904, p. 6, in War Office, 'Replies to Questions …', WO 106/44.

[76] Fisher to Esher, 19 November 1903, in Marder ed., *FGDN* I, p. 291.

shift within the balance of strategic decision making. The arguments they put forward in favour of a 'striking force' assumed the continuance of the Navy's traditional monopoly over imperial strategy, which hitherto had been guaranteed by its control over the movement of men by sea. As we have seen, however, the government had weakened the Navy's grip on this foundational aspect of British strategy during the discussions of the reinforcement of India the previous year.

When Nicholson's committee had considered the issue of Indian reinforcement in 1901–2, particular emphasis had been placed upon the Admiralty's advice regarding the transport of troops during wartime. The naval authorities' opinion that it would be impossible to guarantee the safe transit of troops for an undefined period after the outbreak of hostilities with a maritime power had been fundamental both to Nicholson's suggestion to strengthen the permanent garrison of India and to his decision to refer the issue to the CID. After the Admiralty's acknowledgement that dispatching troops without escort was a matter for the government to settle, the CID had proceeded on the assumption that risks would have to be run with the first tranche of men destined for India. Whilst final agreement with the authorities in Calcutta over the number of men to be sent proved elusive, the consensus in London from early 1903 onwards was that an initial reinforcement of 30,000 men should be sent within the first three months of a conflict with Russia. The Admiralty accepted this fact and assented to assist in preparing 'general precautions' if the government was willing to contemplate the possible loss of one transport in ten.[77] A firm decision on the scale of the reinforcement was delayed by the rapid escalation of Kitchener's demands for men. However, in March 1904 the CID confirmed that 'if the naval conditions allowed, and supposing South Africa remained quiet, 30,000 men could be sent to India at the outbreak of hostilities'. The Indian authorities were instructed to anticipate the 10 per cent attrition rate predicated by the Admiralty.[78] By enabling the military authorities to proceed with plans to send men to India without naval escort, the CID subtly shifted the balance between military and naval planning onto a more equitable footing than had been the case hitherto. Prior to the Boer War the Admiralty had effectively exercised a veto over the movement of troops by sea. After 1903, the government granted the War Office an equal share in the formation of imperial strategy due to the demands of India.

The naval department revisited its advice regarding the movement of troops by sea in the summer of 1904. Some internal documents suggest that the Admiralty gave serious consideration to proposals to assign an armoured cruiser escort drawn from the Channel Fleet to convoy transports to India; however, these plans never came to fruition, probably due to the resistance of the flag officers involved.[79] Writing to the India Office in mid-July, the Admiralty re-iterated the Navy's inability to provide an escort at the outbreak of war, but suggested that 'no reason is seen why, with luck and precaution, the whole force should not arrive in safety', provided

[77] Battenberg, 'Reinforcements for India', 12 May 1903, CAB 6/1/15.
[78] CID, 'Minutes of the 36th Meeting, March 24, 1904', CAB 2/1/36.
[79] 'Protection of Reinforcements for India in war. CID 81', 1904, ADM 116/3111.

the ships sailed separately. As the troops would be disembarking in a friendly port and thus would require no naval support upon their arrival, they could sail individually and thereby blend into the mass of other British flagged shipping crisscrossing the oceans.[80] Perhaps encouraged by this information and aware that 'the conveyance of the first reinforcement to India is absolutely essential', the General Staff prepared plans for independent sailings. Aided by the fact that 'the Russian Fleet is at present moment a vanishing quantity' after the losses it had sustained during the Russo-Japanese War, sending troops via the Cape route appeared a realistic means of avoiding the contested waters of the Mediterranean.[81] The conclusion of the *entente* with France and the successful containment of the Russo-Japanese War by Paris and London offered further encouragement, as these developments appeared to reduce, though by no means eliminate, the prospect of co-ordinated Franco-Russian aggression. The movement of men by sea without naval protection appeared to becoming less risky than had hitherto been the case.

The General Staff placed their arrangements for reinforcing India before the CID in May 1905, submitting that the government 'keep in mind' the desirability of providing a naval escort. More significant than this request, however, was the conclusion of the memorandum they submitted to the committee. 'From a military point of view', the General Staff stated, 'it is essential that there should be no delay in the dispatch of troops.'[82] In itself, this was not a particularly noteworthy statement. Only 5,300 men and 2,000 horses would need to sail immediately, with a further 25,000 following within three months. This window may even have been sufficient to allow the Navy to provide a convoy for the second instalment of men. Moreover, the plans were the product of explicit direction from the CID. The General Staff was thus merely translating the government's strategic intent into practical arrangements. However, the embodiment of plans to dispatch troops from the British Isles immediately after the outbreak of war without the direct co-operation of the Navy was a departure worthy of note. Whereas the much-discussed 'striking force' would be deployed with naval support, the Indian reinforcement would not. The troops for India were also likely be the first force to leave Britain and speed was of the essence in their doing so. This development may appear to be so minor as to appear almost inconsequential, yet here was the first indication of the impact the government's attempts to shift the Army away from its defensive posture could have upon the aggregate of naval and military planning that amounted to British grand strategy. With the Navy's de facto control over British strategy loosened by the requirements of defending India, the space for a more independent military strategy to flourish had emerged. Nowhere was this more clearly illustrated than by the War Office's investigations into the possibility of subsidizing auxiliary cruisers of its own to protect the convoys destined for India.

---

[80] Admiralty to India Office, 13 July 1904, CAB 38/5/72.

[81] Col. Drake, 'War with Russia: A Project for the conveyance of the First Reinforcement to India, if necessary without convoy', 13 April 1905, WO 106/48 E3/1, fo. 475.

[82] Memorandum by the General Staff, 27 May 1905, in 'Protection of Reinforcements from the United Kingdom to India', CAB 38/9/44.

The Admiralty had paid an annual subsidy to several ship owners in order to secure the use of their vessels as auxiliary cruisers in wartime since the 1880s.[83] Structural alterations were made to the craft to enable them to mount a modest armament and they were intended to be employed in a range of trade protection and scouting duties. Once it became clear that the Navy would not provide an escort to the first tranche of reinforcements for India, the General Staff identified this stock of armed merchant cruisers as a potentially expeditious means of increasing the protection afforded to the convoy without escort from regular warships of the Royal Navy. Fast, capacious, seaworthy, and sufficiently armed to deter attack from similar enemy vessels, the ships appeared perfectly suited to the role. Suggestions were made to approach the Admiralty about the availability of their stock of merchant cruisers for the purpose (despite the fact that the Admiralty had ended the practice of paying subsidies to merchantmen in 1903).[84] If the naval authorities proved resistant to the proposal, however, the War Office was prepared to consider subsidizing ships of its own. Proposals were duly made to fit out ships as 'armed transports'. The rationale for such measures was set out in no uncertain terms: 'if the principle be accepted that, in time of war, the two great military services of the Crown are to operate without concert or concentration, then some organisation such as that which is foreshadowed in this project becomes imperative'.[85] Here was a succinct encapsulation of the effect of the government's intervention in defence administration between 1903 and 1904. In his attempt to achieve greater efficiency through a more pronounced division of labour, Balfour had in fact removed the key element which had hitherto served to bind military and naval strategy together: the Admiralty's control over the seaborne transport of troops. With this restraint removed, the already tenuous linkage between the planning of the respective services evaporated as the CID failed to produce a coherent combined strategy. The defence of India, and the government's response to it, thus resulted in a divergence between military and naval strategy which the committee proved incapable of resolving.[86] As one scholar has noted, 'so far had the War Office moved that it was now forced to construct its own naval strategy to fit in with its military plans'.[87] The impact of this de-coupling became evident over the course of the subsequent year.

THE QUESTION OF WHAT WAR MEANS

The spring of 1905 saw important changes in the landscape of Great Power politics. Russia suffered major defeats in the Far East at the Battle of Mukden in March and at Tsushima in May. The Tsar's forces suffered around 90,000 casualties at Mukden

[83] S. Cobb, *Preparing for Blockade, 1885–1914: Naval Contingency for Economic Warfare*, London: Ashgate, 2013, Ch. 6.
[84] Seligmann, *RNGT*, pp. 46–64.
[85] Drake, 'War with France and Russia, Germany neutral', 1905, p. 86, WO 106/48/E3/3.
[86] This theme is powerfully advanced in d'Ombrain, *War Machinery*, especially Chs II and VI.
[87] Gooch, *Plans of War*, p. 183.

alone and his Baltic fleet, having made the long trip to the Far East, was decimated two months later. By the summer the war had cost Russia eleven first-class battle-ships, the loss of which effectively consigned her to the third rank of naval powers. 'Tsushima is equivalent to Trafalgar', the Admiralty in London laconically observed.[88] These defeats prompted a wave of internal unrest, and a deteriorating financial, political, and military position significantly diminished the prospects of Tsarist expansionism in Asia or elsewhere for the time being. For Britain, this reduced the immediacy of needing to find a military solution to the defence of India, a fact that was confirmed by the agreement of the Anglo-Russian conven-tion in 1907.

If events in Asia eased the burden upon Britain, however, they also presented opportunities for other powers. Temporarily unburdened of the prospect of a two-front war against the Franco-Russian alliance, Germany sought to rupture the Anglo-French *entente* by challenging the status quo in Morocco. A crisis erupted in June as the French cancelled all military leave and war appeared imminent. Cooler heads prevailed and tensions were defused for the time being, but the prospect of a renewal of Franco-German hostilities obliged the British armed services and government to consider the best course of action available in the event of a European war.

The military and naval preparations conducted during 1905 reflected the uncer-tain international picture Britain faced. Whilst the threat of a Russian attack on India had receded by the end of the year, the prospect of Britain becoming embroiled in the Russo-Japanese War due to her alliance obligations remained real until the conclusion of peace in September. Moreover, despite the signing of the *entente* with France the previous April, the Dual Alliance between Paris and St Petersburg meant that whilst hostilities in the east continued, the potential for an Anglo-French confrontation in support of their allies could not be discounted (although both sides worked to avoid such an eventuality). German belligerence and ambition marked her out as another potential source of danger to Britain. Relations between London and Berlin had been difficult since German colonial ambitions in Africa had become evident in the early 1890s, but tensions had grown as the Kaiser sought concessions in China and in the Middle East around the turn of the century.[89] The growth of the German Navy, her uncompromising style of diplomacy, and her assertiveness within Europe were also causes for concern. This fact was reflected in the increased amount of attention both services paid to the Kaiser's armed forces after 1900.[90] The Admiralty and War Office therefore continued to plan and prepare for hostilities against Russia, France, and Germany,

[88] Marder, *Anatomy*, p. 441.

[89] M. S. Seligmann, *Rivalry in Southern Africa: The Transformation of German Colonial Policy*, London: Palgrave Macmillan, 1998, Ch. 5; Otte, *Foreign Office Mind*, pp. 215–19, 235.

[90] H. A. Lawrence, 'Military resources of Germany and probable method of their employment in a war between Germany and England', 18 January 1902; Robertson to Nicholson, 18 January 1902, E.2/4, WO 106/46; Selborne, 'The Navy Estimates and the Chancellor of the Exchequer's Memorandum on the Growth of Expenditure', 16 November 1901, pp. 10–11, CAB 37/59/118; Seligmann, 'Switching Horses'.

or the worst possible scenario: war against all three. If the services were in accord as to the range of potential opponents, however, their views on how to prosecute a conflict against any or all of them most certainly were not. Indeed, the various schemes considered during 1905 revealed fundamental disagreements about grand strategy, the utility of sea power, and the best course to adopt in the event of hostilities against a Continental power.

The War Office had considered operations against an enemy's colonial possessions to be an important part of British strategy for some time. Plans for assaults against French territories had been elaborated under Wolseley's guidance and this work continued under Roberts. Nicholson's mid-1901 appreciation on the 'Military Needs of the Empire' had embodied this mode of thought. 'Two things are...necessary to the successful conduct of every war', the document had noted: the protection of one's own interests and 'the infliction on the enemy of such injury as will induce him to consent to terminate the war on terms which will afford us a guarantee of peace and compensation'. Relying upon a defensive or passive posture would not fulfil the second condition and would risk prolonging a conflict and making an inconclusive settlement more likely. As Russia was largely immune to British military assault from the sea, in the event of war against the Dual Alliance, the War Office advocated an ambitious series of operations against French colonies in order to inflict such injury as was necessary to bring the enemy to the negotiating table. French naval infrastructure at Bizerta, Dakar, Martinique, Diego Suarez, and Jibutil 'should be captured as soon as the fleet is in a position to co-operate...if it be possible, simultaneously'. An impressive total of 115,000 troops were allocated for these tasks.[91]

The importance the military authorities attached to such operations had been re-iterated in May 1904, when the General Staff proposed a system of army organization capable of supplying a striking force of 90,000 men, 'the most probable objectives [of which]...would be French colonial naval bases'.[92] Correspondence between the DMO and the Admiralty during the Morocco Crisis confirmed the ongoing centrality of such schemes to General Staff thought. Major-General Grierson stated his view that operations against French naval bases such as Saigon and Dakar were 'highly desirable' and stressed the potential for attacks on French Indo-China and French colonies in West Africa.[93] The Admiralty, however, was noticeably cooler in its attitude. This fact was not lost on Grierson, who noted that whilst 'much money and labour has been expended in preparing schemes to capture Martinique, Biserta, Diego Suarez, Noumea, Dakar and Saigon...the naval view appears to be that the maritime situation will not be appreciably affected by capturing these places'.[94] The DMO was correct in his characterization of the

---

[91] E. A. Altham, 'Military Needs of the Empire in a War With France and Russia', 10 August 1901, pp. 30–9, CAB 3/1/1.

[92] General Staff, 'The Strength of the Regular Army and Auxiliary Forces, having regard to Peace and War Requirements', 1 May 1904, pp. 4–5, CAB 3/1/22A.

[93] Grierson, 'Military Policy in the Event of War with France', July 1905, ADM 116/3111. The correspondence is reproduced in Appendix II of Marder, *Anatomy*.

[94] Ibid.

Admiralty's views, which it had expressed openly to the CID in mid-1903. On that occasion Battenberg had penned a critical appreciation of the relevant section of the 'Military Needs of the Empire' in which he had argued that French colonial bases would become useless as soon as their stores had been expended as they would be unable to re-supply them due to Britain's control of sea communications. The DNI described French bases as *'ulterior objectives'*, concluding that 'there is no need to keep any troops specially ear-marked for these over-sea expeditions'.[95] His successor adopted a similar attitude in response in 1905. Captain Ottley, who had moved from the CID to replaced Battenberg as DNI in February, re-iterated that the capture of outlying colonial possessions was unnecessary if they had already been cut off from effective re-supply. Drawing a somewhat colourful analogy, Ottley noted that 'a man may suffer severely by the amputation of a limb, but when the operation is over his health is not further affected by anything which is subsequently done to the severed member. It may be dissected into the smallest shreds for all that it matters to him.'[96] The difference of opinion between the two departments, Grierson noted pointedly, was 'not so much on the general question of strategy as upon the whole question of war policy, if not indeed upon the question of what war means'.[97] The same could be said of the attitudes of the two services to operations against the home territory of European powers.

Whilst the War Office had considered minor raids against naval installations and infrastructure in France during the 1890s, the department had never regarded major attacks on metropolitan France as a realistic prospect.[98] This was a simple reflection of numbers: the French Army was vastly larger than the British and would be operating on home ground and on interior lines. Similarly, by the turn of the century proposals for amphibious operations against Russia were widely considered impractical on military and logistical grounds. Strengthened fortifications in the Baltic and Far East reduced the number of realistic targets and more effective transport infrastructure had improved Russia's ability to move troops and supplies towards threatened areas by rail. Early military appreciations of war against Germany reflected similar thinking. In February 1903 Colonel Altham of the Directorate of Mobilization and Intelligence produced a short précis of British military policy in the event of an Anglo-German war. After examining the potential targets for combined operations, he concluded that 'the destruction of her seaborne trade...is the more effective weapon', discounting colonial operations on the grounds that the relative unimportance of the Kaiser's overseas empire reduced the effect that capturing such territories might have. Due to the disparity in overall population and military manpower, Altham also made clear his view that 'the possibility of

[95] Battenberg, 'Remarks on Offensive Over-sea Expeditions suggested by the War Office as feasible in the Memorandum on the Military Needs of the Empire in a War with France and Russia (No. 1A, 12th August, 1901)', 1 July 1903, CAB 3/1/14A.

[96] Ottley, 'Remarks on "C"', July 1905, p. 3, ADM 116/3111.

[97] Grierson, 'Further Memorandum on Military Policy in the Event of War with France', July 1905, p. 2, ADM 116/3111.

[98] C. à Court Repington, 'Report on Measures for Interrupting a French Mobilisation on the Shores of the Channel', 28 March 1894, DMO/14/16; Wolseley to Chapman, 30 November 1894, DMO/14/17, BL.

any offensive action on the soil of Germany proper would be madness'.[99] Upon reading Altham's production, the NID did not demur from its conclusions.[100] However, this did not necessarily mean that elements within the Navy did not favour direct attacks upon enemy territory. When Chapman had proposed mounting pre-emptive amphibious strikes against French port facilities in order to forestall an invasion attempt in 1894, he had met with a very positive response from the Admiralty. After reading the proposals the DNI, Captain Bridge, had even suggested that similar operations might form an important element of overall British strategy in the event of war with France. 'In my view', Bridge wrote, 'operations of the kind proposed by Captain à Court[101] ought to be kept up throughout nearly the whole course of a war, and our aim ought to be to give our enemy's coast near his "offensive" torpedo-boat stations no peace at all.' 'If we land at many points and repeat landings incessantly', the DNI argued, 'the disconcerting effects...will greatly assist us.'[102] Faced with the prospect of co-operating with France in a war against Germany in the summer of 1905, the Admiralty reproduced precisely these sort of arguments, underlining the fundamental differences between the two services on the issue of British strategy.

At the turn of 1905 both services had been considering Britain's options in the event of a Franco-German war. Grierson commissioned a war game to be conducted at the Staff College to investigate the situation in the event of a German violation of Belgian neutrality in the event of a European war.[103] The scenario was based upon active British military co-operation with the French and Belgians close to the frontier with Germany and the results suggested that a British expeditionary force might play a significant part in such a campaign.[104] Due to the disparity in numbers between the British and German armies, co-operating with the French and Belgians appeared to offer the best prospect for making a meaningful military contribution to a future Continental war.

The Admiralty adopted an entirely different approach. Naval preparation for war against Germany was more mature than the military's: studies of operations against Germany had been produced in the NID since late-1901 and detailed plans had been elaborated and updated ever since.[105] As the Morocco Crisis developed during the spring, the naval authorities had mobilization arrangements and preparations for war completed and Fisher felt confident to boast that the Fleet was

[99] Altham, 'Memorandum of the Military Policy to be adopted in a War with Germany', 10 February 1903, CAB 3/1/20A.

[100] Battenberg, 'Notes by the Director of Naval Intelligence on the above Memorandum', 18 February 1903, CAB 3/1/20A.

[101] The then Captain Charles à Court, later Charles à Court Repington (military correspondent of *The Times*), was a rising star in military intelligence and worked on the amphibious schemes under Chapman.

[102] Bridge to Chapman, 6 April 1894, DMO/14/17, BL.

[103] Directive by Grierson, 24 January 1905, in War Office, 'Records of a Strategic War Game', 1905, p. 3, WO 33/364.

[104] For Grierson's general comments, see War Office, 'Records of a Strategic War Game', 1905, pp. 152–6, WO 33/364.

[105] Grimes, *War Planning*, Ch. II.

ready for sea within a matter of hours.[106] The Admiralty had good reason to be sanguine about the Navy's prospects. If Britain was not fighting against either France or Russia, or, indeed, if she was in alliance with either or both powers, her naval preponderance in the North Sea would be overwhelming. Under such circumstances, studies conducted in the NID during 1904 had examined the possibility of seizing the island of Heligoland, attacking German North Sea ports, and penetrating the Baltic.[107] If co-operation with France offered great opportunities to exploit Anglo-French sea power, it also brought attendant difficulties, however. Foremost amongst these was that naval operations alone might not be sufficient to relieve the pressure of a German military assault on France. The events of 1870–1 had shown the potential for a swift conclusion to a land campaign and demonstrated the need for similarly rapid action from the sea. For British support to France to be credible, it therefore had to be fast acting and to distract German forces from the Franco-German frontier. Economic pressure would doubtless play an important role in a solely Anglo-German conflict, but for it to work in the context of an Anglo-French combination against Berlin, defeat on land had to be staved off for long enough to enable its effects to take hold.[108] The Admiralty therefore set about attempting to develop a coherent combined arms strategy intended to relieve the pressure on France.

That Fisher and his colleagues contemplated more than a purely naval campaign was made clear during the spring. As the crisis over Morocco worsened during April, Fisher wrote to the Foreign Secretary that 'we could have the German Fleet, the Kiel Canal, and Schleswig-Holstein within a fortnight'.[109] This was not mere hyperbole. War orders issued to the Channel Fleet in May instructed the C-in-C to watch and bring to battle the enemy fleet, safeguard British trade, prevent invasion, and 'to assist the Military Forces in any operations which may be ordered on the Enemy's Coast'.[110] Precisely what the Admiralty had in mind became clear during the summer.

Fisher issued instructions to the NID to prepare for rapid mobilization on 24 June. This began a hurried correspondence with the C-in-C Channel Fleet, Admiral Wilson, to whom control of operations would be entrusted in the event of war. The Admiral submitted a paper several days later outlining his views on the best course of action in the event of hostilities breaking out. 'No action by the Navy alone can do France any good', Wilson wrote, 'we should be bound to devote the whole military forces of the country to endeavour to create a diversion on the coast of Germany in France's favour.' He continued, 'as the main object would be to draw off troops from the French frontier, simultaneous attacks would have to

[106] R. Bacon, *The Life of Lord Fisher of Kilverstone*, London: Redder & Stoughton, 1929, II, p. 81; Marder, *Anatomy*, pp. 498–9; J. Steinberg, 'The Copenhagen Complex', *Journal of Contemporary History*, Vol. 1, No. 3, Jul., 1966, pp. 38–40.

[107] Battenberg, 'The Organisation for War of Torpedo Craft in Home Waters', 4 July 1904, *Naval Necessities* II, pp. 508–19, ADM 116/3093; Grimes, *War Planning*, pp. 52–6.

[108] This fact is significantly under-rated in Lambert, *Planning Armageddon*, pp. 35–60.

[109] Fisher to Lansdowne, 22 April 1905, in Marder ed., *FGDN* II, p. 55.

[110] Admiralty, 'Orders for Commander in Chief, Channel Fleet', 6 May 1905, ADM 116/900B.

be made at as many different points as possible...If Denmark were on our side, a very effective diversion might be made by assisting her to recover Schleswig Holstein.' Wilson requested that, as soon as war appeared imminent, he be placed in communication with the Army in order to arrange troops for such descents, that small craft for transporting troops be arranged, and that obsolete battleships be fitted to support the operations by bombarding coastal defences.[111] This view coincided with Fisher's earlier remarks about the Danish peninsula and one contemporary recorded that the two admirals concerted a plan of campaign together along these lines, although none has survived.[112]

Ottley, who was in correspondence with Grierson regarding operations against French colonies, was well aware that securing co-operation from the General Staff might prove more complicated than Wilson imagined. As Franco-German tensions reached their height in June, he therefore attempted to employ the CID as an instrument with which to secure a military force to enact the Admiralty's preferred strategy.

Ottley collaborated with Clarke, his superior during his previous posting as Naval Assistant to the CID, to steer the military authorities towards accepting a maritime approach to potential Anglo-German war. Whilst continuing to correspond with Grierson, the DNI drafted a document on 'Preparations of Plans for combined Naval and Military Operations in War'. Clarke commented on early drafts, making numerous recommendations.[113] The final product can be seen both as a genuine effort to improve inter-service co-operation and as an attempt by the Admiralty to re-assert its control over British grand strategy.[114] The first portion of the memorandum addressed the general requirement for a planning apparatus capable of coordinating plans for combined operations during peacetime, in order that Britain would be prepared to strike at the very outset of war if required. Thereafter, however, Ottley linked his proposals with an amphibious strategy for war against Germany. Moving from the general to the particular, the DNI began by acknowledging the importance of the CID's ruling on home defence before re-asserting the Admiralty's true role as the arbiter of grand strategy due to its control over the movement of men by sea. 'The Prime Minister has recently shown the invasion of the British Isles to be impracticable', he wrote, 'hence it follows that a British mobile army locked up on British soil is strategically wasted in war...before it [the Army] can be usefully employed it must (in every case) be transported across the sea.' Conceding that 'in recent years our Military authorities have not suggested the invasion of the main territory of any Continental Power as a practical scheme', Ottley continued:

...it is clear that in the special circumstances arising out of the recent Morocco embroglio, Great Britain—in alliance with France—would not merely be in possession

[111] Wilson to the Admiralty, 27 June 1905, quoted in Marder, *Anatomy*, pp. 504–5; Wilson to Fisher, 9 March 1906, FISR 1/5, CAC.

[112] Bacon, *Fisher* II, p. 81.

[113] A draft of the paper with Clarke's comments can be found in CAB 17/5 and a further annotated version is present in CAB 17/95, fos 11–19.

[114] Williamson Jr, *Politics of Grand Strategy*, p. 52; d'Ombrain, *War Machinery*, p. 77.

of such overwhelming Naval preponderance as would permit her, under certain circumstances, to risk her ships to an extent not formerly contemplated, but also, from the mere fact that she would have been fighting side by side with Russia's ally she would have possessed an effective guarantee against Russian hostile action on the North-West Frontier of India. A part at least of the British Military reinforcements hypothecated for service in India would thus have been available for service nearer home. The question whether (in the circumstances imagined) British action against Germany should be limited merely to sea operations, or whether a British expeditionary force might not be landed in Schleswig-Holstein, or elsewhere, so as to relieve the pressure upon France through the passes of the Vosges, immediately arises.[115]

Translating Wilson's proposed plan of campaign for a political audience, the DNI concluded by stressing the need for any such operations to be conducted as swiftly as possible in order to disrupt a German attack on France. Here, then, was the Admiralty's attempt to re-assert the grip over British grand strategy it had lost when India dominated the CID's discourse during 1903–4.

Fisher sent the paper, with an amended title of 'British intervention in the event of France being suddenly attacked by Germany', to the Prime Minister.[116] Balfour was supportive of the plans, in part because each additional layer of integration and complexity made the CID more difficult for the next government to interfere with. With his grip on power becoming increasingly tenuous, the Prime Minister was committed to ensuring the legacy of his reforms of Britain's defence administration.[117] With this in mind the formation of a permanent joint body of the sort envisaged by Fisher and Ottley, 'to consider and prepare such schemes for joint naval and military operations as might be found practicable and desirable', was discussed and agreed by the CID in July.[118] For a short time conversations between the two departments appeared to be yielding fruit. Captain Ballard of the NID discussed joint operations with the Assistant Director of Military Operations, Colonel Charles Callwell, in August.[119] Callwell referred Ballard to one of his subordinates, Captain Adrian Grant Duff, for further information, noting that the topic of combined operations 'will probably be the first thing considered by the sub. com. of the CID when the holidays are over'.[120] Writing to Grant Duff, Ballard asked him for a military perspective on two subjects. The first was what urgent action might be possible to relieve German pressure upon France. In this case Ballard felt that 'we should have to hurry up and take extra risks by sea at least'. Secondly, there was a less pressing scenario in which Britain would have more time to prepare for concerted action against Germany. Significantly, Ballard discounted the idea of amphibious operations in the event of a solely Anglo-German

[115] Ottley, 'Preparations of Plans for combined Naval and Military Operations in War', 16 July 1905, CAB 17/95, fos 8–9.
[116] See the copy in Add MS 49711, fos 65–9.
[117] Mackay, *Balfour*, pp. 183–5; Esher to Balfour, 5 and 13 October 1905 in Brett ed., *Esher* II, pp. 114–15 and 117–18.
[118] See the minutes in CAB 2/1/76 and 77.
[119] Ballard to Callwell, 28 August 1905, WO 106/46/E2/6, fo. 26.
[120] Callwell note of 29 August 1905, WO 106/46/E2/6, fo. 27.

conflict from the outset of these discussions.[121] The Admiralty was only advocating military intervention in the event of a conflict waged in support of France against Germany as a means of relieving the pressure on the French frontier.[122] This is an important distinction to strike as it showed an appreciation of diplomatic and military realities—something lacking in recent attempts to privilege economic warfare within British naval thought during the crisis.[123]

Grant Duff forwarded Ballard a paper prepared by the General Staff on 'British Military Action in the Case of War with Germany', which appeared encouraging. The document suggested that a seaborne British army might provide 'immense assistance' to the French and that '120,000 troops would probably hold fully 400,000 German regular troops and Landwehr tight in the Baltic provinces, and would relieve the French'.[124] Colonel Drake expressed similar views, noting that 'a force of 120,000 men based on the sea and employed in a Strategical Stroke in the Theatre of Operations in co-ordination with the French Army would have considerable influence on the course of a campaign'.[125] Callwell, absent on holiday, was another well-known advocate of such operations and seemed likely add his weight to such proposals.[126]

Other members of the General Staff were less supportive, however. Grant Duff himself wrote back to Ballard suggesting that since 'the arrangements on the coast in question are so efficient, and our numbers are so small . . . it is very difficult to see in what way we can intervene to any really useful purpose'.[127] He followed this up with a robust internal critique of the Admiralty's proposals on 9 September, where he concluded that 'there is no feasible military operation on the Baltic coast promising adequate results to the risks run' and that 'without a powerful army to back our sea power we can exert little influence on the peace of Europe'.[128] The other Assistant DMO, Colonel Robertson, also sounded a note of caution, suggesting that he would endorse the preparation of a paper on the topic, but only if an official request was made by the DNI or the First Sea Lord.[129]

In the absence of such a request and as a result of the lack of suitable targets on the German Baltic coastline, Callwell was obliged to admit to Ballard on 3 October that military operations against German territory were unlikely to be practical in the immediate future. On this basis the General Staff adhered to the lukewarm

[121] Ballard to Grant Duff, 2 September 1905, WO 106/46/E2/6, fos 37–8.
[122] This reflected Wilson's views: see Marder, *Anatomy*, p. 504.
[123] Lambert, *Planning Armageddon*, pp. 35–60.
[124] Ballard to Grant Duff, 9 September 1905, ADM 116/1043B II, fos 210–11; General Staff, 'British Military Action in Case of War with Germany', 28 August 1905, WO 106/46/E2/6, fos 50–2. The copy of Grant Duff's memorandum in the Admiralty papers is dated 3 October; however, Ballard accurately describes its contents in his letter of 9 September, suggesting that the version here was misdated.
[125] Drake to Callwell, note dated 30 September 1905, WO 106/46/E2/6, fo. 43.
[126] D'Ombrain, *War Machinery*, pp. 78–9.
[127] Grant Duff to Ballard, 7 September 1905, WO 106/46/E.2.
[128] Grant Duff, 'British Military action on the Baltic Coast in the event of a war between Germany and Great Britain and France in alliance', 9 September 1905, WO 106/46/E2/6, fos 44–7.
[129] Note by Robertson, 26 September 1905, WO 106/46/E2/6, fos 40–1.

appreciation of the topic they had submitted to the CID the previous year.[130] This infuriated Fisher, who wrote to the Prime Minister enclosing the paper on 'the Elaboration of Combined Naval and Military Preparation for War' several days later. He also commissioned his Naval Assistant, Captain Thomas Crease, and the NID to produce a paper outlining the benefits and organizational details of a small striking force of 5,000 men for rapid deployment.[131] The document Fisher sent to Balfour rehearsed some of Ottley's earlier suggestions that had led to the appointment of the CID sub-committee on joint operations and was doubtless intended to prompt the Prime Minister into action. The First Sea Lord made his intentions explicit in a covering note to Balfour's influential private secretary, Jack Sandars: 'I am very hot on this Committee', he explained, 'for as I told Esher *it's the only engine capable of drawing the Army out of its Quagmire "of one man waiting for another"!*' Revealing his ambition to use the body to re-assert the Admiralty's control of strategic planning in the round, he laid out his wish that the new committee 'will work a revolution at the War Office! They will be *forced* to ready, *forced* to get on, *forced* to co-operate and finally *forced* to be efficient!'[132] Fisher's actions were in vain. The sub-committee never met and with the fall of Balfour's government in December the future of the CID itself appeared uncertain.[133]

THE LEGACY OF THE MOROCCAN CRISIS FOR BRITISH STRATEGY

Fisher's attempt to institutionalize a means of ensuring naval control of grand strategy had failed. Yet the First Moroccan Crisis was not the moment when a General Staff-inspired 'Continental' approach became accepted as Britain's strategy in the event of a European war.[134] The Admiralty did not become the junior partner in defence planning and a preference for a 'maritime' strategy remained ascendant within the CID and the government. Indeed, the episode contained more encouragement for advocates of an amphibious approach than is commonly accepted.

As had been clear from Ballard's original letter to Callwell on the topic of combined operations, the Baltic scheme which had been rejected by the General Staff was but one, 'urgent', option under consideration by the naval hierarchy. The Admiralty was not irrevocably committed to the idea of landing a major expeditionary force in the Baltic at the expense of other alternatives, nor was it unwilling to co-operate with the military in formulating new plans. The paper Fisher commissioned on the 'Organisation of an Expeditionary Force' addressed many of the

---

[130] Callwell to Ballard, 3 October 1905 and attached précis, WO 106/46/E2/6, fos 28–30.

[131] Crease and Hankey, 'Organisation of an Expeditionary Force', October 1905, CAB 63/1.

[132] Fisher to Sandars, 10 October 1905, Add MS 49711, fos 120–1, BL; d'Ombrain, *War Machinery*, pp. 79–80.

[133] Hankey, *Supreme Command* I, p. 62.

[134] Williamson Jr, *Politics of Grand Strategy*, pp. 65–88; d'Ombrain, *War Machinery*, pp. 78–90, 209–25; McDermott, 'The Revolution in British Military Thinking', pp. 172–7.

organizational and logistical barriers the General Staff had raised to the successful execution of the scheme—most damagingly the amount of time taken for the Admiralty to organize the necessary transports.[135] The Admiralty circumvented this issue by proposing to use battleships held in reserve—which still maintained a high state of readiness—to transport troops and by providing detailed figures on the men and equipment necessary.[136] This was still some way from a workable agreement between the two services, but it did at least demonstrate a willingness on the Admiralty's part to respond positively and in detail to concerns raised by the military. Scope remained for effective compromise between the two services, even if much work would be required to enact it.

As for the General Staff, the body had yet to realize its full potential as a planning organ in the wake of the major upheavals which had accompanied its creation. Its capacity to exercise a major influence over government policy remained extremely finite, not least due to frustrations stemming from the ongoing difficulties at the War Office regarding the re-organization of the Army. Lyttelton, the CGS, had absented himself from the office for much of the summer due to his opposition to Sir William Butler's Royal Commission into corruption in the Army in South Africa. Arnold-Forster complained bitterly that he found it 'preposterous' that he should be working 'without the assistance of my principal military adviser', but the CIGS retained his post due to strong political connections—his brother Alfred was Colonial Secretary.[137] This lack of leadership limited the War Office's capacity to argue the case for a convincing or enduring alternative to the Navy's plans. Clarke bemoaned the Staff's shortcomings on a regular basis and initially excluded Lyttelton and Grierson from the conversations he organized to prepare a co-ordinated British response to a potential Franco-German war in December 1905.[138] That General John French, Commander of the 1st Army Corps—almost certainly the force to be used in any amphibious operations—attended the first meetings of Clarke's planning group as the senior military representative illustrates the extent to which the CID's strategic assumptions were construed apart from those of the General Staff. Nor did the Staff's influence wax with the arrival of the new Liberal administration. Campbell-Bannerman, who succeeded Balfour as premier, had after all opposed the formation of such a body in the 1890s due to its potentially insidious influence over national policy. He was thus hardly likely to allow himself to be bundled into accepting plans for war on the Continent by the professional staff at the War Office.

The General Staff was also not so unified in its views, nor as committed to operations in Europe as is supposed by some.[139] The ongoing flexibility of thought within the Staff was evidenced by the internal disagreements the Admiralty's Baltic scheme provoked. The naval proposals attracted support from officers like Callwell

---

[135] For the General Staff's criticisms, see General Staff, 'Military Operations on the Baltic Coast in the Event of War with Germany Great Britain Being in Alliance with France', 1905, WO 106/46/E2/6, fos 32–4.

[136] Crease and Hankey, 'Organisation of an Expeditionary Force', October 1905, CAB 63/1.

[137] Arnold-Forster diary, 19 June 1905, Add MS 50345, fo. 53, BL.

[138] d'Ombrain, *War Machinery*, p. 84. [139] Gooch, *Prospect of War*, vii–viii.

and Drake, and General French appeared to favour sending the Army to Antwerp. The military authorities were thus more willing to contemplate combined operations than might have been expected if they had already settled definitively on providing direct support to the French or Belgians on the Continent. Despite their reservations, the General Staff did investigate the feasibility of attacks in the Baltic in considerable detail and produced a lengthy appreciation on the topic in November.[140] Moreover, a mobilization scheme for dispatching two army corps to fight alongside the French or Belgians was not completed until January 1906.[141] Even when one was prepared, Lyttelton made clear that the plans were but one contingency 'amongst other problems which are receiving the attention of the General Staff'.[142] Both of these facts indicate a greater degree of flexibility of mind than has been depicted by some.[143] Finally, the scepticism officers like Robertson and Grant Duff exhibited towards the Admiralty's proposals reflected a continuity of thought evident in the Intelligence Division's appreciations on the topic in 1903—and as far back as the 1880s and 1890s. Launching the diminutive British Army against the home territory of a European power possessed of a mass conscript force and an effective railway infrastructure held no more appeal in 1905 than it had in a decade previously. That it was a General Staff, rather than the Intelligence Division, enunciating these opinions, did not fundamentally alter the arguments emanating from those at the War Office who viewed amphibious attacks against Continental powers with scepticism.

Ultimately the series of conferences Clarke arranged between December 1905 and January 1906 to oversee British planning during the political paralysis engendered by the general election could only pick between options available in the event of an imminent outbreak of war. Due to the service's lack of preparedness to launch an immediate amphibious operation, the body concluded that 'any military co-operation on the part of the British Army, if undertaken at the outset of war, must take the form either of an expedition to Belgium or of direct participation in the defence of the French Frontier'.[144] Yet, this conclusion was a temporary one intended to meet the needs of the moment and did not represent a commitment to military involvement in support of France. Clarke continued to work towards an amphibious approach for the remainder of his tenure as Secretary to the CID and neither service emerged from the episode with its reputation enhanced sufficiently to claim a definitive political victory. Uncertainty about the Admiralty

[140] Grant Duff, 'Memorandum on the Feasibility of Landing a British Force of 100,000 Men on the Coast of Germany, in the event of Great Britain Being in Active Alliance with France in a War Against Germany, and the Probable Effect on the Military Situation', 11 November 1905, WO 106/46/E.2:10.

[141] Ewart recorded that Lyttelton first mentioned the possibility to him on 5 January: Ewart diary, GD527/1/1/135/8, NRS. See also Macdiarmid, *Grierson*, pp. 215–16, which suggests that the DMO began work in late December and submitted his plans on 16 January.

[142] Lyttelton to the Adjutant General, 16 January 1906, WO 32/7098.

[143] d'Ombrain, *War Machinery*, pp. 81–90, 206–25; McDermott, 'The Revolution in British Military Thinking', pp. 172–7.

[144] 'Notes of a Conference Held at 2, Whitehall Gardens, January 6, 1906', CAB 18/24; d'Ombrain, *War Machinery*, p. 82.

Transport Department's ability to provide the shipping required for the amphibious assaults Ottley and Fisher proposed left an enduring impression of unpreparedness on the part of the naval authorities.[145] This negativity was magnified by the inconsistency between Fisher's widespread advertisement that the Navy was ready for immediate action and his apparent lack of plans for it to do so.[146] Equally, despite stressing the dangers of delaying an amphibious raid and the need to act quickly to assist the French, the War Office could not commit to placing the 1st Army Corps in France before twelve days after mobilization had begun.[147] Whether this would be fast enough to have any effect on the fighting on the Continent was unclear. Doubts also remained as to the efficiency of the arrangements for other units.[148]

After the Liberal government arrived in office in January 1906, it shunted discussions of strategy firmly onto the political back burner, eschewing firm decisions on the issues raised during the crisis. The CID met only twelve times during the remainder of the year, its future role unclear.[149] No meaningful commitment to a policy of military intervention on the Continent was thus entered into and the urgent necessity—laid bare during the crisis—of enforcing a more complementary approach on the two services went unsatisfied.

* * *

These qualifications about British strategy after 1906 notwithstanding, the period 1904–6 witnessed the impact of the CID's initial proceedings upon British grand strategy. By making decisions on specific issues without ever assuming the overall responsibility for joint planning, the government had unwittingly shifted the balance of strategic decision making away from the maritime and towards the military. To an extent this reflected the imperative to reconcile the contradictory demands of economy and military efficiency. The Army's ability to defend India whilst retaining the flexibility to deploy to other theatres at the same time was an important aspect of overall imperial strategy. However, by shifting the focus of military planning to operations outside Britain and allowing these to be planned without co-operation with the Admiralty the government conveyed a significant share of the responsibility for offensive operations to the War Office. The Navy's ability to guarantee the security of the home islands was the foundation of this approach, but it also robbed the Admiralty of its say over the use of the Army. This was reflected in Fisher's increasingly desperate attempts to re-assert naval primacy over the planning process through the joint operations sub-committee in 1905.

---

[145] Repington to Marker, 26 January 1906, Add MS 55277, fos 36–8, BL, noted now 'my idea is that our sailors have thought out nothing'. Also see Clarke's comments quoted in d'Ombrain, *War Machinery*, pp. 85–9.

[146] Repington to Marker, 2 January 1906, Add MS 55277, fo. 30, BL, noted that 'we are at half-cock at sea & ready to start at 2 hours notice. Jackie Fisher tells me he means to act'; Grey to Haldane, 6 January 1906 MSS 5907, fo. 10, Haldane Papers, [N]ational [L]ibrary of [S]cotland, noted that 'Fisher says he is ready'.

[147] Williamson Jr, *Politics of Grand Strategy*, pp. 78–9.

[148] Haldane, *Autobiography*, pp. 187–8.

[149] d'Ombrain, *War Machinery*, pp. 84 and 211; Esher, 'Memo on the work of the Defence Committee in Anticipation of Possible Hostilities', 20 January 1906, ESHR 16/10, CAC.

In the short term, the government's actions had the comparatively limited effect of curtailing the Admiralty's amphibious ambitions during the Morocco Crisis. Moving forward, however, the divergence between naval and military planning and the freedom afforded the General Staff by the CID's initial ruling on home defence began to exert an increasingly negative, constraining influence upon Admiralty strategy. This process was exacerbated by the differing nature of the challenge posed by Germany, which increasingly came to dominate the Navy's planning process after 1904. Despite the greater distance across the North Sea, for a series of reasons Germany posed a more formidable threat of invasion than France had done for the previous two decades. The extent to which defensive considerations influenced naval strategy had to increase in response. Even as Fisher fought for control of British strategy during the winter of 1905–6, the requirements of meeting a surprise German invasion attempt had begun to shape the Navy's preparations for war.

5

The German Threat

In 1905 the Chancellor of the Exchequer, Austen Chamberlain, circulated a note to his colleagues on the CID. In it, he recounted a conversation he had shared with a friend in France during which the two men had envisaged a German invasion of Britain. 'Germany was afraid to attack England with 900,000 French soldiers on her flank', the note read, 'but could she be certain of immunity from French interference she would throw her troops across Belgium & Holland, seize the ports over against England & land an army on our shores.' The passage continued:

> My friend assumed that the English fleet would destroy the German fleet very shortly after the outbreak of hostilities, but it appears to be the French view, & is doubtless still more decidedly the German one, that under modern condition this would not prevent the Germans from landing a large force in England, probably after a very heavy sacrifice of life in getting them over, but this would be a legitimate war risk in view of the immense effect to be produced.[1]

Chamberlain's note encapsulated the essence of British concerns about the threat of a German invasion: a sudden operation conducted at the outset of war which would use speed to negate the defensive power of the Navy to strike a devastating blow at the very heart of the Empire.

Similar scenarios had first been postulated in the early 1870s at the time of the Franco-Prussian War, when the competence and efficiency demonstrated by the Prussian Army had created a considerable impression in British minds. Prussian arms and their directing influence in the Great General Staff were afforded such respect that when the War Office staged Britain's first major peacetime military manoeuvres in 1871, the scenario selected for the exercises was a hypothetical German invasion.[2] In a similar vein, during the middle of the decade the Quartermaster General's Department undertook detailed surveys of the south-east coastline to ascertain the most likely landing spots for an invading army approaching from the Low Countries or from across the North Sea.[3] Suspicions of France relegated Germany to the position of a subordinate concern for British military planners for most of the 1880s and 1890s; however, the Kaiser's empire returned to the strategic agenda as the turn of the century approached due to her belligerent foreign policy

---

[1] Chamberlain, 'Invasion of England & France by Germany from a French point of view', 1905, AC7/5B/13, Cad.

[2] Clarke, *Voices Prophesying War*, p. 36.

[3] 'Reconnaissance of the Country between the Wash and Lyme Regis: Prepared in the Intelligence Branch of the Quarter-Master-Generals Department', 1876, WO 33/29.

and colonial ambitions.[4] Fate had placed the United Kingdom in the ideal geographical position to block German access to the 'place in the sun' she desired and this, to the minds of some, made conflict between the two nations only a matter of time. To these concerned observers, many of whom demanded increases in military spending and preparedness to mitigate the danger, Britons displayed a disconcerting reticence to take responsibility for the protection of their global empire. Many of the most prominent exponents of the threat from Germany were united in the belief that the German challenge would ultimately manifest itself in the form of the invasion of the British Isles. Vice-Admiral Penrose Fitzgerald encapsulated this body of thought when he wrote to Leo Maxse, editor of *The National Review*, stating that 'Germany's ambition is to attack by force of arms upon the first available opportunity. The provocation we give her is that we stand in the way of her declared ambitions. That is all, but that is enough'.[5]

GERMAN PLANNING FOR THE INVASION OF BRITAIN

Whilst the German military and naval establishments moved away from the idea of mounting an invasion of Britain after 1900, for a brief period the idea of staging a pre-emptive strike against the United Kingdom received serious consideration in Berlin. Ironically, these plans were motivated by the same recognition of Germany's relative weakness at sea identified by scaremongering writers in Britain, a reality which led elements of the Kaiser's naval leadership to advocate exploiting the narrow window of opportunity that might present itself at the outset of war to launch a decisive blow against the heart of the British Empire.

Impetus for the discussion of waging war against Britain was provided by the diplomatic estrangement between London and Berlin resulting from the Kruger telegram of 1896. In February of that year the Chief of Staff of the German High Command, Rear Admiral Alfred Tirpitz, proposed a strategy of concentrating 'everything that can crawl' in the North Sea and proceeding to mount a sudden strike on the Thames Estuary.[6] Tirpitz's logic was simple: the longer an Anglo-German conflict went on, the more successful Britain would be in destroying the German fleet, blockading her coastline, and mounting raids on her territory. A concentrated, surprise thrust against British shipping in the Thames at the outset of war might exploit the relative weakness of the British reserve fleet and the time it would take the Royal Navy to concentrate its dispersed forces into the Channel and North Sea to score a significant victory.[7]

The idea of a pre-emptive attack on the Thames gained traction within the German naval establishment during 1896–7 and increasingly became associated with the idea of an accompanying military strike. Writing in May 1897, one officer

---

[4] P. M. Kennedy, *The Rise of the Anglo-German Antagonism, 1860–1914*, London: Ashfield, 1980, Chs I–II; Otte, 'War-in-Sight' and *Foreign Office Mind*, pp. 198–202, 215–19, 223–31.
[5] Fitzgerald to Maxse, 18 November 1905, quoted in Morris, *Scaremongers*, p. 98.
[6] Lambi, *The Navy and German Power Politics*, pp. 118–19.
[7] Kennedy, 'German Naval Operations Plans', pp. 48–52.

in the Admiralty Staff argued that 'a landing in England must in my opinion be seriously considered in a solid connection with the offensive blow', a view shared by several other senior officials.[8] Naval planners duly made contact with the General Staff in order to gain a military appreciation of the practicality of a joint naval–military strike against the British Isles. The desirability of seizing ports on the Dutch and Belgian coastline to provide a jumping-off point for an invasion of Britain was also investigated. Reasoning that 'a victory over England cannot be won by the fleet alone', the Admiralty Staff envisaged seizing Dutch or Belgian coastal bases as a precursor to a military descent on British shores.[9]

The military authorities took almost six months to reply to the Admiralty Staff's request. When a response finally arrived in December 1897 the Chief of the General Staff, Count Alfred von Schlieffen, expressed tentative support for both amphibious operations against Holland and for a strike against England. He endorsed the notion of striking before the British had time to collect the full extent of their naval forces in the North Sea and proposed conducting experiments to establish whether the German North Sea ports could embark large numbers of troops rapidly and in secret.[10] However, Schlieffen imposed strict conditions upon military participation in the Navy's schemes. Foremost amongst these was that the Navy had to be able to guarantee the maintenance of communications with any army that might be landed in Britain. Should this be unattainable, Schlieffen reasoned, the landing force would ultimately be obliged to surrender, regardless of any tactical successes it might achieve: 'when the last gun cartridge has burned out the victor must lay down his gun'.[11] Unable to make any such commitment, the Admiralty Staff was ultimately obliged to abandon plans for a pre-emptive landing in Britain. Faced with resistance from the General Staff, a reinforced British Home Fleet, and the competing requirements of providing a squadron of ships in the Far East, the Admiralty Staff ceased to view a swift offensive as the best method of prosecuting a war against Britain. Despite the occasional re-emergence of schemes to strike directly at Britain after 1900,[12] advocates of such an approach were increasingly isolated from the trends in both military and naval thought.[13] Improving relations between Paris and London also reduced the prospect of a war between Germany and either Britain or France in isolation. Reasoning that 'the English army will not undertake to come to Germany, the German [army] will not be able to reach its opponent on the other side of the Channel', Schlieffen concluded that 'the first declaration must therefore be the signal for Germany to mobilize her entire army and if necessary to anticipate France'.[14] Serious consideration of a landing in Britain thus slipped in abeyance in Germany, not to be revived until the Second World War. Yet, the crucial condition Schlieffen imposed on military participation in an attack on Britain—the ability to preserve communications with

---

[8] Quoted in Lambi, *The Navy and German Power Politics*, p. 124.
[9] Reproduced in J. Steinberg, 'A German Plan for the Invasion of Holland Belgium, 1897', *Historical Journal*, Vol. 6, No. 1, 1963, pp. 117–19.
[10] Moon, 'Invasion', pp. 659–60; Kennedy, 'German Naval Operations Plans', pp. 52–3.
[11] Lambi, *The Navy and German Power Politics*, p. 127.   [12] Marder, *Anatomy*, p. 461.
[13] Lambi, *The Navy and German Power Politics*, p. 216.   [14] Ibid., pp. 243–4.

the Army—was not considered so vital on the other side of the North Sea. As preparations for an invasion were consigned to the realm of the impractical in Germany, some decision makers in Britain grew increasingly concerned that the Germans might be able to subjugate the country before Schlieffen's 'last cartridge' had been expended.

EARLY ASSESSMENTS OF THE GERMAN THREAT

The British armed services began to devote greater attention to the challenge of war against the Kaiser's empire around the turn of the century. Both the Admiralty and the War Office quickly identified that Germany posed a fundamentally different challenge to that which Britain had faced during the years of tension with France and Russia. With minimal colonial possessions to defend, Germany's nascent fleet was permanently concentrated in the North Sea and Baltic, placing it within ten hours' steaming from the British east coast. She also possessed the world's second largest merchant marine and some of the most extensive port and railway infrastructure in Europe, giving her ample shipping resources to embark an invading army swiftly and efficiently. Germany's geographical location exposed her commerce to British interference in wartime, but it also afforded her access to Britain's long and weakly defended eastern coastline. The Admiralty's method of preventing a French invasion—interposing a British squadron between the enemy fleet and the United Kingdom and relying upon the logistical difficulties of collecting sufficient shipping to preclude a *coup de main*—would not necessarily translate effectively to war against Germany. Allied to the formidable reputation of German arms and of the logistical and planning skills of the Great General Staff, these factors combined to foster a growing sense of threat to the British Isles by the turn of the century.

The growth of the German fleet had been revealed as a factor in the Admiralty's strategic calculations as early as the Fashoda Crisis. The passage of the first Naval Law in April 1898, which provided for the construction of a fleet of nineteen battleships and over forty cruisers over the next seven years, ensured that Britain would be unable to ignore German naval strength in future.[15] The Admiralty's interest in developments in Germany prompted the dispatch of the first naval attaché to Berlin in November 1900. The officer selected for this task, Commander Arthur Ewart, quickly formed the impression that the growth of German naval power was directed specifically against British interests.[16] Ewart's reports confirmed the existing suspicions of the Naval Intelligence Department and of the First Lord, Lord Selborne.[17] During a Cabinet debate on naval expenditure in late

[15] J. Steinberg, *Yesterday's Deterrent: Tirpitz and the Birth of the German Battle Fleet*, London: MacDonald, 1965.
[16] Kerr to Selborne, 28 April 1902, Selborne Papers, BOD., MS 31; M. S. Seligmann, *Spies in Uniform: British Military & Naval Intelligence on the Eve of the First World War*, Oxford: Oxford University Press, 2006, pp. 185–6.
[17] Marder, *Anatomy*, pp. 462–4.

1901 Selborne warned his colleagues that 'the naval policy of Germany ... is definite and persistent' and highlighted the fact that at the present rate of construction Germany would have 26 battleships 'massed in the North Sea' by 1907.[18]

The German Navy featured heavily in the discussions which preceded the formation of a permanent British Home Fleet in 1903. In late 1901 the Royal Naval College had conducted a series of war games, one of which simulated a war between Britain and a Russo-German combination in the North Sea. The balance of power within this coalition—which mirrored existing levels of relative strength—highlighted the growing power of the German Navy: seventeen of the twenty-four battleships of the combined 'Allied' force were German, as were the majority of cruisers and flotilla forces.[19] Captain Custance, the DNI, became convinced that a Home Fleet was necessary to 'cover the whole of the East Coast'. 'The magnitude of the force which may be required in the North Sea', he continued, 'will be practically determined by the power of the German Navy.'[20] Admiral Lord Walter Kerr, the Senior Naval Lord, agreed, noting that 'I think we shall have to take the German factor into consideration more than hitherto.'[21] During his time as Financial Secretary to the Admiralty, Arnold Forster re-iterated the threat the German fleet posed to the vulnerable east coast on a regular basis. After visiting Wilhelmshaven in 1902 he produced a series of 'Notes' on the topic of German naval power, which Selborne circulated to the Cabinet. The document stated that, 'in view of the great increase of the naval power of Germany ... and of the perfect organization of the German army under the direction of the German General Staff, it is necessary to contemplate the possibility of an attempted landing on the east coast'. He judged that an increased British naval presence in the North Sea, facilitated by new bases on the east coast, was vital to guard against this threat.[22] This theme was not confined to official documents. Erskine Childers' popular thriller *The Riddle of the Sands*, published in early 1903, condemned the lack of a British presence in the North Sea as inviting a surprise German assault. 'We have no North Sea naval base, no North Sea fleet, and no North Sea policy', he charged.[23] The book was influential enough for Selborne to have the NID examine it and the Cabinet was sufficiently perturbed by the situation to sanction funds for the development of a base in the Forth around the time Childers' novel appeared, despite the ongoing financial crisis stemming from the Boer War.[24]

---

[18] Selborne, 'The Navy Estimates and the Chancellor of the Exchequer's Memorandum on the Growth of Expenditure', 16 November 1901, pp. 10–11, CAB 37/59/118.

[19] NID, 'Precis of Strategical War Games carried out at the Royal Naval College, Greenwich. January to May 1902', November 1902, ADM 231/37/675.

[20] Custance, 'Memorandum on the Strategic Position in the North Sea', 28 May 1902, in Boyce ed., *Crisis*, p. 145.

[21] Kerr to Selborne, 28 April 1902, Selborne Papers, MS 31.

[22] Arnold-Forster, 'Notes on a Visit to Kiel and Wilhelmshaven, August 1902, and General Remarks on the German Navy and Naval Establishments', 15 September 1902, p. 15, CAB 37/62/133.

[23] E. Childers, *The Riddle of the Sands*, London, 1903, p. 279.

[24] Selborne to Battenberg, 27 April 1904, MS 44, fo. 9, Selborne Papers; Marder, *Anatomy*, pp. 466–7.

Concerns about a German attack on Britain were also expressed at the War Office.[25] In January 1902 the department produced an internal appreciation of the 'military resources of Germany and probable method of their employment in a war between Germany and England'. The author of this document was unequivocal in stating his view that an invasion would be well within Germany's military capability and that the topic was likely to have been well studied by the General Staff. The memorandum encapsulated what one naval official would later term 'German invasion theory' and merits lengthy quotation:

> The harbours of the Baltic [sic] Coast are not easily accessible to English ships of war and it is conceivable that transports loaded with troops at these ports might be brought loaded at the wharves of Hamburg and Bremen. From this point to the coast of the Eastern Counties is a distance of 300 miles, under favourable conditions 24 hours passage.
>
> The German authorities would hope that if the English fleet were temporarily absent from the Eastern end of the Channel, or if owing to favourable conditions a German fleet were able to hold the narrow passage between Calais and the coast of Kent, the time would be utilized to throw a force of say 300,000 men across the North Sea upon the Eastern coast of England.
>
> It is reported that transport for at least one half of this force would be available within a brief period.
>
> They would be prepared to accept the certainty that the communications by sea of such a force would be immediately severed, and the local supremacy referred to above would be lost, but they would consider that such a force once landed could live upon the country with ease and would be able to maintain themselves unreinforced for many weeks. Even if this force were ultimately forced to surrender or were destroyed, its loss would not be vital to the existence of the German Empire or army...[26]

Lieutenant Colonel Robertson, head of the Foreign Intelligence section of the Directorate of Mobilization and Intelligence, endorsed the document, adding his view that the German General Staff had 'long devoted careful study to the question' and suggesting that 'the most favourable opportunity will present itself during the first few days of a war', before the strength of the Royal Navy was brought fully to bear. He concluded that 'there are many good reasons why Germany should attempt invasion if the opportunity offers; and if she has decided to do this—a matter in which there is practically no doubt—she may be trusted to fully work out her plans beforehand'.[27] Whether these views reflected accurate British intelligence of the tentative German planning for a pre-emptive landing conducted between 1896 and 1899 is unclear. The War Office had maintained an attaché in Berlin since the 1860s; however, few reports dating from the period 1900–2 survive and those that do make no mention of the discovery of a German invasion plan.[28] It seems more likely that the indiscreet pronouncements made in the press

---

[25] Tyler, *The British Army and the Continent*, pp. 16–17; Marder, *Anatomy*, p. 465.

[26] H. A. Lawrence, 'Military resources of Germany and probable method of their employment in a war between Germany and England', 18 January 1902, pp. 6–7, E.2/4, WO 106/46.

[27] Robertson to Nicholson, 18 January 1902, attached to Lawrence, 'Military resources...', E.2/4, WO 106/46.

[28] Seligmann, *Spies in Uniform*, p. 160.

by several German military officers may have informed the military's concerns.[29] When the War Office assessed the feasibility of the German invasion again during the CID's enquiries into home defence in 1903, Robertson re-iterated that 'the idea of invading England has for long received the attention of German experts, and is not deemed by them to be nearly as impracticable as we are apt to think it'.[30] He continued:

> Baron von Edelsheim,[31] another officer attached to the General Staff, has explained how Germany, with her exceptional transport facilities, could throw upon the English coast within little more than thirty hours a force of 100,000 men, whose desperate but well-considered task it would be to win or be annihilated.[32]

The Admiralty agreed that 'more shipping would be available' for such an enterprise than in the case of France.[33] This was a telling admission. France's lack of merchant tonnage had been one of the Admiralty's primary arguments against the feasibility of a rapid cross-Channel invasion for the past two decades. The larger German merchant marine and extensive infrastructure at the German North Sea ports meant that a pre-emptive invasion attempt from across the North Sea could not so easily be dismissed on the grounds of logistics. The presence of the Royal Navy would be vital to forestalling a German landing.

CONCENTRATING IN HOME WATERS

The Admiralty had acknowledged the need to meet the steady growth of German naval power by developing a fully commissioned Home Fleet in May 1903. When established the new squadron comprised eight battleships and two armoured cruisers. However, the pace of German construction and the concentration of Tirpitz's fleet in northern European waters soon threatened to render this force inadequate to ensure British superiority in the waters around the United Kingdom. By the summer of 1904 Germany could boast twelve modern battleships ready for service in the North Sea. Due to the Channel Fleet's status as reinforcement to the Mediterranean, the Germans thus outmatched the nascent British Home Fleet. The C-in-C Channel Fleet, Admiral Wilson, warned Lord Selborne that, with Germany hostile, 'the Channel Fleet would have to be kept in Home waters instead of being sent to the Mediterranean'.[34] Even if Germany remained neutral at the

---

[29] Marder, *Anatomy*, p. 461. For the British press speculation on the topic, see Moon, 'Invasion', pp. 135–43; Morris, *Scaremongers*, pp. 101–2.

[30] W. R. Robertson, 'The Military Resources of Germany, and Probable Method of their Employment in a War between Germany and England', 7 February 1903, CAB 3/1/20A.

[31] Edelsheim was one of the officers who had provided interviews to the press discussing the feasibility of an invasion of Britain, adding weight to the notion that the War Office was basing its views upon the German press, rather than more secret sources: see Marder, *Anatomy*, p. 461.

[32] Robertson, 'The Military Resources of Germany', p. 6, CAB 3/1/20A.

[33] Battenberg, 'Notes by the Director of Naval Intelligence on the above Memorandum', 18 February 1903, CAB 3/1/20A, pp. 9–10.

[34] Wilson to Selborne, 6 March 1904, in Boyce ed., *Crisis*, p. 174.

outset of a conflict between Britain and the Dual Alliance, her diplomatic stance was sufficiently ambiguous to oblige the Admiralty to make due provision for German belligerency were Britain to be already engaged against another power. Failure to do so might tempt an opportunist declaration of war by Germany, resulting in a temporary loss of the command of the North Sea and a potential invasion, or the serious disruption of British trade. The German fleet therefore acted as a powerful constraint on the Admiralty's ability to detach forces to the Mediterranean and further afield.

The need to balance against Germany prompted in-depth discussions about recalling vessels from the Pacific to strengthen the Home Fleet. Eleven days before the Dogger Bank incident precipitated a war-scare with Russia, the outgoing Senior Naval Lord, Kerr, minuted Selborne stating:

> I am thinking much about what steps we should take in view of the recent additions to the German Fleet. They have now 12 1st class Battle-ships in permanent commission. The DNI has made some proposals, the principal one being the re-call of two of the China battle-ships.... The German Fleet as now composed has been I am sure, much on your mind, as it has on mine. One cannot shut one's eyes to the possibility of a Russo-German combination some day.[35]

Battenberg concurred, writing to Selborne that 'I wish we could get 2 Oceans home from China and with the 2 in reserve, replace the 4 Royal Sovereign in the Home Fleet. That is our weak spot—Germany and Russia have now between Kiel and Libau 17 first class battleships in commission.'[36]

By contrast the Admiralty was not particularly impressed by the danger of a purely Franco-Russian naval combination.[37] The French Navy was wracked by crippling financial constraints and a divided leadership which vacillated between building battleships and the more radical ideas of the *Jeune Ecole*, with disastrous results for procurement, efficiency, and morale.[38] The NID was well informed of these developments, as successive attachés reported on the confusion evident in French naval policy.[39] Developments in Russia appeared equally disordered.[40] The NID reported that the Russian fleet possessed no seaworthy destroyers at the end of 1903 and that the Black Sea Fleet did 'not possess a single cruiser which, according to English standards, could be reckoned in the second class, still less in the first'. Russia's lack of shipbuilding capacity obliged her to modernize older battleships, rather than build replacements. This process was utterly unsatisfactory for any first-class naval power and the NID noted disparagingly that the re-fitted

[35] Kerr to Selborne, 11 October 1904, in Boyce ed., *Crisis*, p. 181.

[36] Battenberg to Selborne, 16 October 1904, in Boyce ed., *Crisis*, p. 182.

[37] Seligmann, 'Great Security Mirage', pp. 21–4.

[38] Ropp, *Development of a Modern Navy*, pp. 283–305 and 324–59; Marder, *Anatomy*, pp. 468–75.

[39] Ottley, 'The French Naval Budget, 1903' in NID, 'Papers on Naval Subjects', April 1903, ADM 231/36/676; NID, 'Reports on Foreign Naval Affairs, 1904, Vol. I – France', August 1904, ADM 231/39/712.

[40] For the shortcomings in Russian naval procurement, see N. Papastratigakis, *Russian Imperialism and Naval Power: Military Strategy and the Build-Up to the Russo-Japanese War*, London: I. B. Tauris, 2011, pp. 55–8.

vessels 'would not stand a chance, ship for ship, against any of our Mediterranean battleships'.[41] These assessments were borne out by Russian failings against the Japanese in the Far East, which prompted Battenberg to suggest that 'the superiority of Great Britain in battle-ships may therefore be considered as being, in reality, greater than the figures...would indicate'.[42] When war with Russia over the Dogger Bank Crisis appeared imminent, Fisher crowed that 'the Russian Fleet is ours whenever we like to take it. The Lord has delivered them into our hands!'[43]

He was less sanguine about the Navy's current position vis-à-vis Germany, however, and made strengthening the forces stationed in the North Sea a priority upon assuming office as First Sea Lord. After arriving in post on Trafalgar Day 1904, Fisher commissioned Battenberg and the Naval Intelligence Department to chair an investigation into whether the existing distribution of the Navy's fleets remained appropriate to the needs of Britain's international position. The group's deliberations were temporarily interrupted on 22 October by the crisis resulting from the Russian Baltic Fleet's actions in the North Sea, but the prospect of war against Russia did not obscure the committee's gaze from what it considered to be the broader challenge facing the Admiralty: that of the steady growth of German power. The Battenberg Committee's central recommendation was that 'as the Kiel Fleet is considerably stronger than the Toulon Fleet, it follows that the Home Fleet should be considerably stronger than the Mediterranean Fleet'.[44] Germany had thus overtaken France as the primary threat to British maritime interests. On the basis of these recommendations the Admiralty re-distributed British naval forces early the following year. The existing Channel Fleet was relocated to Gibraltar and re-styled as the Atlantic Fleet. This change of nomenclature was accompanied by alterations to the composite of the force, which received the Navy's swiftest armoured vessels in order for it to perform the dual reinforcing role it had served since the 1890s more efficiently. The recently formed Home Fleet assumed the mantle of the 'Channel' Fleet, but unlike its predecessor would operate primarily in home waters. The new squadron was strengthened to consist of twelve battleships and six armoured cruisers, making it numerically equal to the German fleet at Kiel. The Mediterranean Fleet was reduced to eight battleships accordingly.[45] It is revealing of the Admiralty's priorities that when three additional ships were recalled from China during the summer, they too were added to the Channel Fleet, raising its strength to fifteen such vessels.[46] By early 1905 there was thus no doubt

[41] NID, 'Reports on Foreign Naval Affairs, 1904, Vol. I – Russia', p. 135, August 1904, ADM 231/39/712.

[42] Report of the Battenberg Committee, 10 November 1904, p. 2, ADM 1/7736.

[43] Fisher to Selborne, 6 November 1904, in Marder ed., *FGDN* II, p. 48.

[44] Battenberg, Typescript Memorandum on the Battleships Strength of the Home and Mediterranean Fleets, 7 November 1904, MB1/T5/28, Battenberg Papers, Hartley Library, University of Southampton. Numerous drafts of the papers relating to this re-distribution can be found in 'Redistribution of the Fleet in Home and Foreign Waters, Minutes on the First, Second, Third and Fourth Reports of Progress of Committee presided over by the Director of Naval Intelligence', 6 December 1904, ADM 1/7736.

[45] See report dated 10 November, 'Redistribution of the Fleet in Home and Foreign Waters', ADM 1/7736.

[46] Admiralty to C-in-C Channel Fleet, 3 July 1905, ADM 144/17, fo. 234.

that maintaining a fleet superior to that of Germany in the North Sea was a key tenet of Admiralty policy. Simply stationing more ships in home waters did not provide an adequate degree of security, however. As had been exposed in *Riddle of the Sands*, the lack of supporting infrastructure on the east coast made operating in the North Sea for a prolonged period a major challenge for the Navy. How best to secure command of the seas between Wilhelmshaven and the British east coast quickly became a key focus of British naval planning.

The NID and Naval College had studied operations against Germany since 1901. The plans they had produced comprised the mix of the aggressive inshore destroyer operations, attacks on coastal infrastructure, and close watches that had been developed during the period of tension with France in the 1880s and 1890s. However, fighting against Germany posed new challenges. Destroyers would be required to work at much greater distances from their bases, reducing their endurance and increasing the number of boats required to maintain a constant presence on station. Moreover, the opening of the Kaiser Wilhelm Canal between Kiel and the Elbe in 1895 meant that the Admiralty had to consider the possibility of the German fleet entering the North Sea either from the German Bight or via the Baltic route. The imperative to monitor two points of egress into the North Sea placed additional demands on the Navy's scouting forces, and constrained the Home Fleet's freedom of action as it would have to maintain itself in a position which enabled it to intercept a German force emerging from either debouch. This predicament prompted the Admiralty to develop schemes to obstruct the entrance to the canal with sunken hulks, thereby confining the German fleet to either the Baltic or North Sea. It was hoped that this would enable Britain to dominate the North Sea whilst only having to observe the entrance to the Kattegat, rather than dividing the Navy's attentions between Scandinavian waters and the German North Sea coast. If the blocking operations proved successful in closing the channels to large vessels then the DNI envisaged the British fleet operating 'somewhere within 30 miles of the Skaw' along with an attendant force of destroyers.[47]

Fisher supported these proactive inshore deployments and used the prospect of a British fleet passing through the Belts into the Baltic as rhetorical weapon on numerous occasions.[48] His oratory was supported by credible preparations. Hydrographic reports on potential anchorages in Scandinavian waters and in the Baltic were distributed to Admiral Wilson in February 1905,[49] the Channel Fleet

---

[47] Battenberg, 'The Organisation for War of Torpedo Craft in Home Waters', July 1904, *Naval Necessities* II, pp. 512–14, ADM 116/3093.

[48] Steinberg, 'The Copenhagen Complex'; R. Mackay, *Fisher of Kilverstone*, Oxford: Clarendon, 1973, pp. 330–1, 333–4; A. Lambert, 'Great Britain and the Baltic, 1890–1914' in P. Salmon and T. Barrow eds, *Britain and the Baltic: Studies in Commercial, Political and Cultural Relations, 1500–2000*, Sunderland: University of Sunderland Press, 2003, pp. 215–36; A. Lambert, '"This Is All We Want": Great Britain and the Baltic Approaches, 1815–1914' in Jørgen Sevaldsen ed., *Britain and Denmark: Political, Economic and Cultural Relations in the 19th and 20th Centuries*, Copenhagen: Copenhagen Museum Press, 2003, pp. 147–69; Grimes, *War Planning*, pp. 58–63, 65, 68–71; R. Dunley, 'Sir John Fisher and the Policy of Strategic Deterrence, 1904–1908', *War in History*, Vol. 22, No. 2, Apr., 2015, pp. 155–73.

[49] Admiralty to C-in-C Channel Fleet, 21 February 1905, ADM 144/17, fos 277–86.

frequented the Kattegat regularly,[50] and plans for an ultimately abortive summer cruise to St Petersburg were made the following year.[51] Fisher's posturing was sufficiently believable for the Kaiser to order the General Staff to consider invading Denmark in order to close the Belts to the Royal Navy in the event of an Anglo-German conflict.[52] The constraining factor in the Admiralty's plans was the requirement to maintain a fleet in the North Sea capable of defeating a German attempt to attack the east coast or the valuable Channel trade routes. Sunken hulks or coastal mines might seal the entrances to the North Sea in theory, but in practice such obstacles might eventually be cleared and the Admiralty remained reluctant to see the Channel Fleet penetrate the Baltic lest its absence encourage a German sortie in the south. Their Lordships issued specific guidance on this point: Admiral Wilson's orders instructed his Channel Fleet to 'prevent any attempt at invasion or landing of troops in any part of the United Kingdom'. He was free to dispose his forces as he saw fit 'provided adequate measures are taken to prevent invasion'. This meant that 'unless actually in pursuit of the Enemy you are not to pass into the Baltic without their Lordships permission'.[53] The Admiralty therefore subordinated offensive operations in the Baltic to the security of the British coastline.

The naval leadership and Fisher himself were consistent in their view that the capital ships of the British Fleet were central to the Navy's ability to prevent an invasion.[54] Destroyers and submarines formed an important part of the country's naval defences: the orders to the flotilla craft underlined this fact: 'in case of an attempted invasion it will be their duty to endeavour to torpedo the vessels carrying troops'. However, flotilla craft were not viewed as capable of interrupting an invasion if the armada was protected by enemy battleships. Indeed, the Navy's light forces were explicitly instructed to avoid engaging enemy capital ships unless under the most favourable of circumstances, merely doing 'all in their power to harass the expedition until the arrival of the Fleet'.[55] Fisher brooked no departure from this essential formula after 1904,[56] working consistently to increase the number of armoured warships in home waters by recalling vessels from foreign deployments and improving the efficiency of the older armoured vessels of the naval reserve. Manpower freed up by scrapping obsolete vessels was transferred to the reserve and used to provide older battleships and armoured cruisers—so-called 'emergency ships'—prepared to respond swiftly in time of crisis.[57] These armoured vessels

---

[50] Fisher to Corbett, 28 July 1905, in Marder ed., *FGDN* II, p. 63.

[51] Folder 'Proposed visit of Channel Fleet to the Baltic. Owing to troubles in Russia the entire cruise abandoned', ADM 1/7865.

[52] Grimes, *War Planning*, pp. 58–9.

[53] Admiralty, 'Orders for Command in Chief, Channel Fleet', 6 May 1905, p. 4, ADM 116/900B.

[54] For an alternative argument, see Lambert, *Revolution*, pp. 122–3.

[55] Admiralty, 'Memorandum to Commanders in Chief Channel Fleet and Home Ports and Admiralty (D)', May 1905, p. 3, ADM 116/900B. The memo is clearly an updated version of Battenberg's paper from the previous year.

[56] D. G. Morgan-Owen, '"History is a Record of Exploded Ideas": Sir John Fisher and Home Defence, 1904–10', *International History Review*, Vol. 36, No. 3, 2014, pp. 550–72.

[57] 'Here follows the elaboration of the previous Print by Sir John Fisher, which he gave to the Committee of Seven. General Outline', *Naval Necessities* I, p. 63, ADM 116/3092.

would bolster the defensive flotillas, stiffening the latter's ability to defend the British coastline.

If the Admiralty viewed the presence of a British fleet in the North Sea at all times as a strategic necessity in the event of war with Germany, obstacles to maintaining a squadron there did remain, however. This was particularly true at the very outset of war, when the lack of naval infrastructure on the east coast made positioning the Fleet in a suitable position a source of some difficulty.

'INSTANT READINESS FOR WAR'

Whilst Fisher projected confidence that his reforms had ensured the impossibility of 'even a dinghy' reaching the British coastline, the Admiralty regarded the threat of a surprise torpedo attack on a British fleet at the outset of war with a good deal more concern. The threat of such a *coup de main* had been well appreciated since the 1880s due to the development of the French *defense mobiles* in the Channel, a fact attested to by the extensive series of protected anchorages and harbours built along the south coast in which the fleet could seek shelter.[58] In 1901 the Admiralty had informed a joint-service conference on coastal defence that a pre-emptive torpedo attack under the cover of darkness was 'at once the most probable' and 'the most dangerous' form of likely attack on Britain.[59] This assessment appeared to be confirmed by the Japanese surprise assault on the Russian fleet in Port Arthur in February 1904, which provided a powerful example of the potential effectiveness of such an attack. The Japanese succeeded in damaging three Russian capital ships, blockaded the port, and thereby facilitated an unopposed landing at Incheon. Surprise had been used to circumvent an adversary's naval strength and to dispatch a military expedition across a contested sea. The implications for Britain were clear.[60]

In simple terms a surprise torpedo attack could be guarded against in one of three ways: building a protected anchorage in which ships could shelter; putting the fleet to sea and thereby making it difficult to locate; or moving the battleships out of range of enemy torpedo craft altogether. In the case of a war between Britain and Germany where the decisive theatre was almost certain to be the North Sea, the extensive fleet-support infrastructure on the English south coast would be of little utility. A fleet ensconced in Portsmouth or Plymouth would be further from the north-east coast than a German force crossing from Wilhelmshaven. The Nore, the only anchorage to the north of Dover that could accommodate a large fleet, had the pronounced disadvantage of a narrow and difficult tidal entrance through the Medway. The width of estuary rendered it very susceptible to enemy mining and it was considered an unsuitable fleet anchorage in wartime.

---

[58] Grimes, *War Planning*, 30–1.

[59] 'Report of a Conference between Admiralty and War Office Representatives to consider Conditions governing the Coast Defence of the United Kingdom in War as affected by Naval Considerations', February 1901, pp. 2–3, CAB 3/1/9.

[60] Marder, *FDSF* I, p. 344.

This lack of naval infrastructure on the east coast had prompted discussions about the necessity for a North Sea base since the turn of the century. Work to develop a site at Rosyth in the Firth of Forth had begun in 1901; however, completion of a major infrastructure project of this nature would be costly and protracted even under the best of circumstances. Progress was further complicated by ongoing debates in naval circles as to whether a dockyard and fleet anchorage were both required, and even whether the Queensferry Bridge made the Forth an unsuitable site altogether, vulnerable as it might prove to being blocked by an attack on the rail bridge.[61] When the prospect of war against Germany arose during the Morocco Crisis in late 1905, the Navy therefore had no suitable anchorage in the North Sea on which to base the Channel Fleet. The Admiralty's preferred alternative—putting the fleet to sea where it would be difficult to locate—was an extremely sensitive diplomatic step during a period of strained relations. The Channel Fleet was a highly visible symbol of British power and intent, whose position would be widely remarked upon during a period of international tension. Its deployment was thus subject to political approval. Unwilling to rely upon the wavering nerve of the Cabinet to protect the fleet, Fisher was obliged to adopt the only alternative available: removing the Channel Fleet from the radius of action of German flotilla craft.

As tensions with Germany escalated during the summer, Fisher asked Captain Ottley of the Naval Intelligence Department to prepare a statement outlining the most suitable dispositions of the British fleets for action against Germany. Sadly, Ottley's reply to Fisher's request did not survive the consolidation of the Admiralty records conducted in 1958.[62] The only trace of its having existed is a quotation from the document in Marder's work, which unfortunately makes no reference to where the DNI believed the Channel Fleet should be stationed before war broke out.[63] However, a document outlining the 'Dispositions of the Fleet in England Preparatory to an Outbreak of War with Germany' is preserved in Fisher's private papers. The Admiral's most recent biographer, who catalogued the collection, believed it to be part of the memorandum Ottley prepared for the First Sea Lord in June 1905.[64] If not June, then it seems almost certain that the document originated from the second half of 1905. This can be ascertained from the fact that the paper lists a series of vessels—HMS *Duke of Edinburgh*, *Argyll*, and *Donegal*—which were then undergoing trials and began to commission in January 1906—as shortly to become 'ready'.[65] The memorandum in Fisher's collection reveals that

[61] 'Notes by Sir John Fisher on New Proposals for the Information of Committee of Seven', 14 May 1904, Part III, in *Naval Necessities* I, p. 29, ADM 116/3092; 'Report of Committee on Armaments of Home Ports, 1905', p. 19, MSS/80/200, Box 3, Ballard Papers, NMM. Also see Marder, *FGDN* I, pp. 420–4; Mackay, *Fisher*, pp. 303, 314, 336–7.

[62] M. S. Seligmann, 'A Great American Scholar of the Royal Navy? The Disputed Legacy of Arthur Marder Revisited', *International History Review*, Vol. 38, No. 5, 2016 , pp. 1040–54.

[63] Marder, *Anatomy*, pp. 502–3.

[64] See the pencil date in his hand appended to the top of the document from when he catalogued the papers. Mackay, *Fisher*, vi.

[65] 'Dispositions of the Fleet in England, preparatory to an outbreak of War with Germany', FISR 5/12, CAC. Mackay, who catalogued Fisher's papers, noted at the top of the document that he believed it was written in June 1905.

the Admiralty intended to concentrate the Channel Fleet at Portland in order to safeguard it from a surprise torpedo attack. The emphasis placed on anti-torpedo measures was made clear from the outset, where the best location for the battle fleet during a period of strained relations with Germany was described as 'at Portland, dolphins closed'.[66] All of the Navy's fully commissioned flotilla forces and the 1st Cruiser Squadron were to be arranged in a protective barrier across the Strait of Dover, with orders to 'open fire on any torpedo craft attempting to pass, to capture, ram, sink and destroy them'. As soon as hostilities began, the 2nd Cruiser Squadron was instructed to proceed to the island of Heligoland, off the German North Sea coastline, as fast as possible and then to sweep back towards the Channel, in order to catch any German raiders returning to port. It was only after this anticipated 'first brush' was over that offensive operations in the North Sea would begin.[67] The only British battleships in the North Sea during this opening period of hostilities would, therefore, be the nucleus crew vessels of the naval reserve held at Sheerness, and even these vessels were directed to proceed into the basins at Chatham in order to protect them from torpedo attack.[68]

Due to the imperative to protect the Fleet from a pre-emptive strike, these dispositions betrayed the Admiralty's principle of maintaining a superior force of armoured warships in the North Sea at all times in the event of an Anglo-German war. Collecting the Channel Fleet at Portland would protect it from torpedo attack, but withdrawing so far into the Channel would significantly prejudice the fleet's ability to protect the east coast from a German strike at the outset of war. The seriousness with which the naval leadership viewed the situation was reflected in the attention the Navy's key planning organ—the Naval College—devoted to the issue during the winter of 1905–6. Fisher used the college to 'thrash out systematically all sorts of war problems' through intensive study and war gaming, the results of which regularly informed Admiralty planning.[69] During the Morocco Crisis, the college commenced testing a series of scenarios depicting a pre-emptive German attack on the British Isles. The outcome of the exercises demonstrated the vital importance of being able to observe both the German coastline *and* the Baltic entrances in order to ensure the detection and interdiction of German raiding parties. Locating the enemy in the expanses of the North Sea proved problematic: the final report admitted that success in defeating one landing had only been achieved 'owing to a mistake in drafting the sailing orders [of the transports]'. Concerningly for the Admiralty, one expedition of troops, embarked in four large, swift ocean liners, had succeeded in reaching the strategically vital munitions works at Barrow-in-Furness entirely unseen.[70] These findings confirmed the seriousness of the position at the outbreak of hostilities, when reliable monitoring of German movements

---

[66] Dolphins were a form of anti-torpedo net defence for moored warships.

[67] 'Dispositions of the Fleet in England, preparatory to an outbreak of War with Germany', June 1905, FISR 5/12, CAC.

[68] Ibid.

[69] Lambert, 'The Naval War Course', pp. 219–51; Grimes, *War Planning, passim*.

[70] 'War Plans, 1907' in P. Kemp ed., *The Fisher Papers*, London: Spottiswoode, Ballantyne, & Co., 1964, Vol. II, pp. 452–3.

would not be possible and the enemy would be able to put to sea undetected. Despite Fisher's insistence that the official figure for the number of German troops that might be landed in Britain might safely be reduced to '5, or to nothing at all',[71] the Admiralty's own internal considerations of the topic seemed to demonstrate that the initial period of hostilities might prove more problematic than the First Sea Lord cared to admit. The impression that Fisher might be protesting too strongly was not lost upon either Clarke or Balfour.

'THE GERMANS HAVE DRAWN UP PLANS'

The First Sea Lord's 'amazing exaggerations' about the defensive strength of the Navy, as Arnold-Forster described them, were made in the context of ongoing arguments with the War Office about the future of the auxiliary forces.[72] Balfour's invasion paper had not resolved the question of home defence in its entirety, dealing as it did only with an invasion of 70,000 men or more. The question of the forces required to deal with smaller raiding parties was less clear, intruding as it did into broader debates about providing an effective reserve for the Regular Army. The Admiralty had conceded that sorties of up to 5,000 men might conceivable evade the Fleet and reach the shore, and the Prime Minister had commissioned the naval authorities to examine which places on the east coast might be vulnerable to such attacks in December 1903.[73] With the Regular Army constituted and organized for operations overseas, how to respond to minor landings would clearly have important implications for the future of the auxiliary forces, the role, size, and cost of which had yet to be resolved since the damning report of the Norfolk Commission in early 1904. Still smarting from the implications that the CID's decision on home defence might have for the pool of trained manpower in Britain, the War Office adopted a resigned attitude in its assessments of the problem. Re-iterating the need for 'a reserve of fighting material imbued with sufficient military spirit', the military authorities warned that the training and efficiency of the auxiliary forces was 'not sufficient to enable them to oppose continental troops in the field'. As things stood, it would be significantly more efficient to maintain a smaller number of regular troops to fulfil the role of overwhelming raids of up to 5,000 men.[74] These arguments ignored the insurmountable political obstacles to dramatically curtailing the auxiliary forces size and function. As Brodrick had experienced prior to 1903, the Volunteers and Militia had powerful patrons in Parliament and within Cabinet. A compromise arrangement whereby the size and cost of the auxiliaries could be reduced and their efficiency improved appeared to represent the most realistic way forward. The important duty of rapidly overwhelming hostile raids appeared to offer a ready justification for such reforms, entailing as it would better

[71] Arnold-Forster diary, 1 March 1905, quoted in Moon, 'Invasion', p. 295.
[72] Arnold-Forster diary, 1 March 1905, Add MS 50345, fo. 1, BL.
[73] Minutes of the 27th Meeting of the CID, 12 December 1903, CAB 2/1/27.
[74] Lyttelton, 'The Strength of the Regular Army and Auxiliary Forces, having regard to Peace and War requirements', 1 May 1904, pp. 2–3, CAB 3/1/22A.

training and mobility and a more compact force.[75] 'The raid theory, in which I confess I do not believe', Clarke wrote, 'may be useful to serve as a peg on which to hang a justification of a more intelligible organisation for the Volunteers.'[76] With this objective in mind Clarke therefore returned to the question of raids and began collecting practical data upon which Balfour could build a case to reform the auxiliary forces during the spring of 1905.[77]

Clarke collated information from both services and from a range of other sources. The General Staff maintained its position that additional regular troops would be a more cost-effective means of ensuring that raids were overwhelmed promptly, particularly at the outset of war. Borrowing from Maurice's *Hostilities without Declaration of War*, they viewed a *coup de main* as the most dangerous form of attack as it would catch Britain with her auxiliaries unprepared and with the regulars preparing for dispatch abroad.[78] In response to a catalogue of historical examples from the War Office, Captain Ottley produced a characteristically stylish parody of the General Staff's case, a task which he combined with advertising the success of Fisher's recent re-organization of the Navy's fleet commands. 'How wildly fantastic, how totally devoid of the faintest shred of vraisemblance this idea is', Ottley wrote, 'the terrific engine of our sea-power... will interpose between this country and the old spectre of invasion a shield of perfect efficacy!'[79] The Admiralty apparently also ran a number of war games to test the feasibility of a military raid on a major port: the General Staff's justification for maintaining large garrisons at bases such as Portsmouth.[80] The findings of these simulations buttressed Ottley's effusions, conveniently supporting Fisher in his efforts to argue for reductions in military spending.

Beyond the service departments, Clarke also reached out to sources in Germany for information on the logistical feasibility of a surprise raid. The British intelligence network in Germany, such as it was, was composed primarily of military attachés and consular officials in key cities. Whilst neither could be described as official 'spies', their roles allowed them to gather a significant amount of information regarding German attitudes to Britain, infrastructure in their local areas, and aspects of military and naval policy. For Clarke's purposes, the British consular officials in the German North Sea ports were of particular significance, as they could provide figures regarding the tonnage of merchant vessels usually present in their particular port cities.[81] In early June, the CID wrote to the British officials in the primary German North Sea ports for information regarding the volume of merchant shipping 'available for the transport of Troops from German ports in the

[75] Clarke to Sandars, 27 June 1904, Add MS 49700, fos 52–3, BL.
[76] Clarke to Balfour, 25 March 1905, Add MS 49701, fo. 110, BL.
[77] Clarke to Balfour, 15 March 1905, Add MS 49701, fos 96–7, BL.
[78] Clarke to Balfour, 23 March 1905, Add MS 49701, fo. 103, BL.
[79] Ottley, '"Suddenness" in Naval Operations', 1 March 1905, Add MS 49710, fos 195–204, BL.
[80] Clarke to Balfour, 23 March 1905, Add MS 49701, fo. 103, BL.
[81] Seligmann, *Spies in Uniform*, pp. 81–6.

North Sea'.[82] Such figures would be vital to any meaningful study of the question of a surprise German landing, as the Admiralty had consistently emphasized during the 1890s and early 1900s. Clarke's enquiries generated a mixed response, one official writing back to express his regret at his 'inability to supply the information' due to having 'no means at [my] disposal whereby it can be obtained'.[83] Not all consular officials were so easily defeated, however.

The most extensive and useful reply came from the conscientious British consul in Hamburg, William Ward, who faithfully observed the volume of merchant shipping in the port himself. The consul reported that, on any given day in June, an average of 219,869 tons of German and 76,363 tons of British shipping could be found in the ports in the Elbe, Weser, and Ems estuaries. Whilst the proportion of these vessels available for military purposes would 'to a considerable degree depend upon the circumstances of the political situation', ample tonnage to carry a significant number of troops was certainly present.[84]

Clarke's studies were augmented by more professional sources of intelligence, namely the military and naval attachés posted to Germany. British military intelligence in particular consistently warned of German plans to launch a surprise assault on the British coast. The source of the majority of these reports was Lieutenant Colonel Count Gleichen. During the autumn the attaché had warned that 'the German aim would be to divert, beat off, or elude the British Fleet and land an army on our shores, sufficient to crush all opposition and to dictate terms of peace from London'.[85] He therefore reasoned that:

> The British Fleet must, in order to be successful, not only be theoretically in command of the sea, but must be actually present, in overwhelming force, at the right place, before the commencement of hostilities: if not, a German transport-fleet might give our ships the slip, and land an army on British shores.[86]

Gleichen was convinced that 'the Germans have drawn up plans, and keep them up to date, for an invasion of England',[87] a view he broadcast throughout his tenure in Berlin.[88] The regularity of these ominous warnings has meant that they have not received particularly detailed consideration from most scholars. However, perhaps unknowingly, the military attaché had struck directly at the heart of the strategic dilemma facing the Admiralty with his claim that the Navy had to be 'actually present, in overwhelming force, *at the right place*, before the commencement of hostilities'. As we have seen, at around the time Gleichen was writing, the Admiralty

---

[82] W. Ward, 'Estimate of the average registered tonnage of British and German steamships actually present in port on an ordinary working day in June, 1904, and available (after being duly fitted up) for carriage of troops and war material, in the German North Sea Ports', 27 June 1905, CAB 17/61, fos 187–90.

[83] R. Henderson to Clarke, 10 July 1905, CAB 17/61, fo. 194.

[84] Ward, 'Estimate of the average registered tonnage…', CAB 17/61, fos 189–90.

[85] Gleichen, 'Chapter XIII. Strategical Considerations with Regard to England', 9 November 1905, CAB 17/61, fo. 44.

[86] Gleichen, 'Strategical Considerations', CAB 17/61, fo. 45.

[87] Ibid., fos 49–51.   [88] Seligmann, *Spies in Uniform*, pp. 161–5.

had indicated that this would not be the case at the outset of war, when the Channel Fleet would have been sheltering at Portland.

Clarke's investigations did not result in rapid action on Balfour's part during the summer. Fisher in particular grew frustrated at the Prime Minister's prevarication over the joint operations sub-committee, but Balfour was preoccupied with ensuring that the CID would survive a change of government in the event of a Liberal victory at the forthcoming general election and proved unable to devote sufficient time to the issue to make any meaningful progress. The politicians then became focused upon the deteriorating situation in Europe and the demands of the forthcoming election.[89] Yet during November, in the midst of the campaign, Balfour took the decision to complete work on a definitive summation on the issue of hostile raids.[90] Perhaps the work represented a welcome distraction from the vicissitudes of party management, or maybe the Prime Minister was motivated simply to complete the process of army reform he had initiated in 1902–3 prior to the election. Whatever his reasoning, that he viewed the issue as urgent enough to consider whilst simultaneously leading his party to the polls is worthy of note. He commissioned Clarke to collect a final round of evidence during the middle of the month to assist him in his labours.[91] The most revealing appreciation that passed the Secretary's desk was an Admiralty paper on 'The Landing of German Troops in England', which set out the Navy's plans to defend the British coastline in some detail. The document re-iterated the naval leadership's long-stated position that it would be impossible for the Germans to collect sufficient merchant tonnage to convey a military expedition without arousing attention. It skirted the crucial question of where the Channel Fleet would be at the outset of war, stressing that the reserve forces in the North Sea would provide sufficient security to the east coast:

> The Channel Fleet is constituted so that it shall be able successfully to oppose the German Fleet in commission, but it is possible that the German Fleet may attain all that they desire, if by attracting the British Fleet, they draw them off from opposing the landing of the troops.
>
> If this is so, that portion of the British reserve of ships ready at 6 hours notice [the 'Emergency Ships'] is far more than enough to oppose the landing of troops even if they are accompanied by the whole German Fleet in reserve, many of which cannot be got ready under fourteen days.

Provided warning of an invasion fleet having sailed was received, the Admiralty estimated that the British Fleet would be able to intercept a raiding party making for the Tyne some 150 miles away from the north-east coast.[92] The requirement for intelligence of German movements was a major qualification, however. There was no guarantee that the Navy's cruiser and destroyer patrols would detect a German military expedition in the expanses of the North Sea, especially during the long hours of winter darkness or in conditions of reduced visibility such as often

---

[89] Mackay, *Balfour*, pp. 183–9, 214–26.   [90] Ibid., pp. 179–80.
[91] Ward to Law, 25 November 1905, CAB 17/61, fos 178–9.
[92] Admiralty, 'The Landing of German Troops in England', 18 November 1905, p. 2, CAB 17/22.

prevailed in the fogs and squalls common in the region. The flexibility afforded by the Kiel Canal meant that such a force might either emerge from the German river estuaries on the North Sea coastline, or sail from Kiel in the Baltic via the Kattegat, further complicating the Navy's task in locating its quarry. Moreover, nothing was said about the possibility of a pre-emptive strike, the threat so much discussed by the press, in popular literature, and by the General Staff.

Having gathered all the available information, Balfour set to work producing a memorandum for the CID on the topic of hostile raids. If he had hoped to reach a definitive verdict before the general election for political purposes, the demands of the campaign and leading his divided party to the polls frustrated his ambitions. However, despite the Unionists' catastrophic defeat at the election, Balfour remained sufficiently motivated to continue work on his raids appreciation and had a memorandum ready for circulation before the year's end. Displaying characteristic acuity, the former Prime Minister saw through the Admiralty's attempt to divert attention from the risks the Navy would run in the North Sea at the outset of a war with Germany.

'IT SEEMS TO BE JUST POSSIBLE'

The document Balfour produced between November and December 1905 considered the danger both of a French cross-Channel expedition and a German attempt to raid the Elswick works on the Tyne. The former Prime Minister was categorical in his dismissal of the first contingency, noting the formidable naval forces always in the Channel and the impossibility of concealing the necessary preparations due to the insufficiency of the merchant tonnage usually held in French Channel ports. His confidence did not, however, extend to the scenario of a German raid on the strategically vital armaments industry of north-eastern England. Balfour calculated that the crossing from the German port at Cuxhaven to the Tyne and disembarkation of troops would require a period of around sixty-four hours. He therefore reasoned that if the Channel Fleet was sufficiently distant from the threatened area of coast—a figure he put at 300 miles—then a landing might be successful it its absence:

> It seems to be just possible that if the weather was calm; if the Channel fleet was remote from the German Ocean; if the raiding Power could make the necessary preparation in absolute secrecy; if no hint of hostility or even of unfriendliness had reached the ears of the British Government; and if the enemy, in order to attain their object were prepared for the certain sacrifice of their expeditionary force and the possible defeat of their navy—if (I say) all these conditions were fulfilled, it seems not impossible that a landing might be effected near the mouth of the Tyne without serious interference from the sea...[93]

---

[93] Balfour, 'Possibility of a Raid by a Hostile Force on the British Coast', 12 December 1905, pp. 8–13, CAB 3/1/34, fo. 147.

The emphasis Balfour placed on the Channel Fleet being 'absent' or 'remote from the German Ocean' strongly suggests that he had read the Admiralty's paper on 'The Landing of German Troops in England' and that he was aware of the naval leadership's intention to remove the Channel Fleet to Portland during a period of strained relations with Germany. The distance from Portland to the mouth of the Tyne was considerably in excess of the 300 miles he suggested would enable a landing to occur before interference from the Channel Fleet. Balfour identified the same danger Gleichen had hinted at in his report on Germany a month earlier: if the British Fleet was not *at the right place* during the opening moves of an Anglo-German conflict, it would place the north-east coastline at risk of a pre-emptive military strike. He struck upon the essence of the strategic dilemma the Admiralty was to grapple with for the subsequent decade: how to prevent an invasion without exposing the Fleet to undue risk in the North Sea. What most historians have not appreciated, however, is that the Admiralty had little faith in Balfour's proposed solution to this problem.

The former Prime Minister postulated that increasing the strength of the submarine defences of the Tyne would provide adequate security against any surprise attack. This recommendation was not surprising. Balfour had shown a consistent predilection towards a naval solution to the problem of home defence since becoming Prime Minister and did not want to provide advocates of compulsory service with any excuse with which to demand additions to the auxiliary forces. He was also keenly interested in the utility of new technology and its applications for national and imperial defence. Fisher had worked hard to impress on him the value of underwater weaponry and of submarines in particular since 1903.[94] Whilst serving as C-in-C Portsmouth, the Admiral had assailed Balfour's private secretary with a veritable deluge of letters, memoranda, and official documents in an effort to convince the Tory leader that the submarine boat had made invasion 'impossible'.[95] On these grounds it was perhaps no surprise that Balfour concluded that providing a submarine defence for the Tyne might prevent even a raiding party from getting ashore in the vicinity. However, whilst Fisher's confidence in submarines appeared absolute in 1903, he had placed considerable (if subtle) qualifications on his views at the time. Reasoning that 'the landing places for an Invading Army are few', the Admiral had assumed that the seizure of a major port would be required to mount an invasion in force. 'All such suitable places on the Coasts of the United Kingdom can be counted on the fingers of one hand', he continued, 'and if provided with three Submarine Boats such would absolutely intimidate any transports from using them.'[96] Fisher's statements may have been accurate when applied to a full-scale cross-Channel invasion of upwards of 100,000 men and all their supplies, such as would have required the seizure of a port for a prolonged period. Its logic, however, did not necessarily extend to cover smaller landings of lightly equipped troops,

---

[94] Lambert, *FNR*, pp. 65–7, 86–90.

[95] Fisher to Sandars, 29 December 1903, pp. 3–4, Add MS 49710, BL; Mackay, *Fisher*, pp. 298–305, and *Balfour*, pp. 167–9.

[96] Fisher, 'Appendix A', p. 2, in 'Invasion and Submarines', ADM 116/942.

which could be conducted with considerable rapidity and, if necessary, on an open beach.

The limits of the Admiralty's faith in submarines to prevent a landing had been revealed earlier in 1905, during a discussion about the level of defences required to protect Malta. On that occasion Captain Ottley noted in an internal document that, whilst the addition of submarine boats to the existing defences of the island would 'add enormously to the difficulties and dangers of a hostile landing', 'in the present state of development of this type of vessel, it would hardly be safe to say that they would render land attack altogether impossible'.[97] Submarine boats remained vulnerable whilst on the surface, slow, lacking in visibility, and limited in range of action.[98] With enemy ships in the area, the craft would be obliged to dive, limiting their speed to 9 knots in the case of the newest 'B'-class boats and reducing their visibility even further.[99] Thus, whilst the Admiralty came to share Balfour's concerns at the vulnerability of the north-east coastline during the opening stages of an Anglo-German war, there is good reason to doubt the extent to which the naval leadership was prepared to rely upon the solution the former Prime Minister proposed to remedy the problem. Admitting this fact was a political impossibility for Admiral Fisher, however. In the context of the intense inter-service feuding over British strategy which was occurring in December 1905–January 1906, any statement bearing upon the relative responsibilities and importance of Army or Navy was highly sensitive. With the new Liberal government apparently willing to support the deployment of the Army to France or Belgium, all measures that might assist Fisher in his campaign to curtail military spending and influence were welcome at the Admiralty. He therefore mentioned nothing about whether submarines would provide an effective defence of the Tyne, or of the large tracts of vulnerable Scottish coastline to the north, endorsing Balfour's views enthusiastically and saying nothing more on the matter.[100]

Prioritizing bureaucratic politics over strategic exigency in this manner was a dangerous and irresponsible course for Fisher to adopt, a fact which became increasingly clear as 1906 drew on. The initial investigations conducted at the Naval College during the winter of 1905–6 had suggested that the threat Balfour had identified was a very real one. This was confirmed repeatedly by further investigations conducted during the following year. The first phase of the 1906 summer manoeuvres aimed to test the Navy's response to a surprise attack on the Channel Fleet or major home ports during a period of diplomatic strained relations. The findings were broadly positive, supporting Fisher's contention that large garrisons for well-defended ports might be reduced without risk. The final period of the manoeuvres was more problematic for the Admiralty, however. After a week of tactical exercises, a second staged scenario aimed to replicate an attack on British

[97] Ottley, 'Infantry Garrisons', 19 July 1905, ADM 116/3414.
[98] Mackay, *Fisher*, pp. 311 and 382, criticizes the size and capabilities of early submarines.
[99] M. F. Sueter, *The Evolution of the Submarine Boat, Mine and Torpedo from the Sixteenth Century to the Present Time*, Portsmouth, 1907, p. 160, I/5/1, Bethell Papers, Liddell Hart Centre for Military Archives.
[100] Admiralty to the CID, 17 May 1906, CAB 3/1/36A.

trade.[101] A lack of participation from commercial shipping stymied attempts to test the arrangements for the protection of seaborne commerce, but the exercises highlighted the vulnerability of the coastline during periods when naval forces were dispersed on other duties. Colonel Repington, the military correspondent of *The Times* who was to become a prominent antagonist of Fisher's over the issue of home defence, gleefully reported in a letter to his friend Raymond Marker that 'the naval manoeuvres have made the dinghy school look excessively foolish, as May with 4 battleships swept the Channel & landed at Scarborough unfought'.[102] This inspired an article the following month in which Repington entreated his readers not to be 'hypnotised by the phrases of schoolmen without practical acquaintance with war and its fluctuating chances' and to 'study the problem of invasion from the point of view of the enemy'.[103] Neither the official reports of the manoeuvres, nor *The Times* must have made pleasant reading for Fisher.

A pre-emptive German military strike again played a prominent part in a *Kriegspiel* conducted at the Naval War College during the autumn of 1906. Whilst the landing force was ultimately used as a feint, when news of an expedition sailing reached London the Channel and Atlantic Fleets were rushed to a point of concentration off the Humber in order to cover the east coast—demonstrating the potential for a threat of invasion to disrupt the normal course of naval operations.[104] In the same month Captain Philip Dumas, the naval attaché to Berlin, warned the Admiralty that complacency regarding Germany's capability to assemble an invasion attempt in secret would be dangerously unfounded. In a paper on the 'Invasion of England by Raids from North Sea Coast Towns', submitted on 25 November, Dumas stated that:

> I am, of course, aware that any such invasion has been declared to be impossible, but, as my researches and study of the subject have led me to a precisely opposite conclusion, though I consider that it is extremely unlikely that it would ever be attempted, I deem it my duty to lay some of the facts before you.
>
> I also wish to point out that we possess at present absolutely no means of obtaining timely warning from those districts in which any such raiding parties would be formed should strained relations cause them to come within the region of practical policy.

Dumas claimed that the German authorities were eminently capable of assembling sufficient troops, shipping, and stores without arousing any suspicion and pressed the Admiralty to improve the efficiency of British intelligence arrangements in Germany to remedy the problem.[105] In private, the attaché was sceptical about the prospect of such an undertaking and hinted that he had emphasized the danger in order to induce some action on the Admiralty's part.[106] Nevertheless, despite these

[101] NID, 'Great Britain. Naval Manoeuvres, 1906', ADM 231/47/817.
[102] Repington to Marker, 9 July 1906, Add MS 55277, fo. 76, BL.
[103] Repington, 'Moltke and Over-Sea Invasion', *The Times*, 29 August 1906, p. 6.
[104] 'Short Summary of other War Games' in Kemp ed., *Fisher Papers*, Vol. II, pp. 446–7.
[105] Dumas, 'Invasion of England by Raids from North Sea Coast Towns', 25 November 1906, in M. S. Seligmann ed., *Naval Intelligence from Germany: The Reports of the British Naval Attachés in Berlin, 1906–1914*, Aldershot: Ashgate, 2007, pp. 52–6.
[106] Seligmann, *Spies in Uniform*, p. 191.

ulterior motives, the timing of his report is suggestive. That Dumas chose the topic of invasion as the vehicle with which to draw attention to the need for improving British intelligence arrangements may suggest that he suspected the Admiralty would be sensitive to a report on this particular issue. Indeed, it is entirely plausible that he had been instructed to compile a report on the topic by the naval leadership.

That the naval authorities themselves viewed the topic with far greater serious-ness than is often supposed became clear in January 1907. Two months after dis-patching his warning about a surprise German attack, Dumas submitted his annual review on the German Navy. On that occasion he admitted that 'I believe such a raid to be possible though not probable, but under any circumstances, with a cruiser squadron in the vicinity, the arc of search is not great, and so its departure should be rapidly discovered and reported.'[107] More interesting is the response Dumas' report prompted at the Admiralty. Upon reading the document, Ottley produced a lengthy commentary. In it he revealed his conviction that:

The 'certainties' or, at least, the 'strong probabilities' in an Anglo-German war appear to be limited to

1. An instant German torpedo attack on our Fleet, and
2. Very probably a raid on the East Coast, or North of Great Britain.[108]

This was a significant admission on Ottley's behalf. It demonstrated how, in the eighteen months since Balfour had produced his paper on raids, the Admiralty's belief in the likelihood of a German torpedo attack on the British Fleet had extended to encompass a military raid on the British Isles. That Ottley considered such a threat to be *very probable* completely contradicts the viewpoint prevalent amongst historians that the Admiralty considered a German 'bolt from the blue' to be 'impossible', during Fisher's initial period as First Sea Lord (1904–10).[109] Far from being an imagined peril, the prospect of a German landing was viewed with genuine concern in the corridors of the Admiralty. How best to meet this danger became one of the most pressing operational questions Fisher faced from 1907 onwards.

---

[107] Dumas to Lascelles, 29 January 1907, p. 7, ADM 116/1043B, fo. 265.

[108] Unsigned paper, 'Copy M0171/07', commenting on a submission from Captain Dumas, the naval attaché to Germany, ADM 116/1043B, fos 256–61. The paper is likely to have been drafted by Ottley in February–March 1907: see Lambert, *Planning Armageddon*, pp. 80–1, n. 105.

[109] Moon, 'Invasion', pp. 338–9 and 340–6; Marder, *FDSF* I, pp. 345–6, 348–50; Mackay, *Fisher*, pp. 381–3, 384–6, 392–3; D. M. Schurman, *Julian S. Corbett: Historian of British Maritime Policy from Drake to Jellicoe*, London: Royal Historical Society, 1981, pp. 79–98; Morris, *Scaremongers*, pp. 131–2, 135–47; Gooch, 'Bolt from the Blue', p. 12; Ferguson, *Pity of War*, p. 8.

6

The North Sea Guard

The need to prepare a response to a potential Franco-German conflict had brought tensions between the two services and the CID secretariat to a head during January 1906. At the CID, Clarke judged that dispatching the Army to the Continent was the best option available given the lack of plans and preparation for co-ordinated joint action elsewhere, but in so doing embittered the Admiralty towards the committee and revealed the strategic deficit remaining in British defence administration. The CID had made no serious study of how to prosecute a war against Germany, leaving the two services to produce wildly divergent, independent approaches. If the committee aimed to address those issues that were 'naval, military, and political' in nature, much greater involvement in the planning processes of the service departments appeared an urgent necessity. As the threat of war receded, however, the more pressing question was not how to improve the CID's performance, but whether the new Liberal government would abolish the body altogether. The new PM, Campbell-Bannerman, had been a determined opponent of a British general staff whilst Secretary of State for War in the 1890s and had criticized the CID whilst leader of the opposition.[1] With a mixture of relief and hesitant optimism Esher recorded a conversation with the new premier in which Campbell-Bannerman stated that he 'would make no change until the working had been well tested'.[2] This equivocal position did not augur well for the committee's future, however, as previous experience suggested that an interested and involved PM in the chair was vital to the body's effectiveness. Whether the veteran Liberal would apply himself with the vigour and incisiveness of which Balfour had proved himself capable was uncertain. The challenges he would face were certainly no less arduous than those with which his predecessor had grappled.

Foremost amongst these difficulties would be how to overcome the legacy of bitterness and inter-service suspicion remaining from the acrimonious disputes over British strategy during the Morocco Crisis. The recommendations of Clarke's informal sub-committee had infuriated Fisher, and the Admiral became increasingly obdurate and uncooperative towards the CID as a result. By obstructing further discussion of strategic issues Fisher hoped to delay acceptance of the General Staff's plans long enough to ensure that they became a political impossibility.

---

[1] G. R. Searle, *The Quest for National Efficiency: A Study in British Politics and Political Thought, 1899–1914*, Berkeley and Los Angeles: University of California Press, 1971, pp. 223–7.

[2] Esher, journal entry, 13 December 1905, in Brett ed., *Esher* II, p. 128.

Given time, he hoped that the Liberals' strong Radical wing and Campbell-Bannerman's well-known opposition to Continental military involvement would enable him to restore the Admiralty's authority over strategic decision making. Yet as the Admiralty's concerns about the Navy's ability to detect and intercept raids destined for the east coast waxed during 1906, Fisher remained evasive in discussions of defensive considerations. The First Sea Lord did not want to damage the Admiralty's position in the eyes of the government by admitting that, under certain circumstances, it seemed possible that a German force could cross the North Sea with a reasonable chance of avoiding detection. Such a revelation might strengthen the hand of the General Staff and advocates of conscription in calling for additions to the Army and thus lessen the Admiralty's authority in discussions of British strategy still further. Fisher therefore pursued a purely naval solution to the problem of raids whilst withholding his concerns from the committee and the government. This high-risk approach was to enable him to navigate a formal investigation into the topic of home defence in 1907–8, but did nothing to solve the strategic predicament facing the Navy. Moreover, by deceiving the CID, the First Sea Lord placed his successors in an increasingly awkward position by bequeathing them an inheritance of half-truths and ambiguity.

* * *

The new Liberal administration was met with a stern test of its resolve even before it had arrived in power. Several of Campbell-Bannerman's pronouncements on the desirability of arms limitation had been picked up in the foreign press during the election campaign and were subject to widespread derision in France.[3] This sparked criticism from the Unionist benches that the new government would be too weak to defend British interests abroad, in this case embodied by the *entente* with France. Influential elements within the incoming government thus moved quickly to ensure that their Radical credentials and interest in arms control were not perceived as weakness by other powers—to the approval of the new opposition.[4] Richard Burdon Haldane, who assumed the poisoned chalice of the War Office, expressed his 'great fear' that foreign governments might perceive the administration as weak and encouraged resolve, informing his military advisers that 'the best way to preserve peace was to let the Germans know that we meant to fight'.[5] His colleague at the Foreign Office, Sir Edward Grey, concurred. Grey had considered Germany a source of danger since the turn of the century and advised Haldane that 'a situation might arise presently in which popular feeling might compel the govt. to go to the help of France'.[6] Grey resisted promising British support, but allowed unofficial contact to be made between the respective militaries in mid-January. Paris welcomed British co-operation, from the outset making clear that

---

[3] 'The Limitation of Armaments', *The Times*, 24 December 24th, 1905, p. 3.
[4] Williams, *Defending the Empire*, pp. 81–2.
[5] Ewart diary, 2 March 1906, GD527/1/1/135/8, NRS.
[6] Grey to Haldane, 6 January 1906, MSS 5907, fos 10–11, NLS; W. Mulligan, 'From Case to Narrative: The Marquess of Lansdowne, Sir Edward Grey, and the Threat from Germany, 1900–1906', *International History Review*, Vol. 30, No. 2, 2008, pp. 273–302.

France placed a particular premium on the rapid deployment of the British Army to the Continent, preferably within five or six days of the outset of hostilities. The General Staff concurred in this assessment, stressing the vital importance of rapid mobilization and deployment both to the outcome of operations in France and to Anglo-French relations.[7] Knowledge of these conversations was restricted to an inner ring of Cabinet ministers for reasons of party unity, but at the War Office 'there was little doubt that, if Germany fostered an unprovoked quarrel upon France, we should not be likely to leave the latter country in the lurch'.[8] The military conversations, which the General Staff subsequently identified as the origin of the 'With France' scheme which saw the British Expeditionary Force (BEF) deploy in 1914, have assumed greater significance in light of subsequent events than they possessed at the time.[9] They were not without immediate consequence, however. The suggestion that the Regular Army should be dispatched to the Continent as soon as possible in the event of a Franco-German war increased the onus on the Admiralty to make good its guarantees that a major landing in the United Kingdom was impossible in the face of British naval power.

The hiatus caused by the election and the situation in Europe had delayed any detailed consideration of Balfour's paper on raids, and it was to this topic that the committee returned to work on during the spring. The service departments were requested to respond to the former Prime Minister's assessment, in anticipation of it becoming an official CID document. The Admiralty issued a perfunctory note, expressing its concurrence with Balfour's findings.[10] Fisher had little to gain from quibbling with what amounted to an endorsement of his policy, despite his doubts about the ability of submarines to defend the vulnerable north-east and Scottish coastline. The General Staff produced a more thorough appreciation of the memorandum, which reflected how the Morocco Crisis had strengthened the case for military operations on the Continent. The Staff suggested that Balfour had overestimated both the tonnage and the number of men required to mount a surprise raid on a target such as the Elswick armament works on the Tyne and reminded the committee that the auxiliary forces would be unable to react to a hostile landing prior to general mobilization. They therefore warned that surprise raids might be used as a means of delaying British military participation in a general European war. An enemy might 'devote his attention to making a diversion on our coast in the proximity of the capital or any of our great commercial centres, in the hope of pressure being brought to bear upon the Government to retain regular troops in the country which may urgently be wanted for oversea expeditions'.[11] The sub-text was clear: if the Navy could not be relied upon to prevent small but potentially

---

[7] Repington to Marker, 26 January 1906, Add MS 55277, fo. 37, BL; Williamson Jr, *Politics of Grand Strategy*, pp. 70–7.

[8] Ewart diary, 8 February 1906, GD527/1/1/135/8, NRS.

[9] Nicholson, 'Action taken by the General Staff since 1906 in preparing a plan for rendering military assistance to France in the event of an unprovoked attack on that power by Germany', 6 November 1911, WO 106/49A/1.

[10] Admiralty to the CID, 17 May 1906, CAB 3/1/36A.

[11] Lyttelton, 'Remarks by the General Staff', 23 March 1906, p. 1, CAB 3/1/36A.

damaging raids with absolute certainty, then additional military provision would be required in order that the Regular Army be free to proceed overseas at the outbreak of war.

The precedent of 1870–1 suggested that a future Franco-German conflict might be concluded in a matter of weeks, making the rapid deployment of as many men as possible to the Continent an urgent necessity if Britain wished to influence the outcome in a meaningful fashion. Relying upon the delay resulting from the vast distances involved in a Russian movement towards India to raise more men for the Army, as Balfour had intended since 1904, would not be possible in the event of a general European war.[12] The requirement for rapid deployment on the maximum possible scale was reflected in the policies Haldane pursued at the War Office. Continuing Balfour's work of disentangling the Regular Army from any defensive responsibilities, the new Secretary of State explained to the CID his intention to 'assign definite functions to the Yeomanry and Volunteers for home defence, so that, in case of necessity, the country might safely be denuded of regular troops in time of war'.[13] This would provide for an expeditionary force of six divisions totalling some 158,000 men. Despite Haldane's later claim to have prepared this force in anticipation of the need for intervention on the Continent, at the time the destination of this army remained unspecified.[14] However, the emphasis on speed and the government's support for military conversations with the French was suggestive that operations in Europe had at least risen up the military's agenda after Morocco.[15] This was corroborated by the enthusiasm with which the General Staff pursued contacts with their French counterparts after 1906.[16]

Fisher's reaction to the General Staff's paper has not survived. It cannot have made pleasurable reading for the First Sea Lord, however. Beyond his objections to military co-operation with the French, the Staff's position created a problem for the First Sea Lord. For the previous eighteen months he had preached that the strength of the Navy would be sufficient to prevent any raid on the British coastline and that the size of the Army should be reduced accordingly. By early 1906, he appeared to have achieved this objective. Haldane reduced the scale of military preparedness to meet a hostile attack on the British Isles, eliminating the remaining London defences and obsolete coastal guns, and cutting ten battalions of infantry in an effort to restrict the Army Estimates to £28 million.[17] All that remained for Fisher was to convince the new government to induce the General Staff to co-operate in the Admiralty's amphibious schemes. Yet in his hour of apparent victory, the Admiralty was increasing its own assessment of the likelihood of a German raid reaching the British coast. Admitting that raids might be a realistic prospect threatened not only to justify additional spending on the Army,

---

[12] Balfour, 'Supplementary Note on the Military Needs of the Empire', 19 December 1904, CAB 38/6/124.
[13] Minutes of the 89th Meeting, 28 June 1906, CAB 2/2/89.
[14] Gooch, *Plans of War*, pp. 184, 262–4, 281–9, and *Prospect of War*, vii–viii; E. M. Spiers, *Haldane: An Army Reformer*, Edinburgh: Edinburgh University Press, 1980, pp. 81–3.
[15] Williamson Jr, *Politics of Grand Strategy*, pp. 90–2.
[16] d'Ombrain, *War Machinery*, pp. 89–90.   [17] Spiers, *Haldane*, pp. 57–9.

but to do so directly at the Navy's expense. Moreover, maintaining the Regular Army as an amphibious striking force was crucial to Fisher's vision of a maritime approach to a future Anglo-German war. Weakening the striking force due to defensive considerations was thus almost as undesirable as a rise in the Army Estimates. The Navy's ability to live up to the claims Fisher had made for it would thus be crucial to the enabling the Admiralty to regain the controlling influence over British strategic decision making it had lost in 1903–5. What Fisher required was to solve the problem of pre-emptive German raids quickly, and without reference to the War Office or the government. The First Sea Lord therefore adopted a highly secretive and controversial new distribution of British naval resources in order to improve the Navy's ability to meet the threat of a *coup de main* against Britain's north-eastern littoral. By linking these plans with economies in naval spending, Fisher sought to win the favour of the new Cabinet.

THE HOME FLEET REFORMS

In his first public speech after assuming office, Campbell-Bannerman had informed an audience at the Albert Hall that 'I hold the growth of armaments is a great danger to the peace of the world.'[18] Whilst the Liberal Imperialist element within the new Cabinet promised a degree of continuity with previous foreign policy, the party's desire for economies in defence spending was common knowledge. The Treasury was quick to pressure both service departments to reduce their expenditure. Radical suspicions of the Army and their sympathy for a blue-water imperial strategy meant that Haldane arrived at the War Office with a considerable weight of expectation on his shoulders. His target of a ceiling of £28 million for the Army Estimates was higher than many desired, but at least represented a start. The Admiralty too was subjected to political pressure to economize. The new Chancellor, Herbert Asquith, informed the naval leadership that the construction programme would have to be curtailed and that future infrastructure projects would be funded from within the Estimates rather than by a separate Loan Bill. Lord Tweedmouth, the new First Lord, was astounded to learn that 'a new Naval Works Loan Bill—even confined to provision for completion of existing works—is quite out of the question' and that his Estimates were to be scoured for reductions by the Cabinet.[19] Asquith swept Tweedmouth's feeble protests aside and only two armoured warships were ordered under the 1907–8 programme, with a third contingent upon foreign developments.[20]

The First Lord was also tasked with identifying additional economies from within the Navy's budget. Fisher duly assembled the Controller of the Navy,[21] the Accountant General, and the DNI to discuss potential savings. It was agreed that

---

[18] 'Sir H. Campbell-Bannerman at the Albert-Hall', *The Times*, 22 December 1905, p. 7.
[19] Asquith to Tweedmouth, 23 May 1906, Tweedmouth MSS, 254, [N]ational [M]useum of the [R]oyal [N]avy, Portsmouth.
[20] Tweedmouth to Asquith, 25 May 1906, MSS 254, NMRN; Mackay, *Fisher*, p. 358.
[21] The Third Sea Lord—responsible for procurement and *matériel*.

Russia's demise as a naval power and improving relations with France justified a reduction in the number of armoured warships maintained in full commission.[22] Japan's success in the east and the renewal of the Anglo-Japanese alliance had already enabled the Admiralty to recall the five battleships of the China squadron the previous June. During the Morocco Crisis these vessels had temporarily reinforced the Channel and Atlantic Fleets;[23] however, they were not required to ensure British superiority in European waters under normal circumstances. After discussing the issue with his colleagues, Fisher reported to Tweedmouth that transferring six battleships and four armoured cruisers into the reserve could provide an economy of around a quarter of a million pounds a year. Whilst a relatively modest sum, the saving would help to offset additional expenses incurred elsewhere and at least demonstrate a willingness to meet the Chancellor's demands.[24] The decision was duly sanctioned during the summer, and the Admiralty informed the senior C-in-Cs afloat of its intentions in a confidential letter in August. This communication explained that the quality of new vessels entering service during the next six months meant that a concomitant reduction in the number of units in full commission could safely be made without causing any reduction in overall capability. The manpower thereby released was to be re-distributed throughout the reserve, raising the strength of the nucleus crews to three-fifths in larger vessels and four-fifths in the flotilla forces, resulting in an increased level of readiness.[25] The distribution of ships in commission would also be changed, to concentrate the most modern battleships together in the Channel Fleet. Over the course of the following year, the Channel would be further bolstered by the arrival of the most modern new vessels including HMS *Dreadnought* and the new *Invincible* class armoured cruisers.[26] These changes were not solely motivated by financial considerations, however, and they contained within them the seed of what became Fisher's plan to mitigate the danger of German raids.

The link between Fisher's reallocation of the Navy's forces and his desire to bolster defensive provision in the waters around the British Isles becomes apparent when one considers the role he envisaged the ships held in reserve playing. The Admiralty viewed the vessels of the reserve as fully capable of fighting with their reduced complements, meaning that they could play an important part in a war in the North Sea despite not being in full commission. 'The wanting portion of the nucleus crews are not essential for the actual fighting and seagoing efficiency of the vessels so manned', Fisher explained, 'the extra portion of their crews if not embarked in time by the sudden sailing of the Fleet (say at a few hours notice) could be sent to their vessels afterwards ...'.[27] By increasing the crew complements of the armoured

[22] Ottley, 'The Balance of Naval Power'; Ottley and Ballard, 'Further Report of Committee on Relative Strength of the British Navy and Its Constitution, Distribution, and Personnel', 6 June 1905, both in Kemp ed., *Fisher Papers* II, pp. 59–68, 68–70.

[23] Grimes, *War Planning*, p. 63.

[24] Fisher to Tweedmouth, 29 May 1906, MSS 254/41, NMRN.

[25] Admiralty to C-in-Cs, 18 August 1906, in 'Admiralty Policy, Replies to Criticisms', October 1906, pp. 38–41, MSS 253/53, Crease Papers, NMRN.

[26] Fisher, 'The Size and Distribution of the Fleets in Commission' in 'Admiralty Policy, Replies to Criticisms', October 1906, p. 32, MSS 253/53, NMRN.

[27] Fisher, 'Preparation for War, The Subsidiary Services of War', 1905, pp. 1–4, FISR 5/12, CAC. Reprinted in *Naval Necessities* II, pp. 10–5, ADM 116/3093.

vessels of the reserve from 40 per cent to 60 per cent, Fisher's confidence in the vessels' availability for '*immediate* fighting' grew.[28] Battenberg considered the plans as 'a brilliant success', the product of 'Fisher's genius' in re-organizing the reserve.[29] In practical terms, they provided Britain with a significant operational advantage over the Kaiser's navy. The German system of crewing their fleet through a system of three-year conscription meant that even their fully commissioned ships were not prepared for immediate action for large parts of the year, as the new intake of men undertook their training.[30] Moreover, a large number of vessels in the Royal Navy's reserve were of comparable size, speed, and armament to the more recent additions to the High Seas Fleet. Fisher's reforms would therefore enable the Navy to con-centrate a quantitatively and qualitatively superior force in the North Sea more quickly than the Germans. This would confer a particular advantage at the outset of war, a fact the Admiralty had stressed to Balfour the previous autumn. In the paperwork it had prepared to inform Balfour's 'raids' paper, the Admiralty claimed that two battleships, two armoured cruisers, and twenty-three destroyers of the reserve could be at sea within nine hours of the order to sail being received. After fifteen hours the numbers of capital ships would have tripled and within three days some forty armoured warships would have become operable. In contrast the Admiralty estimated that the German reserve fleet would take at least two weeks to mobilize. Increasing the efficiency of the reserve forces thus enabled Fisher to reduce the Navy's reaction time and to provide a powerful second line of vessels with which to establish command of the North Sea as soon as possible after the outbreak of hostilities. These measures were integral to the naval leadership's efforts to defeat a pre-emptive German raid on the east coast, a fact that Fisher impressed in no uncertain terms upon Balfour. If the High Seas Fleet were deployed with the intention of diverting the attention of the Channel Fleet away from an invasion armada, then 'the British reserve of ships ready at 6 hours notice is far more than enough to oppose the landing of troops even if they are accompanied by the whole German Fleet in reserve'.[31] The centrality of these reforms to the Navy's ability to repel a German invasion attempt was underlined by the manner in which they evolved in close parallel with the escalation of the Admiralty's assessment of the German threat in 1906–7.

The first in what would become a series of modifications to the original plans occurred in October, when the general announcement of the Admiralty's inten-tions was made. Fisher revealed that he now intended to group the best vessels of the reserve into a new 'Home' Fleet, based upon the Nore.[32] Battenberg

---

[28] Fisher, 'The Size and Distribution of the Fleets in Commission' in 'Admiralty Policy, Replies to Criticisms', October 1906, p. 36, MSS 253/53, NMRN.

[29] Battenberg to Thursfield, 23 January 1907, in M. Kerr, *Prince Louis of Battenberg: Admiral of the Fleet*, London: Longmans, Green, & Co., 1934, p. 218.

[30] M. S. Seligmann, 'The Anglo-German Naval Race, 1898–1914', in T. Mahnken, J. Maiolo, and D. Stevenson eds, *Arms Races in International Politics: From the Nineteenth to the Twenty-First Century*, Oxford: Oxford University Press, 2016, pp. 24–5.

[31] Admiralty, 'The Landing of German Troops in England', 18 November 1905, CAB 17/22, fos 50–2.

[32] Admiralty to C-in-C Channel Fleet, 23 October 1906, ADM 144/17, fos 345–6.

subsequently claimed that Fisher had appropriated this idea from him in order to forestall criticism of the reduction in the number of vessels in full commission.[33] If so, then the First Sea Lord was largely successful in achieving his aim of positive press coverage. *The Times*, which had previously been critical of Fisher's willingness to indulge the government's predilection for prioritizing economy over effectiveness, recanted, praising 'the strategic wisdom of the Board of Admiralty'.[34] Even the notoriously critical C-in-C Mediterranean, Vice-Admiral Lord Charles Beresford, thought that 'the new ideas in the letter would appear to give a very effective and efficient Fighting Squadron, and add enormously to the Channel defence'.[35] Yet, within a month of the Home Fleet scheme becoming public the Admiralty had altered its plans again, this time in a more dramatic and controversial manner. On 22 November a letter was sent to Admiral Wilson, C-in-C of the Channel Fleet, informing him that when the HMS *Dreadnought* and new *Invincible* class armoured cruisers commissioned they would now join the fledgling *Home Fleet*, rather than his flag.[36] This was followed in early December by the news that the Admiralty intended to form a fully manned division of the Home Fleet at the Nore, consisting of the most modern armoured vessels of the reserve and all of its flotilla craft.[37] The Nore Division was to become an independent, fully commissioned fighting fleet. The Admiralty projected that by the end of 1907 the force would comprise six battleships (including *Dreadnought*), eight of the newest armoured cruisers, forty-eight destroyers, and twenty submarines, all fully manned. This would be achieved by assigning the newest *Lord Nelson* battleships and *Shannon* class armoured cruisers to the Nore, rather than the Channel squadron.[38] These announcements revealed a clear shift in policy, which historians have hitherto been unable to justify on strategic grounds.[39] On first inspection, such confusion appears well founded. Placing the most powerful warships in the Navy into what had until recently been a reserve squadron was certainly a superficially strange decision. Battenberg, for one, was unable to fathom any legitimate explanation for such a dramatic departure from earlier plans.[40] Yet, despite being well versed in the detail of the nucleus crew system, by this stage the former DNI was far removed from the Admiralty, commanding the 2nd Cruiser Squadron. This obscured the prevailing currents of strategic thought in Whitehall from his gaze and blinded him to the shift in priorities at the Admiralty which occurred over the winter of 1906–7.

At around the same time as it was informing Wilson that he would no longer receive HMS *Dreadnought*, the Admiralty instructed the Naval War College to renew its study of the feasibility of German raids. Upon the completion of

---

[33] Battenberg to Thursfield, 23 January 1907, quoted in Kerr, *Battenberg*, pp. 218–19.
[34] *The Times*, 24 October 1906, p. 9.
[35] Beresford to Tweedmouth, November 1906, p. 5, MSS 254/110-37, NMRN. Also see Mackay, *Fisher*, p. 365.
[36] Admiralty to C-in-C Channel Fleet, 22 November 1906, ADM 144/17.
[37] Admiralty, 'The Home Fleet', December 1906, p. 10, MSS 253/59, NMRN.
[38] Admiralty, 'The Home Fleet', December 1906, p. 4, MSS 253/59, NMRN.
[39] Mackay, *Fisher*, pp. 361–3; Morris, *Scaremongers*, p. 131; Lambert, *FNR*, pp. 160–1.
[40] Battenberg to Thursfield, 23 January 1907, quoted in Kerr, *Battenberg*, pp. 218–21.

these simulations Ottley requested that the President of the college, Captain Slade, summarize its findings for the First Sea Lord. 'The critical time', Slade reported, 'is from the rupture of diplomatic relations to about two days after the actual outbreak of hostilities, and in my opinion if she is going to try a *coup de main* against us, it will be then or much later in the war as the result of a long course of preliminary operations.'[41] This assessment is likely to have informed Ottley's conclusion that a military raid appeared one of the 'certainties' or, at least, the 'strong probabilities' of war with Germany.[42] Slade went on to reason that 'the importance of always having a strong force *in* the North Sea cannot be overrated, and it will probably be only the absence of this force which will tempt Germany to try and bring off such a coup'. 'The only safeguard', he recommended, 'is a strong naval force always at home ready to act at a moment's notice.'[43] Printed in the margin of the document, adjacent to the section stating the need for '*always having a strong force in the North Sea*' is a note from Fisher:[44] 'N.B. The Home Fleet'. The First Sea Lord also began referring to the new Nore Division as a 'permanent Home Guard'.[45] How the Admiralty intended to surmount the barriers which had prevented it from employing the Channel Fleet in this role remained unclear, however. Surely the Nore Division would be vulnerable to the same threat of torpedo attack that had led the Admiralty to remove the Channel Fleet from the North Sea during a period of strained relations?

No explicit explanation of the Admiralty's intentions for the Nore Division in early 1907 exists, but it is possible to gain a sense of Fisher's intentions from circumstantial sources. In the spring the First Sea Lord met with the new C-in-C Channel Fleet, Vice-Admiral Beresford, to discuss the question of war with Germany. Fisher provided the C-in-C with a series of printed plans, outlining the parameters of Admiralty strategic thought. The historian Julian Corbett had been employed to write an introduction to the document, in which he mirrored the earlier Home Fleet prints in referring to the Nore Division as 'an invincible Home guard'. Beresford was unimpressed. He submitted a caustic rejoinder the following month in which he castigated the Home Fleet as 'an invitation for our enemies to attack' and 'a fraud upon the public and a danger to the Empire'.[46] Why this might be so was revealed in July, when Captain Slade provided a tantalizing hint as to the role the Home Fleet would play in a letter to Corbett. Slade explained that 'the "guard" fleet need not be as strong as the fighting fleet...The guard is only a detachment of the fighting fleet which is placed in a position where it can observe & if necessary hold the enemy until the main force can come up.'[47] The Nore

---

[41] Slade to Fisher, 11 February 1907, in 'War Plans', pp. 21–2, MSS 253/20-32, NMRN. Italics in the original.
[42] 'Copy M0171/07', commenting on a submission from Captain Dumas, the naval attaché to Germany, ADM 116/1043B, fos 256–61.
[43] Slade to Fisher, 11 February 1907, in 'War Plans', pp. 21–2, MSS 253/20-32, NMRN.
[44] M. S. Seligmann, 'Germany's Ocean Greyhounds and the Royal Navy's First Battle Cruisers: An Historiographical Problem', *Diplomacy & Statecraft*, Vol. 27, No. 1, 2016, p. 179.
[45] Admiralty, 'The Home Fleet', December 1906, MSS 253/59, NMRN.
[46] Beresford to Admiralty, 8 May 1907, and enclosed remarks on 'War Plans', p. 18, ADM 116/1037.
[47] Slade to Corbett, 18 July 1907, CBT 13/2/2, Corbett Papers, NMM.

Division was thus seemingly to be employed independent of the Channel Fleet, in an advanced position in the North Sea, and to be ready to strike in the event of an emergency. That it was intended specifically to meet the threat of a German raid was confirmed later in the year. Before the Admiralty's intentions were revealed in full, however, Fisher was faced with the unwelcome prospect of renewed political interest in the question of home defence which threatened to expose his inchoate scheme.

CONSCRIPTION, HOME DEFENCE, AND UNDERHAND DEALINGS

The CID's investigations into the question of home defence between 1903 and 1905 had done little to bring any sense of finality to the on-going debate about the needs of the Army. Navalists such as Fisher and his carefully cultivated allies in the press maintained that the Army should be a more modest size and that its function ought to be subordinated to the Navy as part of a maritime imperial strategy. The First Sea Lord entreated Tweedmouth to impress this point upon the new Cabinet, writing to him on Christmas Day 1905 that '*now* is the time for a *pause* and a reduction in military strength'.[48] Conversely, significant elements within the Army, the Germanophobe press, and the Unionist Party remained convinced that strengthening Britain's military forces was a matter of vital national urgency, not only for the security of the country but for the balance of power in Europe. Whilst powerful sections of this lobby remained genuinely concerned at the prospect of a hostile invasion, others increasingly came to view the popular preoccupation with the threat of hostile attack as the perfect vehicle with which to advance their agenda for compulsory service and a more powerful Army. This attitude was encapsulated by H. A. Gwynne of *The Standard* in a letter to Raymond Marker, Kitchener's Military Secretary, in mid-1905. 'When I talk of an invasion of England', the editor wrote:

> you must remember that I always have at the back of my head that...if you talk to the people of England about the dangers of a war with Russia, and of the great strain that would come upon this country in such a case, they would not realise what it all meant, but talk to them of invasion and bring before them a picture of a possible raid, and they will bestir themselves...I go rather beyond perhaps the extreme probabilities of the case because I want to rouse England to the fact that she is in danger.[49]

The most consistent public advocate of universal training was the aged Field Marshal Lord Roberts, for whom Gwynne had run a press campaign during the Boer War. Roberts had retired from the CID in late 1905 in order to take up the chairmanship of the National Service League and to present the case for compulsory national service to the country. The following year he had added his name to

---

[48] Fisher to Tweedmouth, 23 December 1905, in Marder, *FGDN* II, p. 65.
[49] Gywnne to Marker, 16 May 1905, Add MS 55277, fo. 166, BL.

William Le Quex's sensational novel, *The Invasion of 1910*, which depicted a fictionalized German attack on Britain and was serialized by Lord Northcliffe in the *Daily Mail*. Roberts vetted the manuscript and provided a foreword in which he made an impassioned plea for compulsory service in order to meet the German threat.[50] The Field Marshal advertised his views with considerable vigour for a man of his age, delivering numerous speeches in the House of Lords and around the country, and cultivating relationships with journalists such J. L. Garvin, editor of *The Observer*.[51] However, whilst he was the most dogged and well-loved advocate of compulsory service, Roberts was not a shrewd political operator and the bluntness with which he rehearsed the same tired arguments reduced the impact of his efforts. After a meeting of the National Defence Association in the summer of 1906 at which Roberts had held the chair, one co-conspirator lamented how 'a more useless person for the job no one could find...the real work is done by a smaller body'.[52] More subtle methods were required to secure the consensus necessary to force the Liberal government to address the deficiencies apparent in Britain's military preparedness.

Most influential in this regard was the military correspondent of *The Times*, Charles à Court Repington.[53] Formerly a promising army officer, Repington had served with distinction in the Intelligence Division and during the Boer War, but had been forced to retire his commission in 1902 after an extra-marital affair resulted in a public divorce scandal. Thereafter he quickly established himself as an influential commentator on defence matters, securing the prestigious appointment of military correspondent for *The Times*. Initially an opponent of invasion scaremongering,[54] Repington's advocacy of direct British military support for France led him to conclude that compulsory service was the only sure means of enabling Britain to play a meaningful role in the event of a future war with a fellow Great Power. He was also suspicious of the Admiralty's doctrinaire instance that 'command of the sea' would guarantee the inviolability of British shores, which he labelled a 'shibboleth'. Repington considered that the weakness of the British military enfeebled the Foreign Office in its efforts to secure the balance of power and made Britain an unreliable partner for continental France: 'unless we show a disposition to share in the real struggle at the decisive point, good bye to all ideas of a French alliance!'[55] He therefore came to see the threat of invasion as a vehicle through which to alert the British people to the need for more widespread and serious military training and preparedness. Intrigues such as these marked Repington out from previous advocates of universal training: he thought in

[50] R. J. Q. Adams and P. Porier, *The Conscription Controversy in Great Britain, 1900–1918*, Columbus, OH: Ohio State University Press, 1987, p. 4.

[51] Morris, *Scaremongers*, pp. 230–2.

[52] Repington to Marker, 5 July 1906, Add MS 55277, fos 76–7, BL.

[53] The best summary of Repington's activities in this regard is A. J. A. Morris, *Reporting the First World War: Charles Repington, The Times and the Great War*, Cambridge: Cambridge University Press, 2015, pp. 73–87.

[54] Morris, *Scaremongers*, p. 117.

[55] Repington to Esher, 14 January 1906, in A. J. A. Morris ed., *The Letters of Lieutenant-Colonel Charles à Court Repington: Military Correspondent of The Times, 1903–1918*, Stroud: Sutton, 1999, p. 80.

political terms and was familiar with the back channels necessary to secure access to the heart of the establishment. However, he also appreciated the value of Roberts' name and reputation and the credibility it afforded to his plans. He therefore began co-operating with the Field Marshal openly to challenge the Admiralty's views on national defence. By doing so, he hoped that he might overturn Balfour's decision to assign the principal role in guaranteeing national security to the Navy and thereby revive the debate on compulsion.

Attacking the Admiralty was a task to which Repington took with considerable gusto, having developed an increasing personal animus against Fisher after the Admiral's intransigence during the Morocco Crisis. Throughout the summer, the military correspondent wrote articles and delivered speeches, in which he attempted to 'destroy' Balfour's ruling on home defence.[56] The former Prime Minister maintained an active interest in defence matters and the CID from the opposition benches and monitored Repington's activities closely. Demonstrating a fair-minded willingness to re-open the debate, Balfour even shared the stage with Repington on several occasions to discuss the issue and provided encouragement to *The Times* correspondent's campaign. Repington worked hard to cultivate the Unionist leader's support. As the founder of the CID and leader of the opposition, Balfour retained considerable influence. Furthermore, although the Unionist Party was non-committal on the topic of universal training for political reasons, a significant section of its MPs were sympathetic to the cause and could be counted on to pressure Balfour on the issue.[57] A series of attacks on the Admiralty during the autumn were made all the more stinging by the support Repington garnered from retired admirals such as Gerald 'Sharky' Noel and Cyprian Bridge and by the coverage provided to them by *The Times*. Repington delighted in bringing 'a whole flotilla of Navalists down on me', as 'until we have put an end to all the damned nonsense that is written about sea power we shall never get our national Army'.[58]

'HOW THE WIND IS BLOWING'

By January 1907, criticisms of Admiralty policy were causing Fisher a considerable degree of concern. Captain Herbert Richmond, the First Sea Lord's naval assistant, confided to his diary his disappointment at having been recalled from leave a week early on 15 January in order to assist in the defence of Fisher's policies. 'It rather spoilt my plans', Richmond complained, recounting how:

> I went in to Jack Fisher on my arrival and he started me in with various jobs of work:
> To begin with there was a memorandum from the Foreign & Colonial Offices object-
> ing to the new distribution of the Fleet and this I was told to reply to...the whole
> thing was a straw which shewed how the wind is blowing and the intense opposition
> which is being fostered from all quarters to the 1st Sea Lord...The Home Fleet, just

[56] Repington to Marker, 5 July 1906, Add MS, 55277, fo. 76, BL; Morris, *Repington*, pp. 76–8.
[57] Williams, *Defend the Empire*, pp. 138–55.
[58] Repington to Esher, 22 November 1906, in Morris ed., *Repington*, p. 113.

established, adds fuel and I am now busy in putting forward the arguments shewing it is considered an improvement on the preceding arrangement.[59]

Yet despite the Admiralty's best efforts, deflecting criticism of either Fisher or the Home Fleet proved difficult. Opponents of Fisher's regime were heartened by the discord evident between Beresford and the Admiralty and mounted a fierce campaign against his administration during the spring. Doubts over the Admiralty's Home Fleet reforms provided an unrivalled opportunity for advocates of compulsory service to challenge the primacy that Balfour's ruling on home defence had afforded to the Navy in matters of national security. Fisher therefore faced attacks both from within the Navy and from those who sought to disrupt the influence he had had upon Army reform and defence policy as a whole since serving on the Esher Committee.

Repington delighted in fostering opposition to Fisher, but recognized that the only means to extract a political commitment to a system of compulsion from a reluctant government would be to have the issue of invasion re-examined at Cabinet level.[60] To this end, he sought to exploit his relationship with Balfour to return the matter to the Committee of Imperial Defence. In May Repington, Roberts, and their supporters met with the Conservative leader in order to discuss the possibility of Balfour giving a lecture at the RUSI after Repington had delivered a paper of his own on the subject of invasion. At this meeting, or another soon thereafter, Repington appears to have shown Balfour a detailed draft of the presentation he intended to give, entitled 'Invasion and Home Defence',[61] and provided him with a series of 'Notes on Invasion'. These papers furnished details of German capabilities provided by Repington's contacts in the General Staff and by information collected on trips to Germany, which had been funded by wealthy backers of the national service cause.[62] Balfour was sufficiently impressed to write a long letter to Sir George Clarke in which he advocated that the CID conduct a re-consideration of the issue of national defence.[63] Convinced that the Navy ought properly to remain the first line of national defence, Clarke sought to curb the worst of Repington's excesses in his own pieces for *The Times*.[64] The Secretary's pseudonymous expositions on naval power delighted Fisher,[65] yet Clarke was defending the principal of a maritime imperial strategy, not the Admiralty. Since the Morocco Crisis, the Secretary had harboured deep-seated concerns about Fisher's capacity as a strategist and more recently had opposed the construction of HMS *Dreadnought* and Fisher's Home Fleet plans, dissecting both in letters to the Prime Minister.[66]

---

[59] Richmond, diary entry for 1 February 1907, RIC/1/7, Richmond Papers, NMM.
[60] Morris, *Scaremongers*, pp. 120–1.
[61] Repington to Roberts, 23 May 1907, NAM 1971-23-199.
[62] Morris, *Scaremongers*, p. 120.
[63] Balfour to Clarke, 20 July 1907, reproduced in CID, CAB 16/3A, fos 3–4.
[64] Morris, *Scaremongers*, pp. 118–22, 131.
[65] Fisher to Clarke, 12 September 1907, in Marder ed., *FGDN* II, pp. 131–3.
[66] Esher to Clarke, 18 February 1906, in Brett ed., *Esher* II, p. 144; Fisher to Esher, 18 February 1906, in Marder ed., *FGDN* III, pp. 30–1; Clarke to Campbell-Bannerman, 15 November 1906, and 'Note on the Redistribution of our Naval Forces', Add MS 41213, fos 236–40, BL.

In spite of personal misgivings about Repington's motives, Clarke therefore endorsed Balfour's proposal, agreeing that its contents 'deserve consideration'.[67] 'The main consideration', he questioned, 'is, can we count upon the presence of a sufficient and perfectly *ready* naval force in the North Sea?'[68] Clearly the Secretary viewed his wider aim of subordinating the Admiralty and the War Office to the overall direction of the CID as more important than silencing the demands of Repington and Roberts.[69] Clarke's attempt to use Repington's campaign in order to secure his own political objectives ensured that the Home Fleet would be at the centre of the resulting debate. Unbeknownst to him, this was precisely the situation the First Sea Lord wished to avoid, as secrecy was integral to the entire rationale of the 'Home Guard' and its mission to protect the east coast.

Upon learning that the government was considering Clarke's recommendation, Fisher was livid. Beyond undermining the Navy's strategy for the opening moves of an Anglo-German war, a renewed investigation of the topic threatened to re-open the broader issues of policy Balfour had settled in 1903–5. If successful, Repington's case might result in increased spending on the Army, thereby strengthening the hand of the General Staff in the on-going contest to shape British strategy in the event of war in Europe. Anglo-French military staff talks were still continuing and in August the DMO had intimated to Paris that four British infantry divisions and a cavalry division could be in the line within eighteen days of mobilization.[70] Fisher knew of these contacts as the Admiralty Transport Department was involved in the discussion of moving troops across the Channel.[71] On a more personal level, the application of close scrutiny to the Home Fleet reforms might expose Fisher to attacks from Beresford and other opponents within the Navy, weakening his position as First Sea Lord. He complained bitterly to Tweedmouth on 17 August that 'the defence of the country against oversea attack is in the hands of the Admiralty, and I strongly deprecate the suggestion of a Sub-Committee of the CID being appointed to investigate it'. He then set about producing a lengthy refutation of the arguments Repington and Roberts had presented, in an attempt to have their agitation quashed before it could result in an official inquiry.[72] Fisher argued for adherence to Balfour's original findings, insisting that only the Admiralty could provide expert opinion on the 'adequacy of the naval defence of these islands' and that 'the best security' against invasion was 'the North Sea Division of the Home Fleet'.[73] Tantalizingly, he even alluded to the Admiralty's highly secretive intentions for the 'Home Guard': 'The exact rendezvous of the various divisions of the British Fleet in home waters, the nature of the telegraphic orders it will receive, the positions which, during a period of strained relations, the

[67] Clarke, 'Note by the Secretary', August 1907, CAB 3/2/42.

[68] Clarke, 'Note by the Secretary', August 1907, p. 4, CAB 3/2/42.

[69] On the key role of the CID, see Clarke to Campbell-Bannerman, 17 July and 10 November 1906, Campbell-Bannerman Papers, Add MS 41213, fos 196, 232.

[70] Williamson Jr, *Politics of Grand Strategy*; Mackay, *Fisher*, p. 381.

[71] d'Ombrain, *War Machinery*, p. 91.

[72] Fisher to Tweedmouth, 17 August 1907, quoted in Mackay, *Fisher*, p. 382.

[73] Fisher, 'Covering Memorandum by the First Sea Lord', 22 August 1907, in Admiralty, 'Invasion and Raids', FISR 8/43, Fisher Papers, CAC.

flotillas of destroyers and submarines will be found, are matters upon which no information is ever likely to be available to outsiders.'[74] Fisher's contribution was supported by a similar production from the new DNI, Captain Slade, who had succeeded Ottley in the autumn of 1907. Slade re-iterated the need for secrecy, claiming that 'one of the essential qualities of a good defensive position is that it enables the defended to surprise the attacker with his counter-stroke, but if we publish what this counter-stroke is going to be, we abandon half the advantage of the defensive position'.[75] The vigour with which the First Sea Lord expounded the virtues of the Home Fleet was insufficient to convince informed observers as to the credibility of his policy, however. Lord Esher, a close friend and supporter of Fisher's, wondered quizzically in his journal 'What has he to conceal? He made a great point of the impossibility of divulging a naval plan of campaign. Everyone agrees to that. But there is no necessity for anything of the kind.'[76] Little did Esher know, Fisher had a lot to hide. The Admiralty was apparently intending to operate the Navy's most powerful new warships in an advanced position, considered to be too dangerous for the Channel Fleet, with the intention of ambushing any pre-emptive strike the Germans might have launched against the east coast. Sharing these plans would void the secrecy integral to their successes and require a new approach to dealing with the problem of raids. Committed to his Home Guard, Fisher remained steadfast.

Despite the Admiralty's best efforts to fight a rearguard action against the formation of an inquiry, on 9 November Repington reported triumphantly to Lord Roberts that the 'Cabinet decided to hold the inquiry we desire, & it will begin November 27th'.[77] If Fisher did not have enough reason to be wary on grounds of his policy, the surreptitious support Beresford was providing to the 'invasionist' camp underlined the direct threat to his own position. Whether spurred on by the results of the tactical exercises his fleet had conducted during the summer—which he felt had underlined the inadequacy of Fisher's re-distribution—or by his own bitter resentment of Fisher, during the autumn the C-in-C Channel Fleet had begun actively to conspire and to undermine the Admiralty by providing sensitive information to Repington. On 22 October the latter had written to Lord Roberts, explaining that 'I have also had some confidential talk with Lord Charles Beresford and also with Sturdee his Chief of Staff, and I am most anxious that these and other practical men shall be examined, for they seem far from satisfied that they can defend these shores with existing arrangements, or rather the want of them.'[78] Discussing the possibility of an official inquiry into home defence, the rebellious Admiral warned Repington that 'I know my old friend Fisher very well, and am perfectly confident that what he wants to do is to pack it with his own people...What

[74] Ibid., p. 1.
[75] Slade, 'Memorandum by Head of Naval War College', 16 August 1907, in 'Invasion and Raids', p. 22, FISR 8/43, CAC.
[76] Esher diary, 28 November 1907, in Brett ed., *Esher* II, p. 263.
[77] Repington to Roberts, 9 November 1907, NAM 1971-01-23-62.
[78] Repington to Roberts, 22 October 1907, pp. 2–3, NAM 1971-01-23-62.

we want is a public enquiry.'[79] Given the covert nature of the Admiralty's plans to frustrate a German surprise attack and Beresford's history of leaking confidential information,[80] it is easy to see why Fisher attempted to divert attention away from the Home Fleet scheme. The extensive list of witnesses Repington hoped to call rendered any hope of maintaining the confidentiality of the Admiralty's intentions for the Home Fleet virtually impossible. The 'invasionists' submitted a list of possible candidates for examination which included, amongst others, the Prince of Wales, the previous three First Naval Lords and Directors of Naval Intelligence, the commanders of all the major British fleets and 'Lord Rothschild & other financial experts'.[81] Repington even hoped that 'witnesses should see all papers & be told what points they will be examined upon'.[82] Such a list of naval attendees would represent a serious challenge to the authority of the current Board of Admiralty. Furthermore, the presence of so many non-military or naval persons offered scant prospect of maintaining the secrecy of any strategic plans that might be discussed. Ultimately, the list was drastically curtailed and even Repington and Lord Lovat were excluded from parts of several meetings deemed to be too sensitive for civilians, underlining the concerns of the CID about covert information being leaked. However, by the time proceedings had begun it seems that the committee had lost Fisher's confidence almost entirely. The First Sea Lord viewed Repington with particular hostility and suspicion.[83]

The meetings opened as planned on 27 November, much to Fisher's chagrin. The First Sea Lord approached the proceedings with a characteristically robust attitude, writing to Balfour after the first meeting that 'we've got that Invasion Bogey in hand which I thought you had laid at rest for ever. *I hope we shall smash it completely this time.*'[84] However, this chauvinism was calculated to conceal what must have been very genuine personal and political concerns. Fisher's troubles worsened during the autumn as the Admiralty's latest assessments suggested that the Germans might succeed in landing a force sufficient to subdue the country if the Home Fleet were absent from the North Sea.

THE FREMANTLE COMMITTEE

In anticipation of the CID inquiry, the Admiralty returned to the War College for an updated appreciation of the Navy's ability to respond to a pre-emptive German raid. The new President of the college, Rear Admiral Robert S. Lowry, received a message from Slade in early November asking him to assemble a group of officers

---

[79] Beresford to Repington, 17 November 1907, NAM 1971-01-23-62.

[80] Mackay, *Fisher*, pp. 365–6.

[81] 'Invasion Enquiry—Suggested List of Witnesses', CAB 1/7/9, fo. 157; a handwritten copy of this list, dated 12 November 1907, can be found attached to Repington to Roberts, 12 November 1907, NAM 1971-01-23-62.

[82] Repington to Roberts, 25 November 1907, NAM 1971-01-23-62.

[83] Fisher to John Leyland, 22 September 1907, and Fisher to the Prince of Wales, 16 October 1907, both in Marder, *FGDN* II, pp. 136, 147.

[84] Fisher to Balfour, 29 November 1907, Add MS 49712, fo. 21, BL.

to look into what was to become known as 'German invasion theory'.[85] Lowry convened a small committee of four senior captains to conduct the investigation. The most senior officer in the group was Captain Sydney Fremantle, who would go on to become Director of the War Division at the Admiralty and to command the First Battle Squadron in 1919 during the fateful scuttling of the German fleet in Scapa Flow. Fremantle recalled in his memoirs how 'I was soon taken off the routine work of the War Course, and given by Admiralty Order the special job of presiding over a small committee of four which was to report on the subject of a possible "bolt from the blue".' The group began by producing an historical survey detailing precedents for hostilities beginning before an official declaration of war, mirroring Maurice's *Hostilities Without Declaration of War*. This part of their report, which has not survived, was submitted to the Admiralty at some point in mid-November, whereupon word came from Whitehall that Their Lordships 'demanded a full report as to the most advantageous disposition of our ships at a time of strained relations'.[86] More specifically, the War College was requested to establish 'the best strategical position for the British North Sea Fleet in view of a possible German invasion, undertaken during a period of strained relations'.[87] The Fremantle Committee was thus charged with testing the Admiralty's solution to the vulnerability Balfour had identified in his raids paper. This was achieved in a series of war games conducted at around the time the CID inquiry began at the end of the month, the final report being produced on 18 December.[88]

Fremantle preserved a précis of the group's findings in his private papers. The central conclusion was that with the Channel Fleet removed from the North Sea, the Germans stood a good chance of being able to reach the east coast undetected and of landing a sizeable force of lightly equipped troops there. For the purposes of the war games which informed these conclusions, the Channel Fleet was held at Liverpool—an alternative location for concentration during a period of strained relations which would shorten the steaming time to the Scottish and North Sea coast when compared with Portland. With the fleet so disposed:

> If the CHANNEL FLEET sail via the CHANNEL, in no case can they arrive in time to be of any use, whereas if they come by the Northern route, their Cruisers can arrive in time to be of material value when the disembarkation is in the FIRTH OF FORTH or to the Northward.[89]

The prescience of Slade's warning that 'the importance of always having a strong force *in* the North Sea cannot be overrated' was confirmed. Indeed, minor raids might be the least of the country's worries if the Germans were prepared to risk embarking a large force of troops at the outset of war:

> … with the BRITISH Fleet to the Southward [i.e. at Portland] and not mobilised, if news of the Transports having started is received within about 12 Hours of their

---

[85] Slade to Corbett, 3 January 1908, CBT/6/5/22, NMM.

[86] S. R. Fremantle, *My Naval Career, 1880–1928*, Essex: Tiptree, 1949, pp. 127–8.

[87] Report of the Fremantle Committee, 18 December 1907, p. 5, FRE/321/2, Fremantle Papers, NMM.

[88] Fremantle, *My Naval Career*, pp. 127–8.   [89] Report of the Fremantle Committee, p. 18.

departure, the GERMANS have a very fair chance of landing an Army of 80,000 men with a proportion of guns and vehicles at any place on the East Coast from YARMOUTH to NEWCASTLE—and that, with the HOME Fleet mobilised, but at CROMARTY, they have an equal chance at any point from HULL to the Southward. This chance is considerably increased if news of the landing is our first intimation of their having sailed …[90]

Here was justification for Fisher's superficially strange decision to commission a new Home Fleet from the naval reserve. The problem that Balfour had identified in his raids paper appeared to be far more serious than the Prime Minister had appreciated at the time.

These findings placed additional importance on the second phase of the War College's simulations, which aimed to establish 'the best position for the HOME Fleet (NORE Division) and the minimum requirements to ensure safety from invasion under similar conditions'. The first phase of the study had shown that the Home Fleet could not be deployed too far north without exposing Lincolnshire and Norfolk to an enemy landing. A suitable location central to the area of coast to be defended was necessary. However, this was complicated by the ongoing problem of the lack of a suitable anchorage on the east coast. The Fremantle Committee proposed utilizing either the Humber or Yarmouth, both of which were in a roughly central position on the stretch of coast to be defended. Preference was given to the latter on the basis that it was the closest point to the Elbe and as such likely to be attacked itself. Both anchorages were small, but this disadvantage would count for little as the Home Fleet would put to sea at the first sign of diplomatic tensions and await orders by wireless.[91]

Fremantle and his colleagues suggested that the Navy's speed of response could be further improved by ensuring that the Home Fleet contained the fastest vessels available, with a high proportion of armoured cruisers. Speed would be an important asset for the force for both strategic and tactical reasons. Clearly, the faster such a squadron could sweep the North Sea in search of an approaching convoy, the more effectively it could disrupt its approach to the coastline. The committee also viewed armoured cruisers as posing a particular menace to a large invasion armada due to their manoeuvrability and speed. 'Armoured cruisers can, at the best, only be delayed for 2 or 3 hours by GERMAN battle ships if met by them in the open sea', they argued. By using their speed to evade the convoy escorts, the cruisers would pose a serious menace to drawn-out lines of merchant ships pressed into service as troop transports.

Lowry forwarded the report of the Fremantle Committee to the Admiralty on 24 December. Endorsing the group's recommendations, he felt that a Home Fleet of '3 to 6 of our fastest battleships' based at Rosyth and supported by '8 of our fastest and most powerful cruisers' further south at the Humber would be suffi-cient to hold any German force that might venture into the North Sea. This would allow 'the Channel Fleet to be the force to deal the smashing blow—nucleus crew

90 Ibid., p. 1.   91 Ibid., pp. 1–2.

ships in its absence'.[92] Slade viewed the report of the Fremantle Committee with some seriousness. It validated the conclusions he had drawn from his own tenure at the War College about the vulnerability of the east coast at the outset of an Anglo-German war and proved the necessity of the Home Fleet reforms. In the context of the CID invasion inquiry, the documentation from the War College would have been political dynamite had it leaked out, as happened all too often to sensitive documentation at the Admiralty in this period.[93] This is doubtless one explanation for the secrecy surrounding the committee's proceedings: here was an internal naval assessment confirming the essential features of the case Repington and the 'invasionists' were presenting to the CID. Impressed with the need to formalize the Home Guard's function into tangible war orders, the DNI worked feverishly between Christmas and the New Year to prepare instructions for the C-in-Cs afloat. On 1 January 1908 Slade recorded in his diary that:

> Sir J.F. looked in this morning & spoke about the plans problem that I am having worked out at the War College & told me to telegraph Lowry & say to be here at noon on Saturday to discuss them. I have pressed on him the necessity of having orders drawn out for the dispositions of all ships on the slightest sign of strained relations so that we shall be secure against any attempt to spring a mine on us. He agreed & I hope shortly to get it drawn out—We shall then have the ships told off very much in the same way as we have the reserve detailed—All that will be necessary is to keep the list up to date and see that everything is provided for.[94]

By 15 January Slade could record with satisfaction in his journal that 'I put my memorandum on war preparation before Sir J. and he agreed with it, and we are now going on.'[95] The papers prepared by Slade and the mobilization department were transmitted to the Fleet during the first quarter of 1908. They referred to the Home Fleet as the 'North Sea Guard':

> This 'Guard' need not be of very great strength (numerically), its ships, however, should be homogeneous and work together. A force of 10 battleships and 6 cruisers would be sufficient and would allow for 8 battleships and 4 cruisers being always ready for sea.
> Whenever relations are strained this fleet should be sent to sea and remain cruising at a rendezvous in the North Sea within easy wireless touch of the British Coast.
> This could be done without exciting attention if the fleet were based at Rosyth, but not so easily if sent out from Sheerness.
> This fleet is far safer at sea than in harbour, so far as torpedo attack is concerned and its position can be so chosen as to render any surprise attempt at invasion nearly impossible.[96]

The fleet would thus cruise within range of the wireless station at Cleethorpes on the Lincolnshire coastline, near the mouth of the Humber, awaiting intelligence of

---

[92] Lowry to Slade, 24 December 1907, FRE/321/2, NMM.
[93] Morris, *Scaremongers*, pp. 128, 130–1, 133–4.
[94] Slade diary, 1 January 1908, MRF/39/3, NMM.
[95] Ibid., 15 January 1908, MRF/39/3, NMM.
[96] Admiralty, 'Strained Relations. Scheme A', ADM 116/1043B, fos 86–8.

German movements. The Admiralty's intent to utilize Rosyth as a base for the force was confirmed in the summer of 1907 when it sanctioned additional expenditure to increase the scale of armament given to the base. In July the Board also decided to make provision under the 1908–9 estimates for works intended to make the base anchorage suitable for coaling capital ships.[97] Slade still viewed a German 'bolt from the blue' as 'improbable', but the Admiralty had nevertheless gone to considerable lengths to guard against it. What remained was to shield the plans from the CID inquiry, whilst still convincing the government that the Navy could provide for the protection of the country.

THE PROCEEDINGS OF THE CID SUB-COMMITTEE

By commissioning the Fremantle Committee and amending the Navy's war plans based upon its findings, the Admiralty exposed a genuine sense of apprehension at the prospect of a major German raid. Yet rather than admit these fears, Fisher sought to obscure them from the CID, insisting that the naval defence of the country was the Admiralty's responsibility alone and that the Fleet was more than able to fulfil its duties in this regard. In part this was due to the need to protect the content of the North Sea Guard plans, but it was also symptomatic of the attitude with which both service departments had come to view the committee. Frustrated at his inability to control the CID during the Morocco Crisis, Fisher dismissed it as 'a sort of Aulic Council' and provided only lukewarm support to its proceedings during 1906–7.[98] His deteriorating relationship with Clarke exacerbated this process and Esher repeatedly chided the Admiralty for failing to act in good faith towards the body.[99]

Despite the sympathy of many within the War Office for the cause of national service, the forthcoming invasion inquiry also promised to be problematic for the military authorities, however. Haldane and the General Staff were supportive of Repington's quest to provide an effective second line force from which to expand the Regular Army in wartime. As the Director of Military Training, Major-General Douglas Haig, explained: 'the duties of the Territorial Force are Home Defence and expansion of the Regular Army...It is possible however that from the first...command of the sea would be so assured as to allow Home Defence to take a less important place.'[100] The Secretary of State had made as much clear to Parliament earlier in the year and welcomed the invasion inquiry as a possible route to constituting such a reserve.[101] Fisher suspected collaboration between the

---

[97] 'Board Minutes, Tuesday, 16th July 1907', ADM 167/41; Ottley and King-Hall, 'Remarks by D.N.I.', 26 August 1907, p. 1, ADM 1/8030.

[98] Fisher to Esher, 7 October 1907, in Marder ed., *FDGN* II, p. 144.

[99] Esher to Fisher, 4 February and 29 August 1907, in Brett ed., *Esher* II, pp. 219–20, 247–8; d'Ombrain, *War Machinery*, pp. 216–21.

[100] D. Haig, 'Memorandum on the Principles and Policy of Home Defence and the Adaptation of the Territorial Force Organisation to the Same', 1907, ESHR 16/10, CAC.

[101] Spiers, *Haldane*, pp. 98, 109, 169–70; Strachan, 'The Territorial Army and National Defence' in Neilson and Kennedy eds, *British Way in Warfare*, p. 163.

military and the 'invasionists', accusing Haldane of 'throwing himself into the arms of Lord Roberts and the invasion party to get his 300,000 men to resist invasion'.[102] Yet, despite being 'quite sure that the German General Staff has worked out in detail a carefully considered scheme for the invasion of Great Britain', the Staff was acutely aware of the difficulties involved in adopting the traditional War Office position that a large army was required for purely defensive purposes.[103] Stating the need to retain a greater proportion of existing military resources at home would undermine the Army's ability to deploy troops overseas rapidly at the outset of war. As many in the General Staff were firm advocates of direct co-operation with the French Army, this was a decidedly undesirable outcome.

Planning to commit British troops to the support of France had continued apace since the Morocco Crisis and the French military attaché, Colonel Huguet, was a regular visitor to Horse Guards Parade.[104] In the months prior to the invasion inquiry he met with Lyttelton and Major-General Spencer Ewart, the Director of Military Operations, to discuss the 'W.F.' (With France) scheme to deploy the British Army on the French left flank.[105] Ewart encapsulated the conundrum the inquiry posed to the General Staff: 'not being a great enthusiast for passive "home defence" I am always afraid of money being taken away from the regulars for the benefit of the stay at home force'.[106] He felt the implications of any such cuts were clear: 'if our expeditionary force is cut down then "good bye" to the Entente Cordiale with France'.[107] Nevertheless the DMO was obliged to admit to the CID that the relative weakness of the Territorial Force in terms of numbers and preparedness 'seem to point to the necessity, under existing conditions, of retaining some portion of our regular army (say two of the six divisions) in these islands until the embodied Territorial Force has time to acquire some cohesion, confidence and mobility'. Despite his personal scepticism about the likelihood of the scenario contemplated by the 'invasionists', Ewart continued:

> This enforced retention of two regular divisions at home would not necessarily be out of harmony with the arrangements suitable for a war in India or the Near East, for we should probably not require, or be able to embark, the whole of our striking force simultaneously. In the event of war in Europe, in which we ought to exert our full strength from the earliest possible moment, the reduction in numbers would be unfortunate, but it might be the lesser of two evils.[108]

The General Staff's reticence publicly to back the need for compulsion led Repington to fear that the War Office and the Admiralty might even unite to make common cause against him.[109] The presence on the sub-committee of Nicholson,

---

[102] Fisher to Cawdor, 27 January 1908, in Marder ed., *FGDN* II, p. 159.
[103] Ewart to Lyttelton, 1 February 1908, WO 106/47.
[104] Williamson Jr, *Politics of Grand Strategy*, pp. 101, 113; d'Ombrain, *War Machinery*, pp. 89–90.
[105] Ewart diary, 31 July 1907, GD527/1/1/135/8, NRS.
[106] Ibid., 26 October 1907.   [107] Ibid., 7 February 1908.
[108] 'Memorandum on Invasion by the General Staff', 18 February 1908, in CID, 'Appendices to Proceedings', Appendix XXXV, CAB 16/3B, p. 125.
[109] d'Ombrain, *War Machinery*, p. 222; Morris, *Repington*, p. 80.

who became Chief of the General Staff in April 1908, should have eased Repington's mind. The General was at daggers drawn with Fisher from the outset, the latter having played a key role in his ejection from the War Office in 1904. Such was the animus between the two men that the First Sea Lord attempted to have 'that double dealing arch-fiend Nicholson' removed from the group prior to the first sitting.[110]

The anomalous position of the General Staff, sympathetic to Repington's objectives yet politically unable to say so, made the Admiralty's task in countering the invasionists' case somewhat easier by providing official military support for aspects of its argument. Yet it did nothing to distract from the criticisms of the Home Fleet or of Fisher's administration. In an effort to avoid discussing the details of the North Sea Guard, the Admiralty elected to base its defence upon 'principles' of naval warfare and historical precedent. Fisher secured the services of his friend and ally Julian Corbett, a trained lawyer and effective advocate, to assist Slade in handling the Admiralty's brief. The two men were well acquainted after working together at the War College and had collaborated in the preparation of the Admiralty's 1907 war plans.[111] It has long been suggested that Fisher sought Corbett's assistance in order to deflect the committee from the detail of his strategic intentions.[112] If he did so in order to obscure radical plans to rely upon flotilla craft and submarines to prevent an invasion, however, then Corbett and Slade fell at the first hurdle. In their initial submission to the sub-committee, approved after a discussion with Fisher,[113] they stated that 'Naval defence against invasion rests fundamentally not on a battle fleet, as is usually assumed, but on a defensive flotilla.' 'It is, in fact, one of the strongest though least recognized features of Admiralty tradition', they continued, 'we actually exercise the control of lines of passage by flotillas and cruisers. The function of the battle fleet is to prevent that control being interfered with by the enemy's battle fleet.'[114] Fisher turned to these arguments not to conceal a fundamental shift in the strategic ethos,[115] but to distract attention from a more conventional solution to the threat of German invasion: the armoured warships of the Home Fleet.[116]

The Admiralty's theoretical arguments resulted in the sub-committee adopting the General Staff's suggestion that two divisions of troops should be retained in Britain until such time as the Territorial Force gained full efficiency. The only concession the Admiralty made was over the size and number of potential raids, which Fisher increased from 5,000 to 12,000 men due to the capacity and speed of the

---

[110] Fisher to Esher, 16 September 1907, quoted in Mackay, *Fisher*, p. 383.

[111] Schurman, *Corbett*, pp. 66–8, A. Lambert, 'The Naval War Course', pp. 228–38; Grimes, *War Planning*, pp. 84–9.

[112] Marder, *FDSF* I, p. 348; Lambert, *FNR*, pp. 171–2.

[113] Schurman, *Corbett*, p. 86. A copy can be found in his private papers: see 'Memorandum on Invasion, in Reply, & c.', 4 December 1907, FISR 8/43, CAC.

[114] Slade, 'Preliminary Observations on the Course of Former Attempts to Invade, and the Traditional Strategy by which they have been met' in Appendix XVI of CID, 'Appendices', CAB 16/3B, fo. 23. Emphasis added. For Corbett's role, see Schurman, *Corbett*, pp. 79–98.

[115] Lambert, *FNR*, p. 126.   [116] Morgan-Owen, 'History is a Record'.

most modern German ocean-going liners.[117] Ottley, who had replaced Clarke as Secretary to the CID, summarized for Balfour how 'Germany is [in] a far worse position for invading Britain, than is France' but that 'Raids then are raised in the scale from 5000 to 12000 men.'[118] Whilst the size of a potential raid remained contested, Haldane was quick to apprehend (as Clarke had in 1905) that it might form a useful justification for his shortly to be implemented Territorial scheme, and the War Office duly accepted the new figure without further complaint.[119] Both service departments were thus broadly satisfied with the outcome.[120]

Repington was furious at the government's decision to keep the conclusions of the sub-committee secret and suspected foul play. In a last-ditch attempt to force the government's hand, Roberts instigated a debate in the Lords, but another address from the aged Field Marshal had little effect upon the course of events in Whitehall.[121] Fisher had succeeded in concealing the detail of his Home Fleet plans, yet the fact remained that the Admiralty had withheld the extent of its concerns about a German landing from the government in a duplicitous and partisan fashion. Organizing the Navy to fulfil the defensive function the government envisaged for it was clearly a legitimate course for Fisher to pursue, but his unwillingness to discuss the Admiralty's escalating assessment of the German threat revealed much about the state of the relationship between the naval leadership and the CID.[122]

* * *

Fisher handled the setback his policy had suffered during the Morocco Crisis poorly and failed to recognize that his intransigence and stonewalling during the meetings of Clarke's informal planning committee had played an important role in alienating the CID Secretary and new government. Lacking credible plans from the Admiralty, Clarke had seen no option but to endorse Grierson's proposal to send the Army to Europe to the new administration, despite the fact that neither he nor they favoured such a course. The prevarication Fisher engaged in during 1906–7 and the exaggerated arguments he deployed in order to try and avoid the formation of the invasion inquiry further eroded the Admiralty's ability to influence strategy by ostracizing it from the CID. Whatever the committee's limitations and in spite of the government's failure to utilize it to impose coherent direction upon the service departments, the CID remained the only forum in which issues of combined naval and military strategy could be discussed in detail between military professionals and the senior decision makers in the Cabinet. By deceiving

[117] Admiralty, 'Statement by the Admiralty Defining their Responsibility for Protecting the United Kingdom from Oversea Attack', Appendix XXXVI in CID, 'Appendices', CAB 16/3B, fo. 79. For a discussion on the exact number, see 'Minutes of the Seventh Meeting' in CID, 'Report and Proceedings', pp. 154–5, CAB 16/3A, fo. 86.
[118] Ottley to Balfour, 13 March 1908, GD433/2/54, NRS.
[119] Spiers, *Haldane*, pp. 169–71; Adams and Poirer, *Conscription Controversy*, pp. 36–7; Strachan, 'The Territorial Army and National Defence', p. 163.
[120] Ewart diary July 27th, 1908, GD527/1/1/135/10; Slade diary, July 21st, 1908, MRF/39/3, NMM.
[121] Morris, *Repington*, pp. 86–7.   [122] d'Ombrain, *War Machinery*, pp. 223–5, 231.

the CID about how the Admiralty viewed the prospect of war in the North Sea, Fisher ensured that the body operated with a distorted impression of the strategic landscape. This was to have profound implications for the Navy as the politicians felt confident in deploying the Army on the basis of naval advice, whilst all the while the situation in the North Sea was in fact deteriorating precipitously.

For the government's part, Campbell-Bannerman's lack of interest in the CID left Haldane to become the driving force behind its work in 1906–7. Fully occupied with the demands of his department, the Secretary of State for War showed little interest in the committee's co-ordinating function and largely utilized it as a vehicle with which to overcome internal opposition to his plans to reform the Army.[123] There was therefore little scope for the Admiralty to recover the damage done to its plans in 1905–6 even if Fisher had been inclined to do so. The government's unsympathetic handling of the invasion inquiry inevitably pushed Fisher onto the defensive by giving head to some of his most severe critics both within the Navy and without. By 1908, the Admiralty could thus be excused for viewing the CID as unable and unwilling to force the General Staff to give fair consideration to its amphibious plans and therefore as little use to the co-ordination of national strategy. It was at this nadir of the body's fortunes that international conditions conspired to bring strategy back to the forefront of politicians' minds, albeit in a transitory manner.

---

[123] Ibid., pp. 204–6.

7

A Growing Burden

The CID's 1907–8 invasion inquiry touched upon issues of grand strategy in a way the body had largely been unwilling to since the Morocco Crisis. Whilst not a direct investigation into how best to prosecute a war against Germany, the recommendation to withhold two divisions of the Expeditionary Force at the outset of a European war confirmed the government's hesitance to commit British forces to a future Continental conflict. Yet whereas the conclusions Balfour had reached in 1903–4 had fitted into a broader, if incomplete, conception of British strategy during an Anglo-Russian conflict, the invasion sub-committee's findings were largely divorced from considerations of how best to wage war against Germany. No serious thought was given to how the four remaining divisions of the Expeditionary Force could be profitably employed, nor was this question followed up subsequent to the decision to withhold two divisions of troops for defensive purposes. British strategy thus continued to drift, despite the implicit acknowledgement that a war against Germany in Europe had definitively replaced the threat of Russia in Asia as the most dangerous possibility the country faced.

The government only devoted its attention to a war against Germany in the winter of 1908, when a crisis resulting from the Austro-Hungarian annexation of Bosnia and Herzegovina threatened a general European conflict. Yet nothing emerged from this process beyond a re-affirmation that two divisions of the Expeditionary Force ought to remain in Britain at the outbreak of war. A definitive decision was deferred for 'the Government of the day' to make. A similarly episodic approach to strategy was evident in the summer of 1911, when renewed Franco-German tensions over Morocco prompted a further bout of isolated political interest in the country's military preparations. Here again, no firm decisions were reached, although a trend towards direct military co-operation with the French was suspected by some. Britain had no defined strategy and lurched from crisis to crisis, guided only by broad outlines of defence policy established in 1903–4. If the nineteenth century had witnessed defence policy by crisis, the first decade of the twentieth paid host to strategy by the same means. Balfour's efforts had established the contours of Britain's military and naval organization within which strategy could be formed: the Admiralty remained responsible for the protection of the country against invasion, the Regular Army was constituted for offensive operations against ill-defined targets overseas, and the new Territorial Force was nominally purposed for repelling raids in its absence. Yet the failure of the government to employ the CID as an effective forum for co-ordinating naval and military effort left the two service departments to prepare in isolation, the very problem the

committee had been conceived to solve. In this context the General Staff worked
to secure support for deploying the entire Expeditionary Force to the Continent in
support of France. Working at almost cross-purposes, the Admiralty continued to
advocate a more maritime approach, targeting German trade and using amphibious operations to detain enemy troops along the North Sea coastline. However, the
prospect of the major German landing envisaged by the Fremantle Committee
preoccupied naval thought to an ever greater extent. As the Admiralty wrestled
with how best to control the North Sea in the face of growing German naval
power, the General Staff's plans for operations in Europe and ongoing uncertain-
ties as to the quality of the Territorial Force increased the urgency of finding a naval
solution to the 'North Sea problem', as the Army's capacity to defeat an invading
force seemed doubtful. Defensive considerations steadily rose up the naval leadership's strategic agenda, diverting its attention from producing coherent offensive
plans. As had been the case prior to the formation of the CID, British naval and
military strategy interacted organically and without direction, only now the
Admiralty no longer held the whip hand.

THE MILITARY NEEDS OF THE EMPIRE

Since the Morocco Crisis of 1905–6 the General Staff had continued to develop
the Army's capability to deploy abroad. Overseas garrisons were thinned to concentrate troops at home and the auxiliaries grouped into a leaner, more effective
body. Officially this policy was pursued with the requirements of India primarily
in mind.[1] The CID still contemplated dispatching a force of 100,000 men to India
in the event of Anglo-Russian hostilities and preparations for fighting outside the
United Kingdom remained justifiable on those grounds. Arrangements to reinforce
India would, however, also prepare the Army for action in other theatres, a fact
of which contemporaries were well aware.[2] Lord Esher, no supporter of direct
military co-operation with France, reported to the King how 'war with Russia on
the NW Frontier, being the gravest military operation which Your Majesty's Army
could be called upon to undertake, covers by its magnitude all other conceivable
operations'.[3] The government's decision to sanction the transport of reinforcements
to India without naval escort obliged the Admiralty Transport Department to
furnish the General Staff with all of the information required to plan to send the
Expeditionary Force to France.[4] Armed with these details and the arrangements
made during the Morocco Crisis, the General Staff updated shipping arrangements to integrate them more effectively with the latest French mobilization plans
in the summer of 1907. With Grey's approval the details were shared with the

---

[1] Hankey, *Supreme Command* I, p. 61.
[2] Williamson Jr, *Politics of Grand Strategy*, p. 95.
[3] Esher to the King, 21 January 1907, in Brett ed., *Esher* II, p. 218.
[4] Admiralty to War Office, 1 June 1907, WO 106/47, fos 229–30.

French staff in July, strengthening the impression that Britain was willing to send an army to France's aid.[5]

It would be a mistake to ascribe a doctrinaire commitment to co-operation with the French to British military planners, however. The General Staff's advocacy of providing the military assistance that Paris so desired remained flexible and contingent. The Staff displayed a commendably realistic attitude to the invasion inquiry, acknowledging the necessity of maintaining regular troops in Britain at the outset of war. This attitude was influenced in no small part by Ewart in his capacity as DMO. The Major-General was a fair-minded officer with the capacity to look beyond partisan service considerations and the wrangling of bureaucratic politics. His brother Arthur was a former naval attaché to Berlin and now captain of the battleship HMS *Duncan* of the Channel Fleet, and Ewart formed a close working relationship with his counterpart at the Admiralty, Captain Slade. A measure of his collaborative attitude can be gleaned from the final submission the Staff made to the inquiry, in which Ewart suggested that under certain circumstances it might in fact be advisable to retain a third division of the Expeditionary Force (amounting to half the strength of the Regular Army) in Britain until the Territorial Force had achieved efficiency.[6] The DMO presented a similarly moderate case when affairs in the Balkans prompted a renewed consideration of British strategy in the autumn of 1908.

Tensions in Europe flared in late September due to a failed attempt by German embassy staff in the port city of Casablanca to secure passage to Hamburg for three deserters from the French Foreign Legion. The French port authorities exposed the attempt and re-ignited the simmering Franco-German tensions in the region, precipitating a major diplomatic row.[7] Days later, on 6 October, Austria-Hungary announced its intention to annex the former Ottoman territories of Bosnia-Herzegovina. The affair made public secret Russian machinations to secure passage of the Straits in exchange for acceding to Vienna's actions, embarrassing St Petersburg and raising the spectre of a regional conflict. France was reluctant to become involved in Russia's Balkan policy, but Berlin gave Austria-Hungary its full backing. The implications of the alliance system therefore threatened to escalate a Balkan crisis into a general European war. Asquith formed a special sub-committee of the CID to investigate the options open to Britain if war did erupt. Before the first meeting, Ewart and Slade accompanied Ottley to the Foreign Office to discuss the possible contingencies the military authorities faced. The DMO also visited the Admiralty two days later, where he and Slade agreed to re-convene in the following days to concert a plan for

---

[5] Nicholson, 'Action taken by the General Staff since 1906 in preparing a plan for rendering military assistance to France in the event of an unprovoked attack on that Power by Germany', 6 November 1911, WO 106/49A/1.

[6] 'Memorandum by the General Staff Showing the Distribution of Troops for Home Defence', 24 July 1908, CAB 16/5, Appendix XLII, dos 82–4.

[7] G. E. Silberstein, 'Germany, France and the Casablanca Incident, 1908–1909; an Investigation of a Forgotten Crisis', *Canadian Journal of History*, Vol. 76, No. 3, Dec., 1976, pp. 331–54.

presentation to the politicians.[8] The proceedings of an extraordinary session of the CID promised to be the first direct discussion of British strategy since the Morocco Crisis. As had been the case in 1906, however, they failed to provide meaningful guidance to the service departments.

Despite the co-operation evident between Ewart and Slade, the Admiralty and War Office approached the proceedings with divergent agendas. Ewart believed that the committee, named the 'Military Needs of the Empire', was intended 'to deal with our European liabilities'. The DMO described it as 'the most important enquiry we have had' on the grounds that 'it discusses the real use of the Expeditionary Force'.[9] The General Staff's submission to the group reflected this attitude. It dismissed the Admiralty's proposals for amphibious schemes, insisting that 'the idea of a diversion by way of the Baltic does not appear to have anything to commend it from a military point of view'. 'Direct support for the French army', it reasoned, 'offers a better prospect of useful result.' The DMO therefore presented a scheme to deploy four divisions of the Expeditionary Force and a cavalry division, either to France or to Belgium.[10] The soldiers adhered to the limitations placed upon the number of men that could be sent to France by the 1907–8 invasion inquiry and remained flexible enough in their thinking to contemplate operating in Belgium as well as France. A compromise option of landing a British force at Antwerp to threaten the flank of a German advance into France remained plausible. The War Office's open-mindedness did not extend to some of the more circuitous operations envisaged by the Navy, however. The military authorities remained convinced that British military intervention would need to be at the 'decisive point' were it to relieve pressure on France. As to how Britain was to prosecute a war after staving off a rapid French defeat, the General Staff was notably reticent to explain.

As had been the case in 1906, the Admiralty fundamentally disagreed with the General Staff's strategy of direct military co-operation with France. The naval authorities contemplated strategies both for the immediate requirement to deflect German pressure on France at the outset of war and to prosecute a prolonged conflict thereafter. In the first instance, the Admiralty remained committed to an approach predicated upon detaining German forces through the threat of seaborne descent on their coasts. The on-going popularity this approach enjoyed in naval circles had become evident during the hearings of the invasion inquiry, when both Slade and Fisher had enthused about the potential number of German troops that could be paralysed by threatening amphibious operations against the German or Danish coastline. 'We have one plan for attacking a portion of the coast where it would be very desirable to have a military force', Fisher had stated, enigmatically. He continued, 'there is no use the Navy having a great success in doing something on the enemy's coast unless they have got a military force to take advantage of

---

[8] Slade diary, 4 and 6 November 1908, MRF/39/3, NMM.
[9] Ewart diary, 6 November 1908, GD527/1/1/135/10, NRS.
[10] 'Memorandum by the General Staff', November 1908, WO 106/47, fos 292–300.

it...the success of the Navy cannot be carried to its proper conclusion unless you have got a military force able to land and take advantage of it'.[11]

Amphibious assaults also formed an important part of how Fisher envisaged conducting a more protracted campaign. Here the naval authorities demonstrated greater breadth in their thinking than the General Staff—encompassing the possibility of a protracted conflict and responses to a range of German actions. The naval authorities had continued to develop plans to land troops in Denmark should Germany violate Danish neutrality during the summer. These had been prompted by on-going negotiations about the legal status of the entrances to the Baltic, access to which the Admiralty regarded as a vital means of exerting naval pressure on Germany. Occupying Denmark would enable Germany to close the Belts with minefields, denying the Navy access to her vulnerable Baltic littoral and securing her trade with Scandinavia (a key source of iron ore) from British attack.[12] The Admiralty had made contact with the War Office during the summer to discuss potential British military action to keep the Belts open, but with little result. Major Grant-Duff of the Operations Division had stated bluntly that a military expedition to Zealand 'could accomplish nothing when it got there, and might not improbably end in total disaster'.[13] Slade acknowledged the difficulties involved, noting that in the event of a solely Anglo-German conflict such an operation would be unnecessary. Yet the DNI remained convinced that penetrating the Baltic represented the most effective means of relieving the pressure on France in the event of an Anglo-French combination against Germany. 'In this case', Slade informed Ewart, 'it would probably be necessary for us to run risks which would be quite unjustifiable if we were acting solely on our own account.' He continued:

> It might be very important to keep the passage open to the German Baltic coasts, so as to force her to provide for their defence, and so prevent a certain proportion of her forces, at any rate, from being despatched to the French frontier. What that proportion would be is a matter which only the GS can say, but, with these coasts open and exposed to an attack anywhere, it would probably necessitate a larger force being held inactive than any that we could hope to hold down when acting in other directions.[14]

The DNI also prepared plans for an amphibious striking force of 15,000 men which might 'seize Antwerp...and from there to operate on the flank of the German line of advance'.[15] Here appeared to lie the prospect of common ground

---

[11] Admiralty, 'Statement by the Admiralty Defining their Responsibility for Protecting the United Kingdom from Oversea Attack', Appendix XXXVI in CID, 'Appendices', CAB 16/3B, fo. 79. For a discussion on the exact number, see 'Minutes of the Seventh Meeting' in CID, 'Report and Proceedings', pp. 154–5, CAB 16/3A, fos 87–8.

[12] Grimes, *War Planning*, pp. 111–26.

[13] A. Grant-Duff, 'A Military Expedition to Zealand in Support of the Danes Against German Invasion', 14 July 1908, WO 106/47, fo. 215.

[14] Slade, 'Expedition Against Zealand', 19 October 1908, WO 106/47, fo. 203.

[15] Slade to Corbett, 16 December 1908, quoted in d'Ombrain, *War Machinery*, p. 92.

between the services. Unfortunately the CID proved insufficiently responsive to occupy it.

The dissonance between advocates of direct co-operation with the French and the Baltic scheme reflected the same disagreement on 'the general question of strategy' that had so appalled Grierson in 1905.[16] Whilst Slade laboured to convince the military authorities to reconsider his plans, Fisher was resigned to what seemed their inevitable rejection. Days before the first session of the Military Needs Sub-Committee he told Slade that 'we had better not say anything at all about it', preferring to discuss the desirability of leaving command of the Mediterranean and Channel to the French in order to free British forces for operations in the North Sea.[17] True to his word, when Asquith asked whether the Admiralty would require any troops to support the activities of the Navy, the First Sea Lord declined, noting caustically that 'it took time for them to mobilise, and naval measures would have to be taken without delay'.[18] The only mention he made about the use of troops was in connection with dispatching an army to Denmark—an operation he knew the General Staff considered to be unfeasible. Military advice to this effect saw the politicians discard the scheme in short order. Fisher's unwillingness to put the case for alternative combined operations—such as Slade's Antwerp option—to the sub-committee at greater length and in more detail was short-sighted. His private correspondence confirms his on-going advocacy of such a strategy:[19] in January he claimed to be secretly preparing transports for embarking troops at a moment's notice.[20] Commenting on a proposal from Esher to send a limited force of cavalry to the Continent, Fisher explained to his friend how:

> the General Staff criticism is, on the other hand, the thin end of the insidious wedge of our taking part in continental war as apart absolutely from coastal military operations in pure concert with the Navy—expeditions involving hell to the enemy because backed by an invincible Navy (the citadel of military force). I don't desire to mention these expeditions and never will, as our military organisation is so damnably leaky![21]

The First Sea Lord proved unable to contain his views throughout the duration of the Military Needs proceedings, however. A colleague who was present recorded that at one of the meetings 'Fisher expressed the view that the British Army should be absolutely restricted to operations consisting of sudden descents on the coast,

---

[16] Grierson, 'Further Memorandum on Military Policy in the Event of War with France', July 1905, p. 2, ADM 116/3111.

[17] Slade diary, 28 November 1908, MRF/39/3, NMM.

[18] CID, 'Minutes of the First Meeting, December 3rd, 1908', CAB 16/5, fo. 8.

[19] Marder, *FDSF* I, pp. 384–90; Williamson Jr, *Politics of Grand Strategy*, pp. 109–10; Grimes, *War Planning*, pp. 140–6; A. Lambert, 'The German North Sea Islands, the Kiel Canal and the Danish Narrows in Royal Navy Thinking and Planning, 1905–1918' in M. Epkenhans and G. P. Gross eds, *The Danish Straits and German Naval Power, 1905–1918*, Potsdam: MGFA, 2010, pp. 35–62; A. Lambert, 'The Possibility of Ultimate Action in the Baltic: The Royal Navy at War, 1914–1916' in M. Epkenhans, J. Hillman, and F. Nägler eds, *Jutland: World War I's Greatest Naval Battle*, Lexington, Kentucky: Kentucky University Press, 2015, pp. 79–116. For alternative interpretations, see Mackay, *Fisher*, pp. 405–7; Lambert, *Planning Armageddon*, pp. 38–60, 117–21.

[20] Fisher to Esher, 17 January 1909, in Marder ed., *FGDN* II, p. 220.

[21] Fisher to Esher, 15 March 1909, in Marder ed., *FGDN* II, p. 232.

the recovery of Heligoland and the garrisoning of Antwerp.' The First Sea Lord had apparently continued on:

> ...there was a stretch of ten miles of hard sand on the Pomeranian coast which is only ninety miles from Berlin. Were the British army to seize and entrench that strip, a million Germans would find occupation; but to dispatch the British troops to the front in a Continental war would be an act of suicidal idiocy...Fisher followed this up with a diatribe against the War Office and all its ways, including conceit, waste of money, and ignorance of war.[22]

Yet Fisher's failure to present any tangible exposition of his ideas rendered his invective counter-productive. The General Staff was open to criticism for blocking naval attempts to conceive feasible amphibious plans, but the Admiral's absolutist rhetoric conveyed an impression of petty awkwardness. Asquith adjourned the meeting in response to his outburst.

As had been the case in 1905–6, the government was thus presented with two options if war were to break out suddenly: a purely maritime campaign of economic warfare unlikely to satisfy French demands for support, or the dispatch of the diminutive British Army to the 'decisive theatre' on the Continent. The lack of combined planning and preparation effectively ruled out an amphibious assault, as the arrangements for such a complex undertaking would be impossible to extemporize in an emergency. It was almost an axiomatic assumption that an ill-defined yet potentially powerful effort to exert pressure on the enemy economy would form the basis of any British campaign against Germany.[23] A naval plan predicated upon economic warfare was thus largely a given. The War Office may not have presented any convincing arguments for what might happen after the initial battles on the Franco-German frontier, but its scheme thus appeared the only means of supplementing the 'steady pressure' of sea power with more direct and immediate assistance to the French.

In a characteristically unsatisfactory fudge, the sub-committee concluded that 'the expediency of sending a military force abroad, or of relying on naval means only, is a matter of policy which can only be determined when the occasion arises by the Government of the day'.[24] Preparations to dispatch troops were approved, but such plans were already well in train and these measures meant little in the context of national strategy: as Esher had argued, an Army with an efficient embarkation scheme could always be sent to different locations. The Military Needs Sub-Committee presented Asquith, who had succeeded Campbell-Bannerman as Prime Minister in April, with an ideal opportunity to address the unsatisfactory state of Britain's preparations for war. Balfour had bequeathed him the requisite administrative machinery and both services were arguably better prepared to fight than at any time since the turn of the century. Yet the Prime Minister was unwilling to adjudicate in the debate between the military and naval

---

[22] Quoted in Bacon, *Fisher* II, pp. 182–3.
[23] French, *British Economic and Strategic Planning*, pp. 33–5; Offer, *Agrarian Interpretation*, pp. 239–43; Lambert, *Planning Armageddon*, pp. 117–22.
[24] Minutes of the Seventh' in CID, 'Report and Proceedings', pp. 154–5, CAB 16/3A, fo. 86.

professionals in the manner Balfour had shown possible in 1903–4. After the final report of the Military Needs group was signed in July 1909 and approved by the full CID, the body dissolved for the summer. The demands of a general election meant that it did not sit again until February 1910.

'IT IS NOT POSSIBLE FOR THE NAVY UNAIDED TO BRING A CAMPAIGN TO A SUCCESSFUL ISSUE'

Whilst the Military Needs Sub-Committee had reached no firm conclusions, the General Staff interpreted its findings as a tacit endorsement of military operations on the Continent. This was an entirely legitimate interpretation of the indications the War Office had received from successive governments. Balfour had laboured to divorce the Regular Army from the defence of the British Isles and re-directed its attention solely towards expeditionary warfare between 1903 and 1905. Thereafter, the Liberals had authorized the original Anglo-French staff conversations in 1906, approved their continuation in 1907, and now endorsed further consideration of the details of dispatching a force to Europe in 1908–9. Yet a contradiction existed between the findings of the CID invasion inquiry and the Military Needs Sub-Committee. If military intervention in support of France was contemplated, then four divisions of British troops were unlikely to have anything more than a moral effect. Six divisions would count for little more militarily, but would still be preferable to the smaller contingent. Government policy thus appeared to pull in opposite directions: contemplating deploying an army to Europe on the one hand, but refusing either to marshal the Army's full strength or to recruit more men on the other. Several weeks before the final meeting of the Military Needs group, Ewart summarized the position in his diary:

> If the 'Triple Entente' with France and Russia is to last, it behoves us to put our military house in order, to perfect our mobilization arrangements, and increase our offensive striking power. Foreign nations are always suspicious of our selfish policy of isolation and Home defence and doubt whether we can be relied upon to take our fair share of the hard knocks on the Continent. If we are to have compulsory service—and I hope it will come—let it carry with the obligation of going to fight the enemy wherever he is to be found. 'Home Defence' is the most poisonous strategical fallacy ever propounded by man. The only true defence is offence. It will never be justifiable to raise more men for Home Defence than the irreducible minimum to which must in any case be kept at home to hold our naval ports, prevent raids, and preserve public order. Lord Roberts and his henchmen are out of date.[25]

This was a criticism of Haldane's decision to make service overseas optional for members of the Territorial Force, which the Secretary of State had calculated would be a political necessity and vital to meeting his target of recruiting 300,000 men into the organization. Home defence thus became the most obvious justification

---

[25] Ewart diary, 12 July 1909, GD527/1/1/135/10, NRS.

for the Territorial Force's existence, but limited its utility as a reserve for the Regular Army in wartime.[26]

Faced with seemingly insurmountable obstacles to the introduction of compulsory service, the Staff focused on increasing the efficiency of the Territorial Force in an effort to liberate a greater proportion of the Regular Army for operations overseas.[27] 'The object to be aimed at', the CIGS argued,[28] 'is that the Army for Home Defence should be able to provide the measure of land defence required for the security of the United Kingdom without keeping in this country the Regular troops wanted for field service elsewhere.'[29] The naval authorities were kept up to date with the General Staff's intentions through on-going discussions regarding transport for the Expeditionary Force. Fisher had grudgingly consented to the Transport Department consulting with the War Office in 1907, but a lack of co-operation from the Admiralty led the General Staff to bring the issue to the attention of the CID in February 1910, arguing that 'it seems essential that a plan for embarkation should be thoroughly worked out'.[30] It subsequently emerged that the Admiralty had in fact prepared the embarkation scheme, but that the documents were 'not forthcoming'.[31] Whether Fisher had purposefully delayed the plans being shared with the General Staff is unclear, but he would hardly have prioritized their swift transmission. Whilst logistics ultimately came to play a role in the General Staff's efforts to secure official endorsement for Anglo-French co-operation,[32] initially they remained secondary to efforts to achieve political endorsement through other, more dubious, methods. This became clear towards the end of the year.

In May the War Office wrote to the Admiralty enclosing a new document that the General Staff had prepared on home defence, intended to replace four existing publications on the topic. Due to the complicated principles and precedents involved, a series of meetings to discuss the memorandum were held during the summer, after which the Admiralty approved what it thought was a final draft of the paper.[33] This version contained nothing to which the naval authorities saw cause to object. However, the War Office then made a series of subtle but important alterations to the document before submitting it to the CID for consideration and approval. The Military Assistant to the CID, Major Adrian Grant Duff, welcomed the memorandum when he saw it, noting that 'if accepted it will lay down fairly clearly and at last the object for which we keep up an army'.[34] His superior,

---

[26] Strachan, 'The Territorial Army and National Defence', pp. 161–3.

[27] General Staff, 'Home Defence: Memorandum Dealing with the Selection of War Stations for the Central Force', 9 October 1909, p. 32, WO 33/485.

[28] The post Chief of the General Staff became Chief of the Imperial General Staff in 1909.

[29] Nicholson, 'Home Defence: Memorandum on the Principles Governing the Defence of the United Kingdom', April 23rd, 1911, p. 3, WO 33/515.

[30] General Staff, 'Questions Requiring Inter-Departmental Consideration', 22 February 1910, CAB 18/16/3; Marder, *FDSF* I, p. 387; Williamson Jr, *Politics of Grand Strategy*, p. 171.

[31] Nicholson to Haldane, 25 September 1911, WO 106/50.

[32] Williamson Jr, *Politics of Grand Strategy*, p. 172.

[33] Note by Bethell on docket, 'Home Defence. Memo. On principles governing the defence of the U.K.', 21 May 1910, ADM 1/8896.

[34] Grant-Duff diary, 4 October 1910, AGDF 2/1, fo. 3, CAC.

Secretary to the CID and former DNI Charles Ottley, was less enthusiastic. Ever a shrewd political operator, Ottley was quick to apprehend the significance of the updated memorandum when it crossed his desk. He produced a lengthy list of criticisms which he referred privately back to the Admiralty.[35] His Naval Assistant, Captain Maurice Hankey RM, was more forthright, and complained bitterly to Fisher about the 'poisonous Home Defence Memo. which the War Office tried to ram down our throats'.[36] Rear Admiral Alexander Bethell, the present Director of Naval Intelligence, was obliged to bring the matter to the attention of the First Sea Lord and First Lord. He explained how:

> the Memorandum as now printed has been altered since the Admiralty concurred in it, without their having been informed of the fact. It will be seen that the wording of Clause 1. Imperial Defence, on page 3, is not the same as in the proof concurred in by the Admiralty, and that the sentence 'for seldom can it be possible for the Navy unaided to bring a campaign to a successful issue' has been altered to 'it is not possible for the Navy unaided to bring a campaign to a successful issue', since the original proof was returned.

In the same section as the passage to which Bethell objected, the paper stated that 'it may be necessary in future, as in the past, to support allies against aggression, or to intervene on the Continent of Europe in accordance with any treaty obligations which may exist' and that '*for the present* it is probable that two divisions of the Expeditionary Force' would be withheld for home defence.[37] The amended version thus presented a strong argument for military intervention on the Continent and approval of this document by the CID would represent a powerful endorsement of the principle. Doubtless embarrassed, Bethell admitted that the differences between the two versions of the memorandum had been overlooked when the War Office had forwarded the Admiralty a copy of the updated paper before submitting it to the CID.[38] In order to prevent the paper reaching the committee, the Admiralty would therefore have to rescind approval already granted.

In an attempt to defuse the situation, Ottley suggested that the First Lord—Reginal McKenna—raise the matter with Haldane. The result of this approach was that the document was referred from the full CID to the Home Ports Defence Sub-Committee (HPDC) for amendment.[39] Quite when this body examined the document is unclear. The records show that the HPDC did not meet officially between the time the paper was referred to it and the end of March, when an

---

[35] 'Remarks on the Memorandum on the Principles Governing the Defence of the United Kingdom' and Ottley to Bethell, 16 January 1911, ADM 1/8896.

[36] Hankey to Fisher, 26 January 1911, quoted in S. Roskill, *Hankey: Man of Secrets*, Vol. I, London: Collins, 1970, p. 109.

[37] 'Home Defence. Memorandum on the Principles Governing the Defence of the United Kingdom', 3 November 1910, CAB 3/2/48A, fo. 36. Emphasis added.

[38] Bethell, 'Home Defence. Memo: on Principles of', 18 January 1911, ADM 1/8896.

[39] CID, 'Minutes of the 108th Meeting, January 26th, 1911', p. 6, CAB 2/2. The HPDC did not meet between 11 January and 28 March (after the paper was submitted), so the means by which the paper was drafted is unclear. See CAB 12/1 for meetings of the HPDC.

altered version was returned to the full CID.[40] Nevertheless, the full CID discussed and approved an updated iteration of the General Staff's production on 24 March. Hankey had hoped that the HPDC might 'take all the poison out of the memorandum', but his aspirations were not entirely fulfilled.[41] The final version of the document included in the CID files reveals that the Admiralty had succeeded in expunging any mention of whether 'naval means alone' could successfully influence affairs in Europe, but that it had done so at the expense of assenting to the General Staff's ambition to weaken the conclusions of the 1907–8 invasion inquiry regarding the retention of regular troops at the outbreak of war.

The approved version of the paper stated that 'the object to be aimed at, therefore, is that the Army for Home Defence should be able to provide the measure of land defence required for the security of the United Kingdom *without keeping in this country the Regular troops wanted for field service elsewhere*'.[42] The Admiralty found it difficult to refute this argument. Admitting that additional troops were required for home defence would sacrifice its political success at the invasion inquiry and strengthen the hand of supporters of compulsory service in arguing for a large Home Army. Moreover, a capable Expeditionary Force remained necessary for the kind of amphibious operations that remained in favour within the NID. McKenna thus endorsed the memorandum, suggesting only that the figure of 70,000 potential invaders—the justification for Haldane's Territorial Force—might be lowered due to the strength of the Navy. Both Haldane and Churchill railed at the suggestion and Asquith therefore dismissed it. Whether the Prime Minister appreciated the significance of the fact that the War Office was clearly working to overturn the conclusions of the 1907–8 invasion inquiry is unclear.[43] The extent to which the changes to the document were a deliberate act of subterfuge is open to debate, but the sensitive nature of the sections that were amended and the broader context of the General Staff's efforts to increase the size of the Expeditionary Force make it difficult to avoid the impression of foul play. The Admiralty ought to have identified the last-minute alterations when it was sent a copy of the memorandum, but the War Office's actions were symptomatic of the lack of co-operative spirit so essential to the success of combined operations which the department had displayed since the abortive discussions between Ballard and Callwell in 1905–6. This obstructionist attitude made political intervention and oversight vital if combined operations were to be examined in a serious, thoroughgoing manner. Asquith's reticence thus allowed the military to exert an undue influence on the course of British strategy by stonewalling the discussion of options outside military co-operation with the French.

[40] See CID, 'Home Ports Defence Committee, Minutes of Meetings (No. 1-38), 17. Aug. 1909–10. May 1921', fos 40–50, CAB 12/1.
[41] Hankey to Fisher, 26 January 1911, quoted in Roskill, *Hankey* I, p. 110.
[42] 'Home Defence', 23 March 1911, CAB 3/2/49A, part III—Alternative draft from Nicholson (which the committee approved—see CAB 2/2/109). Emphasis added.
[43] CID, 'Minutes of the 109th Meeting, March 24th, 1911', p. 8, CAB 2/2.

PLANNING FOR WAR IN THE NORTH SEA

The period after the initial meetings of the Military Needs of the Empire Sub-Committee was a difficult one for the Admiralty. After being obliged to haul down his flag from the Channel Fleet in March 1909, Admiral Beresford had been intriguing furiously in an attempt to topple Fisher. His political and social connections quickly brought his campaign to the attention of the Prime Minister. In the wake of the crisis over naval construction that had threatened to topple the government at the turn of the year, Asquith was sympathetic to the need to investigate the performance of the naval leadership.[44] Balfour had hammered the government in the Commons for its failure to anticipate the pace of German construction and criticism of the Sea Lords abounded in the press.[45] After vacillating between appointing a Royal Commission or using the CID to conduct the inquiry, the Prime Minister formed a new sub-committee to investigate the functioning of the Board of Admiralty and the condition of the Navy. Despite the claims of some scholars, this was an extraordinary use of the CID's time.[46] Balfour had used the CID to involve himself with schemes for Army reform in 1904–5, but had done so on the basis of a consensus of professional opinion as to the inadequacies of the auxiliary forces and of the system of administration at the War Office. His interventions may have been unpopular in military circles, but in the aftermath of the Boer War they had been warranted. The inquiry into Fisher's administration at the Admiralty was altogether more questionable. Esher was furious. 'It is inconceivable to me that they [the government] should be so foolish and weak', he fumed to Balfour, suggesting that the investigation was motivated as much by a desire to deflect awkward questions about naval construction as by genuine shortcomings at the Admiralty.[47] Esher endorsed using the CID, rather than a Royal Commission, to conduct the inquiry, but still deprecated the principle.[48] That the government elected to use the CID to examine the condition of the Navy, rather than to perform the far more pressing role of remedying the schism between naval and military planning laid bare before the Military Needs group the previous autumn, was indicative of the low priority it assigned to co-ordinating a cohesive national strategy.

Widely referred to as the 'Beresford Inquiry', the group began sitting at the end of April. If Fisher had been troubled by the invasion inquiry, then he was disgusted by what amounted to a direct attack on his personal authority. Upon learning of the appointment of the Beresford Inquiry he remarked resignedly to McKenna that 'it looks like the Prime Minister was contemplating throwing the Admiralty to the wolves!'[49] After meeting throughout the summer the group eventually exonerated the First Sea Lord, but the final report was less explicit than either Fisher or

44 Marder, *FDSF* I, pp. 159–71.
45 Ibid., pp. 186–8; Williams, *Defending the Empire*, pp. 162–4.
46 Marder, *FDSF* I, pp. 189–90.
47 Esher to Balfour, 13 and 15 April 1909 in Brett ed., *Esher*, pp. 382–3.
48 d'Ombrain, *War Machinery*, pp. 232–3.
49 Fisher to McKenna, 8 April 1909, in Marder ed., *FGDN* II, p. 242.

Esher would have liked. 'It has been a bitter disappointment', Fisher admitted, 'more bitter because each of the five members of the Committee so expressive to me and to others of the complete victory of the Admiralty'.[50] Disenchanted with the findings and approaching mandatory retirement age (which he had already avoided once by promotion to Admiral of the Fleet in December 1905), Fisher departed the Admiralty at the end of the year. Before doing so, he went to some lengths to ensure that his successor would not attempt to reverse any of the reforms he had instigated since 1904. With this intention in mind, Fisher approached the retired former C-in-C of the Channel Fleet, Admiral of the Fleet Sir Arthur Wilson, to take on the post of First Sea Lord.[51] Widely regarded as the outstanding Flag Officer of his generation, Wilson had regularly been consulted on strategic issues by the Admiralty since his own mandatory retirement in March 1907. He had also recently become a permanent member of the CID at the Prime Minister's invitation.[52] Yet he was not without his drawbacks as a candidate. 'I do not think it is possible to say how his regime is going to affect the Navy', one former subordinate wrote upon hearing of his nomination, 'those who prayed and asked for the supersession of Fisher will find that they have exchanged a very qualified autocracy for an unmitigated absolutism'.[53] An authoritarian and centralizer, Wilson was not ideally suited to the political world in which the First Sea Lord had to operate. Possibly for this reason he took some convincing to accept the post and confessed to 'looking forward with a good deal of dread to my new work'.[54]

Whilst the two men respected one another's opinions, Wilson's views on strategy differed from those of Fisher.[55] This much had become clear long prior to Fisher's championing of Wilson as his successor: differences of opinion between the two had been aired before the CID during the Beresford Inquiry. In March 1909 Fisher had issued a new series of war orders containing an ambitious plan to establish a continuous British presence off the German North Sea coastline in strength sufficient to 'seal in' enemy torpedo craft.[56] By re-fuelling destroyers at sea, Fisher hoped it would be possible to maintain enough boats off the German coastline to suppress the local defences, thereby allowing British armoured vessels to close the hostile shore and provide support to the blockading flotilla forces.[57] Fisher summarized the plan in a letter to McKenna in May: '*destroyers* watch by

[50] Fisher to Esher, 28 August 1909, in Marder ed., *FGDN* II, p. 261.

[51] N. Lambert, 'Admiral Sir Arthur Knyvett-Wilson, V.C. (1910–1911)' in M. Murfett ed., *The First Sea Lords from Fisher to Mountbatten*, Westport, CT: Praeger, 1995, pp. 35–50; *FNR*, pp. 199–203.

[52] See Wilson, 'Remarks on the War Plans', May 1907, in 'War Plans 1907' reprinted in Kemp ed., *Fisher Papers* II, pp. 454–64; Grimes, *War Planning*, pp. 99–100; Fisher to McKenna, 14 April 1909 in Marder ed., *FGDN* II, p. 244.

[53] Pollen to Slade, 24 January 1910, pp. 9–11, MRF/39/1, NMM.

[54] Wilson to Aston, 16 January 1910, AST 4/2, Aston Papers, [R]oyal [M]arines [M]useum, Portsmouth; Marder, *FDSF* I, pp. 211–12.

[55] D. G. Morgan-Owen, 'Cooked up in the Dinner Hour? Sir Arthur Wilson's War Plan, Reconsidered', *English Historical Review*, Vol. 130, No. 545, 2015, pp. 880–4.

[56] Morgan-Owen, 'History is a Record', pp. 565–7.

[57] Admiralty, 'War', p. 7, in 'War Plan G.U. War Orders for The Commander in Chief of the Home Fleet', 1909, MSS 253/84/3, NMRN.

night—*armoured cruisers* by day'.[58] Wilson was more circumspect. Since 1907 he had made clear his view that 'a continuous close watch off all the German ports, in sufficient strength to prevent anything from coming out, would be very difficult and costly to maintain, and, if effective, would bring us no nearer the end'.[59] Rather, the former C-in-C had stated his preference for a limited deployment of destroyers on purely observation duties, noting that 'one or two' off the mouth of each German river estuary would be sufficient to detect major enemy movements. He re-iterated this advice when called to give evidence to the Beresford Inquiry, stating that 'after a great deal of consideration I decided that it was quite impossible to attempt to keep a really close watch off the German ports, because of the risk'. The more realistic approach, he reasoned, was 'the policy of giving the enemy every possible opportunity of getting to sea in the hope that you will catch him when he is at sea'.[60] Wilson also professed himself 'perfectly satisfied as to their [the Germans] not doing us any vital injury in the way of invasion'.[61] He intended to keep the British fleets out of the North Sea entirely at the outbreak of war, suggesting that the 'North Sea Guard' scheme was unlikely to survive his arrival in Whitehall. Wilson was far from alone in viewing the March 1909 war plans as unrealistic. Herbert Richmond, a captain on the staff of the Home Fleet and Fisher's former Naval Assistant, noted in his diary that the plans 'are full of amateurisms'.[62] Richmond's replacement as Naval Assistant, Captain Henry Oliver, concurred, noting simply that 'I did not like the plans.'[63]

These differences meant that, after succeeding Fisher as First Sea Lord in early 1910, Wilson moved to amend the Navy's war plans to reflect his appreciation of the situation in the North Sea. Oliver, whom Wilson kept on as Naval Secretary, observed the changes first hand, recalling how 'the 1st Sea Lord [Fisher] locked up the plans in his safe and when Sir Arthur Wilson relieved him in 1910 he soon scrapped them and made better plans'.[64] Sydney Fremantle, former chair of the War College committee detailed to consider the 'North Sea Guard' in late 1907, accompanied Wilson to the Admiralty as Head of the War Division. He too recalled how 'my principle business was to edit the war plan, and to make it workable'.[65] As we shall see, the findings of the War College committee were to be reflected in the plans Fremantle drew up, albeit in a different manner to those drafted under Fisher.

[58] The term 'battle cruiser' was not in regular use until mid-1911; at this point the vessels were referred to as large armoured cruisers.

[59] Wilson, 'Remarks on the War Plans', May 1907, in 'War Plans 1907' in Kemp ed., *Fisher Papers* II, p. 455.

[60] CID, 'Report and Proceedings', pp. 307–8, CAB 16/9A.

[61] CID, 'Report and Proceedings of a Sub-Committee of the Committee of Imperial Defence Appointed to Inquire into Certain Questions of Naval Policy Raised by Lord Charles Beresford', 12 August 1909, p. 306, CAB 16/9A.

[62] Richmond diary, 8 April 1909, RIC/1/8, NMM.

[63] H. Oliver, 'Volume II of Recollections, written in 1946, covering period 1901–1939', p. 65, OLV/12, NMM.

[64] Ibid.   [65] Fremantle, *My Naval Career*, pp. 151–5.

Exercises conducted during the spring and summer provide a number of hints as to Wilson's intentions. Between 18 April and 2 May the Home and Atlantic Fleets, which between them comprised all of the fully commissioned battleships in home waters, met for a joint cruise. The majority of the time was spent conducting tactical exercises and evolutions. However, a period of the cruise was devoted to ascertaining how best to detect and interdict an enemy force in the North Sea which had 'in view an attack on either shipping, arsenals or other vulnerable objects on the East coast of Great Britain'.[66] Secret orders issued to Battenberg, who commanded the Blue or 'German' force, instructed him that 'the intention of the Blue Fleet is supposed to be the destruction of the Forth Bridge—this will not be known to RED'.[67] The destruction of the Queensferry Bridge, which crossed the Forth below the location of the fleet anchorage, had been a source of concern to the Admiralty throughout the development of the base at Rosyth. Fisher referred to it as 'that beastly bridge' and had cited it as a good cause to abandon work on the base.[68] The destruction of the bridge would effectively seal the anchorage and, if the fleet were anchored above the Queensferry, it would be trapped, leaving command of the North Sea to the Germans until the debris could be cleared. During the exercises, a defensive patrol flotilla was stationed in the Forth, in an attempt to protect the anchorage. This was the only measure of protection feasible in the immediate future, since the previously planned boom anti-torpedo defence had been proven to be inadequate during a practical trial and improvements in the fixed defences were unlikely to be sanctioned or constructed quickly.[69] Given Wilson's previously stated concerns about stationing armoured warships anywhere within range of German torpedo craft, it appears that the exercise was intended to test whether a British fleet in the Forth would be vulnerable to a German *coup de main*. If this was the intention, the results confirmed the First Sea Lord's concerns. Red cruisers detected, but were unable to stop, the Blue force, which fell upon and annihilated the local flotilla defence.[70] Any fleet in the anchorage would have been acutely vulnerable to a subsequent torpedo attack. Vice-Admiral Sir William May, the C-in-C Home Fleet, was moved to remark upon the 'weakness of a scattered patrol', which he considered 'the weakest form of defence'.[71] Further experiments in the summer suggested that the string of islands at the mouth of the estuary—the likely location of future fixed defences—would also be exposed to capture by

---

[66] 'Home Fleet Temporary Memo No. 114', Sheet 3, ADM 1/8119.

[67] Battenberg, 'Cruiser of Combined Fleets in North Sea April 1910 Cruiser Exercise No. 1 Commencing Tuesday 19th April 1910', 24 March 1910, p. 1, ADM 1/8119.

[68] Marder, *FDSF* I, pp. 421–2; Mackay, *Fisher*, pp. 337–8, 419.

[69] See docket, 'Portsmouth Boom Defence, Trial of "Ferret" against', 10 August 1909, ADM 116/1265/B, and Admiralty to War Office, 19 February 1910, Appendix III of 'The Forth', p. 19, in 'Committee of Imperial Defence, Home Ports Defence Committee, Memoranda No. 1M to 43. M, Aug. 1909 to Sep. 1921. With subject Index', CAB 13/1/18, Appendix III, No. 3, p. 19.

[70] Grimes, *War Planning*, p. 164.

[71] May to Admiralty, 13 May 1910, p. 18, in docket entitled 'R.N. War College: Returning report of the Commander-in-Chief Home Fleet on exercises carried by the Home and Atlantic Fleets during April and May last', ADM 1/8119.

raiding parties.[72] It is surely no coincidence that the First Sea Lord commissioned the Hydrographer to re-survey Scapa Flow as an alternative fleet anchorage at around this time.[73]

The summer manoeuvres provide further important clues regarding the development of the Admiralty's war plans. Graham Greene, the long-serving Secretary to the Admiralty, wrote to Slade confiding his concern that 'if any facts get out it will be evident that the whole scheme is based upon our probable action in the event of war with Germany'.[74] The exercises reflected the less aggressive stance hinted at in Wilson's pronouncements to the Beresford Inquiry and in the Home-Atlantic Fleet cruise. The British forces were positioned further away from the enemy coastline, with the majority of the observational duties being undertaken by armoured cruisers better suited to prolonged operations away from shore.[75] This approach was not without its drawbacks, however. The aggressive inshore operations Fisher had advocated may have been more risky and placed a greater burden on the Navy's flotilla forces, but they promised to deliver a reasonably consistent watch on German ports. The problem of a surprise invasion attempt would thus be removed after the opening moves of a conflict, as the Navy would descend on the enemy coastline and make the clandestine escape of a large convoy of troops impossible. Whilst less difficult to institute, Wilson's cruiser patrols did not offer the same degree of observational capability—particularly after dark and in conditions of poor visibility such as often prevailed in the North Sea. Moreover, they would not 'seal in' enemy torpedo craft. This had implications for the movements and basing of the British fleet, which would have to maintain a constant lookout for hostile torpedo craft. The danger would be particularly acute if the fleet were based upon the Forth, which it was believed was within range of German destroyers operating from Wilhelmshaven.[76] Crossing the North Sea undetected was just possible during the long hours of winter darkness, rendering the prospect of a potentially devastating surprise destroyer attack on the weakly defended anchorage a credible one, as had been demonstrated in the spring. The patrolling cruisers proved reasonably effective at discovering enemy movements during the summer manoeuvres, locating at least one attempted raid.[77] The exercises left no doubt as to the Admiralty's perception of German intentions, however. The first objective of the hostile force had been 'to raid or invade Red Territory'.[78] The risk of such an

[72] Oliver, 'Volume II of Recollections', p. 71, OLV/12, NMM; W. James, *A Great Seaman: The Life of Admiral of the Fleet Sir Henry F. Oliver*, London: A. F. & G. Whitherby, 1956, p. 71.

[73] Oliver, 'Volume II of Recollections', p. 70, OLV/12, NMM.

[74] Greene to Slade, 29 May 1910, pp. 6–7, MRF/33/1, NMM.

[75] Admiralty Mobilisation Department, 'Great Britain, Naval Manoeuvres, 1910', December 1910, p. 15, ADM 144/32.

[76] D.G. Morgan-Owen, 'An "Intermediate Blockade"? British North Sea Strategy, 1912–1914', *War in History*, Vol. 22, No. 4, 2015, p. 484.

[77] Edmund S. Poe, 'General Idea for the Blue Fleet', 5 July 1910, in Admiralty, 'Great Britain— Naval Manoeuvres, 1910', December 1910, pp. 22–3, ADM 144/32; R. Keyes, *The Naval Memoirs of Admiral of the Fleet Sir Roger Keyes*, Vol. I: *The Narrow Seas to the Dardanelles, 1910–1915*, London: Thornton Butterworth, 1934, pp. 22–3.

[78] Admiralty Mobilisation Department, 'Great Britain, Naval Manoeuvres, 1910', December 1910, p. 4, ADM 144/32.

attack was sufficient for the observing cruisers to be instructed to maintain a watch on enemy ports even if the opposing battle fleet put to sea, in order to prevent 'the escape of vessels for the attack of commerce or the invasion or raiding of Red territory'.[79] Here was evidence of the manner in which the demands of forestalling an invasion might conflict with attempts to score a decisive victory over the enemy fleet.

When the draft war orders Fremantle had been working on were finally circulated for comment in January 1911, they revealed the extent to which detecting and interdicting a potential invasion attempt was by now shaping Admiralty strategic thought.[80] Despite Wilson's previously stated opposition to large-scale destroyer operations off the enemy coastline, the orders contained provision to 'mass as many destroyers as possible on the German coast at the commencement of operations, even if this entails the withdrawal of the whole of them when their fuel is exhausted'. The plans explained that 'it is essential that the mouths of the Elbe and Weser should be closely watched during the period immediately following mobilisation by a strong Inshore Squadron'.[81] Should the blockading forces encounter an enemy force escorting transports, the Commodore leading the flotillas was to 'concentrate his attention primarily on the capture and destruction of the transport vessels, and avoid any engagement with the escort, bearing in mind that the main objective in such a case should be the transport vessels'.[82] The destroyers would thus fulfil the traditional function of a defensive flotilla: attacking lightly defended troops transports whilst more powerful units engaged the covering enemy warships. Support would be provided by an advanced armoured cruiser force similar in composition and capabilities to Fisher's North Sea Guard. Wilson had previously stated his view that armoured cruisers would be capable of harassing and engaging enemy battleships, using their superior speed to avoid a direct engagement.[83] This remained the case in 1911, due to the Admiralty's decision to take a technological 'plunge' on the HMS *Dreadnought* and her successors, which had temporarily paralysed foreign construction. This meant that the first German dreadnoughts only began to enter service between May and September 1910, and that the first German battlecruiser, *von der Tann*, did not complete trials until February 1911.[84] When the war orders were being prepared, therefore, Britain's most modern armoured cruisers and battle cruisers were comparable in dimensions and fighting power to the majority of relatively small German battleships then in service. The Admiralty did not hesitate to instruct the cruisers to 'prevent the enemy breaking out without being reported and brought into action'.[85] The

---

[79] 'Blue Battle Squadron Putting to Sea' in Admiralty, 'Great Britain—Naval Manoeuvres, 1910', December 1910, p. 15, ADM 144/32.

[80] Fremantle, *My Naval Career*, p. 155.

[81] May, 'Heligoland Bight Blockade Squadron: Preliminary War Orders for Commodore T. in Command', 23 January 1911, ADM 116/3096.

[82] May, 'Heligoland Bight Blockade Squadron', pp. 5–6, ADM 116/3096.

[83] Wilson, 'Remarks on Preliminary Draft Report', 5 January 1914, pp. 2–3, CAB 17/36, fos 20–1.

[84] *German Warships of World War I, The Royal Navy's Official Guide to the Capital Ships, Cruisers, Destroyers, Submarines and Small Craft, 1914–1918*, London: Greenhill, 1992 edn, pp. 43–9, 67.

[85] May, 'Heligoland Bight Blockade Squadron', p. 1, ADM 116/3096.

essence of the North Sea Guard—a fast, manoeuvrable squadron of capital ships deployed in an advanced position to detect and hamper offensive German operations before they reached the British coast—was thus preserved under Wilson.

Wilson's actions after arriving as First Sea Lord revealed that a significant shift in his strategic thinking had occurred since his appearance at the Beresford Inquiry in 1909. Gone were plans to rely on a 'very limited use' of destroyers off the German coastline, replaced by a temporary surge of flotilla and cruiser forces into the southern North Sea. The Admiralty was unambiguous in its justification for this *volte-face*, stating that such a watch was essential until 'the Straits of Dover are strongly held, all the mobilized ships have taken up their stations, and the Army has been mobilized'. This was a revealing statement. It made a direct link between naval war planning and the level of military preparation in Britain. The Admiralty felt that, during times of military unpreparedness, the Navy had to run a higher level of risk in its attempts to detect and engage enemy raiding parties or an invasion force. Viewed in conjunction with the prevalent trends in military thought—towards deploying the entire Expeditionary Force to the Continent and thereby leaving home defence to the Territorial Force—the way in which military strategy had begun to impinge upon naval planning was clear.

Here was evidence of the insidious effect that the General Staff's intentions could have upon British 'grand' strategy, understood as the sum of independently conceived naval and military efforts, rather than a coherent, top-down attempt at co-ordination. Accepting that sending the largest possible number of men to the Continent in an expeditious manner would be the best means of assisting France led logically to an assumption that the role of the Navy within British strategy was simply to facilitate this process—by protecting communications across the Channel and preventing a landing in Britain, thereby freeing up more manpower. By advocating such a strategy, military planners in favour of Continental warfare paid no attention to the Navy's wishes or preferences; they simply sought to impose their will on the Admiralty by refusing to countenance combined operations and stressing the necessity to support the French. By contrast the Admiralty's planning process *did* consider military plans and factored them into the Navy's own preparations, improving defensive provision so as not to leave the country vulnerable in the absence of the Regular Army. As the CID abdicated its responsibility to co-ordinate naval and military efforts, the Admiralty thus took up the slack and acted to try and inject some coherence to British strategy as a whole—even if by doing so it departed further and further from its preferred amphibious strategy.

THE AGADIR CRISIS

The urgent necessity to reconcile the General Staff's plans with those of the Royal Navy was laid bare during the summer. Tensions in Europe rose again after France attempted to exploit a dispute over local mining rights to justify establishing a military protectorate over Morocco. The official explanation offered—protecting European citizens during a period of domestic tumult—was an unconvincing justification given historic French aspirations in the region. Inflamed by the precipitous French action, German public opinion reacted in a particularly bellicose manner, inducing the Kaiser to consent to the aged gunboat SMS *Panther* being dispatched to Agadir as a signal of intent. In Britain the government was preoccupied with the most serious industrial unrest in a decade. Major-General Ewart, now Adjutant General, recorded how 'Strikes continue all over the country and we have had to send further troops to South Wales. It is a lively look out!' Some within the military department feared that the movement of units away from their mobilization centres might prejudice British intervention in the event of hostilities on the Continent.[86] The CID was occupied presiding over a conference with the Dominion premiers convened to discuss areas for greater co-operation in the sphere of imperial defence. It was only towards the end of July that decision makers in London began to view the European situation with a greater sense of urgency. 'Things are looking rather serious', Maurice Hankey, Naval Assistant to the CID wrote, 'there are some ominous symptoms.'[87] As had been the case during the Balkan Crisis in December 1908, the threat of hostilities in Europe prompted the government to re-visit its military and naval options. Sensing an opportunity to seize the initiative, supporters of dispatching the Army to the Continent precipitated this process by petitioning Asquith to convene a meeting of select Cabinet members and experts to discuss British strategy.[88]

Much of the impetus for this initiative came from the War Office, where Haldane and the new DMO, Brigadier General Henry Wilson, worked hard to impress the need for action upon the Cabinet. Since arriving at Horse Guards the previous summer Wilson had been appalled at the lack of firm arrangements to dispatch the Expeditionary Force.[89] A confirmed advocate of closer co-operation with the French, he viewed resolving these preparations as his highest priority.[90] Wilson viewed the competition between the Admiralty and War Office to shape government policy as a zero-sum game. Thus, in addition to throwing himself and his department into the logistical arrangements necessary to transport all six divisions of the Regular Army to France, he also began arranging evidence collected by his predecessor into an effective case intended to prove that the Navy could not bring a war against Germany to a conclusion by the exercise of commercial pressure alone.[91]

As relations between France and Germany worsened in early August, Wilson despaired of the government's inaction. After lunching with Haldane and Grey on 9 August he recorded in his notoriously indiscreet diary how the Foreign Secretary

---

[86] Ewart diary, 26 July, 17 August, and 19 August 1911, GD527/1/1/135/10, NRS.

[87] Hankey to Grant-Duff, 24 July 1911, AGDF 2/1, fo. 82, CAC.

[88] N. d'Ombrain, 'The Imperial General Staff and the Military Policy of a "Continental Strategy" during the 1911 International Crisis', *Military Affairs*, Vol. 34, Oct., 1970, pp. 88–93; Offer, *Agrarian Interpretation*, pp. 296–7; Lambert, *Planning Armageddon*, pp. 150–1.

[89] C. E. Callwell, *Field-Marshal Sir Henry Wilson: His Life and Diaries*, New York: Charles Scribner's Sons, 1927, pp. 89–94.

[90] Jeffery, *Wilson*, pp. 85–94.

[91] See the various documents in WO 106/47, fos 137–97; Williamson Jr, *Politics of Grand Strategy*, pp. 173–87; Lambert, *Planning Armageddon*, p. 152.

'had no idea what war meant' and that he 'seemed to me an ignorant, vain & weak man quite unfit to be the Foreign Minister of any country larger than Portugal'.[92] At the behest of Nicholson, now Chief of the Imperial General Staff, Wilson prepared a memorandum embodying his views on the military situation facing the country. This document expressed the essence of his desired strategy: to mobilize as rapidly as possible and to dispatch all six divisions of the Expeditionary Force to France. Yet the DMO did not restrict himself to purely military considerations. 'As regards the naval aspect of the problem', he wrote:

> what we ask is that it shall be possible safely to transport troops and supplies across the Channel and in the other directions indicated in this paper, and that the Navy will protect the United Kingdom from organized invasion from the sea. If this cannot be done the scheme falls to the ground.[93]

As ever, the level of defence required in Britain was fundamental to releasing the Regular Army for operations in Europe.

Whilst Wilson was working on his memorandum, Haldane impressed what he felt to be the realities of the situation upon Asquith, McKenna, Grey, and Churchill, with the result that the Prime Minister decided to convene an extraordinary meeting of select CID members the following week.[94] Upon learning of the meeting Hankey expressed his concerns to McKenna, warning the First Lord that neither Fisher nor Esher, both powerful opponents of sending the Army to the Continent, had received an invitation. He warned that Wilson 'has a perfect obsession for military operations on the continent' and that 'if he can get a decision at this juncture in favour of military action he will endeavour to commit us up to the hilt', thereby beginning a process whose logical conclusion was compulsory service and a mass army.[95] Forewarned, the naval leadership therefore had another opportunity to convince the government of the merits of its preferred maritime strategy.

The Admiralty responded to the DMO's activities with a memorandum of its own prior to the meeting. In this document Admiral Wilson presented a robust critique of the General Staff plan: 'If the proposed landing of the Expeditionary Force gave any hope of ensuring the final victory to France...it might be considered worth while...but even the advocates of the scheme do not pretend that this is the case.' In its stead he recommended the Admiralty's long-established scheme of embarking an army to raid the German coastline. This difference of opinion between the two services was by now unsurprising. More significant were the First Sea Lord's remarks about the effect the General Staff's plans would have upon the Navy. In addition to denting the offensive potential of British sea power:

> In the absence of practically the whole Regular Army the Navy will also have the responsibility of preventing raids and the panic arising therefrom thrown on it in an increasing degree.

[92] Wilson diary, 9 August 1911, HHW 1/20, Wilson Papers, IWM.
[93] General Staff, 'The Military Aspect of the Continental Problem', 15 August 1911, p. 2, CAB 38/19/47.
[94] Callwell, *Wilson*, p. 99; Jeffery, *Wilson*, p. 94.
[95] Hankey to McKenna, 15 August 1911, HNKY 7/3, Hankey Papers, CAC.

Any failure on the part of the Army to deal promptly with a raiding party, however small, which lands on our shores, will lead to demands from the public and the press for ships to be attached permanently to the coast and this could only be done by weakening the watch on the enemy.[96]

This argument has generally been passed over in favour of criticism of Wilson's amphibious plans,[97] but given the emphasis placed upon the Army's speed of mobilization in the draft war orders circulated to the Fleet in January, it deserves additional consideration. Officially the Admiralty remained wedded to the statements it had made before the 1907–8 invasion inquiry. These had been re-affirmed in November 1910, when Fremantle had drafted a paper for the First Sea Lord in preparation for a debate in the House of Lords re-iterating that 'invasion on even the moderate scale of 70,000 men is practically impossible'.[98] The document was produced 'for the use of the War Office' and subsequently published as an appendix to the second edition of General Sir Ian Hamilton's book *Compulsory Service*, and was thus widely available.[99]

Behind this imperturbable facade, however, the demands of detecting and intercepting enemy raiding parties or an invasion attempt was exercising an increasingly significant influence over naval war planning. The initial push towards the German coast envisaged in the January draft war orders, the sort of operation to which Wilson had previously been strongly opposed, was in large part a reflection of this demand. *Until* the flotilla forces along the east coast were ready and *until* the Army was prepared to repel an invasion, the Navy would be obliged to guarantee the security of the east coast in the face of the growing German Fleet. The departure of the Regular Army threatened to extend the period during which such risks were deemed necessary to the time it would take for the Territorial Force to become efficient, a matter of considerable debate and conjecture within the General Staff and more widely, but a period likely to be measured in terms of months.[100] A firm expression of political support for Brigadier General Wilson's 'With France' scheme therefore threatened both to deprive the Navy of a striking force for amphibious operations and to oblige the Fleet to adopt a strategic defensive—which would necessarily involve exposing ships and men to enhanced risks with little prospect of inflicting meaningful harm upon the enemy. The stakes were high as the day of the meeting approached.

At the session on 23 August, Brigadier-General Wilson delivered a polished presentation of the General Staff's scheme for co-operation with the French.

---

[96] Admiralty, 'Remarks by the Admiralty on Proposal (b) of the Memorandum by the General Staff', 21 August 1911, CAB 38/19/48.

[97] Williamson Jr, *Politics of Grand Strategy*, pp. 190–1; d'Ombrain, *War Machinery*, p. 102.

[98] Wilson, 'Notes Supplied by the Admiralty for the use of the War Office in the Debate that was to have taken place in November, 1910, in the House of Lords on a Motion by Lord Roberts', 19 November 1910, CAB 17/100, fos 23–4; Fremantle, *My Naval Career*, pp. 152–3.

[99] I. M. Hamilton, *Compulsory Service: A Study of the Question in Light of Experience*, London: John Murray, 1911, 2nd edn.

[100] Hamilton, *Compulsory Service*, pp. 26–9; Adams and Poirer, *The Conscription Controversy*, pp. 34–41; Spiers, *Haldane*, pp. 164–86; Strachan, 'The Territorial Army and National Defence', pp. 162–3.

He recorded in his diary how 'I had all my big maps on the wall and lectured for 1¾ hours. Everyone very nice.'[101] The shortcomings in the First Sea Lord's counter-proposals are well known.[102] The Admiral was viewed as a stone wall by many associated with the CID and he reinforced this image during the morning by stubbornly refusing to co-operate with plans to transport the Army to France. After lunch Sir Arthur outlined ambitious plans to mount a close blockade of the German coastline, to seize or destroy a number of formidably defended coastal installations and islands, and to conduct amphibious raids intended to detain enemy forces from reaching the front in France.[103] The naval aspects of these proposals were more credible than is often allowed,[104] but it is undeniable that the Admiral's presentation produced a negative impression upon the assembled ministers. His blithe assumption that troops would be readily available to conduct the landings he envisaged and that the targets he suggested were appropriate, made without so much as consulting the War Office, rendered his proposals useless in the event of an unexpected outbreak of war. Suddenness would be vital to the success of such a strategy: improvising the meticulous planning and preparation required to give the best chances of success was simply not possible on the fly. Of course the General Staff's consistent refusal to engage with the Admiralty in preparing plans for joint action was a major barrier to any such collaboration, but this did not matter during a period of crisis. The Prime Minister labelled Wilson's plan 'puerile' and told Haldane that he had 'dismissed it at once as wholly impracticable'.[105]

These failings aside, it is important to note that the First Sea Lord enjoyed considerably more success in other aspects of the discussion, particularly those relating to home defence. Admiral Wilson re-iterated his concerns that the dispatch of the entire Regular Army would have a powerful negative effect on public confidence and that the resulting panic 'might result in the movements of the Fleet being circumscribed with serious effect upon our naval operations'.[106] He stressed that 'he did not know whether the number of troops which would remain in the United Kingdom after the departure of the 6 divisions was sufficient to insure that raids would be immediately overwhelmed'.[107] McKenna supported him, underlining the 'great danger of interference with the freedom of movement of the Fleet' and of 'great pressure being brought to bear on the Government to tie the Fleet to the defence of our coasts'. These arguments impressed the Prime Minister sufficiently for Asquith to conclude that only four divisions should be sent abroad until the Territorial Force had achieved efficiency sufficient to allow it to take the field

[101] Diary for 23 August 1911 in Callwell, *Wilson*, p. 99.
[102] For the most prominent criticisms, see Hankey, *Supreme Command* I, p. 81; Williamson Jr, *Politics of Grand Strategy*, pp. 189–94; d'Ombrain, *War Machinery*, pp. 101–3; Gooch, *Plans of War*, pp. 289–92; Strachan, pp. 394–5; Lambert, *Planning Armageddon*, pp. 152–5.
[103] CID, 'Minutes of the 114th Meeting, August, 1911', pp. 11–18, CAB 2/2.
[104] Morgan-Owen, 'Cooked up in the Dinner Hour'.
[105] Asquith to Haldane, 31 August 1911, MSS 5909, fos 140–1, NLS.
[106] CID, 'Minutes of the 114th Meeting, August, 1911', p. 11, CAB 2/2.   [107] Ibid., p. 15.

rapidly.[108] In doing so he deflected an attempt by Brigadier General Wilson to secure an agreement to the dispatch of five divisions to France.[109]

Despite the attempt he later made in his memoirs to depict the August 1911 meeting as decisive in determining British strategy in 1914,[110] at the time Hankey was greatly relieved by Asquith's decision to preserve the status quo. 'The great point is that no decision was arrived at', he informed Fisher, 'this means, in my opinion, defeat for our opponents.'[111] This outcome was confirmed when the Radical members of the Cabinet—John Morley, Lord Loreburn and Lewis 'Lou-Lou' Harcourt—who had been excluded from the meeting learned of the proceedings in early September. Morley in particular was furious, both at having been excluded and at the principle of entering into ill-defined military commitments to France. An initial row escalated into a potential split in the Cabinet between the Liberal Imperialists—Grey, Haldane, Asquith and Churchill—and their Radical colleagues.[112] The War Office was requested to produce a memorandum detailing the development of its plans to provide military support to France. This document, signed by Nicholson but most likely written by Henry Wilson, admitted that plans to send all six divisions of the Expeditionary Force had been under consideration since April 1910. The defence that 'this enlarged scheme was drawn up not in supersession of, but as alternative to, the original scheme'[113] failed to convince the Radicals in the Cabinet, who condemned Wilson as a militarist.[114] Asquith defused the situation by agreeing that no military or naval commitments should be entered into without the approval of the Cabinet and by placing seemingly strict limits on the degree to which the General Staff was able to intertwine Britain into French mobilization arrangements, yet these barriers did not change the fact that the government had erred towards providing military support to France in preference to the Admiralty's plans in 1905–6, 1908–9, and 1911. As Henry Wilson noted, 'they will stop me going to Paris, I think, but not much else'.[115]

* * *

The Admiralty's performance at the meeting on 23 August convinced the Prime Minister that reform of the naval administration was an urgent necessity. Both Churchill and Haldane lobbied Asquith for the chance to replace McKenna as First Lord, the latter threatening to resign from the War Office unless changes were made at the Admiralty.[116] The most pressing matter at hand was the institution of a naval staff, which was widely perceived to be the most effective means of improving the Admiralty's strategic planning process and of fostering coherent discussions

[108] Asquith to Haldane, 31 August 1911, MSS 5909, NLS; Williamson Jr, *The Politics of Grand Strategy*, p. 193.
[109] CID, 'Minutes of the 114th Meeting, August, 1911', p. 17, CAB 2/2; Williamson Jr, *Politics of Grand Strategy*, p. 193.
[110] Hankey, *Supreme Command* I, p. 82.
[111] Hankey to Fisher, 24 August 1911, FISR 1/10, no. 59, CAC.
[112] Williamson Jr, *Politics of Grand Strategy*, pp. 196–200.
[113] Nicholson, 'Action taken by the General Staff since 1906…', WO 106/49A/1.
[114] Wilson diary, in Callwell, *Wilson* I, p. 106.
[115] Ibid., p. 107.   [116] Marder, *FDSF* I, pp. 246–7.

between the services. 'The Admiralty', Haldane wrote to Grey, 'must have a better intellectual basis.'[117] Ultimately Churchill won the day, exchanging his seat at the Home Office with McKenna and assuming the position of First Lord in October. One of his first actions was to remove Admiral Wilson from his post. Fundamental to this decision was Wilson's rigid opposition to the institution of a staff structure, an organization he regarded as entirely unsuited to the Navy and as an intrusion into the First Sea Lord's prerogative to shape strategy.[118] Confessing himself 'very glad to get away',[119] Wilson nevertheless retained his seat on the CID—an appointment that was to prove significant over the next two years.

The political desire to improve the effectiveness of the Admiralty's planning process was understandable. Successive First Sea Lords had presented what amounted to the same strategy to the government on three separate occasions, stubbornly refusing to acknowledge military advice that the operations they contemplated were not realistic and failing to make adequate preparations to conduct them. Administrative changes would only go so far in remedying what amounted to a fundamental difference of opinion, however. The Navy's planning process was more effective than is generally accepted—a fact evidenced by the decision to recall both Fisher and Wilson to the Admiralty after the outbreak of war to improve strategic direction.[120] Indeed, by 1911 the Admiralty was beginning to occupy the territory the CID ought rightfully to have been master of, and to try and create a degree of coherence between naval and military planning. Here was a crucial difference between the services and a point upon which the General Staff is open to criticism—the military wilfully ignored the need to support its sister service, whereas the Navy sought actively to make good the vulnerabilities that the Staff's plans produced. The Admiralty's planning process may have appeared less professional to the politicians than the General Staff's (although the reality is rather more doubtful), but it was the Navy which displayed the willingness to concert a strategy in which the two services complemented each other.

After dismissing Wilson, Churchill was soon confronted by the same dilemma his predecessor had faced: how to adjust the Navy's war plans to accommodate the potential departure of a large portion of the Regular Army from Britain at the outbreak of war, without prejudicing the Fleet's ability to take offensive action against the German Navy. This challenge defined the subsequent two-and-a-half years of work at the Admiralty.

---

[117] Haldane to Grey, 2 October 1911, MSS 5909, fos 151–4, NLS.

[118] Wilson to Churchill, 30 October 1911, in E. E. Bradford, *Life of Admiral of the Fleet Sir Arthur Knyvet Wilson*, London: John Murray, 1923, pp. 229–35; Marder, *FDSF* I, pp. 256–7.

[119] Wilson to his sister, 27 November 1911, quoted in Bradford, *Wilson*, p. 227.

[120] Morgan-Owen, 'Cooked up in the Dinner Hour', p. 905.

8

Surrendering the Initiative

Admiral Wilson's departure from the Admiralty in the autumn of 1911 precipitated six months of flux in naval strategy. By this time the steady growth of German
naval power, the fortification of Heligoland and other stretches of the North Sea
coastline, and the challenges posed by developments in submarine and torpedo
technology had all rendered aggressive inshore operations on the far side of the
North Sea highly problematic for the Royal Navy. Yet no obvious alternative
approach to war against Germany remained without surrendering the watch upon
German ports which had been so fundamental to all of the Navy's previous planning. The resulting uncertainty led to a period of debate and conjecture over the
turn of the year. Senior flag officers in the Fleet, led by the newly promoted C-in-C
Vice-Admiral Sir George Callaghan, raised 'grave objections' to proposals which
would risk exposing the Home Fleet in German coastal waters.[1] Proponents of
using flotilla forces to conduct watches of German river estuaries remained,
although how to provide the necessary support appeared progressively less clear.[2]

The Admiralty reached the conclusion that inshore operations would no longer
be feasible early the following year, informing the Fleet that 'the Blockade by the
British Fleet of the whole German Coast on the North Sea is to be considered
cancelled'.[3] This decision represented a seismic shift in naval thought. All previous
planning for war against Germany had been predicated upon maintaining some
form of watch on the German debouches to the North Sea. The dangers inherent
in abandoning direct observation had long been recognized: not being able to
detect German movements had been the basis of all of the Admiralty's concerns
about the vulnerability of the east coast during the crucial opening moves of an
Anglo-German war. Allowing the Germans to proceed into the North Sea
undetected had numerous other negative ramifications. In the first instance it re-
opened questions over where to base the Fleet which had previously only been an
issue during the period of 'strained relations'. If enemy torpedo craft were able to
penetrate deep into the North Sea without detection, then the Fleet either had to
be based at a securely defended anchorage or kept out of range of German destroyers.
The exercises held off the Firth of Forth in early 1910 had revealed the existing

---

[1] Callaghan, 'War Plans Pages 1 to 24—X Notes on Operations in the North Sea', 9 January 1912,
ADM 116/3096.
[2] Callaghan, 'War Plans —VII War Stations', 9 January 1912; Arbuthnot to C-in-C Home Fleet,
18 December 1911, ADM 116/3096.
[3] Admiralty to Callaghan, 1912, in docket, 'War Plans, Remarks on Certain Points In', ADM
116/3096.

defensive arrangements at the anchorage to be unsatisfactory, yet more effective fixed defences were still not in place. The Admiralty would thus either have to accept the risk to a fleet based in the Forth, or move it out of range—to Portland, a west coast port, or the undeveloped natural anchorage of Scapa Flow in the Orkneys—remote from supporting infrastructure and the exposed east coast. Locating the fleet so far from its theatre of operations would re-open the difficult questions Balfour had posed in 1905: how to defend the east coast if the fleet was removed from the North Sea. The greater the distance between the fleet anchorage and the most vulnerable stretches of the mid-east coast, the greater the risk of a major landing became. The Fremantle Committee had calculated that a fleet based at Cromarty would be unlikely to prevent the landing of 80,000 Germans south of Hull if the armada being sighted from shore was the first indication of hostile activity. Using Rosyth, some 190 miles due south, would shorten the fleet's reaction time considerably. Scapa Flow, however, was almost 150 miles north-north-east of Cromarty. West coast or Irish ports were even more remote. A fleet operating from an anchorage safe from enemy torpedo attack would thus be too far away to guarantee breaking up a German landing covered by the High Seas Fleet. The situation that had motivated the Admiralty to run increased risks at the outset of war between 1906 and 1911—with either the North Sea Guard or by 'massing' destroyers in the Bight—might now be extended to the entirety of an Anglo-German conflict in the North Sea.

Eschewing efforts to contain German torpedo craft within the Bight would also require the permanent attachment of destroyer flotillas to the fleet itself, as associating light craft with the battleships would be necessary in order to provide the latter protection from marauding enemy torpedo craft. Yet operating so many different vessels together produced myriad command and control challenges and also absorbed most of the Navy's most seaworthy modern destroyers. These factors combined to face the Admiralty with the unenviable task of establishing a substantially new approach to operations against Germany during the course of 1912, in the context of formidable technological, infrastructural, and logistical constraints.

Yet despite the seriousness of the situation in the North Sea, admitting their concerns to the CID remained an unappealing prospect to the naval leadership. Lord Roberts and the National Service League continued to run an active campaign in favour of conscription, citing the threat of invasion as a key justification for compulsory military training. Roberts grew progressively more forceful in his public criticisms of the Territorial Force, questioning 'whether a force thus constituted is an army at all' and repeating the 'impossibility of constructing a defensive Army equal to this country's needs on a basis of voluntary enlistment'.[4] Many within the General Staff were sympathetic to this viewpoint, including Henry Wilson, who was briefing the new Unionist leader Andrew Bonar Law on the force's deficiencies.[5]

---

[4] Article by Roberts in the *National Review*, quoted in Adams and Poirier, *The Conscription Controversy*, pp. 44–8.

[5] F. Maurice, *Haldane, 1856–1915: The Life of Viscount Haldane of Cloan*, London: Faber & Faber, 1937, p. 289.

Placing the deteriorating situation in the North Sea before the CID therefore risked playing into the hands of those who wished to raise a national army, the ultimate employment of which was likely to be on the Continent. Discussions of strategy during the Morocco Crisis, the Balkan Crisis, and Agadir had all pointed to a political willingness to dispatch the Regular Army to assist the French and enlarging the pool of trained manpower available threatened to facilitate an extension of this policy. Yet the requirements of home defence also appeared to be the most effective tool available to the Navy in order to curtail plans to dispatch the entire Expeditionary Force to Europe. Asquith had accepted the principle of limiting Britain's initial commitment to four regular divisions in 1908–9 and had re-affirmed this stance in August 1911. If the Navy could secure a re-affirmed endorsement of the status quo produced by previous CID judgements, two divisions of regular troops were viewed as sufficient to provide the degree of re-assurance required to relieve pressure on the Fleet and to render British shores inviolable to even minor raids. If effective arguments could be put forward, the troops might ultimately even become available for amphibious operations in concert with the Navy. Whereas the War Office had used home defence as a justification for an inefficient auxiliary establishment prior to 1904–5, the Admiralty was now obliged to use it to prevent the General Staff's ambition to commit Britain to fighting a war in Europe from undermining the Navy's freedom of action.

'A CONSIDERABLE ELEMENT OF CHANCE AND OF RISK'

As had been the case since Fisher oversaw the creation of the North Sea Guard in 1906–7, the Admiralty remained committed to finding a solely naval means of guaranteeing its responsibility to prevent a major landing even whilst it engaged in bureaucratic manoeuvres with the General Staff. Its first attempt to remedy the Navy's deteriorating capacity to prevent an invasion was to experiment with a system of patrols ranging across the middle of the North Sea during the spring and summer of 1912. Five cruiser squadrons and four destroyer flotillas were detailed to watch a series of areas stretching from the mouth of the Baltic to the Hook of Holland. It was hoped that these observational forces would provide a watch effective enough to enable the Battle Fleet to operate safely from Rosyth, from where it could provide support to the patrols.[6] In effect the blockade of the German coastline would thus be retreated into the mid-North Sea. The thorny question of how to offer protection to the east coast during the opening period of a war remained unsolved, however. The Admiralty intended to adopt the reasonable if conservative approach of collecting the Fleet on the west coast of Scotland, outside of range of potential danger. Yet this would revive the now familiar problem of leaving the east coast and the patrols guarding it vulnerable to pre-emptive German action. The Admiralty asked the General Staff whether it would be possible to provide the artillery

[6] Admiralty, 'Memorandum to Accompany War Orders', April 1912, ADM 116/3096.

and men necessary to make Scapa Flow a secure anchorage—a compromise solution but a preferable one to using a west coast base—but the question remained unresolved due to political opposition to spending money defending an additional anchorage when works at Rosyth were already under construction.[7]

The reliability of the Admiralty's plans was put to the test during the summer manoeuvres. The exercises were framed to assess the capacity of the patrols to detect and intercept German raiding parties making for the east coast. Churchill, who had proven a very engaged and proactive First Lord since arriving at the Admiralty in October 1911, took a characteristically prominent part in shaping the scheme. The resulting scenario replicated the situation the country faced in the absence of the Expeditionary Force—down to the detail of only 20,000 regular troops remaining in the country—a clear indication of way in which defensive considerations were rising to the top of the Admiralty's agenda.[8] The exercises placed particular emphasis on the opening moves of an Anglo-German war, positioning the Battle Fleet on the west coast of Scotland and detailing the attacking force to 'cover the descent of a military expedition on the Blue coast in vessels known to be ready for immediate sailing'.[9]

The defensive patrols did score some notable successes during the course of the manoeuvres. Nevertheless, Callaghan's 'German' fleet succeeded in landing 28,000 men at Filey on the Yorkshire coastline.[10] Admiral May, the former C-in-C, acted as Chief Umpire. In his report he noted that 'by acting at once, the element of surprise is in favour of Red, and Blue battleships may be too far away to interfere'.[11] Here was the same dilemma the Admiralty had grappled with since 1905: how to keep the Fleet positioned so as to prevent a German landing without exposing it to torpedo attack.

In response to the success enjoyed by the side representing the Germans, Churchill took immediate steps to secure political support for additional spending on east coast infrastructure. In August he petitioned the Prime Minister for funds to improve the defences at Cromarty and Scapa Flow in order to enable the Fleet to concentrate closer to the decisive theatre of operations.[12] This would not solve the difficulties involved in detecting enemy movements in the North Sea, however. Concerningly, after examining the experience of the manoeuvres, the War Staff reached the conclusion that no ready solution existed to this problem in the short term. Captain Ballard, the Navy's most experienced strategic planner, summarized the situation:

> If circumstances permit of the necessary dispositions being made, the situation of a hostile Fleet which has left its ports to attack British territory or trade may be ascertained at one or more of the following stages of its proceedings:

[7] Wilson diary, 16 April 1912, HHW 1/32/4, IWM.

[8] Churchill, 'Memorandum on the 1912 Manoeuvres', 25 May 1912, CHAR 13/9/59, CAC.

[9] Admiralty, 'Naval Manoeuvres, 1912', pp. 1–2, ADM 116/1176B.

[10] May, 'Naval Manoeuvres, 1912, Narrative of Events by Umpire-in-Chief', ADM 116/1176B.

[11] May, 'Naval Manoeuvres 1912: Remarks by the Umpire in Chief', p. 14, MAY/10, May Papers, NMM.

[12] Churchill to Asquith, 10 August 1912, CHAR 13/12/20, CAC.

(a) Immediately on sailing;
(b) At some point on its passage;
(c) At the point where it delivers its attack.

To effect the desired object at (a), a close and perpetual watch by day and night on the hostile exits is necessary. This was the strategy of the old wars, but under modern conditions it involved an exceptional degree of risk to the ships employed... [German] submarines, torpedo craft, and mines are a constant menace to the blockaders, and his cruisers can emerge and drive off the destroyers on the blockade at any time unless the latter are closely supported by an armoured squadron which itself may be driven off by submarines or the blockaded battle fleet...

If, on the other hand, no steps are taken to ascertain the enemy's movements until he has reached his point of attack, as at (c), his intentions can only be frustrated by ensuring that wherever he may arrive a force superior to his own will engage him, within at most a few hours, or he will succeed in effecting his purpose. If long stretches of coast and lines of outer commercial blockade have to be protected against the enemy's fleets in this way—as would be necessary in the case of a defence of our position against Germany—such a plan would involve the maintenance of separate battle fleets at many points such as the Thames, the Humber, the Forth, Cromarty and Scapa Flow, besides cruisers and destroyers. This system of defence is, in fact, the most expensive of all...

There remains only the third alternative, viz. to ensure if possible that the enemy shall be sighted on his passage so as to give time to bring the main defending fleet in contact with him before he reaches his objective or at any rate soon after... It is not considered that the general results of the Manoeuvres afford any justification to alter the views expressed on this point.[13]

Churchill could not help but appreciate the implications of what Ballard was saying: the threat of raids was a real one and the Admiralty would not be able to solve it in the immediate future. The First Lord found this revelation an unpalatable one. He bemoaned the War Staff's inability to deliver an adequate solution to the problem to Brigadier General Wilson, venting about 'the total lack of knowledge of war, higher leading, and Staff work in the Navy', and speaking in envious tones of the DMO's staff at the War Office.[14]

Frustrated as the First Lord may have been, to his credit he did not conceal the situation from the Prime Minister as his predecessors had. In a summary of the manoeuvres he prepared for Asquith during the autumn, Churchill was frank in his assessment of the risks the Navy was running. He explained how 'a considerable element of chance and of risk that important hostile movements will not be reported and intercepted in the early stages is inseparable from all dispositions other than a close blockade'. The implication of these difficulties was that:

a German battle fleet seeking to maintain itself in the North Sea would be defeated; that German flotillas endeavouring to attack British battle fleets would be gradually worn down and broken up, and their supporting cruisers brought to action or forced

---

[13] Ballard, 'Remarks on War Orders for an Observation Force in the North Sea in connection with the lessons of the 1912 Manoeuvres', 16 September 1912, pp. 1–2, ADM 116/866B, fos 285–7.
[14] Wilson diary, 19 October 1912, HHW 1/32/10, IWM.

to fly; that landings would be interrupted; and that forces landed would have their oversea communications immediately severed; are all conclusions which may be reasonably held. None of them, however, obviate the possibility of a determined enemy, not afraid of risking the loss of 15,000 or 20,000 men, making a series of simultaneous or successive descents upon different portions of the British coast, and landing men in bodies from 5,000 to 10,000 strong.[15]

The Admiralty therefore advised the Prime Minister of the importance of retaining a 'compact force' of regular troops in the country at the outset of war, to respond to such raiding parties.

THE 'WHOLE QUESTION OF FOREIGN POLICY AND STRATEGY'

Churchill made this recommendation fully aware of the direction of travel of military planning. He had been in close touch with Henry Wilson during the Agadir Crisis and had felt the full force of the DMO's arguments to dispatch six divisions of troops to the Continent on that occasion and subsequently. Despite the Cabinet's instructions to proceed with caution, Wilson had continued to work to perfect arrangements for the dispatch of the entire Expeditionary Force even after the Morley-led revolt over Anglo-French staff talks during the autumn of 1911. Wilson visited eastern Belgium in March 1912, after which he attempted to revive long-deceased plans for Anglo-Belgian military co-operation.[16] He also continued to seek opportunities to secure political endorsement for the principle of dispatching all six divisions of the Expeditionary Force. An indication of his intentions can be gleaned from his reaction when the Under-Secretary of State for War, Colonel John Seely, made an over-exuberant claim as to the War Office's ability to deploy 150,000 men to Europe. After hearing of Seely's mis-step Wilson noted mercilessly in his diary 'now that he is in a mess I will pin him down to the 6 Divs: as Exped: Force'.[17]

Churchill knew of Wilson's aspirations and was broadly supportive of them. The First Lord invited the DMO to the Admiralty on a regular basis and ensured that he met with the First Sea Lord and Chief of the War Staff. After one such occasion in January, Wilson recorded in his diary how 'we had a long and intimate talk about things, and I am greatly pleased with their outlook...the most satisfactory evening I have spent for years'. These personal links enabled Wilson to make progress with the transport arrangements to send the Army to France, which Churchill ensured were expedited.[18] Yet they also enabled the First Lord to monitor the activities of the General Staff. This left him under no illusion that the military department remained fixed in its view that the entire Expeditionary Force should be sent

---

[15] Churchill, 'Notes on the Manoeuvres: Prepared for the Prime minister by the First Lord', 17 October 1912, ADM 116/3381.

[16] Williamson Jr, *Politics of Grand Strategy*, p. 215.

[17] Wilson diary, 13 and 14 March 1912, HHW 1/32/3, IWM.

[18] Wilson diary, 17 and 18 January 1912, HHW 1/33/1, IWM.

to the Continent as fast as possible, to the exclusion of other considerations. Mindful of his naval advisers' views that raids could no longer be intercepted with any degree of certainty, the First Lord became convinced that the government ought to restrain the General Staff for the time being and re-commit to the retention of two divisions of regular troops in Britain until the Territorials had assumed real military value.

To this end Churchill sought to build a consensus in favour of re-opening the CID's consideration of the possibility of invasion. After submitting his appreciation of the manoeuvres to Asquith, the First Lord exploited his friendship with the Seely to secure backing from the War Office for a renewed invasion inquiry. Churchill and Battenberg, whom he had recently installed as First Sea Lord, impressed upon the Secretary of State for War that the departure of the entire Expeditionary Force would severely prejudice the Navy's own strategy by obliging it to subordinate offensive action to the demands of covering the east coast. Impressed by the strength of naval feeling on this point, Seely discussed the need for a new CID inquiry with the Prime Minister on 2 January. He explained how the naval authorities now considered that raids of up to 8,000 men might reach the British coast in large, swift liners. Landing a force of 70,000 men had become more problematic than ever, but it appeared that the Navy had increased its estimation of the likelihood of raids at the outset of hostilities. 'It would follow that we should require forces of all arms instantly ready for war', Seely deduced, 'on the other hand, we should *not* require a large central force, as provided for by the Territorial Army.'[19] The Navy's new assessment of the situation might, therefore, necessitate a re-consideration of how to structure not only the Expeditionary Force, but the Army as a whole.

The petitions impressed Asquith. In addition to the arguments they made about strategy and force structure, the suggestion that the Territorial Force as currently constituted might not meet the nation's requirements appealed on political and financial grounds. Recruiting Haldane's target of 300,000 men had proven unattainable, so reducing the already tenuous strategic justification for the size of the force—home defence, even though ulterior motives were clearly present—might enable the government to conceal this failure.[20] The CID discussed the requirement for a new invasion inquiry on 7 January and Hankey was duly set to work on a draft proposal.[21] Pleased that Asquith had proven amenable to his proposals, Churchill worked to impress upon the Prime Minister how important developing a secure east coast anchorage was to alleviating the Navy's difficulties. The two discussed the issue at length during a tour of the Scottish coast aboard the Admiralty yacht at the end of January. This was followed by visits to armaments works in the north-east, a prime target for destruction by a German raid.[22]

As was by now usual CID practice, a sub-committee was formed to conduct the renewed investigation into invasion. Sittings of the new body began in March

---

[19] Seely to Asquith, 3 January 1913, CAB 17/35, fo. 16.   [20] Spiers, *Haldane*, pp. 182–4.
[21] Wilson diary, 7 January 1913, HHW 1/33/1, IWM; Hankey to Asquith, 13 January 1913, CAB 17/35.
[22] Roskill, *Hankey* I, pp. 124–5.

1913, whereupon it quickly became clear that the questions at hand were far larger than solely home defence. Before the proceedings began Repington had antici-pated that any decision on the topic would have far-reaching consequences for the employment of the Expeditionary Force and for British strategy as a whole.[23] His prediction was quickly proven accurate. Despite Asquith's attempts to limit the scope of the discussion, the inquiry ballooned into a de facto discussion of how to approach a war against Germany. From the outset Churchill assumed that the gov-ernment had accepted the General Staff's plans to dispatch all six divisions of the Regular Army to the Continent and that he needed to reverse this trend. 'The situ-ation...which should be examined', he argued, 'was that in which Great Britain would be placed after the dispatch oversea of all the regular divisions.' If the hypothesis of the previous inquiry—that two divisions would be retained for home defence—held good, then 'the Admiralty were satisfied that the fear of raids was groundless'.[24] This line of argument was calculated to expose the divisions over national strategy within the Cabinet. Lloyd George felt it 'inconceivable' that the whole Expeditionary Force should be sent abroad. McKenna was equally dubious. Yet Seely, Haldane, Asquith, and Grey all contemplated precisely such a course—as had Churchill himself before becoming aware of the realities of the situation at the Admiralty. 'It would be sounder policy', Grey argued, 'to assume entire depend-ence upon the Territorial Force for Home Defence, as circumstances might render the co-operation of the regular forces either impossible or inadvisable.'[25]

Seeing an opportunity to formalize the principle of dispatching the entire Expeditionary Force, the General Staff argued the necessity of such a course with renewed vigour. Henry Wilson was quick to apprehend the scale of the issue at stake for British strategy. After being excluded from the proceedings owing to his intransigence, the DMO worked hard to impress the importance of bringing the discussion around to the 'whole question of foreign policy and strategy' upon the CIGS, General Sir John French.[26] Wilson's point was a simple one: to avoid nar-row considerations of how large or small a raiding force might be, but to focus instead on how the government intended to conduct a future European war and to shape the armed forces accordingly. If the politicians intended to presage their dip-lomacy upon supporting the French, he was sure that the next logical step was to agree to dispatch as large an army as possible to their aid. This line was reflected in the memoranda the War Office submitted to the inquiry, which argued in favour of 'the dispatch of the whole Expeditionary Force, trusting to the remaining Regular troops and to the Territorial Force to resist the contemplated attack'.[27] Nevertheless, despite coaching from Wilson, French was not a shrewd political

---

[23] Esher, 'Notes of a Conversation', 14 February 1913, Asquith MS 24, fos 115–20, Asquith Papers, Bod.

[24] 'Minutes of the 2nd Meeting Held on April 1, 1913' in CID, 'Report and Proceedings of a Standing Sub-Committee of the Committee of Imperial Defence Appointed by the Prime Minister to Reconsider the Question of Attack on the British Isles from Oversea', 15 April 1914, p. 34, CAB 16/28A, fo. 22.

[25] Minutes of the second and third meetings, CAB 16/28A, fos 23–5.

[26] Wilson diary, 4 March 1913, HHW 1/33/3, IWM.

[27] Seely, 'Memorandum by the Secretary of State for War', OA 24, CAB 16/28B.

operator like the DMO. During a meeting on 18 April the CIGS let slip that 'the General Staff had not contemplated the retention at home of two divisions for six months'. Grierson's diary suggests that a year might have been a more accurate figure.[28] Planning of this character was in direct contravention of the instructions the Prime Minister had issued in the wake of Agadir and would have been explosive if revealed to the entire Cabinet. Asquith was appalled, protesting that he had made a commitment to Parliament to retain two divisions.[29] Faced with incontrovertible evidence of his government's failure to control the evolution and development of British strategy, the Prime Minister appeared hapless.

The opening months of the invasion inquiry saw the group flit between issues of technical detail—such as the local defences and ease of access to east coast ports— and fundamental questions of national strategy: how large the Expeditionary Force should be and whether it should be available for instant deployment to Europe. Throughout the spring and summer Churchill worked to find a solution that would free the Regular Army for offensive operations whilst simultaneously pro-viding the degree of security the Navy required.[30] In May he even explored the possibility of making 12,000 naval reservists available to the War Office to man coastal defences.[31] This gesture was a sign of the First Lord's support for the dis-patch of the Expeditionary Force, but the real question was the efficiency of the military forces that would remain in the British Isles after the dispatch of the Regular Army. During the summer the focus of the inquiry thus settled upon the efficiency of the Territorial Force. This put the military authorities on to the back foot, as many within the Army and the War Office were highly critical of the TF, believing it an insufficient reserve for the Regular Army. Churchill, too, had his doubts about the Territorials. Addressing the suggestion that one division of regular troops might be sufficient to stiffen the TF sufficiently to resist a major raid, the First Lord was dismissive:

> …dependence upon a crowd of Territorials in place of one good Regular division might be compared with an attempt to stop a bullet by a mass of cotton wool instead of a quarter-inch plate. What he hoped to gain was the retention in the country of a small and compact Regular force.[32]

Churchill's preferred solution was to increase the size of the Regular Army as a whole. The General Staff echoed this assessment. Sir John French informed the sub-committee that it was 'generally accepted that one regular soldier was equal to three Territorials'[33] and the Director of Military Training, Major-General Robertson, stated bluntly that 'the Territorial Force does not meet the demands which are now made upon it'.[34] Departmental loyalties prevented members of the

[28] Entries for 22 August 1912 in Macdiarmid, *Grierson*, p. 250.
[29] Minutes of the fourth meeting, CAB 16/28A, fo. 30.   [30] Ibid.
[31] Churchill minute, 2 May 1913, CHAR 13/22A/60, CAC.
[32] Minutes of the eighth meeting, CAB 16/28A, fo. 45.
[33] Minutes of the seventh meeting, CAB 16/28A, fo. 40.
[34] Minutes of the seventeenth meeting, CAB 16/28A, fo. 125.

War Office staff from being more explicit and revealing the extent of their often deeply felt private doubts about the TF.

No such restraint was required from Lord Roberts, however, who along with his co-conspirators from the 1907–8 inquiry secured an invitation to appear before the sub-committee. The 'invasionists' stressed that the TF was 51,000 men and 2,000 officers short of its full establishment, lacked training, and was never exercised *en masse*, rendering it of questionable utility in the field.[35] The General Staff eventually re-grouped and mounted a half-hearted defence to the effect that the TF would be capable of dealing with a landing on the scale contemplated by the Admiralty—which had by now risen to some 20,000 men. Arguing that the TF was competent to overwhelm raids of the size contemplated by the Admiralty enabled the War Office to sustain its case that the Expeditionary Force should be free to proceed overseas with no constraint. However, this would only be the case if Churchill's initial premise that larger and more numerous raids were the primary issue at stake remained accurate. By the time that larger questions of naval strategy came up for discussion, it was clear that this was no longer the case.

'NAVAL OPERATIONS WILL BE GREATLY HAMPERED AND COMPLICATED'

When Churchill had outlined the difficulties facing the Admiralty before the first session of the sub-committee, he had explained how the Navy's ability to prevent hostile landings 'depended upon where the blockading line was drawn' and that 'the gradual withdrawal of the blockading line from the enemy's coast facilitated the escape of single ships'.[36] This made raids more likely, but at this stage the Admiralty representatives had insisted that major landings—on the scale of the 70,000 men Roberts had previously advised was the smallest force an invader might send with the object of subduing the country—would be impossible. However, confidence in this figure was shaken during the spring of 1913 by what became known in the corridors of the Admiralty as the 'North Sea Problem'.

Even the most sanguine observer of the 1912 manoeuvres would have been obliged to concede that the defending 'British' side encountered significant problems. The plans intended to detect enemy forces in the North Sea had proven unreliable, making an efficient reaction to enemy movements almost impossible. The Naval War Staff issued a revised series of war orders to the Fleet in November 1912 embodying the lessons drawn from the exercises. However, as Captain Ballard had warned, there was little scope for modifying the existing arrangements, no matter how unsatisfactory they appeared. The Battle Fleet would still be collected

---

[35] 'Memorandum by Lord Roberts, Lord Lovat, Sir Samuel Scott, and Colonel à Court Repington', 14 April 1913, OA 25, CAB 16/28B.
[36] Minutes of the first meeting, CAB 16/28A, fo. 20.

on the west coast of Scotland, where it would remain 'until there is some indication that the German Battle Fleet is at sea or that some important operation is expected'. Warning of an enemy sortie would have to be provided by the widely dispersed destroyer flotillas and cruiser squadrons patrolling areas of the North Sea, none of which had any significant capability to detect enemy forces after dark.[37] The need to protect the fleet from enemy torpedo attack had to take first priority as it was felt that the Germans were likely to try and erode Britain's numerical superiority by mounting attritional attacks with light craft prior to seeking a fleet action. With the Battle Fleet away to the west, cruisers, destroyers, and submarines would have to be relied upon to detect and prevent any attempt by the Germans to mount a landing on the east coast at the outset of war.[38]

The shortcomings of adopting such a reactive stance were the topic of heated debates within the Admiralty at the time the orders were prepared, and their contents soon came under fierce criticism from the Fleet.[39] Callaghan wrote to the Admiralty in March submitting that he had reached some 'disturbing' conclusions about the proposed war plans after exercises conducted during the early part of the year.[40] The C-in-C informed Battenberg that the patrolling forces in the North Sea were likely to prove acutely vulnerable to being overwhelmed by enemy battle cruisers. He reasoned that the Navy's own battle cruisers ought to be in the North Sea from the very outset of war, rather than on the west coast with the Fleet, to provide a degree of support for the light forces and patrols. Moreover, he suggested that 'as soon as war is declared, the Battle Fleets, or at least one squadron, should enter the North Sea'.[41] In Callaghan's view, increasing the support provided to the North Sea patrols and retreating them between 60 and 100 miles further away from the German coastline was vital in order to avoid exposing them to superior enemy forces.[42]

These proposals met with a frosty reception from the War Staff. Captain Ballard made the cutting observation that if Callaghan's plans were adopted and the enemy discovered just how dispersed the Navy's patrols were 'and sent an armoured escort with the transports an invading expedition could force its way to the coast of Norfolk, Lincoln or York without encountering any serious opposition'. Worse still, if 'he made for the vicinity of the Humber at least 8 hours would elapse before a single British armoured ship could reach the spot and interfere with the landing'. In Ballard's view the C-in-C's proposals therefore carried 'arrangements for the safety of the cruisers almost to the point of neglecting the safety of the country'.[43] He considered the presence of armoured warships along the east coast crucial to interrupting a landing covered by German capital ships: the Admiralty was convinced that the patrol flotillas and submarines would not be able to disrupt a

---

[37] Admiralty, 'Proposed War Plans', 25 November 1912, ADM 116/3412, fos 8–20.
[38] M. Kerr to Churchill, December 1912, MB1/T22/165, UoS.
[39] Kerr, *Battenberg*, p. 239.
[40] Callaghan to Battenberg, 8 March 1913, MB1/T23/184, UoS.
[41] Callaghan, untitled typescript report, 8 March 1913, MB1/T23/184.
[42] Morgan-Owen, 'An "Intermediate Blockade"?', pp. 490–2.
[43] Admiralty to Callaghan, 22 July 1913, ADM 116/3088.

disembarkation until after dark. The flotillas were too widely dispersed, had too great a stretch of coastline to patrol, and were too weak to fight off enemy armoured vessels. Submarines, less likely to be hampered by enemy fire, would take a considerable time to reach the threatened area due to their slow speed. The limits of the flotilla forces capabilities were illustrated by a war game conducted during April, when the Tyne patrol flotilla had taken between three and three-and-a-half hours to respond to a landing at Blyth, a mere 5 miles away from their base.[44] After another such exercise in which the local patrols had proven unequal to their defensive task, Churchill vented his frustrations in a private minute: 'the War Staff paper shows very clearly that no force could arrive in time either to prevent the disembarkation of troops or to intercept the returning escort'. 'It is to my mind incredible', he fumed, 'that the dispatch of a hostile expedition of this magnitude would not be known in England... but if this condition is assumed, the rest appears to follow inevitably.'[45]

Thus, as the CID inquiry was in motion, the Admiralty's confidence in its ability to balance the competing demands of protecting the Battle Fleet from enemy torpedo attack and adequately safeguarding the east coast was in precipitous decline. The naval leadership's concerns were reflected in the testimony they provided to the sub-committee as the body began to focus on the naval aspects of the question during the summer. The gravity of the situation was laid bare in a memorandum signed by Churchill, Battenberg, and the Chief of the War Staff, Vice-Admiral Henry Jackson, in June. 'If the British fleet is in its least favourable position', the document admitted, 'it would be possible for Germany to transport the largest military force which she can assemble without noticeable preparations to the East Coast of Britain.' The deduction the Admiralty made from this was that, 'unless the British Army is at home, the British fleet should not be absent from the North Sea'. The naval leadership concluded:

> We fear that unless this adequate military force is maintained in Great Britain, naval operations will be greatly hampered and complicated. There would be grave danger of the British battle fleet being forced to continue for long periods in a war station, much more advanced and therefore much more exposed to torpedo attack than sound naval strategy would enjoin. There is also the grave danger that, at a time when a decisive naval battle is impending or in process, the Government or some Board of Admiralty may be led by the anxiety of having a defenceless country at its back to make some fatal division of the forces necessary to secure victory.
>
> We therefore hold that at all times, until the naval strength of Germany has been broken, the military force retained in the British Isles should not fall below the strength necessary to deal with a concentrated invasion of 70,000 men.[46]

---

[44] War Staff, 'Attack on Armstrong's Works at Newcastle-on-Tyne by a Raiding Party landed at Blyth', 12 April 1913, p. 1, OA 26, CAB 16/28B.

[45] Churchill, 'War Staff Paper on Raids', 1 May 1913, MB1/T24/208, UoS.

[46] Churchill, Battenberg, and Jackson, 'Landings from Oversea', 27 June 1913, OA 48, CAB 16/28B.

Churchill read the memorandum aloud to the sub-committee of the CID on 26 June. It was received with incredulity from the assembled ministers and experts, not least the Prime Minister. The Secretary of State for War was moved to remark that, if accepted, the Admiralty's advice would necessitate changing 'the whole basis of our arrangement for Home Defence'.[47] The ensuring discussion inevitably gravitated back to whether to withhold a portion of the Expeditionary Force in order to forestall the Navy's concerns. Seely admitted that the War Office 'had never accepted' the decision to retain two divisions and maintained that the entire Regular Army should remain free for operations overseas. Haldane supported him. The government's lack of a meaningful vision of how to prosecute a war against Germany could not have been more blatant.

Despite Churchill's insistence that the views he had expressed did not conflict with earlier advice the Admiralty had provided to the government, the extent of the shift in the Navy's position was obvious. As General Ian Hamilton confided to Ellison: '[the] Admiralty and War Office have completely changed round in their two roles of estimating possible numbers of invaders'.[48] The rapidity of this change raised doubts amongst some members of the committee as to whether the Admiralty was distorting its case in pursuit of political aims. The impression of duplicity was reinforced by Churchill's admission that certain portions of the Admiralty's testimony in 1907–8 might have been deliberately misleading. 'In 1908', the First Lord suggested tactfully, 'a controversial spirit so dominated certain members of the Committee that it was impossible to obtain from them an accordance of views upon any subject.'[49] This was particularly true of the value of defensive patrols and the difficulties involved with detecting enemy forces in the North Sea.[50] Indeed, so surprised was he by the views the Admiralty now expressed on the matter that Hankey was moved to produce a memorandum on the difference in opinion evident in the testimony provided in 1907–8 and 1913. He questioned whether, as the naval representatives 'have exploded the idea disseminated by the Board less than three years ago that the coast patrol is a "very effective second line of defence" ... would it not be desirable to consider whether the expenditure might not be devoted to some more valuable form of defence?'[51] Esher suspected that the Admiralty was shaping its case to secure the retention of two divisions of the Regular Army for 'naval strategical purposes' overseas.[52] Asquith was inclined to agree.[53] Little did either man know that securing troops for amphibious assaults was a subsidiary consideration at most for the Admiralty War Staff by this point. The urgency of the naval position was brought home with considerable force during July, as the naval manoeuvres laid bare the seriousness of the situation in the North Sea.

[47] Minutes of the tenth meeting, CAB 16/28A, fos 49–50.
[48] Hamilton to Ellison, 8 August 1813, Hamilton 5/1/66, Hamilton Papers, LHCMA.
[49] Minutes of the first meeting, CAB 16/28A, fo. 20.
[50] Minutes of the tenth meeting, CAB 16/28A, fos 49–50.
[51] Hankey, 'Inconsistency in Admiralty Policy Especially in Regard to the Second Line of Defence', 13 July 1913, CAB 17/100, fos 15–19.
[52] Esher to Asquith, 25 June 1913, in Brett ed., *Esher* III, p. 125.
[53] d'Ombrain, *War Machinery*, p. 109.

THE 1913 NAVAL MANOEUVRES

In May Asquith had suggested that 'the Army and Navy should carry out conjointly serious experiments in landing a raiding force' in order to provide some practical information for the CID inquiry.[54] In fact, Battenberg had proposed embarking a battalion of marines along with three battalions of regular troops almost a year earlier, in order to obtain some more accurate data regarding disembarkation times.[55] This idea had been carried forward throughout the preparation of the Navy's 1913 manoeuvres.[56] The scheme for the exercises replicated that of the previous year: a defensive force with its fleet positioned away to the north would patrol the mid-North Sea with cruisers and destroyers in order to detect and intercept an invading force making for the east coast.[57] As Admiral May, who reprised his role as Chief Umpire, noted: 'the first object of the attacking fleet was to cover the descent of military raids on the Blue coast'.[58]

The 'Red' Fleet—whose task it was to execute the raids—would be commanded by the Second Sea Lord, Vice-Admiral Sir John Jellicoe. Callaghan, the incumbent C-in-C, opposed him on the defensive, 'British' side. Jellicoe planned a series of daring assaults on the east coast, relying on speed and surprise to overwhelm the local defences whilst diversionary attacks elsewhere occupied enemy reinforcements.[59] His approach proved highly successful. Soon after the exercises began, a Red force approached the Humber at speed, 'drove in' the local patrols, and sped up the estuary. Three submarines stationed for local defence were caught on the surface and put out of action by gunfire.[60] Jellicoe's cruisers then anchored in the Humber and engaged the shore batteries, allowing transports to proceed alongside the docks at Immingham and Grimsby, and to begin disembarking their troops. Callaghan's force had been away to the north in the latitude of Inverness and was unable to react in time to interrupt the landing. Having got his troops ashore and wary of being ambushed by superior Blue forces approaching from the north, Jellicoe then successfully retreated back into the North Sea relatively unscathed. After an afternoon of fighting on land, it was decided that the Red force had succeeded in capturing Grimsby, but had later been defeated. A similar outcome was produced by a second series of raids on Blyth and Sunderland shortly thereafter.[61] Jellicoe launched a final raid on 28 July. On this occasion Callaghan's force had retired to port to refuel, leaving Jellicoe with every chance of complete success.[62]

---

[54] Minutes of the sixth meeting, CAB 16/28A, fo. 37.
[55] Battenberg, 'Naval Manoeuvres—July 1913', July 1912, CHAR 13/9/127, CAC.
[56] Admiralty, 'Manoeuvres for 1913', 29 January 1913, ADM 116/1214.
[57] Admiralty, 'Naval Manoeuvres, 1913: General Scheme', June 1913, ADM 116/1214.
[58] May, 'Manoeuvres 1913: Report by Umpire-in-Chief', August 1913, p. 1, MAY/10, NMM (this is a draft version of the final report which contains a number of passages omitted from the final draft).
[59] Jellicoe, 'Naval Manoeuvres—Red Fleet, General Orders & Remarks', 22 July 1913, ADM 116/1214.
[60] May, 'Naval Manoeuvres, 1913', pp. 9–10, ADM 116/1176C.
[61] Ibid., pp. 14–17.
[62] Bridgeman to Sandars, 28 July 1913, c. 765, fos 131–2, Sandars Papers, Bod.

It was at this moment that the Admiralty called a halt to the proceedings 'for fear of giving useful information to the Germans'.[63] Admiral Bridgeman, a guest on Jellicoe's flagship, recounted the episode to Balfour's private secretary, Jack Sandars:

Success of invading force complete. They landed in all 60,000 men on these shores & could have landed 100,000... The manoeuvres were stopped. Jellicoe called onto *Enchantress*. Greeted by Winston with 'Well, Jellicoe, you have made history. The PM will be frightened *out* of his life. But we must stop the manoeuvres.'[64]

In a shorter second phase of the exercises, a more aggressive use of the defending Blue Fleet was attempted. Churchill urged the C-in-C to assume the initiative and to drive Jellicoe's Red force back into the Thames.[65] Callaghan's fleet, preceded by a screen of cruisers and destroyers, conducted a southerly sweep across the North Sea, which succeeded in catching and destroying Jellicoe's transports whilst they were attempting to repeat their earlier success at Blyth.[66] This minor victory paled, however, when compared with the complete failure of a strategy which closely mimicked the Navy's standing war orders during the first phase of the exercises.

Upon the conclusion of the manoeuvres, Callaghan composed a lengthy submission on their outcome for the Admiralty. In it he re-iterated the argument he had put forward since the turn of the year: the War Staff's attempts to maintain the Fleet outside the range of enemy torpedo attack and the necessity to defend the east coast could not be reconciled. The Admiralty would have to decide which of the two was the greater priority. Personally, Callaghan supported collecting the British Fleet outside the North Sea, but recognized that this would depend on more than purely naval considerations; it was a matter of national strategy. He asked the Admiralty to consider the question, 'is the fleet to be primarily used for the defence of our coast, and stationed with this main object in view?' In Callaghan's opinion 'the whole war dispositions of the fleet in Home Waters' depended upon this fundamental point.[67] 'If the primary object of our fleet is to be the prevention of Raid and Invasion', he concluded, 'the battlefleet must cruise much further South than would otherwise be the case, and, in consequence, will be more exposed to the attack of torpedo craft. If this is necessary the risk must be taken, but not otherwise.'[68] The C-in-C felt that running such risks in order to prevent raids was a 'grave strategic error' and that the Army ought properly to be relied upon to overwhelm minor landings.

The government's failure to adhere to or enforce its decision on the number of men that might or might not be committed to the Continent had left the Admiralty facing a strategic crisis. A military strategy with ambitions beyond what the country's resources of trained manpower could fulfil had thrown an

[63] Jellicoe, 'Autobiographical Notes Up to 1914', p. 248, Add MS 49038, Jellicoe Papers, BL.

[64] Bridgeman to Sandars, 29 July 1913, c. 765, fo. 134, Bod.

[65] Churchill to Callaghan, 29 July 1913, CHAR 13/5/45, CAC.

[66] May, 'Naval Manoeuvres, 1913', pp. 21–7, ADM 116/1176C.

[67] Callaghan, 'Naval Manoeuvres, 1913: Remarks on North Sea Strategy', 28 August 1913, p. 2, ADM 116/3130.

[68] Callaghan, 'Naval Manoeuvres, 1913', p. 12, ADM 116/3130.

ever-greater defensive burden upon the Navy, which was now obliged to consider risking ships of vital national importance in order to facilitate the dispatch of an additional two divisions of regulars to France. This much was made clear by the War Staff's reaction to Callaghan's paper. Upon receiving the C-in-C's detailed appreciation, the naval planners produced an incisive critique of the condition of British strategy:

> It is considered that the remedy for the present difficult situation in which the Commander-in-Chief may be placed does not rest entirely with the Admiralty, but is primarily a question for the Government, who must be convinced by all arguments we can bring to bear on the subject that the main force of the Navy must be relieved from minor defensive operations on the coast and of the sole responsibility for stopping raids by attacking them in the open sea, and it is considered that the best assistance that can probably be given in this direction is by putting the military defences of this country on a proper footing ready to meet the changed situation of the present century, for, having abandoned the old policy of a close observation of our enemy's ports, we must be prepared to accept as the result that the first indication of a raid will be its presence off the coast and we must make plans accordingly.[69]

Captain Arthur Vyvyan, assistant to the Chief of the War Staff, encapsulated the dilemma when he remarked that defeating minor raids threatened to exert 'a very powerful and insidious re-action on our naval strategy'.[70]

The extent to which the Fleet should be positioned to defend the east coast raised further questions. If the Navy's primary function within a strategy of military involvement on the Continent was to be a defensive one, consideration ought to be given to whether the enemy battle fleet was in fact the primary objective if it did put to sea. The Assistant Director of the Operations Division, Captain Herbert Richmond, advised making the Admiralty's views on this point explicitly clear to the C-in-C:

> ...the intention of the Admiralty should, I think, be made clear to the Commander-in-Chief, i.e.—the situation in which the enemy puts to sea his main fleet and his transport fleet carrying an invasionary army simultaneously. Should the Commander-in-Chief in those circumstances attack the main fleet or the Transports?...The Commander-in-Chief, Home Fleets, requires clear instructions as to how he should behave in such cases, and whether he should make the Battle Fleet or the transports his objective...I suggest that his instructions should be so framed as to make the intention of the Admiralty regarding that point unmistakeable.[71]

The War Staff equivocated on this point, maintaining on the one hand that the enemy fleet 'should be the first object of our attention', but also noting that 'an invasionary army at sea should in all cases be attacked, even at the risk of not being

---

[69] War Staff, 'Remarks on Comments by the Commander-in-Chief on the 1913 Manoeuvres', 29 September 1913, pp. 6–7, ADM 116/1214.

[70] Vyvyan, 'Remarks on the 1913 Manoeuvres', [?] September 1913, ADM 116/1169; Grimes, *War Planning*, p. 181.

[71] Richmond, 'Remarks by A.D.O.D. Re: C-in-C H.F.'s letter on North Sea Strategy', [?] September 1913, pp. 5–6, ADM 116/1169.

able subsequently to bring to action the enemy's Battle Fleet'.[72] As it was likely to prove extremely difficult to establish the size of a military expedition upon first sighting of an armada of transports, Callaghan was faced with the unenviable prospect of having to use his judgement to determine whether to risk his fleet responding to what might prove to be a small-scale raid, and in so doing risk exposing valuable ships to an ambush, or potentially miss an opportunity to engage the enemy fleet. To add to the Admiralty's troubles, it appeared that the government was contemplating assenting to the General Staff's recommendation to increase the size of the force scheduled for dispatch to France. Hankey circulated a draft report of the invasion inquiry in late September, in which he recommended the retention of only a single division of regular troops.[73] The Admiralty had to act quickly if it was to convince the government to avoid worsening its predicament.

THE CID DECIDES

The naval representatives to the CID had the opportunity to examine a number of witnesses of their own before the sub-committee in November. Over the course of several meetings Callaghan, Jellicoe, and May were all summoned to testify. Sir Arthur Wilson was already a member of the body in his role as a permanent member of the CID. Admiral May, Chief Umpire for both the 1912 and 1913 manoeuvres, informed the assembly that 'I think the situation—to my mind, at all events—has altered considerably as a result of the manoeuvres of the last two years.'[74] Callaghan and Jellicoe supported him in this assessment. The C-in-C stated simply that 'I think it is quite possible for Germany to raid our ports by appearing unexpectedly in misty weather and making a dash up without being seen unless there is some counter force to detain them.' He also pointed out that the Germans would not necessarily have to risk modern ships to cover such raids and that older armoured cruisers, no longer suited to operating with the fleet, would be particularly effective for the purpose.[75] After a technical discussion of coastal armaments, the question of how many men might be landed was eventually raised. This revealed the seriousness of the naval position. Jellicoe, who was judged to have landed 43,750 men during the manoeuvres, admitted that 'there is very little doubt that a very much larger number of men would have got ashore', particularly if the exercises had been conducted during the long hours of winter darkness.[76] A compromise figure of 36,000 men was used for the purposes of further discussion, but Jellicoe made clear his view that the only limit on the size of a possible raid was the number of troops the Germans could embark in secret. The distinction between an invasion and a raid, hitherto made on the grounds of

---

[72] War Staff, 'Remarks on Comments by the Commander-in-Chief on the 1913 Manoeuvres', 29 September 1913, pp. 4–5, ADM 116/1214.

[73] For the date of sending, see Hankey to Asquith, 24 September 1913, CAB 17/35, fo. 230; 'Preliminary Draft Report on Invasion', 29 October 1913, p. 28, OA 52, CAB 16/28B.

[74] Minutes of the eighteenth meeting, CAB 16/28A, fo. 146.

[75] Ibid., fos 149–50.   [76] Ibid., fo. 147.

whether a force could be re-supplied, was thus revealed to be so artificial as to render it valueless. The Admiralty now considered that a force large enough to cause major disruption could be put ashore with comparative ease, albeit with little or only very light equipment. This was beyond the capacity of the existing military provision—calculated on the basis of having to deal only with 'raids'—to handle.

These revelations were a source of deep concern for Asquith. He questioned Jellicoe as to how the conclusions of the 1907–8 invasion inquiry had apparently become obsolete so quickly. Churchill intervened to play down the extent of the naval leadership's concerns, but was obliged to admit that the Admiralty had exaggerated its defensive competence during the previous inquiry. '[T]he position of the Admiralty was that the Army Estimates ought to be greatly cut down—that was Lord Fisher's position... The Admiralty arguments were all pitched in that tone from beginning to end, and lots of statements were made which require considerable modification.'[77] This was as close as the naval leadership came to admitting the duplicity it had engaged in since 1907 to the sub-committee.

On the basis that the only reliable means of meeting the danger of a German landing was to station to the Fleet closer to the east coast, Battenberg and Churchill then attempted to persuade Asquith of the vital necessity for making Scapa Flow and Cromarty secure from torpedo and submarine attack. They did so in parallel with a series of inter-service meetings with the War Office at which they sought a larger commitment of military resources to the defence of key harbours along the east coast.[78] Making the anchorages at Scapa or Cromarty secure against torpedo attack held the prospect of allowing the Fleet to remain much closer to the threatened areas of coastline during the period of strained relations and thus reduce its reaction time. Asquith remained sceptical, however. Baulking at the significant costs involved and mindful of the money already spent on Rosyth—where works were ongoing—the Prime Minister confessed that he was 'wholly unconvinced' of the necessity of such works.[79] Diplomatic relations with Germany had eased and committing to a second large infrastructure project to support naval operations in the North Sea on top of the expanding Estimates, which had exceeded £51 million in 1913–14 due to additional shipbuilding, was a political impossibility for the Liberals.[80] Despite the Admiralty's best efforts, on 21 November Hankey informed Asquith that he remained convinced that 'the highest naval and military authorities are agreed we should now be secure if *one* division was retained'.[81]

With the testimony to the inquiry complete, the Admiralty was forced to try and influence Hankey's views after the meetings had finished. This was attempted through a series of circuitous routes. Brigadier General George Aston RM, currently on the Admiralty War Staff, went through the draft report with Hankey at the CID on 7 January, impressing upon the Secretary that the document was 'dangerous as

[77] Minutes of the nineteenth meeting, CAB 16/28A, fo. 160.
[78] See minutes of the 'High Level Bridge' Conferences, CAB 18/27.
[79] Minutes of the eighteenth meeting, CAB 16/28A, fos 153–4.
[80] T. G. Otte, 'Détente 1914: Sir William Tyrrell's Secret Mission to Germany', *Historical Journal*, Vol. 56, No. 1, 2013, pp. 175–204; Sumida, *IDNS*, table 3.
[81] Hankey to Asquith, 21 November 1913, p. 2, CAB 17/35, fo. 311.

worded at present'.[82] At the same time, Sir Arthur Wilson provided the secretary with a detailed series of notes on the draft report. Asquith held Wilson's views in high regard and the Admiral had adopted a position sufficiently distant from that of the Admiralty during the inquiry to appear as a credible alternative source of naval advice.[83] Indeed, the difference of opinion evident between the incumbent naval leadership and Wilson was significant enough for the Admiralty to try and reconcile its views with those of the retired Admiral prior to the final meeting of the sub-committee.[84] The notes Sir Arthur's provided Hankey reasoned that:

> no new factor has been brought to light which makes it less necessary to maintain two divisions of Regulars in the country till the Territorials are considered fit to take the field than it was in 1908...It appears therefore advisable to adhere to the recommendations of the former Committee to retain two divisions in the Country till the Territorials are fit to take the field.[85]

The Secretary informed Asquith that this point would be the key issue for debate at the final meetings of the sub-committee, at which the draft report would be discussed.[86] Hankey felt that one division and a 'flying column' composed of the 12,500 regulars not included in the Expeditionary Force would be sufficient, but that Admiral Wilson's proposal nevertheless merited consideration by the sub-committee.[87] The group debated this fundamental issue on 17–18 February 1914. Hankey recorded that the War Office maintained that it was unnecessary to withhold any portion of the Expeditionary Force, but that one division was the maximum that would be required should it be decided that the TF required stiffening with regular troops. An opposing faction, led by Balfour, argued for adherence to the previous recommendation to keep back two divisions in the first instance.[88] Prudence prevailed and the conclusions reached in 1907–8 were upheld, although this finding was primarily a political one. Henry Wilson immediately began to petition Asquith, currently performing the duties of Secretary of State for War in addition to the Premiership due to Seely's resignation over the crisis brewing over Irish Home Rule, to retract the ruling. This he apparently achieved in May, when Asquith privately intimated that only one division need be retained, although the extent to which the Prime Minister was committed to either position is unclear.[89] Churchill later claimed the controversy was 'never finally settled', a judgement supported by the initial decision to withhold two divisions in August 1914.[90]

The report of the invasion inquiry appeared to be a political victory for the Admiralty, which had seemingly curtailed the worst effects of the General Staff's

---

[82] Aston diary, 7 January 1914, AST 1/7, RMM.

[83] Minutes of the eighteenth meeting, 25 November 1913, CAB 16/28A, fos 153–4.

[84] Aston diary, 30 January 1914, AST 1/7, RMM.

[85] Wilson, 'Remarks on the Preliminary Draft Report', 5 January 1914, CAB 17/36, fos 27–8.

[86] Hankey to Asquith, 22 January 1914, CAB 17/36, fos 58–9.

[87] Hankey to Asquith, 13 February 1914, CAB 17/36, fos 102–4.

[88] Hankey to Stamfordham, 19 February 1914, CAB 17/36, fos 109–11; d'Ombrain, *War Machinery*, p. 110.

[89] Callwell, *Wilson*, pp. 146–7; d'Ombrain, *War Machinery*, pp. 110–11; Williamson Jr, *Politics of Grand Strategy*, pp. 310–11; Jeffery, *Wilson*, p. 126.

[90] W. S. Churchill, *The World Crisis, 1911–1918*, London: Odhams Press, 1938 edn, p. 119.

plans on naval strategy. Aston recorded his view that the decision to retain two divisions of troops was 'satisfactory'.[91] If the results are assessed in relation to Churchill's initial case that larger-scale raids were now the principal danger, then this viewpoint may appear sound. However, the findings of the 1912 and 1913 manoeuvres had convinced the professional staff at the Admiralty that Churchill may have been too sanguine in his outlook. The Admiralty now contemplated a landing large enough to overwhelm the military forces in the British Isles and remained sceptical of the Navy's ability to prevent it.

'A VERY POWERFUL AND INSIDIOUS RE-ACTION ON OUR NAVAL STRATEGY'

The Admiralty War Staff had worked tirelessly to find solutions to the deteriorating position in the North Sea during the winter of 1913–14. Prospects for the future appeared bright: the number of battleships already building in Britain and the slowing of German construction since 1912 due to financial restrictions meant that the dreadnought race was effectively over. As Churchill minuted Battenberg in May 1914: 'the delivery of 13 capital ships between the fourth Quarter of 1914 and the first Quarter of 1916, as compared with a reinforcement of only 2 to the German navy, is a great military fact'.[92] Developments in submarine technology also appeared to contain the potential to allow for the continuous observation of German ports to be re-established. Submarines had returned a promising performance in the 1912 and 1913 manoeuvres and Churchill, the War Staff, and the Sea Lords were unanimous in their support for using the boats 'for look out purposes' off the enemy coastline.[93] It was estimated that a minimum of twenty-four modern sea-going boats equipped with wireless sets would be required to establish such a watch.[94] Yet technical and operational difficulties meant that this goal would not be achieved for some time. The War Staff conceded that '*until* big submarines are available in sufficient numbers to enable us to revert to the old policy of close observation of the enemy's ports, the duties and responsibilities of cruisers of all classes in the North Sea must be very onerous on account of the extensive area requiring to be watched'.[95] In the interim, a solution to the 'North Sea problem'

---

[91] Aston diary, 19 February 1914, AST 1/7, RMM.

[92] Churchill to Battenberg, 13 May 1914, in R. Churchill ed., *The Churchill Documents*, Vol. V: *At the Admiralty*, 2007 edn, Hillsdale, MI: Hillsdale College Press, p. 1977; Marder, *FDSF* I, p. 420; C. M. Bell, 'Sir John Fisher's Naval Revolution Reconsidered: Winston Churchill at the Admiralty, 1911–1914', *War in History*, Vol. 18, No. 3, 2011, p. 346; T. G. Otte, 'Grey Ambassador: The *Dreadnought* and British Foreign Policy' in Blyth, Lambert, and Rüger eds, *The Dreadnought and the Edwardian Age*, pp. 51–78.

[93] Note by Keyes, 18 September 1912, on docket 'Manoeuvres 1912—general remarks by Flag Officers & Captains of Red Fleet' inside folder 'Manoeuvres 1912', ADM 1/8269; Lambert, *Revolution*, pp. 280–1.

[94] War Staff, 'War Staff Minute of Submarines', 18 July 1913, DEY/31, D'Eyncourt Papers, NMM.

[95] War Staff, 'Remarks on Comments by the Commander-in-Chief on the 1913 Manoeuvres', 29 September 1913, p. 7, ADM 116/1214. Emphasis added.

that would enable the Navy reliably to detect, intercept, and prevent a major landing on the east coast without exposing the Fleet to an unacceptable level of risk from enemy torpedo craft was still required.

The Admiralty's response to this gap in capability was threefold. Firstly, steps were taken to re-organize the coastal patrol flotillas, to improve co-ordination with shore batteries, and to create an integrated coastal defence organization under the leadership of an Admiral of Patrols (AoP). This important function was given to highly effective Commodore Ballard. As the new AoP described, the purpose of his force was 'to prevent the landing of raiding parties from transports which are either unescorted or only escorted in small force'. 'It is not intended', he continued, 'that the dispositions proposed should aim at providing defence against any larger force...the prevention of serious invasion or of attacks by a powerful enemy must be left to the sea-going fleets and battleships stationed along the coast.'[96] To improve the chances of detecting an enemy force before it reached the British coast, the Admiralty also prepared to reorganize the Navy's cruiser forces into a series of mixed-unit formations, consisting of two battle cruisers and four light cruisers each. This arrangement would be expanded in 1915, when the four battle cruisers currently stationed in the Mediterranean would also be returned home for service in the North Sea. Combined formations of this nature would have the advantage of not leaving lighter units exposed to enemy action and also of deploying powerfully armed battle cruisers in a more advanced scouting function than had been the practice hitherto.[97] These measures were accompanied by a fundamental shift in the deployment and usage of the Battle Fleet.

Since the conclusion of the 1913 manoeuvres, Callaghan had re-iterated to the Admiralty that the Fleet ought to be in the North Sea at the outset of war if it was expected to protect the east coast. Stationed away to the west, he argued, 'it would be impossible for the battle fleet to arrive in time to prevent a landing if the attempt was covered by the German battlefleet'.[98] As a compromise between security and better positioning, the C-in-C recommended stationing the Fleet to Scapa Flow during a period of strained relations.[99] This would place the force closer to the threatened area of coastline, but also afford some shelter from enemy torpedo craft. Upon receiving the C-in-C's second submission on the issue, Vice-Admiral Henry Jackson, the CoS, added his weight to Callaghan's proposals. On 4 October he minuted Battenberg, stating his opinion that:

> It is considered the bases of the Fleet in a period of strained relations should be Scapa Flow as the main preliminary war anchorage...As stated by C-in-C, Scapa Flow is the best natural harbour, & its distance from the probable area of operations & from the proposed war cruising ground, is equal to that of Cromarty.[100]

[96] Ballard, 'Proposed War Disposition of Patrol Flotillas', 17 July 1914, MB1/T37/357, UoS.

[97] Morgan-Owen, 'An "Intermediate Blockade"?', pp. 495–6.

[98] Callaghan, 'Review of the W.P. After Manoeuvres, 1913', 3 October 1913, p. 1, ADM 116/1214. A copy of this document along with some useful comments regarding its provenance and the reaction it provoked can be found in MB1/T26/240, UoS.

[99] Callaghan, 'Review of W.P.', p. 2, ADM 116/1214.

[100] Jackson minute to Battenberg, 'Remarks on C-in-C Letter', 4 October 1913, MB1/T26/240, UoS.

Jackson's support meant that, when a draft copy of the new war orders was communicated to Callaghan in December, they contained provision for the Fleet to proceed to Scapa Flow during a period of strained relations.[101] No further direction as to the employment of his force was forthcoming, however. Having still not received any indication of the Admiralty's intentions by May 1914, Callaghan respectfully submitted that he might be informed as to the progress the War Staff had made updating the plans.[102] When new instructions were finally transmitted to him, they contained a dramatic shift in strategic thinking.

The changes conformed to Callaghan's earlier recommendation that the Fleet should be *in* the North Sea, rather than at Scapa Flow, at the outbreak of war if it was to be used to prevent a German attack on the east coast. They also reflected the 'successful' second phase of the 1913 manoeuvres. In a covering note to Jackson, Battenberg explained that:

> It is essential on the outbreak of hostilities the combined force of battleships, battle & other cruisers & flotillas should make a forward movement towards the enemy's coast, then returning by another route to the area enclosed by Lat —&—, Long. —&—, which should be regarded as the station of the main Fleet when not at anchor.
>
> The main object of this 'reconnaissance-in-force' (which should be repeated at certain intervals and arranged so as to traverse fresh ground each time) is to *bring* home to the enemy how hazardous it would be for him to dispatch any raiding expedition or other relatively weak detachments of his main fleet across the North Sea towards the British Coasts.

The First Sea Lord believed that these 'sweeps' would:

> be very disconcerting to the enemy and interfere considerably with any plans, especially in the nature of raids by military detachments, he may have decided to put into execution . . . This should therefore in itself be the most effective defence against hostile raids on the coasts, provided the enemy will everywhere find an adequate military to deal with him, if he should effect a landing. Coast patrols should no doubt be able to attack such expeditions in many cases, before a landing is effected—but the Transports must always be the first objective, not the escorting men of war.[103]

The July 1914 war orders therefore marked a return to earlier plans to deploy a significant force of British armoured warships *into* the North Sea during a period of strained relations with Germany, with the explicit intention of preventing a raid upon the east coast. They confirmed the ongoing centrality of the Battle Fleet to Admiralty strategic thought: the fleet was vital to the defence of the country and so was its position at the crucial moment. Raids were not the only potential form of German military operation covered in the war orders, however. As Richmond had recommended the previous September, the orders contained specific instructions regarding the role of the fleet during a full-scale invasion attempt:

> As the security of the British Isles against serious invasion is mainly dependent upon our maritime superiority, occasions may arise in which the destruction of transports

---

[101] Admiralty, 'War Orders No. 1', December 1913, p. 2, ADM 137/818, fo. 47.
[102] Callaghan to Admiralty, 4 May 1914, ADM 116/3096.
[103] Battenberg to Jackson, 11 May 1914, ADM 116/3096.

conveying a large body of the enemy's troops is a more pressing and urgent necessity than any other, in which case *the transports must receive prior attention even if the enemy's main fleet happens to be within reach of attack.*[104]

The destruction of the German High Seas Fleet, viewed for so long as the undisputed fixation of the Royal Navy in the First World War era by many historians, was thus explicitly ranked as less of a priority than the defence of the British Isles by the Admiralty's final set of peacetime war orders.[105] Significantly for his performance during the war, this was precisely the opposite view to that held by Vice-Admiral Jellicoe. Jellicoe, designated to succeed Callaghan as C-in-C, felt that the hostile fleet should be targeted first 'even with an army in transports practically within reach', but was overruled by his superiors at the Admiralty.[106] Notions that in 1914 the Royal Navy, saturated with Mahan's notion of the primacy of decisive battle, entered the First World War myopically focused upon bringing the enemy fleet to action have failed to consider that the Admiralty took an objective-based approach to naval strategy. So far as the Board were concerned, achieving a second Trafalgar for its own sake was simply not considered to be as important as preventing an invasion in July 1914. This was for the reason that the Admiralty remained the body most able and willing to try and co-ordinate grand strategy in Britain. With the CID impotent to adjudicate between the opposing views of the two services, it fell to the naval leadership to provide overall coherence to the activities of the General Staff—even if by doing so they limited the Navy's own freedom of action.

These war orders reflected the ultimate effect of the government's decision to utilize the Navy as a primarily defensive instrument. The shortcomings of the Admiralty's plans for more 'offensive' operations doubtless played a role in shaping this outcome, but by 1914 the strategic balance had shifted to the extent that the Navy was subordinating the dictates of naval strategy to the requirement to support the government's willingness to dispatch the Expeditionary Force to France. As Jackson reflected bitterly in May 1914, 'If our war plans were based on our actually assuming the offensive at the outbreak of war and carrying the area of action to the enemy's coast, we might afford to give our enemy some start in this respect...but our plans are not prepared on this basis; on the contrary we have to expect raids on our coasts.'[107] What Aston described as a 'strange tendency' to 'sit at the feet of the army' was the situation the Navy found itself in at the outbreak of the First World War.[108] Captain Herbert Richmond of the Operations Division—one of the most powerful naval minds of the period—resignedly noted how:

---

[104] Admiralty, 'War Plans, Part I—General Instructions', July 1914, pp. 4–5, ADM 116/3096. Emphasis added.

[105] Marder, *FDSF* I, pp. 9–11, 344–58, 367–77, and *FDSF* V, pp. 297–312; B. Ranft, 'The Royal Navy and the War at Sea' in J. Turner ed., *Britain and the First World War*, London: Unwin Hyman, 1988, pp. 53–69.

[106] Aston diary, 11 December 1913, AST 1/6, RMM.

[107] Jackson to Battenberg, 20 May 1914, MB1/T33/315, UoS.

[108] Aston, 'Impressions at Admiralty during Past Year', diary entry for 5 June 1914, AST 1/7, RMM.

As it is impossible to bring pressure upon an enemy except by offensive measures, the first point which arises so far as we are concerned is—what offensive measures are open to England. A Naval offensive in the North Sea is meaningless: there mere fact of placing our Battle Squadron outside the German harbour is not in itself offensive if we cannot force our way into their harbours and destroy their fleets there. An offensive denotes that we force the enemy either to fight or to do something which commits him to a worse measure. Are there any means by which we can force them to come to sea, supposing always that they are unwilling to do so?

Offensive operations can be conducted against German Trade and German Colonies...Lastly, there is the case of an alliance with France, which opens further offensive possibilities by means of the employment of the army in the manner which will be of the greatest assistance to the French Army. These appear to be the only courses open to England: both of the first two are weak and one in particular may be ineffectual, but such as they are we require to be able to carry them out thoroughly.[109]

Prioritizing sending the Army to France may have been justifiable if it were a conscious act of policy, made as the result of thoroughgoing consideration and supported by adequate resources. Yet the debates over how to use the Expeditionary Force which occurred in August 1914 confirm that this was not the case. Beyond the diplomatic imperative to support France, the government had no concrete conception of how to fight a war against Germany and had certainly made no serious endeavour to prepare the Army to meet a European foe. Rather, its focus on purely defensive considerations had left the country's primary military strategic asset—the Royal Navy—obliged to focus on defending the east coast in preference to preparing to utilize naval power in an offensive capacity. Whether the presence of the British Expeditionary Force—measured at four or six divisions—on the left flank of the French army merited this price, seems doubtful.

---

[109] Richmond, 'Remarks by A.D.O.D. Re: C-in-C H.F.'s letter on North Sea Strategy', [?] September 1913, pp. 1–2, ADM 116/1169.

Conclusion

On 5 August 1914 a tired Captain Herbert Richmond stole a moment from the frenzy of activity engulfing the Admiralty Operations Division to write his diary. His entry recounted a conversation with Churchill, during which the First Lord had allegedly finished by exclaiming that 'now we have our war. The next thing is to decide how we are going to carry it on.' Richmond was disgusted. 'What a statement!' he wrote, lamenting that Churchill could scarcely have made 'a more damning confession of [our] inadequate preparation'.[1] Often taken as an indictment of the Admiralty's supposedly moribund strategic planning process, Richmond's criticism could just as easily be applied to the country as a whole. Even as he wrote, Britain's political and military leadership remained divided over precisely the question Churchill had posed: whether to send the Expeditionary Force to Europe, where it ought to go, and how many men it ought to consist of were all re-visited in early August 1914.

Despite Richmond's frustration, there was little question as to the role of the Fleet after the outbreak of hostilities. Assembled at Portland for a test mobilization in July, the combined squadrons of the Grand Fleet of Battle had slipped away to their war stations on the Scottish coast before the British declaration of war. Their role was to protect British trade and to defend her shores, thereby facilitating whichever course of action the government elected to follow with the Expeditionary Force. Ironically, in the days to come it was the Navy's advice that it could not guarantee the safe transport of an army to Antwerp that narrowed the Cabinet's options regarding the Expeditionary Force, ending any prospect of direct co-operation between the two services and limiting the government's choices to how many men ought to be sent to France and how they should be used there. The failure to concert military and naval planning in peacetime proved fatal to the ambitions of those within both services who sought to exploit the mobility afforded by sea power to strike at the flank of the German advance. Whether such a strategy would have proven more effective than fighting alongside the French Army can only be guessed at. In the event, the Expeditionary Force met the Germans at Mons and on the Marne and the conditions under which amphibious descents might have proven valuable passed, replaced by the stalemate which was to define much of the following four years.

---

[1] Richmond diary for 5 August 1914 in A. J. Marder ed., *Portrait of an Admiral: The Life and Papers of Sir Herbert Richmond*, London: Jonathan Cape, 1952, p. 92.

Reflecting on Britain's pre-war position after the armistice, Hankey 'felt grateful that our preparations had been sufficient, although only barely sufficient for their purpose'.[2] 'Sufficient' is perhaps the best that could reasonably be said for the situation in 1914. After eight years in power, throughout which time it had been committed to a policy of supporting France in the face of German aggression, the Liberal government had made little attempt to prepare the country to meet the military challenge its diplomacy might presage. It had avoided the costly and politically charged issue of strengthening the Army by gradually contemplating deploying a greater proportion of the regular force to Europe. Yet it had never found a means of sustaining an efficient second line force of adequate size and cap-ability to meet the country's defensive needs and to bolster the Regular Army. Diverting the cream of Britain's military manpower overseas had been the aim of men such as Wolseley, Fisher, and Clarke for decades, but they had envisaged employing her 'little Army' in conjunction with her naval power. In 1914, the Army went to France largely independent of the action of the Fleet. The decision to do so rested upon the twin assumptions that the Navy could offer no realistic means of relieving German pressure on France in the immediate term and that it could render Britain secure from invasion without serious difficulty. The first of these suppositions was superficial, the second inaccurate.

Neither the Admiralty nor the War Office was without blame for Britain's unpreparedness for a European war in 1914. Both services engaged in uncoopera-tive, misleading behaviour, and political manoeuvring to advance their own agendas. This reduced the prospect for compromise and reconciliation, to the detriment of British readiness for war. To take each department in turn: the notion that the General Staff subverted the course of national policy towards a 'continental commitment' is no longer sustainable. As this study has shown, Balfour's govern-ment had to expend considerable and sustained effort to re-direct the focus of military thought towards large-scale overseas operations against another Great Power between 1903 and 1905. Thereafter the Liberals' decision to provide tacit support for sending the Regular Army to France in the crises of 1905–6, 1908, and 1911 means that the General Staff cannot be blamed for responding to such clear signalling and for making the requisite preparations to enact the government's intentions. Where the War Office is open to criticism is for its parochialism and for the manner in which it effectively killed any meaningful consideration of combined operations.

The General Staff's policy of denying that amphibious operations offered any prospect of diverting troops away from the French frontier was not representative of the views of the entire Staff, or of the Army as a whole. Officers like Drake and Callwell were prepared to give far greater consideration to the possible value of seaborne descents than rigid continentalists like Grierson or Wilson. Even the irascible Field Marshal Nicholson appeared to accept the value of such assaults when he appeared before the 1907–8 invasion inquiry. 'We have not got a monopoly of amphibiousness', he informed the committee, 'and I am afraid we

---

[2] Hankey, *Supreme Command* II, p. 865.

shall see that when other nations discover what a good thing that is, they too will become amphibious.' If the Germans could embark an army, he reasoned, 'our six divisions...will never be able to leave our shores.'[3] As Nicholson admitted to the sub-committee, his point cut both ways: if the Expeditionary Force could be detained in Britain by the threat of German seaborne invasion, then it was axiomatic that the reverse would also be true. The outbreak of war saw the compromise option of sending the Army to Belgium to strike against the German flank receive the backing of no less a constellation of senior military figures than Sir John French, Douglas Haig, and even Lord Roberts. Highly credible military strategists thus advanced alternative ways of employing the Army, yet these views were suppressed in favour of strengthening the political case for the 'With France' scheme.

This leads to the broader critique that the War Office never considered strategy on the same level as the Admiralty. The naval leadership failed to produce a convincing plan for prosecuting a war against Germany, but it considered the prospect of such a conflict in a far wider sense than the General Staff. Admiralty thought was predicated upon using the services to complement one another, increasing the impact either could have by operating alone. The naval leadership also gave credence to the idea that a war might be prolonged and that Britain ought to be prepared for such an eventuality. Conversely, elements within the military merely viewed the Navy as a means of facilitating a policy of fighting on the Continent. That the War Office was prepared to go against naval advice and to throw an increased defensive burden on the Fleet for the sake of freeing two divisions of regular troops, whose weight would be inconsequential against the massed forces of a European enemy, exposed a damaging lack of flexibility and collaborative spirit.

By contrast the Admiralty proved willing to respond to the government's apparent intention to use the Expeditionary Force to support the French, shifting the emphasis of naval strategy towards the defensive after 1910. As the CID failed to produce a synergy of effort between the services, the Admiralty thus filled the void, creating a degree of coherence within British strategy as a whole by linking naval planning to the prevailing trends in political and military thought. Yet the naval leadership had also contributed to the unsatisfactory situation which had developed by 1914. The hubris with which Fisher approached the War Office and the issue of combined strategy in 1904–6 was never likely to produce a positive response. Bruised by constant political criticism and the abrupt and intrusive interventions of Fisher and his colleagues on the Esher Committee, one can hardly blame the newly formed General Staff for its unwillingness to co-operate with the Admiralty's plans, which were accompanied by a definite agenda to achieve further reductions in military spending. Thereafter, the general sense of aloofness and superiority with which the Admiralty presented the case for combined operations—advocating their importance without so much as seeking military opinion as to their feasibility—displayed a lack of political sense and hinted at shortcomings in the Navy's staff work and preparations. Simply stating that amphibious

---

[3] Testimony by Nicholson to the seventh meeting of the 1907–8 invasion inquiry, CAB 16/3A, fos 88–9.

landings would detain German troops along their coastline was no more convincing than the General Staff's threadbare argument that six British divisions could turn the tide along the Franco-Belgian border. Perhaps most damagingly, Fisher's deliberate misleading of the CID invasion inquiry in 1907–8—when he knew full well that preventing a German landing was becoming more difficult—was irresponsible and short sighted. Churchill's grudging admission that his friend had dissembled before the sub-committee was a measure of the dangerous legacy Fisher's actions had left for the Navy.

Yet if the ledgers of the two services were marred, ultimate responsibility for the state of affairs in 1914 must rest with the Liberal government which arrived in power in December 1905. Through to a combination of ideological, political, and personal factors, the governments of Campbell-Bannerman and Asquith abdicated the responsibility Balfour had assumed for preparing the defences of the Empire in 1902–5. Neither man possessed the interest in or aptitude for issues of defence policy and strategy that the Unionist leader had. Yet this is not sufficient justification for inaction.

Balfour's handling of the CID was certainly far from perfect. He never established the joint operations sub-committee into an effective forum for co-ordinating inter-service planning; he never produced a coherently articulated outline of how Britain might bring a war against Russia to a conclusion; and, after 1906, he did little to reverse some of the negative trends evident within the CID in his capacity as a permanent member and founder. Yet the fact remains that during 1903–4 in particular he transformed military policy and aligned it with Admiralty thought to produce a rudimentary outline of how Britain might face the Russian challenge to India. It might easily be argued that his government never provided the number of men required to enact the forward policy he tacitly supported and that he is thus just as guilty as Asquith of failing to match military capability to international realities. There is much truth to such a criticism and, had Russia's internal strife not removed the urgency of finding a military solution to the defence of India after 1905, his policy may have been founding wanting. The constructive re-alignment of naval and military focus Balfour achieved, however, was a powerful example of the potential benefits of rigorous and judicious governmental oversight of defence policy. The Prime Minister made reasoned judgements on two protracted controversies which had bedevilled British strategy since the 1880s: the Indian reinforcement and the provision necessary for home defence. In doing so he improved the efficiency and organization of the armed services by streamlining them to face the most pressing challenges of the day, matching existing capability as closely as possible to likely future requirements. His personal intervention during the course of 1903 was vital to these successes, but also showed the amount of prime ministerial time, interest, and energy required to make the CID function. Without any executive authority, the committee was dependent on the Prime Minister to take an active and ongoing interest in an issue for it to be brought to a successful resolution. With a less willing premier, or in circumstances where other matters competed for precious government time—such as Balfour experienced during 1905—the system became markedly less effective.

The lack of such inspiration during the Liberal ministry resulted in the long periods of inaction at the CID in 1906, 1909, and 1913–14. An ever-greater proportion of the committee's work came to consist of issues of technical details that could be resolved by sub-committees without requiring large amounts of ministerial time. It effectively ceased to consider the larger questions of naval, military, and political co-ordination its progenitors had intended it to. Esher was acutely aware of this trend and tried to reverse it, approaching Hankey with the suggestion to reduce the number of ad hoc committees and concentrate decision making in a permanent sub-committee along the lines of Balfour's joint operations group soon after Hankey became Secretary in 1912. Hankey's response underlined the practical barriers to implementing such reform and the on-going fragility of the CID's position *vis-à-vis* the government departments whose activities it was intended to direct: 'the permanent officials could not possibly spare the time for the frequent meetings which would be necessary. They would soon tire of it and boycott us.'[4] Under his stewardship the committee did what it could according to the circumstances of the day. Yet here again one cannot help but wonder why, if he was uninterested in the topic of defence, Asquith neither devolved responsibility to other ministers nor empowered the committee as a forum for collective decision making. Perhaps such innovation, which would have entailed significant departures from the conventions of Cabinet government, was a step too far for a Prime Minister who preferred compromise to confrontation.

This reticence had two particularly damaging effects. First, combined operations never received systematic consideration on an inter-service basis. Despite the advice of Clarke, Fisher, Esher, Ottley, Slade, Arthur Wilson, Churchill, and others, the government never subjected the General Staff to detailed questioning on the topic. This allowed the Staff's increasingly politicized stonewalling to exert an undue influence over British strategy, polarizing the government's options between direct military co-operation with France and a reactive strategy of naval economic warfare. A CID sub-committee investigation might have confirmed the General Staff's view that combined operations had no place in a war against Germany, and if so this would have cleared the way for a new strategic consensus to be formed. Naval and military preparations might thus have been concerted more effectively, even in support of a policy of Continental warfare. Conversely, a body similar to Balfour's joint operations sub-committee might also have become the prototype joint staff required to make the preparations necessary to enact such amphibious assaults a reality.[5] This certainly appears to have been the Admiralty's impression. Fisher and Ottley had lobbied hard for the sub-committee to be formed in 1905–6 and it is significant to note that their successors were attempting to revive it by the outbreak of war. In June 1914 Captain Richmond drafted a paper arguing that, in the Admiralty's view, 'this [Balfour's] sub-committee... is the only body which provides the machinery for the consideration of problems of

---

[4] Hankey to Fisher, 8 May 1912, in Roskill, *Hankey* I, p. 119.
[5] d'Ombrain, *War Machinery*, pp. 75–6.

offensive action in war'.[6] Failing even to try and reconcile the views of the two services on this point—despite the acrimonious exchanges and demonstrably conflicting views on show between 1906 and 1914—was a failure of political leadership and of judgement.

Second, rather than aligning the activities of the Admiralty and War Office to enhance Britain's capacity to fight a war, the government allowed the opposite to occur. Largely through political prevarication, military policy began to subordinate naval strategy to the principle of sending the Expeditionary Force to France. This is not to say that the Admiralty was right and that combined operations ought to have formed the basis of British strategy in 1914. The wishes of the French—who placed far greater importance on British troops than on the Royal Navy—were vital in this regard, as was the need to prevent France from being overwhelmed as she had been in 1870. However, if the government truly believed that British military intervention was vital to French survival, it made no meaningful attempt to prepare the Army for the task which might lie ahead. Formidable political difficulties barred the way to increasing the size of the Army, but these might have been overcome to a limited extent had the will to do so existed. An expeditionary force of even 250,000 men would have been a clear statement of British intent and provided her with greater influence when the July Crisis unfolded.[7] As it was, the government calculated that staking the country's hopes on peace was preferable to preparing more thoroughly to fight a war that might never come. The effect was that planning to send as great a proportion of Britain's modest military resources to France as possible had a considerable and very detrimental effect upon the Royal Navy's offensive contribution to British strategy.

The government's unwillingness to discuss offensive issues meant that decisions it reached on matters pertaining to reactive defence came to determine how Britain could fight a future war. This was particularly true of plans to resist invasion. As home defence was the element within British strategy where the roles of the two services overlapped to the greatest extent, the government's attitude to protecting the United Kingdom—the one issue which it was prepared to expend significant amounts of time investigating in both 1907–8 and 1913–14—became the de facto arbiter of British strategy. Decisions taken on the issue did not define strategy in a specific sense, but they did play an important role in delineating the parameters within which the two services prepared and thought, and in determining the balance each had to strike between offence and defence considerations. As Balfour had shown in 1903, this represented one half of a potentially effective method of defining the broader features of well co-ordinated grand strategy. Unfortunately, after 1905, political reticence left the other side of the coin blank. Hankey claimed that '[in 1914] the country was in many respects well prepared for defence',[8] but this had been achieved at the price of expending much of the country's naval power

---

[6] Draft by Richmond, 20 June 1914, RIC/1/9, NMM.

[7] As argued by L. S. Amery, 'Notes on the Military Situation', 26 August 1913, pp. 20–2, MSS Milner 156/11, Bod.

[8] Hankey, *Supreme Command* I, p. 138.

upon defensive duties, curtailing the scope for a naval offensive, obliging risks to be run with the Fleet, and escalating the potential consequences of a single mis-step by commanders afloat. After assuming command of the Grand Fleet in August 1914, Admiral Jellicoe truly became, in Churchill's phrase, 'the only man on either side who could lose the war in an afternoon'.[9] Had this division of naval and military resource been a conscious choice, it might have been justifiable—what impact sea power could have had upon the potentially decisive land battles of 1914 was unclear at the time and remains so today. Yet as it was—the result of inaction and disregard—Britain entered the war unconsciously having compromised the operational freedom and offensive potential of her most important (and expensive) military-strategic asset. This foreshadowed the conflicted and contradictory manner in which the government managed the war effort in 1914–15 and Britain's inability to concert naval and military effort in a co-ordinated, complementary manner during the First World War.

[9] Churchill, *World Crisis* II (1938 edn), p. 1015.

Bibliography

ARCHIVAL SOURCES

Bodleian Library
Asquith Papers
Milner Papers
Sanders Papers
Selborne Papers

Brighton and Hove Archives Centre
Wolseley Papers

British Library
Arnold Forster Papers
Balfour Papers
Bowood Papers
Campbell-Bannerman Papers
Clarke Papers
Directorate of Military Operations Papers
Jellicoe Papers
Marker Papers

Cadbury Library, University of Birmingham
Austen Chamberlain Papers

Chatsworth House
Devonshire Papers

Churchill College Archives Centre
Churchill Papers
Esher Papers
Fisher Papers
Grant-Duff Papers
Hankey Papers

Hartley Library, University of Southampton
Battenberg Papers

Imperial War Museum
Maxse Papers
Wilson Papers

Liddell Hart Centre for Military Archives
Bethell Papers
Hamilton Papers
Robertson Papers

The National Archives, Kew
ADM 1, 116, 121, 137, 144, 167, 231
CAB 2, 3, 4, 6, 12, 13, 16, 17, 18, 37, 38, 63
CO 537
PRO 30
WO 32, 33, 105, 106, 147

National Army Museum
Ellison Papers
Roberts Papers

National Library of Scotland
Haig Papers
Haldane Papers

National Maritime Museum
Ballard Papers
Bridge Papers
Corbett Papers
D'Eyncourt Papers
Fremantle Papers
May Papers
Oliver Papers
Richmond Papers
Slade Papers

National Museum of the Royal Navy
Crease Papers
Tweedmouth Papers

National Records of Scotland
Ewart Papers
Gerald Balfour Papers

Royal Marines Museum
Aston Papers

PRINTED PRIMARY SOURCES

Boyce, D. G., ed., *The Crisis of British Power: The Imperial and Naval Papers of the Second Early Selborne, 1895–1910*, London: Historians Press, 1990.
Brett, M. V., ed., *Journals and Letters of Reginald Viscount Esher*, London: Ivor Nicholson & Watson, 1934.
Buckle, G. E., ed., *The Letters of Queen Victoria*, 3rd series, New York: Longmans, Green, & Co., 1928–32.
Callwell, C. E., *Field-Marshal Sir Henry Wilson: His Life and Diaries*, New York: Charles Scribner's Sons, 1927.
Churchill, R., ed., *The Churchill Documents*, Vol. V: *At the Admiralty*, 2007 edn, Hillsdale, MI: Hillsdale College Press.

Hattendorf, J., et al., eds, *British Naval Documents 1204–1960*, Aldershot: Ashgate, 1993.

Kemp, P., ed., *The Fisher Papers*, London: Spottiswoode, Ballantyne, & Co., 1960–4.

Lowe, C. J., ed., *The Reluctant Imperialists*, Vol. II: *The Documents*, London: Routledge, 1967.

Marder, A. J., ed., *Fear God and Dread Nought: The Correspondence of Admiral of the Fleet Lord Fisher of Kilverstone*, London: Jonathan Cape, 1952–9.

Marder, A. J., ed., *Portrait of an Admiral: The Life and Papers of Sir Herbert Richmond*, London: Jonathan Cape, 1952.

Morris, A. J. A., ed., *The Letters of Lieutenant-Colonel Charles à Court Repington: Military Correspondent of The Times, 1903–1918*, Stroud: Sutton, 1999.

Preston, A., ed., *In Relief of Gordon: Lord Wolseley's Campaign Journal of the Khartoum Relief Expedition, 1884–1885*, London: Hutchinson, 1967.

Seligmann, M. S., ed., *Naval Intelligence from Germany: The Reports of the British Naval Attachés in Berlin, 1906–1914*, Aldershot: Ashgate, 2007.

Seligmann, M. S., F. Nägler, and M. Epkenhans, *The Naval Route to the Abyss: The Anglo-German Naval Race, 1895–1914*, Farnham: Ashgate, 2015.

SECONDARY SOURCES

Adams, R. J. Q., and P. Poirier, *The Conscription Controversy in Great Britain, 1900–1918*, Columbus, OH: Ohio State University Press, 1987.

Allen, M., 'The Foreign Intelligence Committee and the Origins of the Naval Intelligence Department of the Admiralty', *The Mariner's Mirror*, Vol. 81, No. 1, Feb., 1995, pp. 65–78.

Amery, L. S., 'Imperial Defence and National Policy' in C. S. Goldman ed., *The Empire and the Century*, London: John Murray, 1905, pp. 174–96.

Arnold-Forster, H. O., *The War Office, the Army and the Empire*, London, 1900.

Aston, G., *The Problem of Defence: Reminiscences and Deductions*, London: Philip Allan & Co., 1925.

Aston, G., 'The Committee of Imperial Defence: Its Evolution and Prospects', *RUSI*, Vol. 71, No. 483, 1926, pp. 456–63.

Aston, G., *Secret Service*, London: Faber & Faber, 1930.

Atwood, R., *The Life of Field Marshal Lord Roberts*, London: Bloomsbury, 2015.

Bacon, R., *The Life of Lord Fisher of Kilverstone*, London: Redder & Stoughton, 1929.

Bailes, H., 'Patterns of Thought in the Late-Victorian Army', *Journal of Strategic Studies*, Vol. 4, No. 1, 1981, pp. 29–45.

Bartlett, C. J., 'The Mid-Victorian Reappraisal of Naval Policy' in K. Bourne and D. C. Watt eds, *Studies in International History*, London: Longmans, 1967, pp. 189–208.

Beckett, I. F. W., 'H. O. Arnold-Forster and the Volunteers' in I. F. W. Beckett and J. Gooch eds, *Politicians and Defence: Studies in the Formulation of British Defence Policy*, Manchester: Manchester University Press, 1981, pp. 47–68.

Beckett, I. F. W., 'Edward Stanhope at the War Office, 1887–1892', *Journal of Strategic Studies*, Vol. 5, No. 2, 1982, pp. 278–307.

Beckett, I. F. W., *Riflemen Form: A Study of the Rifle Volunteer Movement, 1859–1908*, Aldershot: Ogilby Trust, 1982.

Beckett, I. F. W., 'The Stanhope Memorandum of 1888: A Re-interpretation', *Bulletin of the Institute of Historical Research*, LVII, 136, 1984, pp. 240–7.

Beckett, I. F. W., 'The Road from Kandahar: The Politics of Retention and Withdrawal in Afghanistan, 1880–81', *Journal of Military History*, Vol. 78, Oct., 2014, pp. 1263–94.

Beeler, J., *British Naval Policy in the Gladstone–Disraeli Era, 1866–1880*, Stanford, CA: Stanford University Press, 1997.

Beeler, J., 'In the Shadow of Briggs: A New Perspective on British Naval Administration and W. T. Stead's 1884 "Truth about the Navy" Campaign', *International Journal of Naval History*, Vol. 1, No. 1, Apr., 2002.

Bell, C. M., 'Sir John Fisher's Naval Revolution Reconsidered: Winston Churchill at the Admiralty, 1911–1914', *War in History*, Vol. 18, No. 3, 2011, pp. 333–56.

Beresford, C., *The Memoirs of Lord Charles Beresford: Written by Himself*, Boston, MA: Little, Brown, & Company, 1914.

Bond, B., *The Victorian Army and the Staff College, 1854–1914*, London: Methuen, 1972.

Bradford, E. E., *Life of Admiral of the Fleet Sir Arthur Knyvet Wilson*, London: John Murray, 1923.

Brooks, J., *Dreadnought Gunnery and the Battle of Jutland: The Question of Fire Control*, Abingdon: Routledge, 2006.

Brice, C., *The Thinking Man's Solider: The Life and Career of General Sir Henry Brackenbury, 1837–1914*, Solihull: Hellion & Co., 2012.

Burroughs, P., 'Defence and Imperial Disunity' in A. Porter ed., *The Oxford History of the British Empire: The Nineteenth Century*, Oxford: Oxford University Press, 1999, pp. 320–45.

Callwell, C. E., *The Effect of Maritime Command on Land Campaigns since Waterloo*, Edinburgh and London, 1897.

Callwell, C. E., *Military Operations and Maritime Preponderance: Their Relations and Interdependence*, Edinburgh & London, 1905.

Childers, E., *The Riddle of the Sands*, London, 1903.

Churchill, W. S., *The World Crisis, 1911–1918*, London: Odhams Press, 1938 edn.

Clarke, G. S., *Imperial Defence*, London, 1897.

Clarke, I. F. W., *Voices Prophesying War: Future Wars, 1763–1749*, Oxford: Oxford University Press, 1992 edn.

Cobb, S., *Preparing for Blockade, 1885–1914: Naval Contingency for Economic Warfare*, Farnham: Ashgate, 2013.

Cobden, R., *The Three Panics: A Historical Episode*, London, 1862.

Colls, R., *Identity of England*, Oxford: Oxford University Press, 2002.

Colomb, P. H., J. F. Maurice, F. N. Maude, A. Forbes, C. Lowe, D. Christie Murray, and F. Scudamore, *The Great War of 189-: A Forecast*, London: William Heinemann, 1893.

Coogan, J. W., and P. F. Coogan, 'The British Cabinet and the Anglo-French Staff Talks, 1905–1914: Who Knew What and When Did He Know it?', *Journal of British Studies*, Vol. 24, No. 1, Jan., 1985, pp. 110–31.

Corbett, J. S., *Some Principles of Maritime Strategy*, London, 1911.

Cruttwell, C. M. R. F., *The Role of British Strategy in the Great War*, Cambridge: Cambridge University Press, 1936.

Darwin, J., 'Imperialism and the Victorians: The Dynamics of Territorial Expansion', *English Historical Review*, CXII, 447, Jun., 1997, pp. 614–42.

Darwin, J., *The Empire Project: The Rise and Fall of the British World-System, 1830–1970*, Cambridge: Cambridge University Press, 2009.

Dunley, R., 'Sir John Fisher and the Policy of Strategic Deterrence, 1904–1908', *War in History*, Vol. 22, No. 2, Apr., 2015, pp. 155–73.

Dunlop, J. K., *The Development of the British Army, 1899–1914*, London: Methuen, 1938.

Ehrman, J., *Cabinet Government and War*, Cambridge: Cambridge University Press, 1957.

Ferguson, N., *The Pity of War*, London: Allen Lane, 1998.

Ferguson, T. G., *British Military Intelligence, 1870–1914*, Fredrick, MD: University Publications of America, 1984.

Fisher, J. A., *Records*, London: Hodder & Stoughton, 1919.

Fremantle, S. R., *My Naval Career, 1880–1928*, Essex: Tiptree, 1949.

French, D., *British Economic and Strategic Planning, 1905–1915*, London: George Allen & Unwin, 1982.

French, D., *The British Way in Warfare, 1688–2000*, London: Unwin Hyman, 1990.

French, D., and B. Holden Reid eds, *The British General Staff: Reform and Innovation c. 1890–1939*, London: Frank Cass, 2002.

Friedberg, A. L., *The Weary Titan: Britain and the Experience of Relative Decline*, Princeton, NY: Princeton University Press, 1988.

Gibbs, N. H., 'The Origins of Imperial Defence', Inaugural Lecture of the Chichele Chair, 1955, reproduced in J. B. Hattendorf and R. S. Jordan eds, *Maritime Strategy and the Balance of Power: Britain and America in the Twentieth Century*, Basingstoke: Macmillan, 1989, pp. 23–36.

Gillard, D., *The Struggle for Asia 1828–1914: A Study in British and Russian Imperialism*, London: Methuen, 1977.

Goldman, C. S., ed., *The Empire and the Century*, London: John Murray, 1905.

Gooch, J., *The Plans of War: The General Staff and British Military Strategy c.1900–1916*, New York: John Wilsey & Sons, 1974.

Gooch, J., *The Prospect of War: Studies in British Defence Policy 1847–1942*, Abingdon: Frank Cass, 1981.

Gooch, J., 'The Weary Titan: Strategy and Policy in Great Britain, 1890–1918' in W. Murray, M. Knox, and A. Bernstein eds, *The Making of Strategy: Rulers, States, and War*, Cambridge: Cambridge University Press, 1994, pp. 278–306.

Gooch, J., 'Adversarial Attitudes: Servicemen, Politicians and Strategic Policy in Edwardian England, 1899–1914' in P. Smith ed., *Government and the Armed Forces in Britain 1856–1990*, London: Hambledon, 1996, pp. 53–74.

Gordon, A., *The Rules of the Game: Jutland and British Naval Command*, London: John Murray, 1996.

Grimes, S. T., *Strategy and War Planning in the British Navy, 1887–1918*, Woodbridge: Boydell & Brewer, 2012.

Grimes, S. T., 'Combined Operations and British Strategy, 1900–09', *Historical Research*, 2016.

Haggie, P., 'The Royal Navy and War Planning in the Fisher Era', *Journal of Contemporary History*, Vol. 8, No. 3, Jul., 1973, pp. 113–31.

Haldane, R. B., *Before the War*, London & New York: Funk & Cagnalls, 1920.

Haldane, R. B., *Richard Burton Haldane: An Autobiography*, London: Hodder & Stoughton, 1928.

Hamer, W. S., *The British Army: Civil Military Relations, 1885–1905*, Oxford: Clarendon, 1970.

Hamilton, G. F., *Parliamentary Reminiscences and Reflections, 1886–1906*, London: John Murray, 1922.

Hamilton, I. M., *Compulsory Service: A Study of the Question in Light of Experience*, London: John Murray, 1911.

Hamilton, R. F., and H. H. Herwig eds, *War Planning 1914*, Cambridge: Cambridge University Press, 2010.

Hankey, M., *Government Control in War*, Cambridge: Cambridge University Press, 1945.

Hankey, M., *The Supreme Command, 1914–1918*, London: Unwin Brothers, 1961.

Hayes, P., 'Britain, Germany and the Admiralty's Plans for Attacking German Territory, 1906–1915' in L. Freedman ed., *War Strategy and Intentional Politics: Essays in Honour of Michael Howard*, Oxford: Clarendon, 1992.

Herwig, H. H., *'Luxury' Fleet: The Imperial German Navy, 1888–1918*, London: Allen & Unwin, 1980.

Hoppen, K. T., *The Mid-Victorian Generation, 1846–1886*, Oxford: Clarendon, 1998.

Howard, M., *The Continental Commitment: The Dilemma of British Defence Policy in the Era of Two World Wars*, Harmondsworth: Penguin, 1971.

James, D., *Lord Roberts*, London: Hollis & Carter, 1954.

James, W., *A Great Seaman: The Life of Admiral of the Fleet Sir Henry F. Oliver*, London: A. F. & G. Whitherby, 1956.

Jeffery, K., *Field Marshal Sir Henry Wilson: A Political Soldier*, Oxford: Oxford University Press, 2006.

Johnson, F. R., *Defence by Committee: The British Committee of Imperial Defence, 1885–1959*, London: Oxford University Press, 1960.

Johnson, R., 'Russians at the Gates of India'? Planning the Defence of India, 1885–1900', *Journal of Military History*, Vol. 67. No. 3, Jul., 2003, pp. 697–743.

Kennedy, P. M., 'The Development of German Naval Operations Plans Against England, 1896–1914', *English Historical Review*, Vol. 89, No. 350, Jan., 1974, pp. 48–76.

Kennedy, P. M., *The Rise of the Anglo-German Antagonism, 1860–1914*, London: Ashfield, 1980.

Kennedy, P. M., *The Rise and Fall of the Great Powers*, New York: Random House, 1987.

Kennedy, P. M., *Strategy and Diplomacy, 1870–1945*, London: Fontana, 1989 edn.

Kerr, M., *Prince Louis of Battenberg: Admiral of the Fleet*, London: Longmans, Green, & Co., 1934.

Keyes, R., *The Naval Memoirs of Admiral of the Fleet Sir Roger Keyes*, Vol. I: *The Narrow Seas to the Dardanelles, 1910–1915*, London, 1934.

Kochanski, H., *Sir Garnett Wolseley: Victorian Hero*, London and Rio Grande: Hambledon Press, 1999.

Kochanski, H., 'Planning for War in the Final Years of *Pax Britannica*, 1889–1903', in D. French and B. Holden Reid eds, *The British General Staff: Reform and Innovation c.1890–1939*, London: Frank Cass, 2002, pp. 9–25.

Lambert, A., *The Foundations of Naval History: John Knox Laughton, the Royal Navy and the Historical Profession*, London: Chatham, 1998.

Lambert, A., 'Great Britain and the Baltic, 1890–1914' in P. Salmon and T. Barrow eds, *Britain and the Baltic: Studies in Commercial, Political and Cultural Relations, 1500–2000*, Sunderland: University of Sunderland Press, 2003, pp. 215–36.

Lambert, A., '"This Is All We Want": Great Britain and the Baltic Approaches, 1815–1914' in J. Sevaldsen ed., *Britain and Denmark: Political, Economic and Cultural Relations in the 19th and 20th Centuries*, Copenhagen: Copenhagen Museum Press, 2003, pp. 147–69.

Lambert, A., 'The Development of Education in the Royal Navy: 1854–1914' in G. Till ed., *The Development of British Naval Thinking: Essays in Memory of Bryan Ranft*, Abingdon: Routledge, 2006, pp. 34–56.

Lambert, A., 'Royal Navy and the Defence of Empire' in G. Kennedy ed., *Imperial Defence: The Old World Order, 1856–1956*, Abingdon: Routledge, 2008, pp. 111–32.

Lambert, A., 'The German North Sea Islands, the Kiel Canal and the Danish Narrows in Royal Navy Thinking and Planning, 1905–1918' in M. Epkenhans and G. P. Gross eds, *The Danish Straits and German Naval Power, 1905–1918*, Potsdam: MGFA, 2010, pp. 35–62.

Lambert, A., 'The Naval War Course, *Some Principles of Maritime Strategy* and the Origins of "The British Way in Warfare"' in K. Neilson and G. Kennedy eds, *The British Way in Warfare: Power and the International System, 1856–1956: Essays in Honour of David French*, Farnham: Ashgate, 2010, pp. 219–53.

Lambert, A., '"The Possibility of Ultimate Action in the Baltic": The Royal Navy at War, 1914–1916' in M. Epkenhans, J. Hillman, and F. Nägler eds, *Jutland: World War I's Greatest Naval Battle*, Lexington, KY: Kentucky University Press, 2015, pp. 79–116.

Lambert, N. A., 'Admiral Sir Arthur Knyvett-Wilson, V.C. (1910–1911)' in M. Murfett ed., *The First Sea Lords from Fisher to Mountbatten*, Westport, CT: Praeger, 1995, pp. 35–50.

Lambert, N. A., 'Admiral Sir John Fisher and the Concept of Flotilla Defence, 1904–1909', *Journal of Military History*, Vol. 59, No. 4, Oct., 1995, pp. 639–60.

Lambert, N. A., *Sir John Fisher's Naval Revolution*, Columbia, SC: University of South Carolina Press, 1999.

Lambert, N. A., 'Strategic Command and Control for Maneuver Warfare: Creation of the Royal Navy's "War Room" System, 1905–1915', *Journal of Military History*, Vol. 69, No. 2, Apr., 2005, pp. 361–410.

Lambert, N. A., *Planning Armageddon: British Economic Warfare and the First World War*, Cambridge, MA, and London: Harvard University Press, 2012.

Lambi, I., *The Navy and German Power Politics, 1862–1914*, Boston, MA: Allen & Unwin, 1984.

Liddell Hart, B., *The Real War, 1914–1918*, London: Faber & Faber, 1930.

Lowe, C. J., *The Reluctant Imperialists*, London: Routledge, 1967, Vol. I.

Luvaas, J., *The Education of an Army: British Military Thought, 1815–1940*, Toronto: University of Chicago Press, 1964.

Macdiarmid, D. S., *The Life of Lieut. General Sir James Moncrieff Greirson*, London: Constable & Company, 1923.

Mackay, R., *Fisher of Kilverstone*, Oxford: Clarendon, 1973.

Mackay, R., *Balfour: Intellectual Statesman*, Oxford: Oxford University Press, 1985.

Mackinder, H., *Britain and the British Seas*, Oxford, 1902.

MacKintosh, J. P., 'The Role of the Committee of Imperial Defence before 1914', *English Historical Review*, Vol. 77, No. 304, Jul., 1962, pp. 490–509.

Marder, A. J., *From the Dreadnought to Scapa Flow: The Royal Navy in the Fisher Era, 1904–1919*, Oxford: Oxford University Press, 5 vols, 1961–70.

Marder, A. J., *The Anatomy of British Sea Power: A History of British Naval Policy in the Pre-Dreadnought Era, 1880–1905*, Hamden, CT: Archon, 1964 edn.

Maurice, F., *Haldane, 1856–1915: The Life of Viscount Haldane of Cloan*, London: Faber & Faber, 1937.

Maurice, F., and G. Arthur, *Life of Lord Wolseley*, London: William Heinemann, 1924.

McDermott, J., 'The Immediate Origins of the Committee of Imperial Defence', *Canadian Journal of History*, Vol. 7, No. 3, 1972, pp. 253–72.

McDermott, J., 'The Revolution in British Military Thinking from the Boer War to the Moroccan Crisis', *Canadian Journal of History*, Vol. 9, No. 2, 1974, pp. 159–77.

Moon, H. R., 'The Invasion of the United Kingdom: Public Controversy and Official Planning, 1888–1918', unpublished Ph.D. thesis, University of London, 1968.

Morgan-Owen, D. G., '"History is a Record of Exploded Ideas": Sir John Fisher and Home Defence, 1904–10', *International History Review*, Vol. 36, No. 3, 2014, pp. 550–72.

Morgan-Owen, D. G., 'Cooked up in the Dinner Hour? Sir Arthur Wilson's War Plan, Reconsidered', *English Historical Review*, Vol. 130, No. 545, 2015, pp. 865–906.

Morgan-Owen, D. G., 'An "Intermediate Blockade?" British North Sea Strategy, 1912–1914', *War in History*, Vol. 22, No. 4, 2015, pp. 478–502.

Morris, A. J. A., *The Scaremongers: The Advocacy of War and Rearmament, 1896–1914*, London: Routledge & Kegan Paul, 1984.

Morris, A. J. A., *Reporting the First World War: Charles Repington, The Times and the Great War*, Cambridge: Cambridge University Press, 2015.

Mulligan, W., 'From Case to Narrative: The Marquess of Lansdowne, Sir Edward Grey, and the Threat from Germany, 1900–1906', *International History Review*, Vol. 30, No. 2, 2008, pp. 273–302.

Mullins, R., 'Sharpening the Trident: The Decisions of 1889 and the Creation of Modern Seapower', unpublished Ph.D. thesis, King's College, London, 2000.

Neilson, K., 'The British Way in War and Russia' in K. Neilson and G. Kennedy eds, *The British Way in Warfare: Power and the International System, 1856–1956*, Farnham: Ashgate, 2010, pp. 7–28.

Neilson, K., 'Great Britain' in R. F. Hamilton and H. H. Herwig eds, *War Planning 1914*, Cambridge: Cambridge University Press, 2010, pp. 175–97.

Offer, A., *The First World War: An Agrarian Interpretation*, Oxford: Clarendon, 1989.

d'Ombrain, N., 'The Imperial General Staff and the Military Policy of a "Continental Strategy" during the 1911 International Crisis', *Military Affairs*, Vol. 34, Oct., 1970, pp. 88–93.

d'Ombrain, N., *War Machinery and High Policy: Defence Administration in Peacetime Britain, 1902–1914*, Oxford: Oxford University Press, 1973.

Otte, T. G., ed., *The Makers of British Foreign Policy: From Pitt to Thatcher*, Basingstoke: Palgrave, 2002.

Otte, T. G., 'From "War in Sight" to Nearly War: Anglo-French Relations in the Age of High Imperialism, 1875–1898', *Diplomacy & Statecraft*, Vol. 17, No. 4, 2006, pp. 693–714.

Otte, T. G., '"The Method by which we were schooled by Experience": British Strategy and a Continental Commitment before 1914' in K. Neilson and G. Kennedy eds, *The British Way in Warfare: Power and the International System, 1856–1956*, Farnham: Ashgate, 2010, pp. 301–24.

Otte, T. G., *Foreign Office Mind: The Making of British Foreign Policy, 1865–1914*, Cambridge: Cambridge University Press, 2011.

Otte, T. G., 'Grey Ambassador: The *Dreadnought* and British Foreign Policy' in R. Blyth, A. Lambert and J. Rüger eds, *The Dreadnought and the Edwardian Age*, Farnham: Ashgate, 2011, pp. 51–78.

Otte, T. G., 'Détente 1914: Sir William Tyrrell's Secret Mission to Germany', *Historical Journal*, Vol. 56, No. 1, 2013, pp. 175–204.

Panayi, P., *Immigration, Ethnicity and Racism in Britain, 1815–1945*, Manchester: Manchester University Press, 1994.

Papastratigakis, N., 'British Naval Strategy: The Russian Black Sea Fleet and the Turkish Straits, 1890–1904', *International History Review*, No. 32, Vol. 4 (2010), pp. 647–53.

Papastratigakis, N., *Russian Imperialism and Naval Power: Military Strategy and the Build-Up to the Russo-Japanese War*, London: I. B. Tauris, 2011.

Parry, J. P., 'The Impact of Napoleon III on British Politics, 1851–1880', *Transactions of the Royal Historical Society*, 6th Series, Vol. 11, 2001, pp. 147–75.

Partridge, M. S., *Military Planning for the Defense of the United Kingdom, 1814–1870*, Westport, CT: Greenwood Press, 1989.

Porter, B., "'Bureau and Barrack": Early Victorian Attitudes towards the Continent', *Victorian Studies*, Vol. 27, No. 4, 1984, pp. 407–33.

Preston, A., 'Sir Charles Macgregor and the Defence of India, 1857–1887', *Historical Journal*, Vol. 12, No. 1, 1969, pp. 58–77.

Preston, A., 'Wolseley, the Khartoum Relief Expedition and the Defence of India, 1885–1900', *Journal of Imperial and Commonwealth History*, Vol. 6, No. 3, May, 1978, pp. 254–80.

Preston, A., 'Frustrated Great Gamesmanship: Sir Garnett Wolseley's Plans for War against Russian, 1873–1880', *International History Review*, Vol. 2, No. 2, Apr., 1980, pp. 239–65.

Ranft, B., 'The Protection of British Seaborne Trade and the Development of Systematic Planning for War, 1860–1906' in B. Ranft, *Technical Change and British Naval Policy, 1860–1939*, London: Hodder & Stoughton, 1977, pp. 1–22.

Ranft, B., 'The Royal Navy and the War at Sea' in J. Turner ed., *Britain and the First World War*, London: Unwin Hyman, 1988, pp. 53–69.

Richmond, H., *National Policy and Naval Strength and Other Essays*, London: Longmans, Green, & Co., 1928.

Robbins, K., *Britain and Europe, 1789–2005*, London: Hodder Arnold, 2005.

Robertson, W., *From Private to Field Marshal*, London: Constable & Company, 1921.

Rodger, N. A. M. R., 'Naval Strategy in the Eighteen and Nineteenth Centuries' in G. Till ed., *The Development of British Naval Thinking*, Abingdon: Routledge, 2006, pp. 19–33.

Ropp, T., *Development of a Modern Navy: French Naval Policy, 1871–1904*, S. S. Roberts ed., Annapolis, MA: Naval Institute Press, 1987.

Roskill, S., *Hankey: Man of Secrets*, Vol. I, London: Collins, 1970.

Satre, L. J., 'St. John Brodrick and Army Reform', *Journal of British Studies*, Vol. 15, No. 2, 1976, pp. 117–39.

Schurman, D. M., *The Education of a Navy: The Development of British Naval Thought, 1867–1914*, London: Cassell, 1965.

Schurman, D. M., *Julian S. Corbett: Historian of British Maritime Policy from Drake to Jellicoe*, London: Royal Historical Society, 1981.

Schurman, D. M., *Imperial Defence, 1868–1887*, J. Beeler ed., London: Frank Cass, 2000.

Searle, G. R., *The Quest for National Efficiency: A Study in British Politics and Political Thought, 1899–1914*, Berkeley and Los Angeles: University of California Press, 1971.

Searle, G. R., *A New England? Peace and War, 1886–1918*, Oxford: Clarendon, 2004.

Seligmann, M. S., *Rivalry in Southern Africa: The Transformation of German Colonial Policy*, London: Palgrave Macmillan, 1998.

Seligmann, M. S., *Spies in Uniform: British Military and Naval Intelligence on the Eve of the First World War*, Oxford: Oxford University Press, 2006.

Seligmann, M. S., 'Switching Horses: The Admiralty's Recognition of the Threat from Germany, 1900–1905', *International History Review*, Vol. 30, No. 2, 2008, pp. 239–58.

Seligmann, M. S., 'A Prelude to the Reforms of Admiral Sir John Fisher: The Creation of the Home Fleet, 1902–03', *Historical Research*, vol. 83, no. 221, Aug., 2010, pp. 506–19.

Seligmann, M. S., 'Britain's Great Security Mirage: The Royal Navy and the Franco-Russian Naval Threat, 1898–1906', *Journal of Strategic Studies*, Vol. 35, No. 6, 2012, pp. 861–86.

Seligmann, M. S., *The Royal Navy and the German Threat, 1901–1914: Admiralty Plans to Protect British Trade in a War Against Germany*, Oxford: Oxford University Press, 2012.

Seligmann, M. S., 'The Anglo-German Naval Race, 1898–1914' in T. Mahnken, J. Maiolo, and D. Stevenson eds, *Arms Races in International Politics: From the Nineteenth to the Twenty-First Century*, Oxford: Oxford University Press, 2016, pp. 21–40.

Seligmann, M. S., 'Germany's Ocean Greyhounds and the Royal Navy's First Battle Cruisers: An Historiographical Problem', *Diplomacy & Statecraft*, Vol. 27, No. 1, 2016, pp. 162–82.

Seligmann, M. S., 'A Great American Scholar of the Royal Navy? The Disputed Legacy of Arthur Marder Revisited', *International History Review*, Vol. 38, No. 5, 2016, pp. 1040–54.

Seligmann, M.S., 'Failing to Prepare for the Great War? The Absence of Grand Strategy in British War Planning before 1914', *War in History*, published online April.

Silberstein, G. E., 'Germany, France and the Casablanca Incident, 1908–1909; an Investigation of a Forgotten Crisis', *Canadian Journal of History*, Vol. 76, No. 3, Dec., 1976, pp. 331–54.

Smith, S. R. B., 'Public Opinion, the Navy and the City of London: The Drive for British Naval Expansion in the Late Nineteenth Century', *War & Society*, Vol. 9, No. 1, May, 1991, pp. 29–50.

Spiers, E. M., *The Army and Society, 1815–1914*, London: Longman, 1980.

Spiers, E. M., *Haldane: An Army Reformer*, Edinburgh: Edinburgh University Press, 1980.

Spiers, E. M., *The Late Victorian Army 1868–1902*, Manchester: Manchester University Press, 1992.

Spiers, E. M., 'The Late Victorian Army, 1868–1914' in D. G. Chandler and I. W. F. Beckett eds, *The Oxford History of the British Army*, Oxford: Oxford University Press, 1996, pp. 187–210.

Spiers, E. M., 'Between the South African War and the First World War, 1902–1914' in H. Strachan ed., *Big Wars and Small Wars: The British Army and the Lessons of the 20th Century*, Abingdon: Routledge, 2006, pp. 21–35.

Steinberg, J., 'A German Plan for the Invasion of Holland Belgium, 1897', *Historical Journal*, Vol. 6, No. 1, 1963, pp. 107–19.

Steinberg, J., *Yesterday's Deterrent: Tirpitz and the Birth of the German Battle Fleet*, London: MacDonald, 1965.

Steinberg, J., 'The Copenhagen Complex', *Journal of Contemporary History*, Vol. 1, No. 3, Jul., 1966, pp. 23–46.

Strachan, H., *The First World War*, Vol. I: *To Arms*, Oxford: Oxford University Press, 2001.

Strachan, H., 'The British Army, its General Staff and the Continental Commitment, 1904–14' in D. French and B. Holden Reid eds, *The British General Staff: Reform and Innovation c.1890–1939*, London: Frank Cass, 2002, pp. 75–94.

Strachan, H., 'The Territorial Army and National Defence' in K. Neilson and G. Kennedy eds, *The British Way in Warfare: Power and the International System, 1856–1956: Essays in Honour of David French*, Farnham: Ashgate, 2010, pp. 159–78.

Sumida, J. T., *In Defence of Naval Supremacy: Finance, Technology, and British Naval Policy, 1889–1914*, London: Unwin Hyman, 1989.

Summerton, N. W., 'The Development of British Military Planning for a War Against Germany, 1904–1914', unpublished Ph.D. thesis, University of London, 1970.

Sweetman, J., 'Towards a Ministry of Defence: First Faltering Steps, 1890–1923' in D. French and B. Holden Reid eds, *The British General Staff: Reform and Innovation c.1890–1939*, London: Frank Cass, 2002, pp. 26–40.

Tucker, A., 'The Issue of Army Reform in the Unionist Government, 1903–5', *Historical Journal*, Vol. 9, No. 1, 1966, pp. 90–100.

Tunstall, W. C. B., 'Imperial Defence, 1815–1870' in J. Holland Rose, A. P. Newton, and E. A. Benians eds, *The Cambridge History of the British Empire*, Vol. II: *The Growth of the New Empire, 1783–1870*, Cambridge: Cambridge University Press, 1940, pp. 806–41.

Tunstall, W. C. B., 'Imperial Defence, 1897–1914' in E. A. Benians, J. Butler, and C. E. Carrington eds, *The Cambridge History of the British Empire*, Vol. III: *The Empire Commonwealth, 1870–1919*, Cambridge: Cambridge University Press, 1967, pp. 563–604.

Tyler, J. E., *The British Army and the Continent, 1904–1914*, London, 1938.

Ward, T. H., ed., *The Reign of Queen Victoria: A Survey of Fifty Years of Progress*, Vol. I, London: Smith, Elder, & Co., 1887.

Wilkinson, S., *The Command of the Sea*, London, 1894.

Williams, M. J., 'The Egyptian Campaign of 1882' in B. Bond ed., *Victorian Military Campaigns*, London: Hutchinson & Co., 1967, pp. 249–53.

Williams, R., *Defending the Empire: The Conservative Party and British Defence Policy 1899–1915*, London: Yale University Press, 1991.

Williamson Jr, S. R., *The Politics of Grand Strategy: Britain and France Prepare for War, 1904–1914*, Cambridge, MA: Harvard University Press, 1969.

Wilson, K. M., 'To the Western Front: British War Plans and the "Military Entente" with France before the First World War', *British Journal of International Studies*, Vol. 3, No. 2, Jul., 1977, pp. 151–69.

Wilson, K. M., *Empire and Continent: Studies in British Foreign Policy from the 1880s to the First World War*, London and New York: Mansell, 1987.

Wilson, K. M., *Channel Tunnel Visions, 1850–1945: Dreams and Nightmares*, London: Hambledon Press, 1994.

Wilson, T., 'Britain's "Moral Commitment" to France in August 1914', *History*, Vol. 62, No. 212, 1979, pp. 380–90.

Yapp, M., 'British Perceptions of the Russian Threat to India', *Modern Asian Studies*, Vol. 21, No. 4, 1987, pp. 647–65.

Index

Admiralty, changing assessment of risk of
invasion, 149–53, 170–4, 196, 205–8,
216–19
attempts to provide coherence to British 'grand'
strategy, 196, 202, 209, 218, 222, 225–6
Admiralty Staff (German), 133
Afghanistan, 15, 46, 55–9, 71, 75–6, 102
Agadir Crisis (1911), 196–201, 205, 208, 211
Amery, Leo, 71, 84–5, 232n7
Anglo-French military conversations, 156–7,
168, 186–9, 208
Anglo-Japanese Alliance, 7, 107, 160
Antwerp, 128, 182–5, 227
Ardagh, Gen. Sir John, 49–50, 60–2, 64, 74
Arnold Forster, Hugh Oakley, 80, 86, 100–13,
127, 135, 145
Asquith, Henry Herbert, 6, 159, 181, 184–5,
189–90, 197–8, 200–1, 205, 207,
209–11, 215–16, 220–1, 230–1
   failure to take responsibility for British
   strategy, 185, 189, 230–1
Atlantic, 25, 30–3, 38, 40
Atlantic Fleet, 139, 152, 160, 193–4
Aston, General Sir George, 220, 222, 225
Aube, Théophile, 17
Auxiliary Forces, 8, 20, 51, 67, 77, 79,
89–92, 98–9, 101–8, 113, 119, 145,
150, 157, 190, (*see also* Militia, Volunteers,
Yeomanry)

Balfour, Arthur James, 5, 8, 31, 72, 84–7,
89–90, 92, 95, 97–101, 103–9, 111–13,
117, 124, 126–7, 139, 145–6, 148–51,
153, 155, 157–8, 161, 166–8, 170–2,
177, 179, 185–6, 190, 204, 217, 221,
228, 230–2
Ballard, Commodore George Alexander, 35,
124–6, 132, 189, 206–7, 212–13, 223
Baltic, 22, 35, 40, 47, 71–2, 107, 118, 120,
122, 125–8, 134, 136, 139–41, 144, 149,
182–4, 205
Battenberg, Admiral Prince Louis, 93–7, 115,
120–2, 132, 138–41, 161–2, 193, 209,
213–14, 216, 220, 222–5
Battle cruisers, 195, 213, 223
Belgium, 128, 131, 133, 151, 182, 208, 229
Beresford, Admiral Lord Charles, 31, 52, 63,
162–3, 167–70
Beresford Inquiry, 190–2, 194, 196
Bethell, Rear-Admiral. Sir Alexander, 188
Bizerta, 28, 199
Black Sea, 22, 27, 30, 38, 47, 71–2, 102
Bonar Law, Andrew, 204

Boer War, 7–8, 45, 68–9, 72–3, 76, 78, 80,
82–3, 85–7, 91, 101, 115, 135,
164–5, 190
Boulanger, General Georges, 17, 19
Brackenbury, General Sir Henry, 47, 49–50,
53–5, 58–60, 62–3, 65–6, 110
Brest, 22, 24, 35, 37
Bridge, Admiral Sir Cyprian, 121, 166
Bridgeman, Admiral Sir Francis, 217
British Army, 2, 4–5, 7–9, 12–13, 15–16,
20–1, 24–5, 33–4, 36–7, 43–70, 71–120,
123, 125–36, 145, 147–8, 150–1, 155–9,
164–8, 172, 174–5, 177–90, 196–200,
202, 204–5, 208–11, 214–18, 220,
225–9, 232
(British) Expeditionary Force, 8–9, 15, 45, 49,
51, 60, 68, 82, 92, 109–14, 121, 124,
126–7, 149, 157–8, 175, 179–82, 187–9,
196–8, 201, 205–6, 208–12, 215, 225–7,
229, 232
Brodrick, St. John, 77, 79–87, 90, 92–3, 95,
100, 102, 104–7, 109, 145
Brownlow, General Sir Charles, 62
Buller, General Sir Redvers, 65–8, 76
Butler Commission, 127

Callaghan, Admiral Sir George, 203, 206, 213,
216–17, 219, 223–4
Callwell, Colonel C.E. 124–7, 189, 228
Calcutta, 15, 55–6, 75–6, 87–8, 101–2, 109,
111–12, 115
Cambridge, Duke of, 54, 61, 63
Campbell Bannerman, Sir Henry, 6, 66, 127,
155–6, 159, 178, 185, 230
Cardwell, Edward, 45–6
Chamberlain, Austen, 131
Chamberlain, Joseph, 86, 100
Channel Fleet, 18, 23, 27–8, 31, 34–5, 37–9,
41, 58–60, 62–3, 115, 122, 137, 139–41,
143–4, 148–51, 160–4, 169, 171–2,
181, 190–1
Chapman, General Sir Edward, 65–9, 78, 121,
Cherbourg, 13, 24, 35
Chief of the (Imperial) General Staff, 107–8,
127, 175–6, 187, 198, 210–11
Chief of the (Admiralty) War Staff, 208, 214,
218, 223
Childers Erskine, 2, 135
Childers, Sir Hugh, 45–6
China, 18, 36, 72, 118–19, 138–9, 160
Churchill, Winston Spencer, 84, 189, 198,
201–2, 206–15, 217, 220–2, 227,
230–1, 233

Clarke, Sir George, 106, 109–10, 112–14, 123, 127–9, 131, 145–8, 155, 167–8, 174, 177, 228, 231
Cleethorpes (wireless station), 173
Colomb, Rear-Admiral Philip Howard, 28
Colonial Defence Committee, 53, 112
Committee of Imperial Defence, formation of, 85–7
　　Agadir Crisis special meeting (1911), 196–202
　　and Indian defence, 87–93, 101–2, 109–14, 115–18
　　and invasion: (1903–04), 93–8, 101, 104, (1907–08), 164–70, 174–8, (1913–14), 207–12, 219–22
　　assessment of, 230–3
　　Joint Operations Sub-Committee of, 126, 129, 148, 230–1
　　Military Needs of the Empire Inquiry (1908–09), 180–6
　　Secretariat of, 109, 112, 155
Continental Commitment, idea of, 3–4, 228
Constantinople, 17, 24, 27–30, 35, 62, 72
Corbett, Sir Julian Spencer, 163, 176
Crease, Captain Thomas, 126
Crimean War, 13
Cromarty Firth, 172, 204, 206–7, 220, 223
Custance, Rear-Admiral Sir Reginald, 38–40, 135

Dakar, 110, 119
Dardanelles, 28–9, 72
Defence Committee of the Cabinet, 30, 78
Denmark, 123, 141, 183–4
Devonshire, Duke of, 98, 101
Diego Suarez, 110, 119
Dilke, Charles, 48–9
Dogger Bank Incident, 138–9
Dover, 13, 142, 144, 196
Dumas, Captain Philip Wylie, 152–3
Dreadnought, 160, 162, 167, 195

Edward VII, 100, 180
Egypt, 15–17, 24, 28–9, 31, 33–5, 37, 39, 44, 46, 55, 58–9, 73, 78, 82–3, 94, 110
Elbe, river, 140, 147, 172, 195
Ellison, Brigadier-General Gerald F., 68, 77–8, 215
Emergency Ships, 141, 148
Esher Committee, 105, 113–14, 167, 229
Esher, Viscount, 100, 109, 112–14, 126, 155, 167, 169, 174, 180, 184–5, 190–1, 198, 215, 231
Ewart, Admiral Sir Arthur, 134
Ewart, General Sir Spencer, 107, 175, 181–3, 186, 197

Far East, 35, 107, 117–18, 120, 133, 139
Fashoda, 34–7, 134
Firth of Forth, 135, 143, 171, 193–4, 203–4, 207

Fisher, Admiral Sir John, 37–41, 112–14, 121–6, 129–30, 139–46, 148, 150–3, 155–70, 174–8, 182–94, 198, 201–2, 205, 228–9, 231
Fitzgerald, Admiral Sir Penrose, 132
Fixed defences, 14, 53, 93, 95, 193, 204
Flotilla, defensive importance of, 25, 42, 45, 96, 135, 141, 143–4, 160, 162, 166, 176, 191, 193–6, 199, 203, 214
Foreign Office, 20, 28, 36, 76, 156, 165, 181
France, 3, 133, 137
　　threat from, 13–42, 45, 52–9, 62–3, 65, 69, 72, 74, 82–3, 87, 105, 118, 120–1, 130, 134, 139–40
　　co-operation with, 5, 7, 109, 116, 118, 121–6, 128–30, 151, 156–7, 160, 165, 175, 177, 180–6, 196–201, 208, 218–19, 225–9, 231–2
Fremantle, Sydney Robert, 171–2, 192, 195, 199
'Fremantle Committee', 170–4, 180, 204
French, General Sir John, 110, 127, 210–11, 229

Garvin, James Lewis, 165
Geography, growth of subject, 1
　　see also strategy
General Staff (War Office), 4–5, 66, 78, 105–16, 119, 123, 125–8, 130, 133–7, 141, 146, 149, 155–8, 167–8, 174–6, 178, 180–2, 184–7, 189, 196–202, 204–5, 208–12, 221, 225, 228–9, 231
Great General Staff (German), 51, 131
Germany, 3, 18, 36, 40–1, 72, 99, 118, 120–57, 163, 167, 177, 179, 181, 183, 185, 194, 197, 203–4, 207, 210, 214–15, 219–20, 224, 226, 229, 231
Gibraltar, 23–8, 30–4, 37–41, 53–4, 59, 94, 139
Gleichen, Brigadier-General Lord Edward 147, 150
Goschen, Lord George Joachim, 36, 38
Grand Fleet, 227, 233
Greene, Graham, 194
Grey, Edward, 156, 197–8, 201–2, 210
Grove, Colonel Coldridge, 64–5, 67
Grierson, Lt-General Sir James Moncrieff, 99, 103, 110, 114, 119–21, 123, 127–8, 184, 228
Gywnne, Howell Arthur, 164

Haig, General Sir Douglas, 5, 174, 229
Hall, Captain William Henry, 19, 22–5, 41, 49, 53, 58
Haldane, Richard Burdon, 156, 158–9, 174–5, 177–8, 188–9, 197–8, 200–2, 210, 215
Halifax, Nova Scotia, 54
Hamilton, Lord George, 21–3, 26, 28–30, 59–60, 67, 76
Hamilton, General Sir Ian Standish Monteith, 104, 215
Hamilton, Admiral Sir Richard-Vesey, 25

Hankey, Colonel Maurice, 6–7, 188–9, 197–8, 201, 209, 215, 219–21, 228, 231–2
Harcourt, Sir Lewis, 201
Hartington Commission, 21, 54, 66, 112
Herat, 75
Hicks Beech, Sir Michael, 83, 87
High Seas Fleet (German), 161, 204, 225
Home Fleet, 35–6, 39–41, 67, 133, 135, 137–9, 159, 161–3, 166–73, 176–7, 191–3, 203
Hood, Admiral Sir Arthur, 16, 24–6, 30, 59
Hoskins, Admiral Sir Anthony, 28–30, 32–3
House of Commons, 21, 79–80, 103–4, 190
House of Lords, 20, 52, 63, 165, 177, 199
Hugeut, Colonel Victor, 175
Humber, 152, 172–3, 207, 213, 216

Imperial Defence, 5, 12–13, 20, 23, 69, 82, 84, 89–90, 113–14, 150, 188, 197
(*see also* Committee of Imperial Defence)
Imperial General Staff, see General Staff
Incheon, 142
India, 2, 8–9, 15–18, 21, 27, 46–7, 52–7, 62–5, 69, 71–8, 82–3, 87–118, 124, 129, 158, 175, 180, 230
India Office, 57, 88, 100–1, 105, 115

Jackson, Admiral Sir Henry Brandwardine, 38, 214, 223–5
Jellicoe, Vice-Admiral Sir John Rushworth, 216–17, 219–20, 225, 233
Jitbutil, 119
Jutland, Battle of, 3–4

Kabul, 76
Kandahar, 15
Kerr, Admiral Lord Walter, 38–9, 113, 135, 138
Kiel, 138–40, 149
Kiel Canal, 122, 140, 149
Kitchener, Field Marshal Earl Horatio, 34, 54, 101, 109
Kruger telegram, 132

Landing Places Committee, 44, 93
Lansdowne, Marquis of, 68, 73
Lloyd George, David, 210
Lowry, Admiral Sir Robert S., 170–3
Lyttelton, General the Hon, Sir Neville, 107–8, 127–8, 175

Mahan, Alfred Thayer, 63, 67, 225
Malta, 18, 24, 26, 28, 31–4, 39–40, 52–4, 96, 151
Manoeuvres, naval, 25, 40–1, 59, 96, 151–2, 194, 206–7, 209, 212, 215–19, 222–4,
military, 131
Marne, 1st Battle of, 227
May, Admiral Sir William Henry, 193, 206, 216, 219

Marker, Colonel Raymond, 152
Martinique, 119
Maurice, Major-General John Frederick, 59, 68
McKenna, Reginald, 188–91, 198, 200–2, 210
Mediterranean, 18–19, 21, 23–4, 26–42, 45, 52–5, 58–9, 63, 69, 72, 116, 137–9, 184, 223
Mediterranean Fleet, 18–19, 21, 23–4, 26, 28–42, 62, 94, 139, 162
Medway, 142
Military Intelligence, Director of (DMI), 59, 62, 65–6, 74, 81
Militia, 51, 73, 82, 92, 98, 103–4, 106, 108, 110, 145, (*see also* Auxiliary Forces)
Mobilization and Intelligence, Director of, 77, 87, 89
Mobilization and Intelligence, Directorate of, 81–2, 91, 102, 120, 136
Mons, Battle of, 227
Moroccan Crisis (1905), 126–9
Morley, Lord John, 201, 208

Naval Intelligence, Department of, 19, 22–3, 25, 35, 49, 53, 121–2, 124, 126, 134–5, 138–40, 143, 152, 189
Naval Intelligence, Director of (DNI), 7, 19, 22, 30, 38–9, 49, 53–4, 93, 95, 97, 120–1, 123–5, 135, 138–40, 143, 159, 162, 169, 170, 173, 183, 188
National Defence Association, 165
National Service League, 164, 204
Naval War College, 152, 162, 170–1, 173, 176, 192
Naval War Course, 171, 176
Naval Reserve, 59, 141, 144, 172
(see Emergency Ships)
Nicholson, General Sir William Gustavus, 77–8, 81–2, 87, 89, 94, 96–7, 104–5, 110, 113, 175–6, 198, 201, 228–9
Noel, Admiral Gerald 'Sharky', 41, 166
Norfolk Commission, 77, 89, 91, 103, 105, 145
Norfolk, Duke of, 98, 101
North Sea, 9, 36, 40–2, 107, 122, 130–65, 168, 170–2, 178, 180, 184, 191–4, 196, 203–7, 212–16, 220, 222–4, 226
North Sea Guard, 168, 173–4, 176, 192, 195–6
North Sea Problem, 212
Northcliffe, Lord, 165

Orenburg-Tashkent railway, 90
Ottley, Rear-Admiral Sir Charles, 106, 120, 123–4, 129, 138, 143, 146, 151, 153, 160, 163, 165, 169, 177, 181, 188, 231
Oliver, Rear-Admiral Sir Henry, 192
Ottoman Empire, 18, 28–9, 181

Persia, 27, 55, 71–2, 102
Pendjeh Crisis, 16, 20, 22, 44, 56

Plymouth, 36, 142
Portland, 24, 144, 148, 150, 171, 204, 227
Port Arthur, 142

Queensferry Bridge, 143, 193

Raids, 94, 101, 105–6, 120, 132, 145–6,
   148–9, 153, 156–62, 165, 169, 171–2,
   176, 179, 186, 198, 200, 205, 207,
   209–10, 212, 216–20, 222, 224–5
Repington, C. á C, 152, 165–70, 173, 175,
   177, 210, 212
Richmond, Captain Herbert, 166, 192, 218,
   224–5, 227, 231
Ritchie, C., 1st Baron of Dundee, 95, 100
Roberts, Field Marshal Lord, 55–7, 62–3, 67,
   76–9, 81–5, 88, 91–2, 94–5, 97, 102–3,
   105, 109, 111, 119, 165–70, 175, 177,
   186, 199, 204, 212, 229
Robertson, General Sir William, 43, 63, 66,
   76–8, 81, 88, 102, 118, 125, 128, 136–7,
   211
Rosyth, 95, 143, 172–4, 193, 204–6, 220
Russia, 7–8, 16–19, 22–3, 27–30, 34–5, 38,
   40, 46–7, 55–7, 62, 72, 74–5, 82,
   88, 90, 105, 107, 109, 114–15, 117–20,
   122, 134, 138–9, 164, 179–80, 186, 230
Russo-Japanese War, 104–5, 116, 118

Saigon, 110, 119
Salisbury, Marquis of, 21, 30, 34, 37, 58, 64,
   76, 80, 84–5, 97
Sandars, John Satterfield, 126, 217
Scapa Flow, 171, 194, 204, 206–7, 220, 223–4
Schleswig-Holstein, 122, 124
Schlieffen, Count Alfred von, 133
Seely, Colonel John, 208–10, 215
Selborne, Earl of, 39, 41, 85–6, 93, 104, 110,
   134–5, 137–9
Simmons, General Lintorn, 52–3
Slade, Rear-Admiral Sir Edmond John Warre,
   163, 169–71, 173, 176, 181–4, 191,
   194, 231
South Africa, 8, 36–7, 68–9, 71–9, 82–3, 86,
   93–4, 100–2, 110, 115, 127
Stanhope, Edward, 43, 54, 56, 59, 61, 63, 80
Stanhope Memorandum, 43, 61–2, 64, 66, 73,
   77–8, 80, 82, 91
Stopford, General Sir Frederick, 110
Strategy, debates on British strategy before
   1914, 2–6
   nature of in contemporary Britain, 11–12
   military, 4–5, 51–2, 109, 114, 116, 177, 180,
   196, 217
   naval, 5–6, 19, 23, 27, 36, 41, 49, 117,
   130, 203, 212, 214, 218, 222, 225,
   229, 232
   economic warfare, 6, 125, 185, 231

amphibious operations within, 5, 45–6,
   55, 57, 64–5, 69, 71, 113–14, 120–1,
   123–4, 126–30, 133, 158–9, 178, 180,
   182–3, 185, 189, 196, 199–200, 205,
   215, 227–9, 231
Strategic theory, blockade, 22, 25–6, 200, 205,
   207
   'command of the sea', 5, 24, 33, 42, 94–6,
   147, 165, 174
   continental, 3, 78, 129, 165, 184, 228
   'decisive point', 5, 165, 182
   decisive battle, 50, 225
   maritime, 6, 11, 65, 92, 112–14, 123,
   126, 129, 159, 164, 167, 180, 185, 198,
   224
   geography in strategy, 22–3, 31
Striking force, concept of, 7, 48, 51, 55, 57,
   64, 71, 73, 104, 106, 108–16, 119, 126,
   159, 175, 183, 199 (see also Expeditionary
   Force)
Sturdee, Admiral Sir Doveton, 169
Sudan, 16, 34–5, 55, 65, 71
Suez Canal, 23–4, 28–9, 31, 34

Territorial Force, 174–82, 186–7, 189, 196,
   199–200, 204, 209–11
Thames Estuary, 19, 132, 207, 217
Tirpitz, Admiral von, 132
Treasury, 14, 55, 75, 80, 83, 85, 87, 89, 92–3,
   95, 104, 109, 159
Tweedmouth, Lord, 159–60, 164, 168

Victoria, Queen, 19, 54, 76–7
Volunteers, 47, 49, 51, 61, 82, 92, 98, 103–4,
   106, 108, 113, 145–6, 158
   (see also Auxiliary Forces)
Vyvyan, Captain Arthur, 218

Ward, Sir William, 147–8
War Staff, Admiralty, 206–8, 212–15, 218, 220,
   222, 224
Western Approaches, 18
Wilhem II, Kaiser, 118, 141, 197
Wilhelmshaven, 135, 140, 142, 194
Wilson, Admiral Sir Arthur, 32, 122–3, 137,
   140, 162, 191–2, 195, 199–200, 202,
   219, 221, 231
Wilson, Brig-Gen. Sir Henry, 81, 197–9, 201,
   204, 207–8, 210, 221, 228
WF 'With France' scheme, 5, 157, 175,
   199, 229
Wolseley, Field Marshal Lord Garnett, 16, 20,
   37, 43–4, 46–8, 50–69, 73–7, 81, 97,
   111, 114, 228

Yarmouth, 172
Yeomanry, 82, 106, 158 (see also Auxiliary
   Forces)